INCREASING READING EFFICIENCY

INCREASING READING EFFICIENCY

REVISED EDITION

LYLE L. MILLER
Chairman
Guidance and Special Education
University of Wyoming
Formerly Coordinator
University Study Skills Center

Holt, Rinehart and Winston, Inc.
New York-Chicago-San Francisco-Toronto-London

"Seek the ideas behind the words."

Preface

In an age of space flight and color TV, we may take for granted some of our basic concepts of communication. Instantaneous communication of ideas through radio, television, international Telstar relays, and constantly improving modern telephone services literally has brought the world to our doorstep. There can be no doubt that we depend extensively on looking and listening to keep us informed today. In the midst of all of these modern developments, however, we find reports of increasing circulation of magazines, continuous publication of new books, expanding library facilities, and an ever increasing volume of printed material being circulated through the mail. In our high-speed world of electronic and atomic wonders, we still find that *reading* is our most fundamental process of interpersonal communication.

With our rapidly expanding field of human knowledge, reading ability has become one of the most important factors of success in many fields today. This is true of the busy doctor or lawyer keeping up with recent developments through his professional journals, of the modern scientists analyzing the work of others through their research papers, of the businessman reading market reports and correspondence, and of the housewife seeking relaxation and relief from her daily problems through reading her favorite magazine. Reading is especially important to the conscientious student who is trying to grasp an understanding of the many new concepts in his chosen curriculum. All of them need to read. More important, however, is the fact that all of them need to read quickly and efficiently.

Colleges are aware of the reading problems of young adults and are attempting to deal with these problems. Remedial reading programs have been available for many years to help the student with specific reading difficulties or deficiencies. Developmental reading programs have developed rapidly in recent years, however, with a focus on the needs and problems of the "average" or "good" readers who need to read more in less time.

Few readers have been able to avoid the pressures of the faster pace of living and learning and the parallel need to read more effectively. Efficient habits of reading are of value to any reader, and many college reading centers have engaged in extensive research on this problem. The first edition of *Increasing Reading Efficiency* (25) was the product of such research in the Study Skills Center and the Reading Research Center at the University of Wyoming. Extensive use of the workbook in many colleges and adult reading programs since then has confirmed the value of this approach to developmental reading.

Experimental work in many high schools and universities has shown that few students are reading at speeds that even begin to approach their real reading capabilities. Although some universities and colleges still place the stress on remedial reading, many instructors in study skills programs have come to feel that this emphasis is misleading, since it tends to discourage many students from participating in reading training programs because they feel that they already have normal reading habits. Experience has shown, however, that *reading training can help any person* who has a sincere desire for self-improvement. Therefore this manual has been developed as a basic drill series for group reading practice. Those individuals who need specific remedial help usually can secure this assistance in addition to this group training. Those who are interested primarily in increasing reading efficiency may devote extra time to practice on longer reading exercises such as those provided in *Maintaining Reading Efficiency* (26).

Letters from many teachers and students who have used *Increasing Reading Efficiency* in many parts of the United States and abroad have convinced the author that this pattern of reading exercises has been of real practical value to thousands of high school and college students and adults. Its popularity led to the development of a companion volume, *Developing Reading Efficiency* (24), which has the same basic pattern of organization but which is focused on the reading needs of students in grades seven through ten. For further reading practice with longer standardized materials, the supplementary

(25) All reference numbers refer to the numbered selected references on page 23.

volume, *Maintaining Reading Efficiency* (26), was developed. *Developing Reading Efficiency* and *Maintaining Reading Efficiency* are available from Developmental Reading Distributors, Laramie, Wyo.

In attempting a revision of *Increasing Reading Efficiency,* therefore, the author has been careful to preserve the basic format and exercise sequence and has attempted to change only a few of the more obviously dated materials and to relate this material to that in the companion volumes. With these changes, the author feels that this revised edition of *Increasing Reading Efficiency* should continue to serve as one of the outstanding workbooks in the developmental reading field.

Use of the workbook

Although this workbook may be used for self-improvement practice in individual cases, it was designed primarily for use with small groups of readers, where competition within the group may serve as a psychological motivation for increased proficiency in the drill exercises. With a planned supervision which stresses both self-improvement and competition with other readers, most group members will be pleasantly surprised by the improvement they can make in a series of reading classes. It is not unusual for many students in a group to double or triple reading efficiency if they make a sincere effort to do so.

Development of the reading exercises

Of basic importance to the exercises in this manual is a provision for increasing eye span and establishing rhythmic eye movements. Also basic is the need to increase rate of mental perception of what is read and so reduce the eye fixation time. These exercises were planned to provide training for these purposes. In addition, the difficulty of the exercises has been standardized sufficiently to allow comparisons between similar exercises. The following are some of the more important attempts at standardization:

1. In all exercises the correct answer may be found with equal frequency in each answer column or position.
2. In the word recognition and word meaning drills, all words used in the key were selected from Thorndike's list of 10,000 most frequently used words (41). All words in the answer columns occur in his list of 30,000 most frequently used words (42). Therefore these exercises may be used also as vocabulary drills for high school and college students.
3. In the phrase and sentence meaning drills, the key words have all been selected from the same 30,000 word list.
4. The section on reading for ideas has been checked by the Flesch Formula (15) and is of an appropriate level of difficulty for high school and college students. Exercises are arranged in order of increasing difficulty from tenth grade level to college senior level.
5. The exploratory reading and the study reading drills have all been equated to a common length and are arranged within each set in order of increasing difficulty from tenth grade level to college senior level. Exercises in these two series are matched for difficulty so that they may be used in pairs to demonstrate the importance of thinking during the reading process.

Arrangement of materials

Although these materials are arranged by groups in the sequence believed to be most advantageous, the groups are designed for some overlapping in class practice. For example, practice on word meaning exercises should be started when the class is only 30 percent through word recognition. This overlapping in the four basic groups of exercises provides better continuity. The idea reading, exploratory reading, and study reading drills should be started at least by the second period of training and should be used regularly thereafter.

If time is limited, the odd-numbered exercises may be used for individual practice and the even-numbered ones for group work. If time permits, however, all the exercises may be used for group practice.

The purpose and method of procedure for each set of exercises is given immediately preceding those exercises. Progress charts are provided on pages 289-295 for maintaining daily records of reading progress during the period of training. Keeping this daily progress chart is an important aspect of self-motivation.

Answer keys are provided in the back of the workbook. Specific suggestions for the teacher have been included in the introductory section. These may be supplemented by reference to the manual, *Teaching Reading Efficiency* (27).

Sources of inspiration

In developing this manual, the author is indebted to several sources for ideas and inspirations. In these reading workbooks he has attempted to incorporate some of the best of the ideas on developmental reading and of effective study. First of all, Dr. Francis P. Robinson (32) stimulated his interest in the field of study skills and reading needs of college students. Although many authors contributed to his understanding of the reading progress, the author was most impressed by the concepts and basic reading drill sequences developed by Stroud and Ammons

(40). The criticisms of hundreds of students in study skills classes and of dozens of graduate students throughout the past decade have contributed to the expansion and polishing of these ideas.

Many authors and publishers have been extremely generous in granting permission to use their materials and to revise these materials slightly when necessary to develop them into standard reading exercises. Those whose materials appear in this final revision are acknowledged by the credit line on the article, but many others had been just as gracious in granting permission to use their materials in developing reading exercises. Many of their exercises have been used extensively in the Study Skills classes at the University of Wyoming.

The necessity for standard lengths of articles and balance of reading difficulty determined the final choice of exercises included in this book, but without the encouragement from *all* those who granted permission to use their materials in this way, this workbook would not have been possible.

Many suggestions and evaluative comments have come from teachers who have used the workbook in their classes. Recognition should be given to the exhaustive evaluative comments provided by critics William Moorhouse, Roy Morgan, and LaVerne Nelson, who were of great assistance in planning modifications for this revised edition.

Special recognition should be extended to Nelda Stevenson and James Bowen, who worked extensively on materials for this revised edition.

Above all, the author is most appreciative of the inspiration of his two children, Tom and Patty, who participated in experimental reading groups and spoke freely of student reactions, and to his wife, Grace M. Miller, without whose patient understanding and continued support and encouragement he would have been unable to complete this revision of *Increasing Reading Efficiency*.

January, 1964   L.L.M.
Laramie, Wyoming

Contents

INCREASING
READING
EFFICIENCY

To the Teacher

With many demands on students for lengthy reading assignments and with an ever-increasing amount of reading material available to adults, the demand on colleges and extension programs for developmental reading programs has increased steadily. The popularity of the first edition of *Increasing Reading Efficiency* (25) has demonstrated its value in assisting college students and adults in the development of their reading skills. A companion volume, *Developing Reading Efficiency* (24), (Developmental Reading Distributors, Laramie, Wyo.), has been equally effective for students in grades seven through ten.

One reaction of teachers using the first edition of *Increasing Reading Efficiency* was that the materials for teachers should be included in the workbook rather than in a separate manual. In response to this suggestion, the revised edition includes this introductory section for teachers and a set of keys located on perforated pages at the back of the workbook.

Teachers who desire more specific suggestions on methods and supplementary materials are encouraged to secure the more comprehensive manual, *Teaching Reading Efficiency* (27), published by Pruett Press, Boulder, Colorado.

Purpose of the workbook

Increasing Reading Efficiency is designed to promote the mutual development of reading speed and reading comprehension through group stimulation. Although the materials may be used for individualized practice, they have been intended primarily for use with groups where competition can serve as a psychological motivation.

Although both rate of reading and comprehension are recognized as important aspects of reading ability, neither one is stressed in itself. Instead this author places the stress on a combination of the two factors which he calls *reading efficiency*. This measures what might be called a "rate of understanding." Reading efficiency is computed by multiplying the rate (in words per minute) by the comprehension score (percentage of correct answers on tested material). This yields a "words-per-minute" figure which serves as a measure of the amount of material understood during a minute of time. Although one recognizes that ideas cannot be accurately measured in "words per minute," this stress on efficiency does seem to overcome some of the concern over comprehension loss in the early stages of training.

Early experimentation in the University of Wyoming Study Skills Center revealed that students seemed to comprehend less after having successfully increased their reading rate. Consequently much thought has been given to the provision of training exercises designed to bring about increases in both rate and comprehension. During the years in which *Increasing Reading Efficiency* has been used in the Study Skills Center, group evaluations have revealed an increase in both rate and comprehension on standardized tests administered at the beginning and end of the ten-week training periods. Paired tests from the workbook, *Maintaining Reading Efficiency* (26), published by Developmental Reading Distributors, Laramie, Wyo., can be used effectively for this comparison.

This dual improvement has been accomplished by introducing students to techniques of self-recitation, reading for ideas, and recognition of textbook clues. These materials are organized in such a way that the effectiveness of this approach is easy to illustrate to the students.

Standardization of the materials

One of the major difficulties in the past in evaluating the results of a training program was the lack of standardized materials. These materials have now been standardized as much as possible in order to make exercises comparable.

In Series I — III, answer frequency per column has been standardized so that in each exercise the right answer will occur five times in each column.

In Series I and II, all key words occur in Thorndike's 10,000 most frequently used words (41) and all words in the answer columns occur in Thorndike's 30,000 most frequently used words (42). Therefore these exercises may also serve as vocabulary drills for high school or college students.

In the phrase and sentence meaning drills, the key words have been checked against the same word list. These exercises have been arranged in an order of gradually increasing difficulty.

The paragraph reading material in Series V, VI, and VII has all been reduced to standardized lengths so that rates may be obtained from tables. This material has been rated by the Flesch formula (15) and has been arranged in order of increasing difficulty — from tenth grade through college graduate level, with most of the material falling in the range of high school seniors or college freshmen.

The first exercises are designed primarily as speed exercises. In Series I, the major emphasis should be on the establishment of rhythmic eye movements and increased eye span. In Series II, understanding is emphasized, and most readers will slow down. Each error indicates a misunderstanding of two words which may serve as reading blocks. Hence students should be encouraged to develop vocabulary lists and study words missed to increase vocabulary.

Series III continues this stress on understanding but deals with groups of words and emphasizes increased eye span and the grasping of ideas rather than words.

Series IV concentrates on rapid grasping of basic ideas in a sentence.

Series V provides practice in high speed reading for basic ideas. The tests on these materials consist of two questions relating to basic thoughts or ideas in the material. Here both rapid reading and correct understanding are important. The questions are of the same type for each exercise. Questions are designed to pick up recurrent thoughts, basic themes, or over-all purpose in the article.

Series VI places stress on more accurate reading for short periods of time. Here, again, the tests follow similar patterns for each exercise, but in this case they require more attention to detailed ideas and facts presented in the material.

Series VII demonstrates an application of the Self-Recitation technique and does much to give students definite evidence of the values of this study technique. It is designed to help them develop habits of *thinking* as they read. The exercises are matched with those in Series VI for readability, length, and type of questions asked, but here the reader is required to stop, think, and answer at intervals as he goes along.

Sequence of exercises

Experience has shown that giving the Drill Exercises in overlapping sequence usually proves stimulating to the students. All exercises should be clocked by stopwatch, and time, in seconds, should be called out for each student as he finishes. Frequently a "pacing" technique of calling out 10- or 20- second intervals helps to keep up the motivation, especially if the group exhibits signs of fatigue.

This book can be used for reading improvement in many types of training groups. In general, the writer recommends a 10-week training period to provide time for additional practice and application. A 5-week training period has been demonstrated to be less satisfactory but still productive.

As an illustration of a procedure for the overlapping of exercises — for college students or adults — one might consider the sequence used in the Extension Classes at the University of Wyoming. The pattern shown on page 4 is that used in a class that meets once weekly for a 1½ to 2 hour session. In this series the even-numbered exercises are used for group drill and the odd-numbered exercises for outside practice. For high school classes, group work could

be done on the first ten exercises of Series V, VI, and VII, leaving the last ten for supplementary practice for the more advanced students. During the last half of the course, workbook practice should be supplemented by longer reading exercises from current materials or from standardized 10-minute reading tests. The supplementary workbook, *Maintaining Reading Efficiency* (26), (Developmental Reading Distributors, Laramie, Wyo.), provides a collection of standardized reading tests appropriate for this purpose.

Motivation

The instructor must be alert constantly to provide encouragement and motivation not only to the group as a whole but to individual students as well. In audition to the pacing techniques mentioned before, he should suggest goals. For example, in Series I, he can suggest that most students should be able to finish in 30 seconds or less. Accuracy in setting realistic goals in different exercises depends upon the developmental pattern of any particular group as well as the teacher's experience with the materials. Encouraging competition with other specific members of the group also is effective in many cases.

Watching the fastest reader and calling a finishing time a few seconds before he is through helps to keep him working at a maximum. Rather than keep the whole group waiting, individual assignments can be made for slow readers, that is, completion of only half an exercise. Extremely slow readers who retard the whole group should be removed from the group, if possible, and given individual help.

Emphasis should be placed on keeping individual progress graphs up to date and encouraging students to compare results of the trends in their reading improvement. During the period between tests, the staff member should circulate among the readers and provide individual encouragement.

If reading machines are available, a class demonstration with two or three class members is a very effective way of spurring individuals to better efforts.

Scoring of questions

Series I is self-scoring since identical words are to be selected. Keys for scoring the other exercises are presented on pages 306 to 318. These keys are grouped according to odd and even numbers in case the teacher wishes to make one set available to students for their own scoring. In the completion questions, individual teachers should use their best judgment in accepting "equivalent terms" for full or half credit. These perforated pages may be left in the book for self-scoring or may be removed by the teacher to discourage advance study. Many teachers prefer to leave the keys for the odd-numbered exercises in the book and to remove the even-numbered keys for standardized testing.

To the Reader

Would you like to have a time-stretcher?

Do you reach the end of the day with unfinished tasks regretfully laid aside? Do you wish sometimes that you had just an extra hour or so in order to finish important tasks? Do you really have time to read the newspapers, magazines, and other recreational materials you would enjoy? Like many other individuals today, you probably find yourself caught between an accelerated rate of living and a mass of written communication. Business today expects its executives and clerical staff to read much more than they did in the past. Schools expect increasingly ←100 longer reading assignments as a means of understanding the more complex world in which we live. Many of us find that at least one third of our time is required for reading of some kind. At the same time we find that our reading habits are not adequate to meet these demands, and we become depressed when we cannot keep the pace and complete the amount of reading we feel that we should.

No one has developed a "time stretcher" to lengthen our days for us, but for years many educators have been studying the problem of slow reading habits. Not until World War II, however, were the ←200 possibilities of more rapid reading developed extensively. The techniques developed during wartime to train men in rapid identification of enemy aircraft and ships were direct applications of some of the theories which had been developed for speeding reading. Based on the success of these wartime experiences, educators set up reading centers in many universities and colleges. Further research led to improvements in techniques and encouraged new approaches to this problem of developmental reading. Reading centers today are using many techniques and group exercise materials that represent great 300→ advances over those used a decade ago.

Reading services are now available to adults through extension classes and to many high school and college students as well. Many participants in these classes have made astounding improvement in reading skills. The average individual trained in one of these reading classes can double his reading speed. Thus he is able to do, in 4 hours, the reading which once took 8 hours. Many individuals have increased their reading efficiency much more than this. Saving these 4 hours for other activities can give you the "time stretcher" of which you may have dreamed.

400→ One reading authority once computed that the saving in time required to do all the reading in the nation, computed at 50 cents per hour, would be more than 5 billion dollars if every American over 15 years of age were given reading training for at least a month (6). Many industrial concerns have recognized this potential saving of manpower and have subsidized reading programs for their employees with very gratifying results. Many students have found free time for greater enjoyment of their college activities by registering for classes in developmental reading. What benefits could you obtain if you were 500→ to double your reading efficiency?

(6) All reference numbers refer to the numbered selected references on page 23.

SUGGESTED SEQUENCE FOR A TWENTY-HOUR READING PROGRAM

All basic series and numbers refer to basic exercises in this book. Pre-tests, post-tests and supplementary reading materials are available in the supplementary exercise book *Maintaining Reading Efficiency* which may be ordered from Developmental Reading Distributors, 1944 Sheridan, Laramie, Wyoming 82070. (Schedule is designed for ten two-hour periods. For a 50-60 minute class, plan only about half the material scheduled. The "5-minute break" divides the material in two sections requiring approximately the same amount of time.)

FIRST PERIOD

Use a standardized 10-minute reading test such as the "History of Brazil" in *Maintaining Reading Efficiency*.

(Score and Collect)

SERIES	NUMBER
I	2, 4, 6

(Explain charts)

II	2
V	2

5-Minute Break

VI	2
VII	2

SECOND PERIOD

I	8, 10, 12, 14
II	4, 6, 8
III	2
V	4

5-Minute Break

VI	4
VII	4

THIRD PERIOD

I	16, 18, 20
II	10, 12, 14
III	4, 6

5-Minute Break

V	6
VI	6
VII	6

FOURTH PERIOD

II	16, 18, 20
III	8, 10, 12, 14
IV	2, 4
V	8

5-Minute Break

VI	8
VII	8

FIFTH PERIOD

SERIES	NUMBER
III	16, 18, 20
IV	6, 8
V	10

5-Minute Break

VI	10
VII	10

SIXTH PERIOD

IV	10, 12, 14, 16
V	12

5-Minute Break

VI	12
VII	12

Supplementary Reading Exercises

SEVENTH PERIOD

IV	18, 20
V	14

5-Minute Break

VI	14
VII	14

Supplementary Reading Exercises

EIGHTH PERIOD

V	16
VI	16
VII	16

5-Minute Break

Supplementary Reading Exercises

NINTH PERIOD

V	18
VI	18
VII	18

5-Minute Break

Supplementary Reading Exercises

TENTH PERIOD

V	20
VI	20

If time allows:

VII	20

5-Minute Break

Use a final standardized 10-minute reading test such as the "History of Japan" in *Maintaining Reading Efficiency*.

(Score in class and discuss comparisons with beginning test.)

1

How Do We Read?

Good reading involves not one skill, but many. Although some individuals can increase their rate of reading without specific training, few can improve, without such help, their comprehension, analytical skill, judgment, skimming ability, and the technique of adjusting their habits of reading to their purpose and the nature of the material. These skills require thorough understanding and practice in a carefully planned program. ✓

The first fact that must be recognized is that our present reading habits are the result of our early experiences in learning to read and our continuing experiences in reading over a period of years. These habits, practiced for many years, are hard to break. 100 We may encounter many feelings of insecurity while we are in the process of substituting new habits for old. Therefore we should give some attention to how we read and how we have established some of our present reading habits.

Development of reading habits

Many articles in popular periodicals have criticized public schools and current methods of teaching reading. We should be cautious in placing the blame for our habits on the schools, however, and should consider several of the factors which have affected our own particular reading habits. Study some of the 200 following factors and see which of them may have had an effect on your habits of reading.

1. Reading is not demonstrable as is speaking, walking, or problem solving. It is impossible to *show* someone how you *read*. It involves recognition of many symbols which have no meaning in themselves and which must be combined in innumerable combinations in order to convey meaning to others. The visible eye movements and fixations are only a small part of the invisible mental process of reading.

2. The great shortage of qualified teachers in the last three decades has resulted in the substitution of many poorly trained teachers who possessed limited interest, desire, or skill in the teaching 300 of reading. Until the problem of the shortage of qualified teachers is overcome, many children will pass through the schools and emerge as adults with serious reading problems.

3. Schools have been developing better methods of teaching. The children in elementary schools today are getting better basic training in reading than we did when we were in elementary school. Teachers now have greater understanding of the factors of reading and of the learning problems of the individual student. In all periods, however, we have found some schools which have developed 400 programs that are more effective than those in other schools.

4. We have come through a period of conflicting philosophy about the basic approach to reading. Some teachers insisted that the "phonics" approach of sounding out syllables was the best method. Others were completely dedicated to the "sight reading" approach of recognizing words as units of meaning and developing a vocabulary by visual association. As a result we had a great variation between different schools and even between teachers in the same school, with a resulting confusion on the part of the students. Fortunately today most of our elementary teachers are recog- 500 nizing that both "sight reading" and "phonics" have a place in developing reading skills. Unfortunately they still are not in complete agreement on the best combination of these two ideas.

5. Our population has become increasingly mobile and, as a consequence, many children do not follow the planned sequence of courses in a single school, but attend many schools during their elementary years. Thus they may miss a basic part of their reading instruction because it has not yet been reached in one school, but has already been covered in another school to which they transfer.

6. Overcrowded schools, in many instances, contrib- 600 uted to poor reading because the problems of the individual student were overlooked and the teaching was directed toward the assumed average of the class. Better schools attempt to discover individual problems in reading through testing programs and observation, and try to provide special attention for slow readers by means of remedial reading classes.

7. Specific instruction in reading has placed emphasis on oral reading and limited attention has been given to helping the student discover various techniques to be used in silent reading. Conse-

quently some people have carried oral reading habits into silent reading practice.

8. Instruction in reading skills often terminated after the fourth or fifth grade. It was assumed by 700 both teachers and parents that, having mastered the basic skills of reading, the student could make the adaptations of those skills to the different reading needs he would face later. Unfortunately many individuals made few adaptations, and many adults today are trying to read adult-level materials using reading skills appropriate for fifth-grade levels of reading.

9. Many adolescents and adults avoid activities involving reading because they have severe reading problems. As a consequence, lack of practice has made their existing habits even more ineffective.

The process of reading

A second important fact to recognize is that we 800 do not read while our eyes are moving. Just as the motion picture is made up of many still pictures flashed before us rapidly, so our reading is a series of visual impressions carried to our brain in a rapid sequence. We stop for each glance and then move on for another glance at another word or phrase. Reading rate, then, is a combination of the amount we see at each glance, the length of time we hesitate for each eye fixation, and the speed with which the eye can move and focus on another unit of material. 900

The first of these factors we refer to as "eye span" — the quantity of reading material we can see at one glance. For some people this may be a single word; for others, one complete phrase; and for others, still larger units of thought. For the very rapid reader, this may be several lines or a paragraph.

The second factor is closely related to the thinking process. It is sometimes referred to as a rate of apperception, or a rate of perception. How long does it take to register the impression of what we see and to transmit it to the brain, and how long 1000 does it take the brain to interpret what was seen? Unless one has had an accident resulting in damage to brain tissue, he probably is capable of a great deal of acceleration in this thinking process.

The third factor of rate is that of eye movement in shifting from one point of focus to another. This is primarily a physical factor requiring the acceleration of rhythmic habits of eye movement.

The average individual is not aware of his complex pattern of reading habits and therefore makes little effort to coordinate the factors affecting his reading efficiency. Recognition of various types of reading 1100 and adjustment of his reading habits to the type and purpose of specific reading assignments is essential. Most individuals have a rather limited range of reading efficiency, however, and therefore have little leeway in adjusting to different types. One of the greatest contributions of a reading program is that of increasing the ceiling on reading speed. As one increases this upper limit of reading speed, of course, he also increases his range of reading efficiency and develops greater flexibility in his reading habits. By 1200 focusing attention on reading habits and placing an individual in a position where he is stimulated to operate at his maximum, we find that most persons are capable of reading at least twice as fast as they had been doing. Thus the normal adult who may be reading at a rate of about 250 words per minute actually is capable of reading 500 words per minute if he is properly stimulated. With practice and concentrated effort on his part, there is little reason why he could not learn to read at 750 or 1000 words per minute. Many individuals have made even greater improvements; records of reading classes include 1300 many cases who have read 2000 or 3000 words per minute. Some reading centers have reported individuals who have achieved rates as high as 50,000 words per minute on certain types of material. The potential maximum reading speed of any individual is unknown, but most reading authorities are convinced that the possibilities for any normal adult are limited only by his own interest and his determination to improve. Only *you* can determine just how fast you can read, but you can be assured that you should be able at least to double or triple your present 1400 reading rate and perhaps to achieve much more than that.

How do we read faster?

Slow readers may possess any one or a combination of poor reading habits. Most of these habits can be changed by recognizing the factors involved in the habit. Glance over the list of poor reading habits below and see which ones may apply to you; then consider what you might do to change these habits.

Vocalizing. Sounding out each word as if you were reading aloud slows you down to a snail's pace. This may be only a mental pronunciation process but frequently it is accompanied by the moving of the 1500 lips as you read. If you do this, try placing your finger tightly on your lips as you read until you have broken the habit of lip reading. Once the lip action is broken, you will find it easier to push yourself to a faster rate where mental vocalization decreases considerably.

Word-by-word reading. Looking at one word at a time to be sure you understand it frequently will obscure the overall meaning of the sentence or paragraph. Remember the old adage about the man who couldn't see the forest because of the trees. To break 1600 yourself of this habit, try reading for ideas instead of words. Try to grasp whole phrases in a glance and sense their meaning.

Word blocking. Stopping to worry about an unfamiliar word breaks the rhythm of your reading and makes you lose the trend of thought or miss some of the main ideas. If you do this often you probably have a poor vocabulary and need to work intensively on building up a greater understanding of commonly used words. In many instances, you can find the meaning of a certain word in the context, however, if you will just keep reading with an emphasis on ideas instead of words. Later on, after you have finished reading, you can go back and check the dictionary for some of the words which troubled you. After looking them up, think about their meaning and try to use them several times in conversation or writing that same day. This will fix the meaning in your mind. But don't let a new word upset you and make you feel self-conscious. Most people encounter new words in their reading and take them in stride, identifying their meaning from other words or phrases with which they are associated.

Number attraction. Some readers come to a complete stop every time they reach a number. They seem to want to study it carefully as if it were a completely different concept of communication. Unless you are studying thoroughly for detailed content, dates, and quantitative ideas, you should try to generalize the numerical idea into verbal symbols such as "many" or "few," "long ago," "recently," "next year," or similar clues that will help in getting general ideas from the material.

Word analysis. Stopping to analyze a strange word as to its origin, structure, prefixes and suffixes may be a sound vocabulary building exercise, but it destroys the trend of thought in reading and may lead to many false impressions as meanings of many words vary with the context in which they are used. We must look for the larger ideas. *Seek the ideas behind the words.*

Monotonous plodding. Keeping the same pace of reading in all materials, from light fiction to heavy study, is tiresome. One needs flexibility in reading habits. They should be as flexible as driving habits. In your car you use the high gear for rapid pleasure driving, but shift to second when road conditions or traffic require greater attention and control. Of course, the low gear is there to use when the situation requires heavy work. Let yourself go on some reading materials and don't worry about comprehension. You are missing much of the enjoyment of recreational reading by applying to it the same type of reading used for study. Learn to adjust your rate to the type of material and the purpose for reading it. Good readers may read at a very slow rate if they want a detailed understanding, but read at a rate of several thousand words per minute on fiction, light correspondence, and other materials they are reading for main ideas or for recreation.

Finger following. Following a line of print with a finger or with a guide of some kind always slows down the reading process because fingers cannot move as fast as eyes. To break this habit, keep both hands in your lap if reading at a desk, or hold the book in both hands. Rely solely on your eyes to follow the printed page.

Head swinging. Moving the head from side to side as one reads is much more laborious than moving the eyes. In addition to slowing down reading, this increased muscular activity will hasten fatigue. If you have this habit, try holding your head firmly in place with your hands and force your eyes to do the moving until the habit is broken.

Clue blindness. Like the driver who is too busy watching the road to see the signposts that direct him to his destination, many readers become too involved in word reading to notice such things as headings, subtitles, styles of type, listings, illustrations, introductions, and summaries. These all are important clues put in by the author to help you understand his concept of what is important. Try looking through some materials, reading only the headings, and the ideas set off by a different style of type or by listings, and see how much you can really get from these clues alone. Use the introductory paragraphs and lead sentences as clues to organization, and the summary statement as a review of material read. Try to develop the ability to glance over some material and get an understanding of the author's style and the types of signposts he has erected for you.

Backtracking. Going back to reread words or phrases is an indication that you doubt your own ability to pick out the important material. It slows you down a great deal because you are constantly thinking back instead of looking ahead to spot new ideas. Consequently you miss ideas until you have gone past them and then you have to go back to pick them up. The more you backtrack, the more necessary backtracking becomes to you. Try to concentrate on reading everything *only once.* You'll be surprised to find that you do get an over-all understanding of it without the mental underlining.

Rereading. Closely associated with backtracking is the habit of going back to read the whole assignment over again to be sure you understand it. Studies have shown that rereading is a fairly ineffective method of reviewing immediately after study (28). If you concentrate on doing a good job of reading in the first place, a few minutes of thinking about what you have read will be far more valuable than rereading. Try laying the reading material aside after you have finished it and thinking over what you have read. This not only will develop a better understanding of the material but will serve as an aid to remembering it later.

Daydreaming. Allowing your attention to wander to other things while you are reading leaves you with the feeling of having covered pages but having no knowledge of what you have read. To overcome this you must develop the ability to concentrate on one thing at a time. This matter of concentration is complex and will be discussed in detail in Sections III and IV.

Programs for improvement

Unless a person has a serious physical or mental handicap, none of the habits mentioned above are serious. All can be overcome with concentrated practice. Thousands of people have overcome them and established flexible reading habits that enable ←2700 them to read several times more efficiently than they did before. Some individuals find that bifocal glasses limit their reading speed. Usually this problem can be overcome by changing to reading glasses.

Colleges and businesses have come to realize the benefits that can be obtained by providing a training situation in which individuals can be motivated to achieve such changes of reading habits. Such reading programs try to force the individual to read faster by applying pressure of various kinds.

Some training centers rely heavily upon mechanical devices such as the reading films, tachistoscopic devices, flash cards, reading-rate controllers, and ←2800 reading accelerators of various types. Some use these devices for group work; others provide them for individual practice. The reading center in your vicinity may have one or more of these types of training devices with which you can practice.

Other centers rely largely upon group drill methods and the psychological pressure of competition within the group as a motivating device. In such situations, the instructor usually will use pacing techniques and a great deal of urging to get students to read faster.

Regardless of the program, much of the progress depends upon the motivation of the individual. Unless ←2900 he really wants to improve his reading and is willing to try out new ideas in an attempt to break old habits, he will gain but little from the experience. If he really wants to improve and will try new approaches to reading, the possibilities seem unlimited for his improvement in reading rate.

How do we understand more of what we read?

All of the techniques discussed above are designed primarily to increase rate of reading, but as we have said before, reading is a complex process of which the rate is only one factor. In this workbook emphasis ←3000 is placed upon *reading efficiency*, which is a combination of factors. In order to understand this term, we should first define clearly what is meant in this book by certain other terms, such as rate and comprehension.

Rate of reading is a numerical expression of the amount of material covered in a unit of time. It is expressed in words per minute. Thus a normal adult reading rate of 250 means that a normal adult should be able to cover 250 words of the material he is reading each minute.

Just covering words or pages would mean little if 3100→ we did not grasp some meaning from what we read. Comprehension, therefore, is an essential factor in good reading. Let us stress, however, that perfect comprehension is not the ideal of good reading, since perfect comprehension would be almost synonymous with memorization of the material, and this is seldom essential. The degree of understanding is measured more commonly in terms of the understanding of the main ideas and facts expressed in the reading. In some reading, it is more important to get a fairly thorough knowledge of these facts than in others. Therefore comprehension also should be 3200→ flexible and should be adjusted to the type of material read and the purpose of reading. One hundred percent comprehension is seldom needed unless one is memorizing material. For most reading a 60 to 80 percent comprehension is adequate. For light recreational reading, detailed comprehension is even less important. In studying, one should be concerned with more detailed comprehension but should not depend on reading alone. Here you need to use a balanced study approach that will make use of other techniques of understanding and remembering material. These will be discussed in detail in Section IV.

3300→ One of the most important factors in improving comprehension is that of having a purpose for reading. This purpose must be personalized to be effective. Mere reading of material because an instructor assigns it, or because your boss or your wife wants you to read it, is not sufficient. You, personally, must see some reason for reading the material and must be looking for something in the material read. There are several ways of developing this personal interest.

First of all, you should *think* before starting to read. Think about the subject matter covered in the material. What do you already know about it? What 3400→ would you like to know about it? What do you know about the person who wrote the article? Is he an authority? Is he well known for his prejudice on this subject? Will his presentation be biased? Can you depend on his statements being accurate and complete, or is he likely to try to persuade you to accept a certain point of view by presenting only partial facts or distorting views of the problem? These are just some of the questions which you should ask yourself before starting to read, but thinking about them will help prepare you for reading the 3500→ article with interest and concentration.

After having spent a few seconds in thinking before starting to read, glance over the article quickly to look for clues. The headings and boldface print will tell you the direction that the article will take in presenting the ideas. This helps prepare you to recognize important points as they are presented.

A third point in helping improve concentration and retention of material is to concentrate on small units, one at a time. Intense concentration on the portion between two headings with a slight pause to rest your eyes and think about the material before going on 3600 to the next section will provide relaxation as well as help to organize your thinking.

Taking a few seconds after each unit, and a longer time at the end of the reading period to think over what has been read and to fix a mental impression, will help you to retain that impression for a longer period of time. In short, an alternation of reading and thinking provides a greater comprehension of what is read.

In order to measure comprehension you must be tested in some way to see how much you remember of what was read. Comprehension usually is expressed 3700 numerically as a percentage score. *The comprehension score is the percent of questions answered correctly in a test on the material read.* A good reader should be able to score at least 60 to 80 percent on such a test, depending on the number of questions asked and the amount of detail involved in the questions.

What is reading efficiency?

Many students, in trying to increase their reading rate, become disturbed when their comprehension drops. Others trying hard to improve comprehension slow down to even slower reading rates in an attempt to get better understanding. Many reading teachers 3800 have found that the faster readers often secure better comprehension scores than the slower readers. Similarly, we find that, at the end of a reading training program, students reading at several times their original rate can read with as great or greater comprehension than they did before starting training. Although most of them go through a period of decreased comprehension while they are working hard on increasing rate, they find that as they become adjusted to reading at a faster rate they are able to build up their comprehension again.

Neither rate nor comprehension really gives us the complete picture of reading skills. Reading at a rapid 3900 rate is of little value if you understand very little of what you have read. On the other hand, reading with a high degree of comprehension is of little value if you never have time to read all the material you are expected to cover. The most important factor is neither the speed at which you read nor the amount you can remember of what you read, but a combination of these: *the amount you can read and remember* per unit of time. In an attempt to express this factor and place an emphasis on the importance of this 4000 combination of skills, we use the term "reading efficiency" to represent the amount of material com-

prehended per minute of reading time. Efficiency is computed by taking the product of the *rate* of reading (expressed in words per minute) and the *comprehension* score (expressed as the percent of correct answers on a test over the material). *Efficiency*, then, is a numerical expression of rate of effective reading represented in words per minute. Let us compare the following sequence of scores to see how this works.

	1st test	2nd test	3rd test	4th test
4100 → Rate	100	150	300	400
Comprehension	80	70	60	75
Efficiency	80	105	180	300

If this individual were to consider only the decreasing comprehension scores during practice he might become discouraged and stop pushing his rate improvement. By stressing the efficiency score instead of rate or comprehension, he gets a better picture of his real progress, however, and although his final comprehension score is still below his initial one, his efficiency score gives a better picture of the amount of material he can grasp in a unit of study time. This individual probably would find that he was accom-4200 plishing at least three times as much work in his periods of reading as was possible before, and the slight difference in comprehension could be offset by other techniques of remembering.

Throughout this book, stress will be placed upon the efficiency scores on reading exercises because efficiency seems the best expression of the effectiveness of reading habits.

Conditions for improvement

In this chapter we have tried to explore some of the possibilities for reading improvement, recognizing some of the bad habits that slow us down, some of the factors that influence these reading habits, 4300 and some of the terms used to describe the results of reading habits. We have presented the idea that anyone is capable of improving his reading efficiency unless prevented from doing so by physical or mental handicaps. The question remains: How can *you* improve your reading efficiency? Three conditions are needed to make satisfactory progress in the improvement of reading efficiency.

First of all, you must be convinced that you want to become a better reader. You must be willing to put in several hours of hard and sometimes monotonous work in reading practice. You must be willing to face the problems of being compared with others, 4400 of competing with others, and of working under pressure that may be irritating. You must be willing to cast aside established habits in order to try new ones. You need to be convinced that the time to be saved in the future, when more satisfactory reading habits have been established, is worth the sacrifice of several hours of the time now. If you can see the long-range value and are willing to work, your possibilities of improvement are practically unlimited.

Second, you will need to work with appropriate materials from which comparisons can be made to determine improvement. Unless the exercises you use are of comparable difficulty, misunderstanding and discouragement may follow. Unless all sets of questions are made up in comparable forms, your comprehension scores may vary because of the difficulty of the test rather than your degree of understanding. There will be a better chance of progress if you work from a workbook which has been standardized and which has comparable tests. The materials used in this workbook represent the results of many years of experimentation and revision in order to develop the best possible sequences of exercises.

Note that all exercises are graded with a readability score. These scores are determined by the application of the Flesch formula (15) to the material. Exercises are arranged in a gradually ascending order of difficulty so that, as you learn to read faster, you also learn to read material of a little greater difficulty.

Finally, you must feel a sense of progress and satisfaction. You must compare results of today with those of yesterday and then set higher goals for tomorrow. The reading charts in this book help you to do that. They are organized in such a way that you can compare results on any particular exercise with others in that series, or with different types of exercises. Keeping your reading graphs up to date will help you to get an over-all view of progress in increasing your reading efficiency. The extent of your growth in effective reading skills will depend upon your desire, your attitude, and your concentration.

II

Kinds of Reading

One of the marks of a good reader is the ability to adjust his reading skills to the type of material he is reading. The greater range of reading efficiency he has, the greater possibilities he has for judging what types of reading skills to apply on different materials. Space limitations in this workbook do not permit detailed analysis of the various types of reading and their application. However a brief consideration of the major types of reading presented at this time may help you to recognize some of them in practice. ⟵100

Scanning

Scanning (or skimming as it is sometimes called) is the technique of reading by the signposts — the clues set up by the author. By using these you can learn to skip materials which are not of immediate interest to you and to locate more quickly those which you really wish to read in detail. Most textbooks are organized to make intelligent skimming possible. All devices such as chapter titles, sectional headings, bold face or italicized type, and underlining are clues to help you with this technique. If you take time to think before you start to read and have a good idea of ⟵200 what you are looking for, these clues can save a great deal of reading time by taking you right to the sections in which you are interested and allowing you to skip the rest. Scanning can also be very effective as a preliminary step to reading something more thoroughly; it gives an overview of what you can expect in the material.

Idea reading

Rapid reading for key ideas is essential to most business reading. The professional man who has not mastered this type of reading may find himself bogged down in his correspondence, his newspapers, his ⟵300 professional journals. Most correspondence includes many formal clichés and standardized expressions. The basic meaning of most articles in professional publications could be condensed into a few simple paragraphs. This reading for the main ideas is a technique of rapid reading in which the eyes move rapidly, catching large phrases at each glance, and registering with the brain only the most significant words in those phrases. Most of the rest of the words are rejected by the eyes without any attempt at the

mental process of registering and remembering. Successful idea reading is perhaps one of the most ⟵400 difficult types of reading to master, yet it is one of the most efficient as one can develop extremely rapid rates of reading with this type. It means being familiar with the make-up of the English language as a means of communication. It necessitates recognition of key sentences and illustrative words and phrases. Rapid recognition of the skeleton structure of the sentence is essential to discovering the basic meaning. Idea reading means making quick decisions as to the relative importance of different sentences and paragraphs as you read. It means quick recognition of the author's clues and rapid association with ⟵500 ideas you already understand that relate to this material.

Exploratory reading

Exploratory, or general content reading, involves more detail than the two types mentioned before. This type of approach would be used for longer articles in magazines, for descriptive literature, and for light fiction. It may be used for similar reading in which we wish to get a fairly accurate picture of the whole presentation of ideas and to pick up a more thorough understanding of some new ideas. Materials on which we apply this type of reading frequently use fewer headings and clues and require reading more ⟶600 carefully to find the important ideas. Students would use this technique on many outside references in which they are to find background material but in which they will not be tested for detail. Emphasis here should be placed on recognizing and understanding main ideas more thoroughly and in relating them to other ideas in the article or to previous knowledge of the subject.

Study reading

Study reading is a type in which the reader must get a maximum understanding of the main ideas and their relationships. This is the type the student must apply to his textbooks, and the professional man must ⟶700 apply to his contracts, legal papers, technical manuals, instructions, and similar materials. Here he frequently deals with materials which he must read and understand *now* and also *remember for future use*. Here again clues are important and a preliminary scanning may be quite helpful, but the actual reading process needs to be an alternating activity between reading for ideas and thinking about those ideas. The actual reading process itself may be quite rapid, but greater time must be taken for detailed consideration and thinking if the ideas are to be organized in logical order and set in your mind to stay. In this type of reading one must make maximum use of such techniques as preliminary scanning, thinking and questioning one-self before reading, concentrating on small units at a time with breaks for thinking and note making be-tween units, and reviewing of the basic ideas after reading is completed to assure lasting understanding. Certain basic sections of the material should be identified for more careful attention through ana-lytical reading.

Critical reading

Another type of reading which must sometimes be applied wisely is that of critical reading. You may find a certain article that tends to stir you to action, such as writing to your congressman or rushing right down town to buy a new and indispensable house-hold appliance. Then you should stop and consider what you have read more carefully. Many of our periodical articles, books, and advertising materials are loaded with carefully used propaganda devices designed to sway our opinions or to sell us on some particular idea or product. Be careful that a rapid reading of the main ideas does not lead to false conclusions.

To apply techniques of critical reading, one should go back and consider carefully what he knows about the source of the reading material and the possible biases or ulterior motives which its publisher or author might have had. He should also consider what he knows of the author and his background and

knowledge of the subject. One should watch the reading material for inconsistent logic and for false analogies. Particularly important is an awareness of emotionally loaded words which appeal to basic emotions and try to stir up emotional reactions for or against something. With experience you can learn to spot some of these types of appeals through a quick scanning for the clues the author provides — then you can beware of these techniques before beginning to read. In any reading we should frequently ask ourselves: "What is the author trying to make us believe and why?"

Analytical reading

Certain sections of study materials require a much more thorough type of reading than those mentioned before. Mathematical theorems and problems, scien-tific formulae and certain definitive statements of key ideas require careful attention to each word and to its relative importance. One must approach such reading with a questioning mind, seeking complete clarifi-cation. Fortunately materials requiring this intense concentration and deliberate thought are seldom long. You can learn to recognize such passages and to slow your reading pace to deal with such sections more adequately.

Identify and adjust

Learning to recognize different types of reading and to judge what types of reading habits to apply to them helps us to become more effective in our over-all use of reading time. We streamline our reading activities to meet the needs of the time and the ma-terial to be read. Such judgment can come only from practice. This workbook will provide an opportunity to practice several types of reading, but you must apply the principles of efficient reading to the materials which you read every day in order to develop really efficient reading habits.

III

Is Reading Enough?

No one would question that reading is essential to understanding, but too many persons jump to the conclusion that reading is the only essential approach to learning. They tend to depend on reading *entirely* for gaining new ideas and for developing an understanding of them. They frequently consider audiovisual devices as merely recreational devices of momentary interest but of little lasting value. Such persons may completely ignore the possibilities of notemaking from speeches, conferences, and telephone conversations as an effective technique. They usually consider note making in conjunction with reading as too much extra work. This dependency on reading may have worked at some levels of education. 100 But the college student and the businessman on his job usually find the demands on their time too great to allow them to do as much reading as they think is necessary.

Perhaps this extreme dependency on reading also makes you fearful of any techniques which might lower your reading comprehension even temporarily. This fear is the basis of much hesitancy in learning. For most people, reading is one of the slower techniques of picking up ideas. A picture sometimes can convey as much information in one glance as several paragraphs of descriptive literature could do. The 200 oral statement often can be made to convey much more meaning through the changes of inflection and the verbal stress on certain words than the same statement could if typed on a piece of paper. Perhaps one reason some people feel so self-conscious about their reading is that they are too dependent upon it and fail to associate it adequately with other means of communication. Reading is a basic skill of communication, but is used most effectively when it supplements and enriches the material gained in other ways. Let us consider some of the techniques which can be used to enrich its meaning. 300

Listening involves skills often overlooked and ignored. A speaker uses many signposts just as the writer does. He uses introductions and summaries during which the listener should be thinking and relating what he hears to what he already understands. Changes of tone, pitch, and rate of speaking are used to emphasize certain points. He uses lead statements as headings to new topics and frequently lists or itemizes points he thinks are important. The listener who is alert to these clues will be able to learn a great 400 deal during his periods of listening.

Notemaking is a very important technique for the busy student. By relying on brief notes he relieves the stress of detailed mental comprehension of many minute facts of temporary importance. Brief, well organized notes taken on important reading assignments provide an excellent basis for review at a later time. An important aspect of good notes, however, is that they are *made* in the writer's own words rather than *taken* as a few random excerpts from the speaker's terminology (5).

Self-recitation of important points helps to keep them in mind. This process of predicting questions 500 to which answers must be found requires occasional pauses to think over what is being read. The questions posed serve as a goal for reading and the pauses for thinking provide brief relaxation for the eyes and strengthen the mental organization of the material read. This is an important aspect of the thinking process applied to reading.

Frequent review of important materials is an invaluable aid in remembering and will make later rereading unnecessary.

In the previous chapter reference was made to several techniques which might be used to improve comprehension. These are all supplementary techniques not actually a part of the reading process 600 itself but closely related to it. At this time let us consider more carefully the actual steps involved in these activities.

Orienting oneself to the reading assignment

Most efficient businessmen operate on some sort of schedule. They plan a certain time of day for reading their correspondence and dictating replies. At other periods they consider reports or devote their time to study of technical material related to their work. By having regular times for certain types of reading work, they get into habits of thinking about these things at regular periods. This helps to establish 700 a "mood" for reading which can be intensified by taking a few minutes to survey the reading to be done, arranging it according to importance, and anticipating the questions which must be answered in the reading. Before starting each item of correspondence or each report, a brief period of thinking serves to coordinate previous information about this particular item and to enable the reader to concentrate intensely on the one item under consideration.

Getting the over-all view

In considering any particular item of reading, a rapid scanning of the pages looking for key ideas will set up general idea goals to be attained and will make the task more meaningful than just covering pages of material.

Reading to find answers to questions

In the preview of the material you will recognize several main topics. As you approach these topics, try to pose questions for yourself to give you a purpose for reading. You will find that looking for answers does much to focus your interest on the material and helps you attain faster rates of reading.

Visualizing and making associations

As you pause, at intervals, try to form a mental picture of the things about which you have been reading. Relate the ideas to something you already know and understand. Establishing associations with known facts will provide a more thorough understanding. This step is particularly important if you feel that the reading material is important for long range usage.

Making notes from materials read

If you are reading to organize material for a speech or a report or if you want some details for later use, take some notes in *your own words* during your pauses. Brief notes with personalized expression help you to bring the verbal recognition into more concise understanding which has lasting meaning for you. If you have difficulty concentrating on important material, making notes forces you to think about it.

Reviewing

Using some time *regularly* to think over materials read during the previous few days and to pull together the important ideas from various sources is an invaluable supplement to the reading process. Thus, ideas picked up from very rapid reading can be fixed more firmly in your mind for later use.

In Summary

These techniques will serve to strengthen your comprehension of what you read. They will make it easier for you to relax and will allow you to read at a maximum rate without fear of losing comprehension. The time you save in rapid reading will provide opportunity to use some of these techniques so important to remembering ideas and their relationships.

IV

A Program for Effective Study

The information in the previous chapters is basic to any sound program of study. Students in high school and college need to develop sound habits of study if they expect to live a balanced life. They must provide time for both academic requirements and social opportunities. Many colleges are attempting to help students establish such habits by the provision of classes in "Study Skill Techniques." Such courses recognize reading as one aspect of study, but also point out that efficient reading alone is not enough to meet the competition of college classes today.

Let us look at some of the factors that are impor-←100 tant in study. We might consider them by asking five questions about effective study:

What?   Who?   Where?   When?   How?

What is effective study?

Many students, even some of those who receive good grades regularly, spend a great deal more time in study than is necessary. They have developed study techniques that are laborious and time consuming. Other students put in many hours in study but seem to get little out of the time spent. They frequently complain about difficulties in certain courses, and the only remedy they can suggest is to put in more time on that subject. In both circum- ←200 stances the students probably are ignoring some basic principles about fatigue and span of interest. Instead of spending *more time* in study, they need to make *better use of time* they do spend. They need to get the most possible good out of each hour spent on a course. This is what is meant by *effective study*. A person who has effective study habits will spend *less* time on the same material and will understand it better than one who has not learned effective methods.

Whose responsibility?

In high school, parents and teachers usually try to build study habits by providing certain times and ⇄300 places for study, and by trying to reduce possible interruptions. As you grow older, however, you find yourself more "on your own." Especially at college you find that no one seems to exert much effort to *make* you study. By now you are supposed to be mature enough to realize that study is essential

to success in school. Therefore it is your responsibility to see that you provide adequate time for study. Other school activities will place many demands on you and you will find it easy to devote to them time 400→ which should be given to study.

Some students realize too late that they have been neglecting their studies and try desperately to cram all their study and review into the last few days before examinations. When they fail the exams, they frequently rationalize and blame the instructor, their roommates, or someone else for their inability to keep up with the requirements of the course. With the keen competition present in college, poor study habits can undermine the entire enjoyment of a college program. An early recognition of this could save much unhappiness.

If you wish to improve your academic record, 500→ you must assume the responsibility *yourself* for keeping up to date in all your school work. The sooner you accept this responsibility seriously, the more likely you are to succeed in your school program. Specific suggestions to help you establish better study habits are given on the following pages.

Where to study?

Some students are able to study almost anywhere. While walking or resting, they may be mentally organizing ideas. Many students, however, do not have this ability to concentrate in the midst of other activity. Even when seated at a study desk, 600→ they may find other ideas creeping into their minds to keep them from thinking about the school work waiting to be done. Since this is true of many students, let us consider some of the factors that do help to make the study desk a more effective place to work.

Auditory distractions usually can be controlled by selecting as quiet a place as possible. A student can reduce, to some extent, distraction from outside noises. This may mean working out arrangements for study hours with roommates and making an agreement not to have guests in the room during certain hours. If you find yourself unable to eliminate 700→ these distractions in your own room, then consider the scheduling of study hours in the library where the atmosphere is kept as quiet as possible. Another possibility is the use of a vacant classroom for that free period between classes.

Visual distractions are frequently present without being recognized. The picture of the girl friend on your desk may take you off on a chain of memories every time you glance at it; the souvenir ash tray you got on your vacation trip last summer may recall many pleasant experiences; the letter you got from home yesterday may start you worrying about the crops at home; the advertising on the desk blotter may stir thoughts of the good times you could have if you only followed the suggestions printed there. The curling smoke from the cigarette in your ash tray may attract your attention and lead your thoughts astray. These and many other items frequently found on study desks can lead students to many minutes of daydreaming during the hours when they *think* they have been studying.

One of the first essentials in improving the place of study is to clear the desk of as many of these diverting influences as you can. If possible, the study desk should be cleared of everything except the textbook you are studying at the moment and the necessary papers and pencils for taking notes.

Next, consider what disturbing items lie in your range of vision as you sit at your desk. Consider carefully any objects that lie in the area of distraction. To do this, check the *angle of distraction* from your study desk. Any object falling within a sixty degree angle on either side of the forward view from your desk is likely to interfere with your concentration. Mirrors are especially disturbing as they expand the area of distraction to include a reflected area as well as the actual one. How many things in your room fall within this range. What do they make you think about? To improve your concentration you would be wise to move your desk so that the expanse covered in this angle of distraction is at a minimum and so that most of the wall space there is blank. Ideally, then, a study desk should be placed in a corner, and the wall above it should be kept clear of distracting influences.

Lighting is also an important factor in concentration. Eye strain and general fatigue are the logical results of poor lighting. Do not depend on a single overhead light. Every student needs a good desk lamp that will provide indirect lighting in the working area. Desk lamps which cause a glare on the books and papers should be avoided. In addition to a good study lamp on the desk, some other light in the room is needed to prevent sharp contrasts between a brightly lighted desk and a dark room. Extreme contrasts make the eyes tire more rapidly. A combination of a good indirect desk lamp and an overhead light is considered ideal for effective study conditions.

Ventilation and temperature are important too. There should be some provision for fresh air without a draft. If you cannot work with a window open, make a point of airing out the study room once a day. A warm room stimulates drowsiness and makes studying difficult. Most people study best in a room that is slightly cooler than the normal living room temperature.

Avoid physical relaxation when trying to study. If you pick the easy chair or the bed as a place to study, don't expect to be able to concentrate very long. By relaxing physically, you invite mental relaxation as well. A good straight chair at a study desk is the ideal location for effective study.

Having one place for study *and study only* is important. If you study at the same place that you play games, do your nails, write your letters, plan your dance programs, etc., you will find it more difficult to get to work. If, however, you use one desk exclusively for studying, you will find it natural to start concentrating when you sit there.

When to study?

Your school program is one of your most important obligations and requires more time than you are likely to give to it without careful planning. The best protection against late assignments and the necessity for "cramming" is to budget your time as you go along and to plan a proper balance between work, study, and recreational activities. One of the best ways to do this is to make out a *Time Budget Sheet* (28). A sample *Time Budget Sheet* is shown on the next page. Copies of these can be obtained through your University Bookstore. The success of such a time budget will depend on how carefully you plan it and use it. Several points should be considered. The suggestions on the back of the *Time Budget Sheet* are worthy of careful consideration.

How to study?

Probably no two students study in exactly the same way. Each student has learned certain techniques which seem easiest for him. If these techniques bring understanding of the materials with a minimum expenditure of time, then the student is probably satisfied with these study habits. If, however, the student feels that he is not getting the desired results or that his methods are too time-consuming, then he should consider a change. If the present study habits are leading only to failing grades and discouragement, they should be discarded and replaced by a new set which shows promise of more effective use of the student's time.

Many students fail to make effective use of new techniques of study because they are unwilling to give up the old techniques, even though these older ones have not produced the desired results. Often it is necessary to *unlearn* poor work habits before you can establish good ones. If you wish to develop a greater efficiency in your study, you must be willing to release some old habits in favor of some new ones.

TIME BUDGET SHEET
COLLEGE FORM

Prepared by
Lyle L. Miller

UNIVERSITY OF WYOMING

Name _____

(Study the suggestions on the back before making out budget)

SQ4R Method

Self R Recitation
S R STUDY PROGRAM
Spaced Review

SELF RECITATION

	MON	TUES	WED	THUR	FRI	SAT	SUN	TOTAL
6 - 7								
7 - 8								
8 - 9								
9 - 10								
10 - 11								
11 - 12								
12 - 1								
1 - 2								
2 - 3								
3 - 4								
4 - 5								
5 - 6								
6 - 7								
7 - 8								
8 - 9								
9 - 10								
10 - 11								
11 - 12								
CLASS								
STUDY								
TOTAL								

These three evening plans interchangeable

SURVEY   QUESTION   READ   RECITE   REVIEW

REPEAT: QRR

SOME HINTS ON PLANNING A BETTER STUDY SCHEDULE

from Lyle L. Miller
Professor of Guidance Education, University of Wyoming

The success of your study schedule will depend on the care with which you plan it. Careful consideration of some of these points will help you to make a schedule that will **work for you.**

1. **Plan a schedule of balanced activities.** College life has many aspects which are very important to success. Some have fixed time requirements and some are flexible. Some of the most common which you must consider are:

   FIXED: eating organizations classes church work
   FLEXIBLE: sleeping recreation study relaxation personal affairs

2. **Plan enough time in studying to do justice to each subject.** Most college classes are planned to require about three hours work per week per credit in the course. By multiplying your credit load by three you can get a good idea of the time you should provide for studying. Of course, if you are a slow reader, or have other study deficiencies, you may need to plan more time in order to meet the competition of college classes.

3. **Study at a regular time and in a regular place.** Establishing habits of study is extremely important. Knowing what you are going to study, and when, saves a lot of time in making decisions and retracing your steps to get necessary materials, etc. Avoid generalizations in your schedule such as "STUDY." Commit yourself more definitely to "STUDY HISTORY" or "STUDY CHEMISTRY" at certain regular hours.

4. **Study as soon after your lecture class as possible.** One hour spent soon after class will do as much good in developing an understanding of materials as several hours a few days later. Check over lecture notes while they are still fresh in your mind. Start assignments while your memory of the assignment is still accurate.

5. **Utilize odd hours during the day for studying.** The scattered one or two hour free periods between classes are easily wasted. Planning and establishing habits of using them for studying for the class just finished will result in free time for recreation or activities at other times in the week.

6. **Limit your blocks of study time to no more than 2 hours on any one course at one time.** After 1½ to 2 hours of study you begin to tire rapidly and your ability to concentrate decreases rapidly. Taking a break and then switching to studying some other course will provide the change necessary to keep up your efficiency.

7. **Trade time — don't steal it.** When unexpected events arise that take up time you had planned to study, decide immediately where you can find the time to make up the study missed and adjust your schedule for that week. Note the three weekend evenings. Most students can afford no more than two of them for recreation, but may wish to use different evenings on different weeks. This "trading agreement" provides for committing one night to study, but rotating it as recreational possibilities vary.

8. **Provide for spaced review —** That is, a regular weekly period when you will review the work in each of your courses and be sure you are up to date. This review should be cumulative, covering briefly all the work done thus far in the quarter.

9. **Practice self-recitation as a device for increasing memory.** Organize your notes in a question and answer form and think in terms of questions and answers about the main ideas of the material as you review weekly. When preparing for exams, try to predict the questions the instructor may ask.

10. **Keep carefully organized notes on both lectures and assignments.** Good notes are one of the best bases for review. Watch for key ideas in lectures and try to express them in your own words in your notes. Watch for headings and bold face type in your reading to give you clues of main ideas for your notes. Take down careful notes as to exactly what assignments are made and when they are due.

11. **Always try to improve your study efficiency.** The SQ4R method of study is a very sound approach to improving comprehension. Details on this method can be found in the library in Chapter IV of "Increasing Reading Efficiency," published by Henry Holt and Company or in Chapter IV of "Developing Reading Efficiency," published by Pruett Press, Inc., Boulder, Colorado.

Order additional copies of this budget sheet from Pruett Press, Inc., 2930 Pearl, Boulder, Colorado.

Space in this book does not allow a detailed discussion of many of the techniques of study. You will find references on study skills in your library or your bookstore. For detailed suggestions on note-making, you may read *Learning More by Effective Study*, by Charles and Dorothy Bird (4). For specific suggestions on classroom and examination skills, you will find *Effective Study*, by F. P. Robinson (33), very helpful. For detailed information on the preparation of reports and term papers, you can find assistance in *The Research Paper* by Hook and Gaver (19). *How to Improve Your Study Habits*, by LeCount and 1800← Bamman (21), is a concise pamphlet — an excellent reference to keep in your notebook.

Three major techniques presented by Francis P. Robinson in his book *Effective Study* (33) have proved to be so helpful to many college students that they merit a presentation here. These techniques provide an excellent means of establishing important ideas in one's mind and retaining them. These may be identified as the three "S. R." techniques since these letters can be used as memory clues for all three techniques. In brief, these techniques may be applied as follows:

A. *Self-Recitation.* Ask questions of yourself as you 1900← study and as you review. Be alert at all times to the questions suggested about major ideas and try to read for answers to them. In reviewing ask yourself questions and see if you can answer them, then check your answers against your notes. In studying for exams, try to predict the questions that the instructor may ask and be prepared for these questions in the examination.

B. *Spaced Review.* Review briefly immediately after study, then review again within a week. Each week schedule review periods where you can review all the material presented thus far in the course. These brief weekly reviews will keep 2000← you constantly up to date and will reduce the necessity for last minute cramming before examinations.

C. *The SQ3R Method,* originated by Robinson (32), has been referred to frequently as the SQ4R Method for purposes of clarification. The following explanation of the six steps of this method has been presented by Miller and Seeman (29).

The SQ4R method of study

1. **Survey.** Glance over the headings in the chapter to see the few big points which will be developed. This survey should take only a few seconds and will show the several core ideas 2100← around which the discussion will be developed.

2. **Question.** Turn the first heading into a question. This will arouse your curiosity and thus aid comprehension. It will help to bring to mind information that you already know. In this way your understanding of that section will be increased. The question will make the important points stand out.

3. **Read.** Read to answer the question. Make this an active search for the answer. You will find that your eyes tend to move more rapidly over the material, slighting the unimportant or explanatory details while noting the important points.

2200→ 4. **Recite.** Try to recite the answer to your question without looking at the book. Use your own words and think of an example. If you can do this you know what is in the book; if you can't, glance over the section again. If you jot down cue phrases in outline form as you do this, you will have an excellent basis for later review and study.

5. **Repeat.** Repeat steps 2, 3, and 4 on each succeeding section. Turn the next heading into a question, read to answer that question, and recite the answer by jotting down cue phrases 2300→ in an outline. Read in this way until the lesson is completed.

6. **Review.** Look over your notes to get a bird's-eye view of the points and their relationships and check your memory as to the content by reciting on the major subpoints under each heading. This checking of your memory can be done by covering up the notes and trying to recall the main points, then exposing each major point and trying to recall the subpoints listed under it.

SQ4R applied to problem solving

A modification of this method to apply to mathematical-type reading where problem solving is in-2400→ volved might be summarized as follows:

1. **Survey.** Look over the problems to see what types of logic they require and what basic formulae will be used. Try to make associations with practical situations in which similar problems might be encountered.

2. **Question.** Looking at the first problem, think through it to be sure you understand what is the unknown factor which you are to find and what are the known facts with which you can work.

3. **Solve.** Work through the problem to find the unknown factor.

4. **Check.** Substitute the answer you have found for the unknown in the original statement and see if it makes sense. Check through the basic formula to see if it balances with this value.

5. **Repeat.** Apply the same three steps to each successive problem in the assignment.

6. **Review.** Check over the whole assignment again

to be sure you have completed all the assigned work and that your answers were reasonable. Be sure you understand the purpose of such exercises and try to think of practical applications of the principles involved in the problems.

Concentrate on end results

The application of these three techniques will free you from much of the tension associated with trying to get thorough comprehension from the reading alone. Frequently, students depend on one reading of the material to grasp its entire content. The methods outlined above decrease the stress on a detailed comprehension in initial reading. They provide other study techniques — scanning, questioning, reciting, and reviewing — to develop the understanding of material. This frees one to read as rapidly as possible with a major emphasis on *seeking the ideas behind the words.*

As you develop this technique of rapid reading, you will usually find that comprehension will improve also. But more important than either is the efficiency of reading — that is, the amount one understands per unit of study time. By increasing the efficiency of the initial reading, you can find time for the other techniques which will help build a more permanent comprehension of the whole body of material.

V

Using This Workbook

The exercises in this workbook have been grouped according to types, each of which plays a distinct part in the development of more efficient reading habits.

Series I — Word Recognition Drills

Word recognition exercises are designed to accelerate rate and to establish some rhythmic patterns of eye movement. As you proceed through these exercises you will find yourself dealing with longer words. Here you will have an opportunity to break the habits of syllabication and to learn to pick up longer words at a single glance.

Series II — Word Meaning Drills

This series of exercises injects the thinking factor, as you are expected to identify synonyms at a rapid $\overset{100}{\leftarrow}$ pace. The arrangement is the same as before, except that you now must think about word meanings. In addition to eye span and rhythmic eye movements, the factor of rate of perception has been added. Since all of the words used in this exercise have been taken from Thorndike's list (42) of the 30,000 most frequently used words in our vocabulary, these exercises also serve to point up weaknesses in your vocabulary list which need study. Any words missed here should be placed on a vocabulary list and studied carefully so that they will not remain as stumbling blocks to $\overset{200}{\leftarrow}$ your reading.

Series III — Phrase Meaning Drills

This series introduces phrases and is designed primarily to increase eye span. At the same time, you continue to practice on rhythmic eye movements and perception of meaning under time pressure. These are the exercises in which you should begin to sense an improvement in rate of reading as you learn to pick up several words at one glance. These exercises begin with short phrases and gradually build up in length until the last few exercises are composed of phrases of several words.

Series IV — Sentence Meaning Drills $\overset{300}{\leftarrow}$

The fourth series consists of exercises in recognition of sentence meaning. Here increased eye span is further stressed, and, in addition, you are expected to recognize the key words that provide meaning for a sentence. This is basic training for the idea-type of reading in which you strip the sentences of their verbal padding to pick up the basic ideas.

Series V — Idea Reading Drills

This series is made up of short articles from which you are to pick up the main ideas or basic themes $\overset{400}{\rightarrow}$ as quickly as possible. On these you should apply your techniques of *idea reading* to attain maximum rates with only a general comprehension of the more basic ideas being presented.

Series VI — Exploratory Reading Drills

This series is composed of readings of longer length and greater complexity. They will provide practice in *exploratory reading*. In these exercises you develop skill in reading at a fairly rapid rate while concentrating for greater detail in terms of general content and ideas rather than specific facts.

Series VII — Study Reading Drills

Here you must stop and *think* to answer questions at intervals in your reading. The basic purpose is to $\overset{500}{\rightarrow}$ demonstrate to you how rapidly material can be covered even when you do take time out for thinking and answering questions. Although not an exact duplication of the *study* reading, in which you develop idea outlines, these drills will provide an objective comparison of this type of reading.

Computing Scores and Recording Progress

On each exercise throughout the book, you are to record time, rate, comprehension, and efficiency. Tables are provided for looking up your reading rates. Each exercise refers you to the table for rates for that exercise.

Keys for scoring exercises are located in the back $\overset{600}{\rightarrow}$ of the workbook. After computing the comprehension and efficiency scores, you should compare these with scores on other exercises to determine your progress. Progress charts are provided on page 289 of this book to record your scores on each reading exercise. Keeping these progress charts up to date will help motivate you to try for continued improvement. Supplementary reading from longer exercises, such as those in *Maintaining Reading Efficiency* (26), will help you to establish more effective reading habits.

On the page preceding each series of exercises, you will find instructions and illustrations of the type of $\overset{700}{\rightarrow}$ work to be done in that series.

VI

Selected References

1. Anonymous — "Our Schools Aren't Good Enough," *The News Letter*, *Bureau of Educational Research*, Columbus, Ohio: *The Ohio State University Press*, Volume XX, Number 2, November, 1954.

2. Anonymous — "The Remembering Skills," *The Supervisor's Notebook*, Chicago: Scott, Foresman and Company, Volume 18, Number 1, Fall, 1954.

3. Anonymous — *Proceedings, First Annual Meeting Southwest Reading Conference*, Ft. Worth, Tex.: Texas Christian University Press, April, 1952.

4. Bird, Charles, and Dorothy M. Bird, *Learning More By Effective Study*, New York: Appleton-Century-Crofts, 1945.

5. Blair, Glenn Myers, *Diagnostic and Remedial Teaching in Secondary Schools*, New York: The Macmillan Company, 1950.

6. Brown, James I., *Efficient Reading*, Boston: D. C. Heath and Company, 1952.

7. Causey, Oscar S., ed., *Evaluating College Reading Programs*, Ft. Worth, Tex.: Texas Christian University Press, 1955.

8. Causey, Oscar S., ed., *Exploring the Levels of College Reading Programs*, Ft. Worth, Tex.: Texas Christian University Press, 1956.

9. Causey, Oscar S., ed., *Techniques and Procedures in College and Adult Reading Programs*, Ft. Worth, Tex.: Texas Christian University Press, 1957.

10. Causey, Oscar S., *The Reading Teacher's Reader*, New York: The Ronald Press Company, 1958.

11. Causey, Oscar S., ed., *What the Colleges Are Doing in Reading Improvement Programs*, Ft. Worth, Tex.: Texas Christian University Press, February, 1954.

12. Causey, Oscar S., ed., *Improving Reading Programs for College Students and Adults*, Yearbook of Southwest Reading Conference for Colleges and Universities, Ft. Worth, Tex.: Texas Christian University Press, 1952.

13. Center, Stella S., *The Art of Book Reading*, New York: Charles Scribner's Sons, 1952.

14. Dallmann, Martha, and Alma Sheridan, *Better Reading in College*, New York: The Ronald Press Company, 1954.

15. Flesch, Rudolph, *The Art of Readable Writing*, New York: Harper & Row, Publishers, 1949.

16. Glock, Marvin D., *The Improvement of College Reading*, Boston: Houghton Mifflin Company, 1954.

17. Hoffman, Lillian R., *The Administration of a Reading Program for College or University Students*, unpublished doctoral dissertation, Laramie, Wyo.: University of Wyoming, 1954.

18. Hildreth, Gertrude H., *Teaching Reading, a Guide To Basic Principles and Modern Practices*, New York: Holt, Rinehart and Winston, Inc., 1958.

19. Hook, Lucyle, and Mary Virginia Gaver, *The Research Paper*, Englewood Cliffs, N. J.: Prentice-Hall Inc., 1952.

20. Judson, Horace, and Kenneth P. Baldridge, *The Techniques of Reading*, New York: Harcourt, Brace & World, Inc., 1954.

21. LeCount, Samuel N., and Henry A. Bamman, *How to Improve your Study Habits*, Palo Alto, Calif.: Pacific Books, 1953.

22. Lewis, Norman, *How to Read Better and Faster*, New York: Thomas Y. Crowell Company, 1951.

23. Metropolitan School Study Council, *Five Steps to Reading Success in Science, Social Studies and Mathematics*, New York: Metropolitan School Study Council, 1954.

24. Miller, Lyle L., *Developing Reading Efficiency, (Rev. Ed.)*, Laramie, Wyo.: Developmental Reading Distributors, 1965.

25. Miller, Lyle L., *Increasing Reading Efficiency*, New York: Holt, Rinehart and Winston, Inc., 1956.

26. Miller, Lyle L., *Maintaining Reading Efficiency, (Rev. Ed.)*, Laramie, Wyo.: Developmental Reading Distributors, 1966.

27. Miller, Lyle L., *Teaching Reading Efficiency*, Boulder, Colo.: Pruett Press, Inc., 1963.

28. Miller, Lyle L., *Time Budget Sheet*, Boulder, Colo.: Pruett Press, Inc., 1962.

29. Miller, Lyle L., and Alice Z. Seeman, *Guidebook for Prospective Teachers*, Columbus, Ohio: The Ohio State University Press, 1948.

30. Pitkin, Walter B., *The Art of Rapid Reading*, New York: Grosset & Dunlap, Inc., 1954.

31. Reynolds, George R., *Teaching Reading — An Interpretation for Parents*, Washington, D.C.: NEA *Journal*, Volume 43, Number 6, September, 1954.

32. Robinson, Francis P., *Effective Study*, New York: Harper & Row, Publishers, 1946.

33. Robinson, Francis P., *Effective Study*, revised edition, New York: Harper & Row, Publishers, 1962.

34. Robinson, Helen M., ed., *Clinical Studies in Reading II*, Chicago: University of Chicago Press, Number 77, January, 1953.

35. Solberg, Kristin B., *A Measurement of Readability of the Texts Used on the Freshman and Sophomore Level in 1952 and 1953*, unpublished doctoral dissertation, Laramie, Wyo.: University of Wyoming, 1953.

36. Stevens, Leonard S., "Did You Stop Reading in the Third Grade?," *Colliers'*, Volume 134, Number 7, October 29, 1954.

37. Staff of the Reading Clinics of the University of Chicago, *Clinical Studies in Reading I*, Chicago: University of Chicago Press, Number 68, June, 1949.

38. Strang, Ruth, *Study Type of Reading Exercises, College Level*, New York: Bureau of Publications, Teachers College, Columbia University, 1951.

39. Strang, Ruth, and Dorothy K. Braken, *Making Better Readers*, Boston: D. C. Heath and Company, 1957.

40. Stroud, James B., and Robert B. Ammons, *Improving Reading Ability*, New York: Appleton-Century-Crofts, 1949.

41. Thorndike, Edward L., *The Teacher's Word Book*, New York: Bureau of Publications, Teachers College, Columbia University, 1921.

42. Thorndike, Edward L., and Irving Lorge, *The Teacher's Word Book of 30,000 Words*, New York: Bureau of Publications, Teachers College, Columbia University, 1944.

43. Triggs, Frances Oralind, *Improve Your Reading*, A Manual of Remedial Reading Exercises, Minneapolis: University of Minnesota Press, 1942.

44. Triggs, Frances Oralind, *Remedial Reading*, The Diagnosis and Correction of Reading Difficulties at the College Level, Minneapolis: University of Minnesota Press, 1943.

45. Whitman, Howard, "Why Don't They Teach My Child to Read?," *Collier's*, Volume 134, Number 11, November 26, 1954.

46. Whittenburg, Clarice, *Training Young Children to Read at the Upper Primary Level*, unpublished outline, Laramie, Wyo.: University of Wyoming, 1955.

47. Witty, Paul, *How to Improve Your Reading*, Chicago: Science Research Associates, Inc., 1956.

SERIES I
Word Recognition Drills

These drills are designed to help you establish rhythmic habits of eye movement. The exercises are of equal difficulty and you should be able to reduce the time necessary to complete these exercises quite rapidly. Keep practicing on them until you are able to complete an exercise in twenty seconds or less.

In these exercises are two columns of words, one with a single word and the other with 5 words. The first column contains the key word. On each line this key word is repeated somewhere among the five words in the other columns. You are to locate this identical word as rapidly as possible and underline it. Then you proceed to the next line and so on till you have finished. As soon as you have finished, raise your hand and the instructor will give you your time in seconds. Record this time and look up your rate in the table on page 297. (Find your time in Column I and then look in Column II for your rate.) Next go back and check your work to see if you have marked any words which were not identical with the key. Count your errors and record them at the bottom of the exercise. Compute your comprehension by multiplying the number of errors by 4 and subtracting the product from 100. Compute your reading efficiency on this drill by multiplying the rate you secured from the table by this comprehension score. Round off the efficiency score to the nearest whole number. Record both the rate and the efficiency on the Progress Chart for Word Recognition Drills on page 289.

These exercises begin on page 27; tables are on page 297; progress charts on page 289.

EXAMPLE

22.	random		random	ranger	ransom	rankle	medal
23.	tape		tap	tape	stun	taper	ape
24.	six	X	six	kiss	hexagon	sexton	sex
25.	we're		ware	let's	we're	were	we've

Time 32 Sec.   RATE (from table on page 297):   R. 281

No. Errors 1   COMPREHENSION (100 — 4% for each error):   C. 96

I-1   EFFICIENCY (R × C): (281 × .96) = 269.76   E. 270

Exercise 1

1. beech   beast   beach   beetle   write   beech
2. civil   meat   civilian   civil   evil   civic
3. desist   desire   desist   design   resist   shoe
4. fabric   fabulous   fabricate   ruining   fabric   fable
5. gun   gun   foil   gum   sun   gunnery
6. supple   supply   support   supplicate   minister   supple
7. miner   concern   miner   diner   mine   mineral
8. pebble   pebble   peddle   treble   medal   flout
9. redden   fish   reddish   gladden   redden   ratify
10. shrub   grub   tangle   shrub   scrub   rub
11. talcum   vacuum   talcum   annoy   welcome   falcon
12. unveil   bewail   unwieldy   object   sail   unveil
13. begot   forgot   begone   beget   begot   friend
14. clasp   clasp   head   clap   chap   class
15. cheat   cheapen   photo   cheat   check   chess
16. deer   dear   beard   dare   ever   deer
17. hadn't   haven't   hadn't   haddock   sign   aren't
18. meed   meed   rose   need   seed   mean
19. minus   minute   plus   case   minus   minor
20. peg   leg   pug   peg   few   pig
21. refer   reference   confer   dealt   defer   refer
22. random   random   ranger   ransom   rankle   medal
23. tape   tap   tape   stun   taper   ape
24. six   six   kiss   hexagon   sexton   sex
25. we're   ware   let's   we're   were   we've

Time _____ Sec.   RATE (from table on page 297):   R. _____

No. Errors _____   COMPREHENSION (100 − 4% for each error):   C. _____

I-1   EFFICIENCY (R × C):   E. _____

Exercise 2

1. adopt   adapt   adopt   arrange   clot   adoption
2. belle   bell   bowl   peal   belle   belt
3. blight   light   oblige   punch   blight   blind
4. devout   devour   vault   devout   bout   about
5. farce   face   false   race   rigid   farce
6. hammer   hamper   stammer   hammer   midst   pound
7. job   syne   job   bog   jog   sob
8. he'd   held   she's   he   he'd   would
9. per   per   par   stir   pet   pert
10. pillar   pillage   pillow   pillar   pill   coarse
11. smelt   felt   rode   smell   melt   smelt
12. thine   time   thine   forest   thing   thin
13. he'll   she   hell   held   he'll   we'll
14. bent   bent   broad   scent   regard   tent
15. closet   cabinet   closed   tabby   clothes   closet
16. mud   muddy   dumb   mud   cud   muddle
17. fatal   fatal   futile   fated   frost   total
18. hap   hop   joy   hole   haste   hap
19. jolly   jelly   jolly   holly   haste   jam
20. mitten   hidden   smite   mitten   often   more
21. pirate   pistol   piracy   pilot   pirate   rate
22. sneak   ratify   sneak   neat   snake   sneer
23. sinful   fully   almost   sinister   awful   sinful
24. teeth   beneath   teem   aback   teeth   tee
25. villa   villa   void   silly   tell   house

Time _____ Sec.   RATE (from table on page 297):   R. _____

No. Errors _____   COMPREHENSION (100 − 4% for each Error):   C. _____

I-2   EFFICIENCY (R × C):   E. _____

Exercise 3

1. abuse   bruise   cord   abuse   bus   about

2. betake   betake   take   better   trace   rush

3. germ   fish   stern   worm   germ   gem

4. dilute   delude   dirt   dilute   rain   dish

5. scrap   bandy   scrip   rap   scrap   scrape

6. harlot   hauteur   harlot   lot   harlequin   marry

7. jumble   mumble   gore   jungle   rumble   jumble

8. stud   stud   study   extra   stub   studio

9. attain   sustain   rock   attain   attend   attach

10. cast   caste   fast   casting   true   cast

11. cycle   bicycle   cycle   master   cymbal   cyclist

12. gilt   silt   gild   gift   gilt   silk

13. pulp   pulp   pulse   pup   pulpit   town

14. beyond   below   beyond   yonder   frost   bead

15. cog   cog   fog   cogent   many   got

16. dirt   skirt   funny   ditty   dirge   dirt

17. felon   simple   fell   long   felon   felt

18. hast   last   hast   masque   haste   aster

19. jury   hurry   junk   jury   juror   fix

20. monkey   monkey   key   money   monarchy   skunk

21. style   mess   study   stile   stylish   style

22. remove   remodel   remnant   remove   move   take

23. wager   bet   wages   wag   wager   wagon

24. ten   tend   ten   bend   fen   ace

25. volume   rescue   voluntary   voluble   luminous   volume

Time _____ Sec.   RATE (from table on page 297):   R. _____

No. Errors _____   COMPREHENSION (100 − 4% for each Error):   C. _____

I-3   EFFICIENCY (R × C):   E. _____

Exercise 4

1. awe   stop   awe   aware   awake   await

2. bog   log   bogus   bog   affix   dog

3. eschew   escort   shrew   screw   topped   eschew

4. ditch   ditty   ditch   witch   mansion   itch

5. flash   moral   flak   flash   lash   flask

6. herd   curd   heard   hero   herd   bird

7. massy   massy   stock   massive   mash   master

8. sultan   pending   sulk   sulky   sultry   sultan

9. plane   true   pane   plane   lane   plain

10. babe   baboon   babble   mercy   babe   baby

11. sober   sobering   sober   bolder   cold   sob

12. etch   etch   civil   etc.   catching   catch

13. goody   good   scorch   goodly   goodman   goody

14. bonny   sonny   bondage   bonny   risk   bone

15. racer   racer   race   eraser   south   tracer

16. dizzy   discreet   forth   divulge   dizzy   fuzzy

17. fleece   maximum   fleece   flee   fleet   feet

18. sunny   summon   summary   verbal   sunken   sunny

19. lard   lard   land   lord   hard   roll

20. muster   mustard   muster   accede   must   master

21. wean   wear   bean   luxury   weak   wean

22. revery   revery   revere   message   very   review

23. solder   rescue   older   solder   soldier   sold

24. thump   thumb   under   hum   hump   thump

25. weekly   meekly   weak   week   weekly   read

Time _____ Sec.   RATE (from table on page 297):   R. _____

No. Errors _____   COMPREHENSION (100 − 4% for each Error):   C. _____

I-4   EFFICIENCY (R × C):   E. _____

Exercise 5

1. anybody   anybody   mixing   anywhere   anyhow   nobody

2. bumble   twist   bundle   bumble   bungle   bumblebee

3. cottage   cotton   phrase   pottage   cottage   cot

4. easily   eagerly   easily   easy   surgery   ease

5. freight   yearling   freighter   eight   free   freight

6. hurtful   hurtful   saddles   healthful   hurt   hurry

7. liver   livid   livery   liver   live   candy

8. notebook   cookbook   pawning   note   notebook   noted

9. prelate   preach   prelude   township   prelate   precede

10. saber   safer   sable   sober   wing   saber

11. stag   staff   vain   stag   stage   tag

12. trespass   tress   trespass   clocking   trestle   trespasser

13. appall   appall   appeal   apparel   misery   appear

14. burner   force   burn   bureau   burner   bunker

15. couple   coupled   reserve   couplet   coupe   couple

16. eddy   edify   eddy   yank   edge   edit

17. frighten   fright   hairpin   freighter   afraid   frighten

18. iceberg   ice   iceboat   iceberg   cooking   icebox

19. lock   lock   locker   idle   loch   local

20. novice   sucker   novice   novel   novelist   novelty

21. sailboat   iceboat   macaroni   sailboat   sailor   soil

22. staple   staple   mixture   stable   table   fable

23. triumph   triumphant   triumph   mulberry   trial   triumphal

24. worry   hurry   stock   worldly   scurry   worry

25. preservation   presentation   preservative   journalistic   preservation   reservation

Time _____ Sec.   RATE (from table on page 297):   R. _____

No. Errors _____   COMPREHENSION (100 − 4% for each Error):   C. _____

I-5   EFFICIENCY (R × C):   E. _____

Exercise 6

1. action   faction   action   fact   act   actor

2. colt   coax   volt   colt   cotton   mother

3. discord   disclose   cord   discourage   discord   office

4. feud   turn   feud   feudal   futile   rude

5. hawthorn   hawthorn   hawk   hauser   fording   thorn

6. kettle   mettle   kernel   kettle   ketch   morning

7. mope   mop   hope   scope   rather   mope

8. repine   sent   repine   repose   pine   reprove

9. sled   led   slowed   lead   sled   moist

10. theater   theater   thaw   heater   theatrical   fooling

11. adieu   mess   die   adieu   adjure   address

12. blank   blast   lower   blink   last   blank

13. disguise   disgust   nesting   dish   guise   disguise

14. fifteen   sixteen   purple   fifth   fifteen   teens

15. heap   leap   heap   heart   heaven   chair

16. kindred   kindness   slacks   hindered   kind   kindred

17. mosquito   moss   faintly   mosquito   quite   mosque

18. picker   lost   picker   picnic   ticker   pick.

19. repulse   repulse   repulsive   repel   pulse   gauntlet

20. sling   slang   sing   sling   slink   force

21. therein   therefore   in   fiddle   therein   wherein

22. wampum   wanton   wander   pumice   course   wampum

23. comforter   comforter   blanket   fixture   comfort   fort

24. philosophic   philosophy   microscopic   physiology   philosophic   earnestness

25. birthright   birthright   daintiness   right   birthplace   birthday

Time _____ Sec.   RATE (from table on page 297):   R. _____

No. Errors _____   COMPREHENSION (100 − 4% for each Error):   C. _____

I-6   EFFICIENCY (R × C):   E. _____

Exercise 7

1. brand   brand   ran   branch   student   brandy
2. doz.   mature   dozen   doz.   buzz
3. foolish   cool   keelson   fooling   foot   foolish
4. holder   hole   holder   letter   hold   older
5. ledge   led   ledger   perform   ledge   edge
6. necklace   necktie   neck   necklace   marauder   lace
7. polite   polite   politic   light   polish   depart
8. rite   dully   rite   right   kite   ritual
9. spade   valve   space   paid   span   spade
10. alphabet   alkali   alphabet   faintness   allegation   alpha
11. breath   breath   breathe   council   beneath   breast
12. drawback   drawer   heading   back   draw   drawback
13. fore   mat   four   ore   fore   forty
14. honest   modest   hornet   honest   honey   punch
15. leisure   leisure   pairing   leisurely   composure   sure
16. negro   shirk   negroid   neglect   neither   negro
17. pony   pond   pony   pooh   puny   smug
18. robe   robes   oboe   toxin   rob   robe
19. special   special   serial   perfect   facial   specify
20. tonight   tonic   versus   tonight   tone   night
21. whoever   whatever   whom   twenty   whoever   who
22. constancy   horseback   constraint   constant   constancy   fancy
23. tolerable   rabble   tolerate   tolerable   review   total
24. consecration   journalistic   consecration   consecrate   conservation   secret
25. allowable   masterful   allows   allowable   lowly   allot

Time _____ Sec.   RATE (from table on page 297):   R. _____

No. Errors _____   COMPREHENSION (100 — 4% for each Error):   C. _____

I-7   EFFICIENCY (R × C):   E. _____

Exercise 8

1. audience   auditor   audible   quadrant   audience   audibly

2. caught   casual   caught   caucus   fish   cauldron

3. damn   damn   dame   prince   dam   damp

4. entrails   entrance   trails   entrails   jackass   entreat

5. glassful   glassful   grateful   locality   glass   glassware

6. inflict   inflame   gossip   afflict   inflict   influx

7. mare   care   mare   halter   hare   margin

8. purity   purify   jurist   pure   destroy   purity

9. subtle   suckle   subtlety   snatch   subtle   subtly

10. celery   celery   celebrity   celebrate   salary   plant

11. daring   dare   punch   darning   darling   daring

12. epitaph   epitaph   epistle   epithet   rating   epoch

13. glory   gory   lorry   glory   gloria   grate

14. initial   initiate   initial   milestone   initiative   inimical

15. marrow   fact   maroon   tomorrow   marrow   marry

16. oven   over   make   oxen   oval   oven

17. quake   quack   fuse   quake   quick   wake

18. seemly   seemingly   seemly   seer   gaunt   see

19. universe   universe   union   occupancy   unit   universal

20. warmth   warmly   warm   warn   destiny   warmth

21. sufferance   suffrage   suffice   sufficient   sufferance   contacting

22. automobile   automotive   auto   automobile   plenteous   automatic

23. ungrateful   ungainly   ungrateful   originality   ungentle   grateful

24. secondary   stand   seclude   second   primary   secondary

25. outlandish   outlaw   land   outlandish   moldboard   outlive

Time _____ Sec.   RATE (from table on page 297):   R. _____

No. Errors _____   COMPREHENSION (100 − 4% for each Error):   C. _____

I-8   EFFICIENCY (R × C):   E. _____

Exercise 9

1. angry   angry   finish   anger   angel   argue

2. brownie   brow   brownie   browse   brown   courage

3. coo   cook   coax   que   coo   rue

4. duration   durable   horseman   duration   during   curable

5. fountain   fountain   foundation   neither   fount   fountainhead

6. howl   cowl   fowl   record   jowl   howl

7. lilac   lilt   prime   like   lilac   lily

8. nobility   section   nobility   nobody   mobility   noble

9. pounce   pour   pound   sphinx   pouch   pounce

10. ruby   ruby   rubber   rubble   silk   rub

11. spouse   next   souse   spouse   spoil   spout

12. annual   courage   annul   annuity   annual   annually

13. bud   bed   bud   lion   budget   buddy

14. core   corn   cork   core   corner   each

15. dwindle   dwindle   study   dwell   wind   dwarf

16. linoleum   linseed   scorch   linnet   linden   linoleum

17. noontide   noodle   midnight   noontide   eventide   noonday

18. preacher   preacher   preamble   preaching   tombstone   reach

19. rump   such   rumple   lump   rump   rummage

20. spun   vail   spun   spurn   spur   pun

21. trash   rash   track   trash   paper   trace

22. woke   wolf   walk   kink   wake   woke

23. humankind   mankind   humankind   human   disgust   humane

24. framework   housework   stronghold   frame   framework   franchise

25. transfigure   horseradish   transfer   torment   transfix   transfigure

Time _____ Sec.   RATE (from table on page 297):   R. _____

No. Errors _____   COMPREHENSION (100 − 4% for each Error):   C. _____

I-9   EFFICIENCY (R × C):   E. _____

Exercise 10

1. ambition   ambiguity   ambition   ambitious   hurrying   amble

2. brighten   brighten   gauntlet   bright   bring   light

3. drip   hook   drift   dribble   drip   trip

4. forgave   forgive   genus   forage   gave   forgave

5. hornet   horn   hornet   honest   figure   horse

6. level   level   lever   shelve   levy   levee

7. portal   port   gouge   postal   portal   portage

8. romp   romp   rump   purple   roam   jump

9. sphere   horrible   sphere   spherical   sphinx   here

10. tortoise   tortuous   torpedo   tortoise   famous   torture

11. ample   amble   sample   future   amplify   ample

12. broaden   board   secure   road   broaden   broad

13. forsook   forsooth   riding   force   forsake   forsook

14. hostile   occupant   hostel   host   hostile   fierce

15. lid   fly   lie   lied   did   lid

16. nickel   nasty   nickel   fickle   sickle   nick

17. postage   hostage   comment   postal   age   postage

18. rosette   rosary   phrase   rosette   rosy   rosin

19. spite   cache   spit   pit   spite   spice

20. trace   trace   train   track   race   traceable

21. windy   kindly   windy   window   wind   winch

22. drunkenness   drunkenness   militarism   drunk   drinking   sunken

23. contradict   contradiction   letterhead   contradict   contractor   contraction

24. nevertheless   nevermore   insistently   nevertheless   unless   never

25. contemplation   contemptuous   temptation   contemplation   content   hieroglyphic

Time _____ Sec.   RATE (from table on page 297):   R. _____

No. Errors _____   COMPREHENSION (100 − 4% for each Error):   C. _____

I-10   EFFICIENCY (R × C):   E. _____

Exercise 11

1. aisle   air   ailment   first   isle   aisle
2. bosom   handsome   ran   boss   bosom   some
3. domestic   enthusiastic   rolling   dome   domestic   mystic
4. flop   flop   lop   flow   float   ruler
5. hillock   capsize   hilltop   bullock   hill   hillock
6. lava   lavatory   lava   have   lave   mason
7. nameless   nameless   namesake   blameless   name   decorous
8. plow   plod   slow   plow   plot   too
9. riches   muse   ditches   rickety   riches   rice
10. somewhat   eighteen   what   some   somewhere   somewhat
11. timber   timber   eager   limber   time   climber
12. alert   ale   alert   avert   ascent   mercy
13. bouquet   shortly   bouquet   boast   croquet   book
14. dost   pretty   does   dost   lost   dust
15. fluid   fluid   flush   lurid   remain   fluent
16. lea   leaf   lea   leeward   smug   leave
17. nativity   horse   activity   nativity   native   naive
18. sorry   sorrow   sorry   morrow   sore   today
19. tip   in   lip   tip   top   tipple
20. whenever   topple   whichever   whatever   whenever   ever
21. righteous   headache   rightful   rightly   cautious   righteous
22. pneumonia   pneumonia   moustache   ammonia   pneumatic   monetary
23. historian   historical   custodian   history   glycerin   historian
24. congenial   congressional   regional   gentile   congenial   feudalism
25. confession   confusion   tricking   confession   confess   confessed

Time _____ Sec.   RATE (from table on page 297):   R. _____

No. Errors _____   COMPREHENSION (100 − 4% for each Error):   C. _____

I-11   EFFICIENCY (R × C):   E. _____

Exercise 12

1. button   button   buttress   suit   buttons   butter

2. cowslip   bulls   coward   slip   cowboy   cowslip

3. fruitful   fruitless   looking   frugal   fruitful   fretful

4. illegal   ill   lawful   illicit   illegal   illness

5. loom   school   loom   loon   loan   look

6. oaken   oaken   type   oxen   oak   oakum

7. prick   prickly   medal   price   pick   prick

8. sample   noose   trample   sample   simple   ample

9. stave   starve   staves   staff   stave   perch

10. truant   truck   truant   ring   truculent   truce

11. arbor   scare   labor   arbor   ardor   arbiter

12. calamity   calcareous   calcite   disastrous   calculus   calamity

13. crash   crash   rash   crass   crater   smash

14. eldest   roost   elderly   oldest   eldest   elder

15. lovable   feasible   force   lovable   lovely   legible

16. obscure   cattle   cur   obscene   obscurity   obscure

17. printer   stark   prince   pint   printer   princely

18. sandy   sandal   sandy   sundry   task   sand

19. stem   stem   stern   stench   stencil   corset

20. tube   tubular   ebb   tube   tuck   tub

21. writhe   mate   whether   wither   with   writhe

22. immediate   immediate   occupancy   mediator   intermediate   immediately

23. fundamental   function   fundamental   prescription   mental   functional

24. efficient   posterior   efficient   proficient   efficacy   effigy

25. appreciation   apprentice   painstaking   appreciation   depreciation   appreciate

Time _____ Sec.   RATE (from table on page 297):   R. _____

No. Errors _____   COMPREHENSION (100 − 4% for each Error):   C. _____

I-12   EFFICIENCY (R × C):   E. _____

Exercise 13

1. bawl   tour   bowl   bale   bald   bawl

2. chord   chord   foot   chore   choice   choral

3. denounce   announce   denounce   dense   punctual   denote

4. exploit   explicit   expect   sparse   exploit   exotic

5. groove   groove   groom   grove   root   salad

6. irrigate   irradiate   irritate   tragic   irrigate   obligate

7. mid   mild   vile   middle   mix   mid

8. pastry   paste   pastry   pantry   pastel   cord

9. shingle   shining   shingle   treaty   single   shingles

10. swim   taxi   swam   whim   swim   twin

11. variable   variable   varied   variance   variegated   messing

12. beaten   sweater   deaden   beater   mice   beaten

13. churl   church   more   churl   curdle   curl

14. deposit   despot   deposit   depot   withdraw   depose

15. extent   tent   extensive   intent   extent   opposite

16. itch   itch   rip   ache   scratch   etch

17. mild   supper   mold   mild   milk   mill

18. pattern   lantern   patty   patter   cushion   pattern

19. shorn   fork   short   shorn   shown   shun

20. vein   vain   vein   feign   veined   prose

21. wig   met   wag   wig   fig   fib

22. syndicate   syndicate   ringing   synthetic   symbol   mental

23. recognition   reception   reclamation   reckless   recognition   sanguinary

24. guarantee   warranty   guaranty   guardian   vicinity   guarantee

25. recapture   salutation   capture   recapture   recapitulate   rapture

Time _____ Sec.   RATE (from table on page 297):   R. _____

No. Errors _____   COMPREHENSION (100 − 4% for each Error):   C. _____

I-13   EFFICIENCY (R × C):   E. _____

Exercise 14

1. camera   cameo   camera   trust   camel   cam

2. creed   creed   creek   cried   creep   erase

3. elm   ton   elk   alms   emblem   elm

4. gad   gadfly   horse   gad   gadget   fad

5. lukewarm   lucrative   lukewarm   luckily   warm   vacancy

6. o'clock   since   ocean   occult   ooze   o'clock

7. product   product   vulgar   produce   prodigy   productive

8. satyr   satin   satisfy   satyr   satire   imply

9. stir   handle   stirrup   skin   stir   stare

10. turnip   turnpike   skip   turn   urn   turnip

11. arrogant   missing   arrogant   ignorant   arrow   arrogance

12. canned   canner   yacht   canned   cannon   canopy

13. criminal   crime   crimp   trucking   criminal   crimson

14. embody   embody   embellish   embattle   head   body

15. gallows   allows   gallows   gallon   gallop   truism

16. official   officiate   vicinity   officious   official   office

17. savory   serve   savor   crouch   savory   save

18. stork   full   stork   stark   store   tore

19. twill   aspic   twice   rill   twirl   twill

20. yoke   bore   yolk   yoke   woke   yogi

21. progressive   progressive   academical   program   aggressive   progress

22. luxuriant   screwing   luxury   sumptuous   luxurious   luxuriant

23. impossible   impose   finishing   impossible   improbable   probable

24. imperative   imperturbable   sticking   impertinent   imperative   imperfect

25. aristocratic   aristocratic   aristocracy   studiously   aristocrat   arithmetic

Time _____ Sec.   RATE (from table on page 297):   R. _____

No. Errors _____   COMPREHENSION (100 − 4% for each Error):   C. _____

I-14   EFFICIENCY (R × C):   E. _____

Exercise 15

1. bargain   bargain   sacking   margin   barge   bargainer

2. chest   quest   cheat   chest   chaste   slot

3. defy   deify   defied   deny   mild   defy

4. execute   executive   execute   occupant   excite   example

5. gravy   gravy   grow   gravity   grave   gravel

6. mention   mental   mansion   attention   mention   element

7. parch   parch   bib   porch   pouch   arch

8. ratify   rational   ratify   rectify   cart   railing

9. usurp   usher   bear   usury   usurp   us

10. bashful   bath   bashful   recount   baseball   basal

11. chill   chide   still   hill   magnify   chill

12. deliver   livery   signora   deliver   delirium   delay

13. mess   mull   table   mass   mess   message

14. readily   readiness   reading   salute   readily   ready

15. sheen   afraid   teen   shine   sheep   sheen

16. sweeper   sweeping   swim   sweeper   sweetly   treatise

17. vagabond   vagabond   thence   vagary   vagrant   vague

18. whilst   white   whittle   victim   whilst   while

19. intricate   phosphorus   intrigue   intricate   intrinsic   intimate

20. shapeless   shameless   happiness   quadrant   shiftless   shapeless

21. suspicious   roughness   suspension   suspicious   susceptible   suspicion

22. exhortation   exhortation   exhort   stronghold   exhilaration   exhibition

23. greenwood   tomahawk   greenback   greenhouse   reduced   greenwood

24. investment   inversion   investment   invention   invitation   vaccination

25. partaker   partition   partaker   particular   yearling   parted

---

Time _____ Sec.   RATE (from table on page 297):   R. _____

No. Errors _____   COMPREHENSION (100 − 4% for each Error):   C. _____

I-15   EFFICIENCY (R × C):   E. _____

Exercise 16

1. ashore   fruit   shore   ashen   aside   ashore

2. caper   capes   near   caper   capital   caprice

3. crucify   crucify   crucible   cruise   dabble   crucifix

4. employ   employer   employ   capable   empower   employee

5. gas   gorge   gash   gasoline   gas   gasp

6. madman   madly   madness   dorsal   madame   madman

7. omen   omission   men   amen   omen   exit

8. scarlet   scarlet   scar   scaracity   scarcely   purple

9. ugly   win   fly   urge   glee   ugly

10. assent   assent   ascent   consent   assert   accede

11. carcass   dirge   canvass   confess   carcass   canvas

12. cube   cub   cubic   high   cube   tube

13. gem   germ   gem   gee   gin   force

14. string   strung   sting   coarse   string   ring

15. virtual   vital   virtual   eraser   virtuous   virulent

16. unceasing   uncertain   mechanize   increasing   cease   unceasing

17. property   frivolity   property   proper   prophet   propaganda

18. incense   incentive   incendiary   incense   license   courage

19. scientific   scientist   scientific   filler   science   terrific

20. magnify   sturdy   magnitude   magnificent   magnetic   magnify

21. encounter   encounter   encumber   counter   encourage   skirmish

22. prosperity   prospective   largeness   prosperity   prosperous   property

23. operation   operation   operator   observation   operate   inducement

24. incurable   curable   incumber   incurable   touring   incursion

25. strawberry   straw   blueberry   strawberry   raspberry   headstrong

Time _____ Sec.   RATE (from table on page 297):   R. _____

No. Errors _____   COMPREHENSION (100 − 4% for each Error):   C. _____

I-16   EFFICIENCY (R × C):   E. _____

Exercise 17

1. affront   affair   carding   affront   affect   front

2. certify   certify   risking   certain   certified   certificate

3. daybreak   daylight   daytime   schedule   break   daybreak

4. godlike   godlike   phrase   golden   godly   manlike

5. inquiry   inquisitor   inquiry   inquest   wailing   query

6. overseer   oversee   overseer   critic   over   overseas

7. quicken   question   battery   quickly   quick   quicken

8. reunion   review   fixing   reunite   union   reunion

9. deathbed   dearth   death   decadence   deathbed   deathless

10. mattock   haddock   mattress   buttocks   merry   mattock

11. conclude   include   conclusion   conclave   conclude   yearling

12. heroism   erosion   zealot   heroism   heroine   hero

13. playground   barometer   playing   playhouse   ground   playground

14. aggravate   aggravating   aggravate   wanderer   aggregate   grave

15. thriftless   thriftless   footlights   shiftless   thrift   thrive

16. murderous   vacantly   murky   murder   murderous   hideous

17. lamentation   legislation   lamenting   lamentation   undeveloped   lame

18. comprehend   comprehensive   tabernacle   hen   comprehend   compromise

19. unspeakable   doubtfully   unstable   speak   unspoiled   unspeakable

20. sepulcher   spectacle   sepulcher   entering   spectator   sepulchral

21. oxen   oxen   often   toxin   sown   box

22. inspector   instance   spectator   touring   inspector   inspire

23. chandelier   chant   chanticleer   chandelier   courtesy   chevalier

24. unpleasant   unpack   unpleasant   pleasant   unpaid   columnist

25. sensation   sensation   sensitive   sensual   busybody   compensation

Time _____ Sec.   RATE (from table on page 297):   R. _____

No. Errors _____   COMPREHENSION (100 − 4% for each Error):   C. _____

I-17   EFFICIENCY (R × C):   E. _____

Exercise 18

1. carrion   carried   carrier   carriage   carrion   switch

2. engrave   engrave   engross   engraving   ruling   engage

3. coachman   mansion   coat   scarlet   coachman   man

4. orchard   orchard   orchestra   orchid   ordeal   pencil

5. prudent   prune   student   prudence   telephone   prudent

6. feature   creature   feature   feat   federal   academic

7. moisture   moist   mixture   moisture   peculiar   hoist

8. undergo   underground   false   underwent   undergo   undergone

9. sixpence   twopence   roofing   sixpence   sixteen   sextette

10. enormous   enough   enormity   immense   courage   enormous

11. tenement   tendency   sentiment   rudiment   tenement   extreme

12. manifest   manifold   manifesto   recorder   manipulate   manifest

13. scullion   stallion   scullion   meaning   scull   scuffle

14. perverse   perverse   perhaps   verse   pervert   rolling

15. skirmish   shrimp   skirt   rescue   skirmish   mission

16. accordingly   accordingly   cablegram   across   cross   accord

17. remainder   remain   remainder   extreme   rejoinder   schooling

18. perseverance   perseverance   pursue   persevere   ransoming   backwoods

19. undoubted   doubted   undo   undesirable   undoubted   prescribe

20. originate   oriental   crowning   origin   original   originate

21. inevitable   inequality   pensively   inevitable   ineffable   inexcusable

22. malicious   impromptu   malice   malicious   delicious   malignity

23. indignation   indignant   indignation   snatching   indigestion   indigenous

24. curiosity   currency   curio   pensively   curiously   curiosity

25. astronomy   astronomical   astronomy   astrology   noontide   astray

Time _____ Sec.   RATE (from table on page 297):   R. _____

No. Errors _____   COMPREHENSION (100 − 4% for each Error):   C. _____

I-18   EFFICIENCY (R × C):   E. _____

Exercise 19

1. abandon   band   abuse   abandon   bandanna   backward

2. disperse   dispersion   disperse   dispell   identify   purse

3. mission   missive   permission   passion   sylvan   mission

4. silvery   silver   slavery   silvery   silvered   saunter

5. taxicab   cab   taxicab   toxin   ability   tropical

6. bluebell   blue   resting   bell   bluebell   blueberry

7. firmness   firmness   firm   first   foolishness   pacifism

8. laborer   excuse   laboratory   bore   laborer   labor

9. dictate   direct   detect   estate   roseate   dictate

10. perfume   perfume   refuse   perhaps   fuming   perfect

11. rejoice   quaint   rejoice   voice   join   revolve

12. thorough   finish   thought   thorough   though   borough

13. abominable   tabernacle   abandoned   abominable   fundamental   practically

14. adversity   adversity   adverse   folding   advisable   verse

15. financial   jealously   final   financial   facial   finance

16. watermelon   salutation   melon   waterfall   watermelon   water

17. responsible   responsive   quadrangle   response   sponsor   responsible

18. dissolution   soluble   dissuade   dissertation   occupancy   dissolution

19. compensate   comparison   compensate   compensation   necessary   pension

20. regardless   retard   regardless   homeless   relative   joyousness

21. resistance   resist   machination   resolute   assistance   resistance

22. mountaineer   maintain   kindergarten   mountain   mountaineer   mount

23. knighthood   knighthood   largeness   night   neighborhood   knight

24. clergyman   clergyman   candlelight   salesman   minister   accountant

25. commonwealth   common   commotion   hallucination   commonwealth   wealth

Time _____ Sec.   RATE (from table on page 297):   R. _____

No. Errors _____   COMPREHENSION (100 − 4% for each Error):   C. _____

I-19   EFFICIENCY (R × C):   E. _____

Exercise 20

1. balance — balance   charge   balcony   balanced   lance

2. charity — chariot   cherish   charge   drift   charity

3. decisive — decision   decisive   exclude   declension   derisive

4. gradual — radiate   graduate   grad   invest   gradual

5. meantime — heading   meander   meanwhile   meantime   text

6. painter — painful   painter   headache   pointer   painted

7. raiment — railway   soldier   raiment   regiment   rainbow

8. janitor — janitor   jangle   jungle   sloppy   banister

9. verdict — convict   vindicative   predict   verdict   allow

10. bandage — occupant   band   bandanna   bandy   bandage

11. faithful — faithful   fitful   faithless   convince   fateful

12. insurance — insurance   insular   dressing   insure   insult

13. grandpa — grandma   grandpa   python   grandfather   father

14. servitude — service   servitude   servile   serve   vomiting

15. pancake — panacea   sturdy   pan   pancreas   pancake

16. uppermost — upper   insistence   uppermost   upraise   upper

17. surgeon — surgery   surge   highland   surly   surgeon

18. witchcraft — witchery   feudalism   handicraft   witchcraft   craft

19. sideboard — sideways   headboard   sideboard   eighteen   boardwalk

20. vexation — sensation   vexation   fixation   vegetation   syllable

21. interchange — interchange   recharge   intercept   exchange   hydrophobia

22. destroyer — battleship   distraught   destine   destroyer   destroy

23. jeopardy — perfidy   jeopardize   leopard   jeopardy   schedule

24. examine — exaggerate   lobbying   examine   exasperate   example

25. everybody — everyone   frivolity   everybody   evermore   anybody

Time _____ Sec.   RATE (from table on page 297):   R. _____

No. Errors _____   COMPREHENSION (100 — 4% for each Error):   C. _____

I-20   EFFICIENCY (R × C):   E. _____

SERIES II
Word Meaning Drills

In these exercises the emphasis shifts to a rapid recognition of *meaning*. Here each key word is followed by five others, one of which means almost the same as the key word. This exercise is the first to give you practice in reading for meaning. Here you want to skim as rapidly as you can, looking for similar meanings.

The directions are the same as for the preceding exercise. Look at the key word in each line and then find the one in the answers which has most nearly the same meaning. Underline that answer and go on to the succeeding line as rapidly as possible. When you have finished, ask for your time and look up your rate in the table on page 297. Wait for the group to finish and the instructor will read the correct answers. Find your number of errors and compute your comprehension by multiplying the number of errors by 4 and subtracting the product from 100. Compute your efficiency to the nearest whole number and record scores on the Progress Chart on page 289.

Since these words are all among the 30,000 most frequently used words, you can use these exercises also as a check on your vocabulary. List all key words missed and all words underlined in error on the vocabulary page and look up their meaning. Try to study and to use these words until you have added them to your vocabulary.

These exercises begin on page 49; tables are on page 297; progress charts on page 289; vocabulary lists on page 285.

EXAMPLE

. . . .

20.	lit	<u>ignited</u>	fit	bit	kit	itch
21.	horn	born	corn	mourn	morn	<u>cornucopia</u>
22.	prefer	close	preamble	creditor	confer	<u>choose</u>
23.	retort X	<u>resort</u>	deport	answer	fort	aerial
24.	spent	rent	<u>exhausted</u>	bent	cant	dent
25.	tight X	<u>light</u>	fight	taut	sight	night

Time 63 Sec.   RATE (from table on page 297):   R.   143

No. Errors 2   COMPREHENSION (100 − 4% for each Error):   C.   92

II-4   EFFICIENCY (R × C): (143 × .92) = 131.56   E.   132

Words to be added to vocabulary list:
retort,
resort,
tight,
light.

Exercise 1

1. brow   sow   <u>forehead</u>   now   bow   scow

2. bully   fully   pulley   gully   tulip   <u>tease</u>

3. cot   <u>bed</u>   rot   tot   bought   aught

4. ease   <u>tranquillity</u>   knees   difficulty   squeeze   sleep

5. freeze   lizard   jab   ice   care   ire

6. noise   choice   mount   notice   source   <u>sound</u>

7. lively   lovely   <u>brisk</u>   liver   blithely   vile

8. notch   crotch   foam   gulch   <u>dent</u>   dotage

9. noble   head   bobble   <u>fine</u>   foal   hobo

10. rag   <u>tatter</u>   fag   tag   gag   bag

11. staff   raft   <u>stick</u>   laugh   quaff   show

12. trend   send   bend   tend   drench   <u>direction</u>

13. worn   born   sworn   mourn   <u>tired</u>   foreign

14. woeful   armful   <u>mournful</u>   artful   baleful   manful

15. dad   bad   cad   <u>father</u>   fad   gad

16. dart   dish   <u>dash</u>   disc   disk   cart

17. errand   <u>trip</u>   head   ferret   wand   tang

18. goal   foal   sole   soul   score   role

19. inn   fin   gin   hotel   skin   hinge

20. meal   feel   peal   peel   powder   <u>seal</u>

21. pagan   sage   fagot   patron   hag   <u>heathen</u>

22. raft   <u>craft</u>   draft   graft   abundance   aft

23. scant   rant   pant   <u>rare</u>   faint   banter

24. catch   match   adapt   crack   cattle   <u>trap</u>

25. tyrant   pirate   hydra   <u>scour</u>   dictator   dysentery

Time _(27)_ Sec.   RATE (from table on page 297):   R. <u>7/</u>

No. Errors _____   COMPREHENSION (100 − 4% for each Error):   C. _____

II-1   EFFICIENCY (R × C):   E. _____

49

Exercise 2

1. bed   fed   red   head   cot   bred

2. civil   devil   shrivel   swivel   level   polite

3. arise   mount   size   maize   nice   barge

4. fable   falsehood   table   stable   staple   gable

5. gum   bum   resin   sum   dumb   hum

6. jam   dam   damn   lamb   predicament   ham

7. mind   find   rind   memory   hind   bind

8. camel   dromedary   cancel   sample   trample   dame

9. weigh   weird   well   measure   sleigh   mellow

10. shroud   conceal   loud   crowd   bowed   proud

11. taint   comtaminate   faint   quaint   saint   paint

12. verdant   aunt   veranda   pant   green   shank

13. amateur   sure   pour   cure   dabbler   lure

14. bribe   tribe   scribe   price   five   live

15. cone   phone   lone   roan   bone   shell

16. dogma   hog   bog   cog   doctrine   foggy

17. flit   hit   dart   kit   slit   bit

18. lucky   duchy   touchy   much   fudge   fortunate

19. lease   please   grease   contract   tease   peace

20. neat   heat   tidy   peat   beat   seat

21. pace   taste   gait   case   haste   chase

22. reside   beside   aside   decide   tide   dwell

23. slap   cap   map   slop   straight   pat

24. occur   fur   befall   sir   stir   burden

25. wallet   pallet   mallet   pocketbook   palate   palette

Time _____ Sec.   RATE (from table on page 297):   R. _____

No. Errors _____   COMPREHENSION (100 − 4% for each Error):   C. _____

II-2   EFFICIENCY (R × C):   E. _____

Exercise 3

1. airy   light   dairy   diary   fairy   lira

2. back   lack   support   tack   sack   sac

3. stink   blink   smell   think   wink   summer

4. dome   cupola   come   foam   home   comb

5. turkey   turnkey   murky   slack   fowl   furl

6. yield   furnish   wield   sealed   reeled   field

7. laurel   honor   quarrel   sorrel   moral   haul

8. naked   sake   slaked   bare   baked   caked

9. plow   allow   plot   cut   how   slow

10. rich   pitch   wealthy   ditch   bit   wick

11. sack   back   ravage   lack   hack   rack

12. tilt   slope   lilt   silt   kilt   gilt

13. wait   fate   date   rate   stay   saith

14. abase   erase   degrade   taste   case   dash

15. beckon   reckon   second   hexagon   seclude   signal

16. defer   confer   refer   postpone   affair   peevish

17. eager   beaver   meager   lever   agent   avid

18. fury   flurry   jury   brewery   aura   anger

19. pen   few   threw   hew   cage   cession

20. mad   bad   bade   crazy   fad   cad

21. olden   golden   stolen   den   ancient   alter

22. prone   phone   drone   gnome   liable   lone

23. rub   dub   tub   scour   tug   sub

24. paste   waste   waist   taste   dastardly   dough

25. trance   dance   enhance   glance   branch   daze

Time _____ Sec.   RATE (from table on page 297):   R. _____

No. Errors _____   COMPREHENSION (100 — 4% for each Error):   C. _____

II-3   EFFICIENCY (R × C):   E. _____

Exercise 4

1. glance   lance   manse   glimpse   dance   enhance
2. quack   lack   rack   charlatan   back   cub
3. colony   call   loan   loon   sol   settlement
4. stile   style   file   aisle   steps   child
5. fetter   hamper   letter   debtor   hew   better
6. yell   yes   cry   bell   knock   yellow
7. keen   seen   sharp   bean   dean   lean
8. mop   pop   sop   cop   pout   flop
9. turban   hat   turbine   suburban   fat   ban
10. rack   backward   tack   jack   afflict   repeat
11. slayer   thrill   player   clay   killer   kitty
12. thaw   melt   haw   jaw   law   maw
13. wage   salary   adage   beige   cage   sage
14. amity   calamity   aim   absurdity   friendship   family
15. baby   fade   child   bake   lady   dabble
16. brief   grief   belief   sheaf   fief   short
17. dump   jump   drop   bump   chunk   dumb
18. fought   sought   aught   struggled   fault   ought
19. drill   fill   grill   bill   pill   practice
20. lit   ignited   fit   bit   kit   itch
21. horn   born   corn   mourn   morn   cornucopia
22. prefer   close   preamble   creditor   confer   choose
23. retort   resort   deport   answer   fort   aerial
24. spent   rent   exhausted   bent   cant   dent
25. tight   light   fight   taut   sight   night

Time _____ Sec.   RATE (from table on page 297):   R. _____

No. Errors _____   COMPREHENSION (100 − 4% for each Error):   C. _____

II-4   EFFICIENCY (R × C):   E. _____

Exercise 5

1. torrid   parched   horrid   florid   morbid   porridge

2. bad   wad   tadpole   had   gad   inferior

3. cowl   hoof   hook   hood   hoop   howl

4. wind   mind   bind   kind   twist   tinder

5. frugal   nominal   struggle   stubble   economical   frustrate

6. ignore   floor   door   overlook   roar   ogle

7. avert   assert   pervert   convert   prevent   habit

8. nymph   goddess   lymph   symphony   limp   gym

9. prey   pray   victim   fray   day   voyage

10. salve   save   have   soothe   halve   delve

11. carol   barrel   song   oral   laurel   sorrel

12. taint   faint   feint   blemish   rant   bailiff

13. writer   fighter   scribe   girder   lighter   stab

14. bat   rat   mat   fat   sat   stick

15. char   mar   far   car   scorch   share

16. endure   cure   bear   sure   pure   benumb

17. gain   gabardine   gander   gauge   get   gentlefolk

18. gown   frown   down   dress   abound   round

19. map   nap   chart   lap   cap   gap

20. menace   dentist   finesse   apprentice   tenacious   threat

21. parade   pageant   tirade   scourge   braid   chard

22. rash   headlong   rare   flash   crash   hash

23. scour   power   dower   tower   courage   clean

24. strut   nut   glut   stray   brutal   brace

25. undefiled   pure   mild   wild   tile   pun

Time _____ Sec.   RATE (from table on page 297):   R. _____

No. Errors _____   COMPREHENSION (100 − 4% for each Error):   C. _____

II-5   EFFICIENCY (R × C):   E. _____

Exercise 6

1. baker   cook   shaper   shaker   rook   took

2. abode   mode   rode   node   pod   house

3. salmon   fish   lemon   salad   balsam   fallow

4. trough   rough   gutter   sought   soft   golf

5. flare   dare   care   bare   blare   blaze

6. herb   grass   barb   bard   bird   garb

7. grade   fade   raid   cage   level   staid

8. insult   affront   cult   result   stint   basal

9. plait   plate   late   rate   place   braid

10. meant   rent   intended   sent   dead   fed

11. sob   weep   rob   mob   rod   bob

12. thrifty   rift   cliff   whiff   shriek   saving

13. weed   seed   ready   really   plant   udder

14. appeal   seal   prayer   real   apple   peel

15. bust   rust   chest   must   cuss   dust

16. cove   rove   dove   hove   inlet   ion

17. edit   reveal   eddy   merit   rain   revise

18. frown   down   scowl   town   sound   sown

19. affirm   blurt   worm   assert   squirm   skirt

20. luck   duc   duck   duct   chance   cluck

21. occidental   accidental   rental   western   wobble   sleep

22. proceed   procure   recess   advance   desist   arrow

23. role   roll   dole   foal   part   pole

24. spell   hell   well   relieve   bell   relish

25. torn   thorn   worn   ripped   born   rope

Time _____ Sec.   RATE (from table on page 297):   R. _____

No. Errors _____   COMPREHENSION (100 — 4% for each Error):   C. _____

II-6   EFFICIENCY (R × C):   E. _____

Exercise 7

1. bauble   bubble   stubble   trouble   gobble   trifle

2. blur   whir   stir   our   obscure   endure

3. denote   remote   rote   vote   quote   mark

4. haven   port   raven   leaven   sort   sport

5. groom   manservant   room   broom   croon   doom

6. knelt   felt   belt   cent   centaur   bent

7. mice   rodents   rice   lice   trice   ice

8. motor   mortar   tartar   carter   snow   dynamo

9. recall   stall   remember   fall   ball   gall

10. shin   bin   fin   gin   leg   grin

11. sworn   vowed   worn   horn   corn   born

12. vapor   taper   mist   caper   maker   favor

13. allay   alley   alloy   ally   relieve   lay

14. boyish   fish   dish   coy   youthful   toy

15. comply   yield   die   dye   fry   cry

16. pill   fill   ball   pall   rill   fall

17. flank   rank   rancor   thigh   hank   thank

18. habit   bit   rabbit   costume   fit   hit

19. regal   legal   lately   beagle   stately   fate

20. mystic   ritual   mist   stick   physic   enigmatic

21. plod   clog   clod   drudge   pod   fog

22. repentance   pence   penitence   pants   stance   lance

23. sinner   system   sister   criminal   dinner   hysterics

24. temptation   location   generation   seduction   inspiration   nation

25. volcano   canoe   eruption   volt   cameo   canto

Time _____ Sec.   RATE (from table on page 297):   R. _____

No. Errors _____   COMPREHENSION (100 − 4% for each Error):   C. _____

II-7   EFFICIENCY (R × C):   E. _____

Exercise 8

1. shrill   keel   keep   still   frill   keen

2. clergy   energy   clerk   allegory   clear   ministers

3. devour   eat   devout   devote   devoid   sour

4. vacant   dummy   cant   empty   rant   pant

5. ham   pork   cam   dam   jam   lamb

6. jingle   tingle   jangle   simple   jungle   single

7. misplace   space   lace   lose   race   trace

8. pepsin   resin   lessen   medicine   lesson   tension

9. regarding   retarding   guarding   lauding   harboring   concerning

10. silverware   fair   fare   sliver   bare   cutlery

11. taxation   ration   relation   levy   sensation   station

12. vile   disgusting   file   tile   pile   guile

13. ammonia   pneumonia   phone   bony   bone   gas

14. broom   loom   brush   doom   boom   tomb

15. conquer   her   stir   vanquish   whir   burr

16. dove   love   pigeon   done   rove   move

17. folder   moulder   holder   solder   bolder   boulder

18. hock   dock   lock   rock   pawn   sock

19. lesser   smaller   dresser   fester   tester   jester

20. net   bet   met   yet   trap   new

21. port   sort   harbor   sport   wart   snort

22. rage   sage   fury   page   cage   beige

23. sly   furtive   cry   high   rye   try

24. thicken   thicket   sicken   chicken   coagulate   lichen

25. waste   taste   washer   waist   squander   haste

Time _____ Sec.   RATE (from table on page 297):   R. _____

No. Errors _____   COMPREHENSION (100 − 4% for each Error):   C. _____

II-8   EFFICIENCY (R × C):   E. _____

Exercise 9

1. alligator   agitator   fascinate   crocodile   mediator   cliff

2. brand   stigma   sand   grand   hand   land

3. consecrate   devote   secret   freight   locate   donate

4. wage   stage   wager   salary   dot   aged

5. fondness   soundness   largess   affection   afoot   jolt

6. hoist   foil   ghost   moist   lift   loiter

7. lecture   picture   fracture   conjecture   discourse   decry

8. necessity   perplexity   need   city   complexity   nationality

9. policy   police   rule   docility   folly   mollify

10. risk   danger   frisk   brisk   wrist   disk

11. spacious   vast   gracious   specimen   narcissus   vacillate

12. token   broken   spoken   army   sojourn   sign

13. buzz   fist   his   jazz   hum   hive

14. assume   room   pretend   doom   broom   psyche

15. statute   statue   flute   random   law   stature

16. crook   brook   book   shook   look   hook

17. emit   permit   remit   submit   venal   voice

18. garnish   varnish   vanish   adorn   vanquish   aroma

19. ability   adversity   legality   power   illiterate   pillory

20. make   male   form   drake   slake   fake

21. oral   sorrel   floral   moral   morale   verbal

22. prow   sow   now   how   row   bow

23. rural   pastoral   fuel   full   gruel   purchase

24. squirrel   quarrel   chipmunk   whirl   furl   square

25. tremble   thimble   assemble   shake   bungle   semblance

Time _____ Sec.   RATE (from table on page 297):   R. _____

No. Errors _____   COMPREHENSION (100 − 4% for each Error):   C. _____

II-9   EFFICIENCY (R × C):   E. _____

Exercise 10

1. ashamed   claimed   humiliated   named   tamed   rash

2. cape   shape   headland   grape   tape   hap

3. crow   row   stow   boast   bow   dough

4. empire   spire   inquire   dominion   bier   dire

5. refute   deny   refund   lute   rest   male

6. incapable   traceable   escapade   enable   enchant   incompetent

7. madden   sadden   dampen   gladden   each   enrage

8. stubborn   stung   inflexible   subsequent   escape   ice

9. property   proper   density   prosperity   possessions   prophetic

10. scarf   muffler   scoff   slough   harp   maze

11. straw   draw   thaw   paw   stalks   ball

12. udder   rudder   shudder   utter   buddy   bag

13. zoological   tropical   biological   topic   surgical   book

14. behold   fold   gold   see   sold   bold

15. chisel   sizzle   cheat   drizzle   gizzard   look

16. deity   lemon   preen   divinity   screen   problem

17. expedite   hasten   extradition   condition   tradition   hexagon

18. grocer   dealer   poacher   roach   brooch   loafer

19. idea   for   flee   concept   sea   cease

20. mince   since   quince   rinse   hash   hind

21. peal   resound   deal   feel   fealty   real

22. recovery   delivery   covertly   mockery   recalcitrant   restoration

23. semblance   blanch   dance   arrogance   form   female

24. suitor   neuter   looter   cuter   wooer   wry

25. unnecessary   commissary   crazy   student   ugh   useless

Time _____ Sec.   RATE (from table on page 297):   R. _____

No. Errors _____   COMPREHENSION (100 — 4% for each Error):   C. _____

II-10   EFFICIENCY (R × C):   E. _____

Exercise 11

1. audible   beard   trouble   word   stirrup   heard

2. cattle   tatter   fetter   tattle   bovine   wine

3. dame   woman   wane   same   fame   luminary

4. fashion   style   file   fasten   false   snub

5. glare   flare   gaze   graze   raze   raise

6. inflammation   ferver   information   cleaver   fever   flyer

7. marble   marvel   warble   limestone   tomb   larceny

8. outing   boating   doubting   flouting   excursion   eunuch

9. purify   clear   purchase   hear   testify   rectify

10. seclude   prelude   conclude   isolate   date   fate

11. subterranean   suburb   years   hidden   bidden   terrace

12. ungracious   dude   rude   lavish   hood   food

13. acorn   nut   ache   adorn   hut   torn

14. bin   came   sin   win   box   name

15. clearness   friendliness   closeness   cleverness   limpidness   lesson

16. develop   envelop   mature   gallop   manure   lope

17. famish   furnish   furnace   carve   family   starve

18. halloo   shout   bald   look   small   too

19. jug   tug   rug   pitcher   slug   richer

20. modify   solidify   grange   change   defy   deify

21. perpetuate   perpetrate   endure   penetrate   sure   awake

22. relic   frolic   soon   clip   croon   ruin

23. sham   slam   room   tan   doom   pretense

24. suspect   respect   distrust   must   rust   trust

25. useful   awful   baleful   capsule   doubtful   helpful

Time _____ Sec.   RATE (from table on page 297):   R. _____

No. Errors _____   COMPREHENSION (100 − 4% for each Error):   C. _____

II-11   EFFICIENCY (R × C):   E. _____

Exercise 12

1. abash   sash   flash   crash   ado   embarrass

2. certificate   testimony   alimony   antimony   delicate   triple

3. dawn   faun   fawn   sand   morn   lawn

4. erruption   corruption   temptation   outbreak   snake   rake

5. gall   fall   stall   cemetery   prosperity   temerity

6. inquire   require   ask   task   fire   fin

7. massive   lassie   flighty   tryout   dread   weighty

8. overseas   oversee   mourn   torn   foreign   tree

9. quest   adventure   best   west   test   wrest

10. senior   elder   junior   juniper   fell   enigma

11. sulphur   suffer   element   cement   sultry   couple

12. pity   flighty   coversation   coversion   compassion   city

13. admit   admire   deceive   receive   calendar   purple

14. bled   fed   lead   read   injured   extinguish

15. club   rub   stud   staff   raft   dub

16. dig   rig   fig   delve   shelve   big

17. fawn   yawn   cringe   spawn   singe   ridge

18. hardware   tools   swear   fool   tear   rare

19. kennel   fennel   stutter   mutter   house   flannel

20. moonbeam   seam   ray   day   deem   say

21. phase   aspic   raze   aspect   beige   craze

22. supervisor   sector   reflector   nectar   factor   director

23. shown   threw   thru   mew   guest   manifested

24. swollen   pollen   expanded   expend   boll   strand

25. vanquish   conquer   varnish   swish   vanish   query

Time _____ Sec.   RATE (from table on page 297):   R. _____

No. Errors _____   COMPREHENSION (100 − 4% for each Error):   C. _____

II-12   EFFICIENCY (R × C):   E. _____

Exercise 13

1. barefoot   bear   shoeless   root   shoot   care

2. calculate   regulate   coagulate   rate   estimate   nominate

3. defraud   laud   hod   paw   caw   cheat

4. excuse   refuse   refuge   condone   amuse   news

5. gravity   laxity   morality   seriousness   anxiety   casualty

6. intoxicated   liberated   sated   concentrated   waited   drunk

7. mental   rental   dental   gentle   intellectual   lent

8. parcel   marcel   bundle   cell   par   trundle

9. rate   date   hate   gate   estimate   fate

10. sage   wage   rage   age   beige   wise

11. suspicion   uncertainty   position   transition   condition   resolution

12. usher   rush   user   she   escort   bush

13. ahead   dead   front   red   said   bed

14. boost   roost   boot   lift   coot   door

15. commit   comment   entrust   comma   comet   come

16. disobey   refuse   hay   hey   bay   say

17. film   haze   craze   helm   limb   kiln

18. heavily   heave   vile   heat   dully   villa

19. lame   dame   infirm   blame   came   fame

20. municipal   principal   munificent   city   cipher   cider

21. plaintive   plainness   captive   plane   deceptive   melancholy

22. relish   lucky   dish   taste   fish   rely

23. silken   soft   welcome   sill   ken   bill

24. tassel   tuft   rascal   vessel   pass   castle

25. vigor   victor   snicker   liquor   stricter   strength

Time _____ Sec.   RATE (from table on page 297):   R. _____

No. Errors _____   COMPREHENSION (100 − 4% for each Error):   C. _____

II-13   EFFICIENCY (R × C):   E. _____

Exercise 14

1. abundant   bun   plentiful   abuse   abusive   dance

2. bet   met   beta   stake   belt   get

3. coach   coachman   teach   broach   roach   loath

4. diligent   industrious   dilute   dilate   dilemma   lie

5. feather   father   farther   gather   weather   plume

6. hark   harp   listen   ark   dark   bark

7. juicy   interest   loosely   ruthless   succulent   ruefully

8. moisten   mosaic   wet   moss   choice   ten

9. persecutor   persevere   perspective   tormentor   persist   person

10. rely   depend   deny   lye   relax   relay

11. situation   site   sit   abbreviation   caption   carnation

12. tenderness   tend   actress   compassion   alertness   aloofness

13. vacillate   late   vacancy   ventilate   violate   oscillate

14. alter   altar   alto   change   halter   falter

15. bride   bridge   ride   pride   wife   side

16. consul   official   consult   council   counsel   con

17. dresser   presser   bureau   dress   lesser   jester

18. foresee   anticipate   fore   see   forearm   forest

19. hopeless   hop   hostess   bottomless   useless   boundless

20. likely   lively   literally   like   lightly   probable

21. nag   fag   bag   keg   torment   gag

22. pouch   couch   pout   pour   bag   vouch

23. resign   design   sign   resin   repine   quit

24. soak   sock   joke   broke   oak   drench

25. threw   drew   flue   flung   shrew   brew

Time _____ Sec.   RATE (from table on page 297):   R. _____

No. Errors _____   COMPREHENSION (100 − 4% for each Error):   C. _____

II-14   EFFICIENCY (R × C):   E. _____

Exercise 15

1. ado   flew   brew   sad   stir   cur

2. bloom   strew   flower   stew   few   flew

3. commonplace   comma   comment   truism   tomato   place

4. dispense   distribute   expanse   expense   tribute   defense

5. financial   romance   pinafore   pecuniary   dance   monkey

6. heavy   levee   weighty   levy   weave   bevy

7. watch   leap   over   observe   patch   wall

8. mound   hill   round   sound   around   hound

9. pillage   oil   pill   village   sill   spoil

10. resist   oppose   desist   sister   fist   pose

11. smear   pulley   fear   beer   rear   sully

12. tacit   silent   facet   tact   tack   sac

13. waterfall   cascade   water   cater   fall   waterfowl

14. anoint   appoint   annoy   ran   rub   sleep

15. bulb   tub   bulk   bull   flower   tuber

16. corrupt   interrupt   truck   rupture   vicious   connect

17. earnest   furnace   ear   serious   sardine   nest

18. freedom   dome   free   kingdom   liberty   leeward

19. hurl   curl   throw   swirl   twirl   turkey

20. lone   bone   solitary   stone   son   condone

21. nursery   hospital   nurse   purse   incubator   ivory

22. pretext   prefix   apology   text   prepaid   pretense

23. rib   bib   crib   fib   tiara   bone

24. sovereign   souvenir   ruler   rein   rain   dominant

25. tact   fact   back   diplomacy   rapt   lack

Time _____ Sec.   RATE (from table on page 297):   R. _____

No. Errors _____   COMPREHENSION (100 − 4% for each Error):   C. _____

II-15   EFFICIENCY (R × C):   E. _____

Exercise 16

1. astray   bay   bayou   day   wrong   wasteful

2. carrier   bearer   terrier   ferry   lexicon   barrier

3. cure   lure   heal   pure   sure   hurdle

4. engineer   guide   sheer   fear   rear   gnaw

5. cloth   there   close   back   crepe   century

6. indignant   filament   angry   pant   rant   andirons

7. malice   spite   talon   louse   shallow   callous

8. orbit   ascribe   fit   hit   path   prayer

9. prudence   prune   wisdom   fence   ascent   wrung

10. safe   secure   waft   missive   saber   salutary

11. stuck   adhered   luck   truck   rude   attune

12. underfoot   undertook   route   below   root   boar

13. absurd   work   foolish   heard   lurid   fabricate

14. beset   debt   let   kept   perplex   session

15. circumference   conference   inference   tense   piratical   perimeter

16. describe   date   rate   fate   relate   rescue

17. earn   burn   ear   learn   garnet   get

18. gulf   rough   chasm   golf   charm   fluff

19. jade   fire   raid   jewel   fade   tadpole

20. mishap   nap   tap   mist   aisle   accident

21. pent   spend   rent   confined   sent   cent

22. refusal   trial   file   denial   filial   defunct

23. server   soothe   lever   weaver   howsoever   tray

24. wise   shrew   show   shrewd   shrank   shred

25. untouched   unhappy   untie   flush   couch   unaffected

Time _____ Sec.   RATE (from table on page 297):   R. _____

No. Errors _____   COMPREHENSION (100 − 4% for each Error):   C. _____

II-16   EFFICIENCY (R × C):   E. _____

Exercise 17

1. affright   terrify   alight   align   alike   taffeta

2. charitable   mesa   variable   benevolent   cant   rant

3. decision   revision   temptation   terror   incision   conclusion

4. evermore   forever   swore   tore   sever   boar

5. lamentable   tableau   table   mournful   men   mama

6. murderer   killer   mud   shudder   death   sturdy

7. retreat   react   readjust   recede   reappear   defeat

8. painful   hurtful   armful   baleful   careful   deceitful

9. railway   rail   railroad   railing   doorway   highway

10. servile   revile   subservient   defile   violent   revelry

11. supplant   haunt   case   race   replace   daunt

12. unusual   hair   fair   rare   snare   air

13. ignorant   ignore   finger   illiterate   rant   significant

14. chopper   hopper   cutter   robber   stopper   copper

15. college   colleague   ledge   league   university   varsity

16. disciple   tipple   ripple   molar   scholar   cider

17. fertile   specific   pacific   tile   ferment   prolific

18. explanation   excavation   relation   donation   sense   constitution

19. irresistible   irresponsible   digest   combustible   powerful   iridescent

20. pastoral   moral   sorrel   floral   choral   rural

21. district   restrict   construct   stricken   disc   region

22. lattice   trellis   lettuce   radish   cabbage   latter

23. believe   deceive   trust   receive   conceive   relieve

24. taffeta   sordid   fete   staff   fact   fabric

25. faraway   sway   distant   stay   tray   quay

Time _____ Sec.   RATE (from table on page 297):   R. _____

No. Errors _____   COMPREHENSION (100 − 4% for each Error):   C. _____

II-17   EFFICIENCY (R × C):   E. _____

Exercise 18

1. ambiguous — antipathy   hurt   obscure   pinch   omelet

2. convene — concave   conceal   assemble   concede   sonorous

3. contemplate — con   consider   conclusive   plate   contempt

4. housework — household   homemaking   horse   homelike   homemade

5. forfeiture — fortune   forefather   feather   penalty   pore

6. nostril — nosegay   trill   fill   nose   trail

7. lettuce — vegetable   terrace   fruit   certify   date

8. neutrality — frugality   lake   rocky   immunity   grey

9. bearable — quarterly   notable   relax   tolerable   tortoise

10. romantic — gigantic   fanciful   frantic   you   save

11. somebody — somber   someday   pomegranate   person   dome

12. respect — depreciate   help   reciprocate   epoch   esteem

13. efficiency — competency   leniency   regent   frog   cedar

14. lookout — flout   watch   doubt   mount   woodland

15. statute — statue   stature   law   match   latch

16. cupboard — closet   headboard   cupola   rubber   clad

17. deceive — receive   beguile   perceive   rod   because

18. eventual — evenly   effectual   fact   fennel   final

19. indictment — foment   indicate   statement   torment   sincerity

20. instructor — factor   adapt   teacher   toy   rector

21. outcast — outbreak   mast   last   duteous   degraded

22. purchaser — pursuer   purser   chase   burden   buyer

23. compound — unite   ponder   pound   around   competition

24. stately — grand   lately   greatly   slightly   quietly

25. disturbance — turbid   turbine   cistern   ran   confusion

Time _____ Sec.   RATE (from table on page 297):   R. _____

No. Errors _____   COMPREHENSION (100 − 4% for each Error):   C. _____

II-18   EFFICIENCY (R × C):   E. _____

Exercise 19

1. angrily   inwardly   silly   indignantly   candidly   fully

2. anxious   noxious   concerned   gracious   rapacious   canyon

3. convince   quince   convert   fence   rinse   onward

4. durable   curate   insure   lasting   fable   lurch

5. hurricane   bean   flurry   cyclone   sour   curriculum

6. however   yet   bower   sour   never   youthful

7. likewise   also   bait   dike   size   bill

8. prejudice   reproduce   bias   fudge   juice   breezy

9. poultry   chickens   sully   paltry   motley   courtly

10. rubbish   publish   pugilist   litter   furious   lubber

11. spotless   seedless   senseless   shameless   stainless   shapeless

12. transfer   convey   defer   confer   refer   gopher

13. banquet   feast   croquet   shut   quit   fang

14. backbone   tone   telephone   phone   sack   spine

15. cataract   contract   waterfall   catarrh   fact   watch

16. ceremonial   testimonial   crane   money   formal   ferment

17. ensnare   ensue   ensure   pare   trap   tart

18. abandon   band   ranch   renounce   don   bank

19. infernal   thermal   hellish   internal   vernal   hermit

20. masonry   fashion   ration   occasion   sash   stonework

21. overlook   book   cook   rover   disregard   dove

22. birthplace   birth   earth   place   dearth   origin

23. satiate   retaliate   prelate   nominate   gather   satisfy

24. discontinue   disc   disk   con   stop   sister

25. philosophical   philanthropy   rhapsody   abdominal   beneficial   rational

Time _____ Sec.   RATE (from table on page 297):   R. _____

No. Errors _____   COMPREHENSION (100 − 4% for each Error):   C. _____

II-19   EFFICIENCY (R × C):   E. _____

Exercise 20

1. desirous   rouse   covetous   liars   cypress   iris

2. peasant   rustic   pheasant   resent   sent   scant

3. credulous   duly   louse   credit   greed   naive

4. redbreast   quest   west   wrest   robin   best

5. gabardine   grenadier   sardine   cloth   grandee   cabin

6. impenetrable   abominable   bachelor   inscrutable   baronial   imaginable

7. highness   elevation   fineness   lightness   sickness   weakness

8. thankful   healthful   grateful   uneventful   vengeful   wakeful

9. produce   process   reduce   conduit   manufacture   modulus

10. satisfy   multiply   petrify   deny   gratify   gather

11. confess   dress   fuss   acknowledge   rest   anywhere

12. floor   mooring   base   booing   doing   cornice

13. highway   day   high   say   road   bey

14. calamity   disaster   salad   credulity   forcibly   formality

15. chemistry   chemise   history   science   dentistry   shelves

16. creator   theater   crater   meditate   producer   preacher

17. exchange   range   flange   trade   derange   text

18. gratitude   thankfulness   servitude   multitude   food   trash

19. interview   consultation   made   one   twinkle   toes

20. impartial   imperial   marshal   martial   farthing   fair

21. sportsman   worst   hunter   abortive   dart   horse

22. rebuild   skilled   filled   trilled   meat   mend

23. sadness   gladness   confess   redress   daddy   depression

24. subsist   resist   exist   consist   desist   eulogy

25. everywhere   mountainous   tree   fuss   obey   omnipresent

Time _____ Sec.   RATE (from table on page 297):   R. _____

No. Errors _____   COMPREHENSION (100 − 4% for each Error):   C. _____

II-20   EFFICIENCY (R × C):   E. _____

SERIES III
Phrase Meaning Drills

In these exercises the emphasis on meaning is extended from words to phrases. In addition these drills should help to increase the eye span as you are to try to grasp the meaning of each phrase at a glance. Do not read them word for word; treat each group as a unit of meaning. Each of the phrases is set off by spaces to allow you to concentrate on group meaning with a single eye fixation.

Look at the key phrase and think about its meaning; then glance at the phrases which follow until you find one that means approximately the same as the key phrase. Try to shift rhythmically from each phrase to the next until you find the right one. Mark this correct answer and go on to the next line. As soon as you have finished the last line, ask for your time and look up your rate on page 299. Use the keys on page 308 or page 314 to check your errors. Compute comprehension and efficiency as indicated in the scoring directions and record rate and efficiency on the Progress Chart on page 289.

Here again the key words in a phrase are a measure of your vocabulary. Take the key words from any phrases you miss and list them in your vocabulary list for further study.

These exercises begin on page 71; tables are on page 299; progress charts on page 289. Keys are on pages 308 and 314.

EXAMPLE

. . . .

17. nose of man   <u>for smelling</u>   such terms as   can define as   you can make   does not imply

18. a meek person   X   along with her   wanted to go   <u>has some kind</u>   has mild temper   may be ahead

19. church song   to be given   <u>morning hymn</u>   one can go   not wish to   many more than

20. act of hunting   free time   never will go   to enjoy life   lead to   <u>a search for game</u>

Time 70 Sec.	RATE (from table on page 299):	R.	257
No. Errors 1	COMPREHENSION (100 − 5% for each error):	C.	95
III-1	EFFICIENCY (R × C): (257 × .95) = 244.15	E.	244

Exercise 1

1. diamond ring   in these days   an average   a precious stone   is obvious   short period

2. spoken word   to say something   will provide   be used to   full extent   against him

3. a passage way   little less   practical way   to all   an opening for   perhaps this

4. share equally   that reason   divide evenly   almost here   have their   with those men

5. very joyous   is taken   never again   other hand   may compensate for   quite happy

6. in the middle   judgment of   such as   about medium   has assumed by   plan to go

7. a mature person   one fully grown   is merely   benefit all   away from   to wait long

8. an outrage   another day   plan to go   so you can   a violent wrong   does not require

9. to precede   college life   to go ahead of   affect all   to believe   not in here

10. human speech   make adjustment   may record   too loud   not yet heard   articulate sound

11. to inspect   same always   likely to   view critically   it is also   tend to do

12. a scamp   a rascal   fine person   looks ahead   always able to   can be expected to

13. not very full   to ignore   of the group   have said   rather meager   decline to state

14. to droop over   may sound   to lean down   are near here   to be seen by   near the top

15. to play   which occur often   are used by   these words   rates low   to amuse

16. large plant   so that he   might be   a big tree   green grass   under no conditions

17. nose of man   for smelling   such terms as   can define as   you can make   does not imply

18. a meek person   along with her   wanted to go   has some kind   has mild temper   may be ahead

19. church song   to be given   morning hymn   one can go   not wish to   many more than

20. act of hunting   free time   never will go   to enjoy life   lead to   a search for game

Time _____ Sec.   RATE (from table on page 299):   R. _____

No. Errors _____   COMPREHENSION (100 − 5% for each Error):   C. _____

III-1   EFFICIENCY (R × C):   E. _____

Exercise 2

1. to remember   set it up   to enjoy life   to recognize again   can be   might lead again

2. pure gold   is equal to   worth more   living along   precious metal   has shown to be

3. bright luster   can read by   great care of   to play as   it may happen   a high polish

4. drain off   to empty out   be considered   perhaps others do   what is this   in this sense

5. an opinion   the use of   a belief held   state support of   because of   good life

6. a short novel   to advance   of the new   prose fiction   to put into   need for more

7. rather narrow   the result of   more than ever   other means than this   of little breadth   too active

8. a member of   in time of   to expend   the story of   in every way   to belong to

9. without limits   infinite in size   his limited views   new order of   subject to   most of us

10. act as host   best way   entertains another   for that   his school   let that do

11. the ground   surface of earth   can be seen   the four levels   all above   blue sky

12. to jab   about half of   to poke something   on each day   method of   to increase some

13. given freedom   to obtain all   as with   made independent of   be sure to   as with him

14. end hostilities   we profess   it appears   he said   to make peace   their names

15. omit something   present time   until later   is made   public life   leave it out

16. a noble person   possessing dignity   the work of   was able to   his own   was urgently

17. large monster   way of   an enormous animal   its cause   the facts   was absent

18. hold court   last year   come down from   administer justice   make wise   be said

19. be inaccurate   should be   it also   lack of   not correct   without loss of

20. hopeful person   he argued   the needs of   stand upon   to guide   one who expects

Time _____ Sec.

No. Errors _____

III-2

RATE (from table on page 299):   R. _____

COMPREHENSION (100 − 5% for each Error):   C. _____

EFFICIENCY (R × C):   E. _____

Exercise 3

1. sign of force   physical vigor   to say so   for those   he grows up   afraid of war

2. looks flat   can develop   even surface   very rarely   no one could
their jobs stop

3. sign of famine   in the period   fine school   scarcity of food   they are   near to home

4. showing spite   was reached   low point of   could be   exhibiting envy   in an age

5. always near   high rent   the future   has also been   rural area   close at all times

6. to expose   to reveal openly   to describe as   leave alone   along the way
return to

7. is desperate   not knowing   in great need   look for work   showing off
buying in

8. of good humor   design for   can often be   a cheerful person   at work   take more

9. in reality   true to life   may assume   in each class   of this type
method of work

10. a shy fellow   on the surface   a new home   to build   a modest person
in conflict

11. without delay   to forget   after these   other times   less than his   with promptness

12. act of haste   we learn   the sense   quickness of action   four days
be a factor in

13. will float   miles away   the point   higher rates   lighter than water
a real income

14. marked faulty   no ambition   cited as   has become great   the rest
made imperfectly

15. to be exposed   open to view   due to this   arise from   to increase   for the aged

16. ruling over   for reasons   act of dominating   coming of age   upper limit
can afford now

17. being partial   the ideal of   in which   show preference   more alike   as defined by

18. as a result of   in the future   to report   believe in   brought about by
too soon after

19. to startle   as a sign   for many days   to do with   to search for
to frighten suddenly

20. to acquit   to assemble   to set free   certain cue   likely to   one part of it

Time _____ Sec.   RATE (from table on page 299):   R. _____

No. Errors _____   COMPREHENSION (100 − 5% for each Error):   C. _____

III-3   EFFICIENCY (R × C):   E. _____

Exercise 4

1. proper place   be sold at   because of   correct position   one year   an election day

2. tame horse   gentle animal   to do better   this age group   in a box   a few years

3. a gentle slope   useful to   a sort of   a hot day   a gradual decline   instead of him

4. to grow small   to control   diminish in size   they give   led by you   no one can

5. ample food   began in   few if any   a long look   to do good   abundant harvest

6. to be confused   child's life   to consider   be flustered   is well to   must not be

7. standing erect   upright position   to walk to   over the top   has called   first period

8. very durable   they are   the source   a large part   to be stable   for peace only

9. being drowsy   as well as   rather sleepy   part of this   term used   said that

10. to be desolate   first day   his life is   sort of damp   to revert   ruinous condition

11. be delinquent   in spite of   which are   neglect of duty   goes on   strong arm methods

12. to groan   expressive of pain   a form of   pay for all   any later   the desire for

13. a fixed limit   the center of   may lead   for less   marked boundary   are some more

14. cease to exist   two weeks   to annihilate   to a degree   so often   the behavior pattern

15. present time   number of   at one place   more usual   this is not   this very instant

16. trudge about   our purpose   by himself   ramble along   is easier to   as a whole

17. chief concern   most valuable part   to assert   in some   are able   new plan of action

18. without grace   under the   to serve fish   made upon   being clumsy   value to us

19. to break down   to secrete   to collapse   most basic part   on the stage   is obvious

20. make difficult   as fast as   who can be   the content of   calls for   to complicate

Time _____ Sec.   RATE (from table on page 299):   R. _____

No. Errors _____   COMPREHENSION (100 − 5% for each Error):   C. _____

III-4   EFFICIENCY (R × C):   E. _____

Exercise 5

1. prompts an action

go beyond it   more to be done   some incentive   possible to define
in some form

2. a forward step

brought to light   seldom mention   the rank order   to move ahead
will be found here

3. on being decisive

pride and joy   in some cases   from the rest   give us the word
man of decision

4. a careless mistake

not using care   when he comes   to leave home   of this group
number of men

5. a catastrophe

can set up   a sudden calamity   to represent all   all afraid to
a passing phase

6. unable to recall

to indicate   the cause of   act of forgetting   of modern life
it is possible to

7. beginning point

real danger here   go to college   among this group   the threshold
a little older

8. of no value

of all sorts   will have less   to earn part   may be presented
completely worthless

9. to understand

gain full meaning   to be desired   an expert in   for that reason
in social events

10. no fixed value

which relates to   no set price   they can help   be alert to
have been listening

11. great enjoyment

show satisfaction   to think so   the time being   to come down
to talk about him

12. to verify the act

comes to mind   confirm the deed   of this nature   well known
an end result

13. to alternate

we talk about   tentative period   to take turns   complex part of
perhaps in a sense

14. rather peculiar

taken for granted   too high   upon the basis   something odd
on the party line

15. most likely

when they agree   at the end of   lags far behind   become more fixed
in all probability

16. making attack

on the offensive   provide for   for some reason   final answer
also appear to be

17. drive with force

on this point   make a thrust   less selective   by such action
a better risk

18. little importance

in this process   often possible   a trivial matter   in any aspect
study made by him

(continued on next page)

19. being unlimited

| almost half of | in contrast to | he should help | have no boundary |

can best be

20. pattern to go by

| need to know | the third session | back them up | did not know about |

serve as a guide

Time _____ Sec.

No. Errors _____

III-5

RATE (from table on page 299):

COMPREHENSION (100 − 5% for each Error):

EFFICIENCY (R × C):

R. _____

C. _____

E. _____

Exercise 6

1. rushing for help

   be taken as   has been paid   tends to change   in this area
   hurrying for aid

2. almost as simple

   keep in mind   nearly as easy   high level of   legion of others
   rate as superior

3. more than enough

   the next series   he may not   in their review   more than needed
   on the test

4. in minute amount

   very small quantity   to possess manly   exist among
   below average   who rates low

5. either of the two

   may accept this   there are two   one or the other   in a study
   fortunate enough

6. a colossal mistake

   as a starting point   in the light   later than   as a sort of
   a great error

7. it became obvious

   may be assumed   plain to see   in terms of   a clear example
   a state of health

8. not concerned with

   the most interested man   to predict what   what things
   not interested in   the most effective

9. shameful action

   scandalous conduct   would not accept   less accurate   new to them
   in the session

10. on the contrary

    loss to himself   more and more   just the opposite   try to classify
    grain of salt

11. from the origin

    as an agency   provides a chance   the influence of   are held to
    at the beginning

12. a small fragment

    no matter how   a surviving part   an excuse for   to feel superior
    to make sure

13. being transparent

    whole new area   a small number   they may turn   obviously clear
    to be fewer

14. break of day

    about dawn   it is interesting   the power to   called to account
    by the same token

15. guilty of crime

    advantage of   it may appear   he who is a criminal
    is usually bound   low nor high

16. to strongly desire

    can be aided   some new ones   may thus help   be more able
    craving something

17. willing to serve

    may be overt   offer your service   may observe   an effort to
    there is trouble

18. keeping clear of

    described as   not at exactly   just before the   avoiding something
    what extent

(continued on next page)

19. true to history   being historical   the progress of   has failed to   does not deny
do occur together

20. of a lazy nature   who are already   in summing up   dislike to work   years earlier
average age of

Time _____ Sec.   RATE (from table on page 299):   R. _____

No. Errors _____   COMPREHENSION (100 − 5% for each Error):   C. _____

III-6   EFFICIENCY (R × C):   E. _____

Exercise 7

1. place of union

    to bring out   a study of   a common junction   for college life
    a broad interest

2. a parting wish

    to bid farewell   within the law   eager to protect   the advice is
    he can learn

3. an endless time

    no matter how   may only be   give everything   eternal existence
    on the side

4. to set free

    for their money   act of liberation   has to talk   no one expects
    to the contrary

5. being confidential

    in the night   little interest   without him   a message from
    keeping a secret

6. that which ceases

    we are here   would not hurt   comes to an end   in the capacity
    just as it was

7. display of wit

    an exhibit of humor   to state this   in any type   aid in general
    it is difficult

8. its proper place

    in the office   major cause of   this is done   correct position
    what he knew

9. out of reach

    not even if   that which is beyond   the form of   is not clear
    the passing of

10. full of activity

    there may be   only a step   has the best   the same was true
    being very busy

11. hold spellbound

    best interest of   all but one   to fascinate   much depends upon
    point of view

12. an angry dispute

    likely a quarrel   sets of forms   were not used   one item of
    another type of

13. great quantity

    who will fail   some phases of   of the function
    considerable amount   the purpose of

14. without delay

    all are omitted   with promptness   all too many   there is much
    the larger task

15. general routing

    to build up   from the office   be extended to   first of all
    regular procedure

16. threatening aspect

    the latter plan   be given first   a severe look   will secure
    does not require

17. unite in a body

    join in a group   a lag from   tend to avoid   the reason why
    of the present day

18. state of silence

    basic to all   does not mean   any other kind   absence of sound
    for other forms

(*continued on next page*)

19. being sincere   may be both   honesty of mind   the fault of   learns most from

                         have claim to it

20. roughly sketched   a correlate of   no small part   some part of   some are operated

                         not completed

Time _____ Sec.   RATE (from table on page 299):   R. _____

No. Errors _____   COMPREHENSION (100 − 5% for each Error):   C. _____

III-7   EFFICIENCY (R × C):   E. _____

Exercise 8

1. promoted in rank

   but hardly more   be wise to   may suggest   rising in power
   any given day

2. should be granted

   working hard   should be allowed   barely escaped   to leave alone
   to describe

3. concerning truth

   in assuming   as late as   as most likely   is far from home
   according to facts

4. to do away with

   to be elected   allowed to search   to dispose of   died instantly
   held until notice

5. achieve the summit

   to reach the peak   must fall back   able to go   not innate
   to avoid going

6. as a result of

   all has been   trying to climb   always able to   brought about by
   it may be true

7. ready to proceed

   is confronted   prepared to go on   in this case   tend to do
   not the thing

8. all by oneself

   are all obvious   will refuse to   he is afraid   to participate in
   exclusive of others

9. lull in activity

   they may be   how to play   not very busy   as is usual
   to do something well

10. act of slaying

    death by violence   habit of refusing   if he has   who reads poorly
    is crucial to

11. worthy of respect

    what to expect   it may be   so far as   decent in character
    in some places

12. without a spot

    may differ from   free from reproach   high level   so much more
    the most part

13. hold in position

    most sinister man   not in accord   has stopped   annoyed to find
    keep from falling

14. a loud clamor

    may be made to   a decided drop   a great outcry   the effect of
    could be observed

15. something vital

    very necessary   in low esteem   the bottom of   the only solace
    which was done

16. over fatigued

    in the future   happens often   very fact of   completely exhausted
    not so clear

17. mountain lodge

    were less active   place for vacations   counter to   social dancing
    the other end of

18. a prompt person

    most crucial   an area in which   in our culture   turn the dial
    one who is punctual

(*continued on next page*)

19. brave person   little relation to   be helpful   a motive for   one who is courageous

same classroom as

20. broken to bits   shattered to pieces   in all events   show as great   are found to

does not support

Time _____ Sec.   RATE (from table on page 299):   R. _____

No. Errors _____   COMPREHENSION (100 − 5% for each Error):   C. _____

III-8   EFFICIENCY (R × C):   E. _____

Exercise 9

1. jumble things up   to conclude by saying   pave the way to   to mix confusedly   an opportunity for   invite your attention to

2. mark of distinction   to be outstanding   remains to be done   a major obstacle   some of these issued   need for a system

3. a time of crisis   can be relied upon   awarded to each   free to choose   a decisive moment   cost of providing information

4. an abundant supply   the lack of time   more than is needed   a large section   one school of thought   to synthesize methods

5. contrary to reason   an emergency situation   will profit   the required ability   result of experience   thought to be absurd

6. very appropriate   be allowed to participate   will not remain   especially suitable   in order to learn   in cooperation with

7. the extent of space   capacity of anything   covering all phases   an adequate answer   a disturbing failure   gaining more

8. grasp the meaning of   on a large scale   to approve   able to speak clearly   to comprehend   in relation to the city

9. an acquired habit   secret sign   usual way of doing something   return in the fall   the greater interest   to organize

10. place of residence   to be washed away   which seemed to him   the other   to remove from sight   where one lives

11. lowest in a rank   a word of caution   held responsible   the last in the series   marked by failure   process of defining

12. that which confines   boundary line   no right to expect   in other instances   to gain prestige   for what he plans to do

13. indicative of grief   kinds of pressure   not too subtle   the first activity   a sound like a moan   conferred with the group

14. picture of a landscape   cannot be disrupted   a scenic painting   standard practice   deserves mention   the final word

15. state of privacy   a joint responsibility   a kind of service   usually small   person being referred   not public in nature

16. to make a recess in   will want to know   for his own needs   to set back   a simple question   an explanation

17. living a lonely life   a solitary existence   at a casual level   a type of program   a small group   to destroy the function of

18. furnish with a subsidy   achieve the goal   tend to disappear   to express oneself   provide financial aid   a nursery school

(*continued on next page*)

19. neat in appearance | an appropriate suggestion | a tidy person | examine the situation | center of it | a separate volume

20. display of kindness | the rapid growth of | best way out | few specific changes | a sense of balance | an act of good will

Time _____ Sec. | RATE (from table on page 299): | R. _____

No. Errors _____ | COMPREHENSION (100 — 5% for each Error): | C. _____

III-9 | EFFICIENCY (R × C): | E. _____

Exercise 10

1. forced to pay a fine — punishment for an offense   to be commended   the basic terms used   remains to be done   level of skill

2. be granted admittance — avoid the difficulty   no one can doubt   an act of entering   used for centuries   a thing observed

3. a definite difference — really consistent   in only one situation   method of improving   sort of estimate   in complete contrast

4. act of condemning — an economic necessity   to pronounce guilty   to be stressed   not a part of   obtaining accurate data

5. make more difficult — universally accepted   a radical change   relationship between   to complicate matters   one point of view

6. an innocent person — free from blame   one of the essentials   to fill in a gap   to be arranged   very accurately described

7. to hurl into space — of special importance   degree of freedom   to throw with violence   of the plan   some previous prejudice

8. henceforth from now — the same problem   a number of ideas   with the real issue   the valid use of   from this time forward

9. looked upon as an enemy — are less expensive   a military foe   an estimated budget   should be made   type of floor covering

10. cease from being — the important ingredient   the rate of speed   the principal reason   to come to an end   after much searching

11. to shape by cutting — words of wisdom   kind of a tree   the art of carving   after much searching   taking over too much

12. a flat-bottomed boat — the immediate circle   a large river barge   to discover when   meet the test   certain satisfactions

13. an object of dislike — beyond the bounds   to get pleasure from   be supported by   to have an aversion to   motivated by love

14. admittance to a hearing — to be part of an audience   may be acute   contacts in business   with wear and tear   a new example

15. belonging to antiquity — feeling of hostility   to help others   anything very old   a staff member   time before midnight

16. gruff in appearance — a dominant factor   to stop growing   varying needs of pupils   rough in countenance   be initiated at

17. a friendly greeting — an ancient landscape   father and son   a losing battle   the new building   pleasant salutation

18. the angry canine — one mad dog   to go forward   misunderstood husband   not to be seen   a disgusted feline

(continued on next page)

19. move forward in haste   at one time   to rush someplace   would be favorable

      likely to wander   superior to long periods

20. secure from danger   found to promote   to retard forgetting   forced to check

      particularly effective   to be in a safe place

Time _____ Sec.   RATE (from table on page 299):   R. _____

No. Errors _____   COMPREHENSION (100 − 5% for each Error):   C. _____

III-10   EFFICIENCY (R × C):   E. _____

Exercise 11

1. a craving for water   field of endeavor   a feeling of thirst   must guard against   not willingly change   not to be disturbed

2. rather indefinite   regarding the other   ability to exist   resolution of conflict   to know something   not certain to occur

3. execute the commands   discuss the alternatives   dispense with it   to be obedient   a source book of   dealing with students

4. something in the future   that which is to come   a sense of resentment   may come from   to take the raps   a complex program

5. a boisterous laugh   result may decrease   excellent argument for   have more control   showing hilarity   not easy to accept

6. exemption from work   some simple rules   an acquired holiday   trustees of human values   from the office   a direct outgrowth of

7. guilty of crime   a cross-section of society   to help answer   a chain of events   a parallel effort of   one who is a criminal

8. to vanish in thin air   by this time   too many people   pass quickly from sight   born of a need   to be defensive against

9. fitting and proper   to be in right accord   apt to respond   on the way toward   our greatest fault   the latter part of

10. on his own accord   might be applied to   was addressed to   our basic insecurity   of his own free will   more obvious signs

11. making a selection   stating our strengths   choosing from several   much more to be said   in a rough way   reactions of others

12. causing to assemble   much to learn   for what they are   as a young profession   because of long life   to come together

13. plainness in manner   beneath the surface   most other fields   simplicity of style   suffer a kind of   from exterior behavior

14. not completed in detail   roughly sketched   often accused of   may be expressed   with whom we deal   will readily recognize

15. considerable strength   from time to time   one of the solutions   the human factor   state of being strong   a couple of hours

16. only a glimpse   a big boon for   source of irritation   give every indication   no particular merit   a short hurried view

17. that which is unique   become less concerned   only one of a kind   to appear at ease   it is essential   jammed with affairs

18. different from usual   everything possible   reason why   changed in appearance   of the group   the largest amount of

(*continued on next page*)

19. cease from motion   to stand still   act of coming to   we cannot assume

                                     thoughtful interest in   in one common connection

20. sign of gratitude   for all that happens   never seem to feel   the liability of

                                     to be thankful   a very perplexing thing

Time _____ Sec.   RATE (from table on page 299):   R. _____

No. Errors _____   COMPREHENSION (100 − 5% for each Error):   C. _____

III-11   EFFICIENCY (R × C):   E. _____

Exercise 12

1. entitled to reverence

   should be an aid   visualized form   consecrated as sacred
   a key phrase   distraction to thinking

2. to commit treason

   level of popularity   the same experiment   be allowed to decide
   betray a trust   to leave school

3. a wrong statement

   it should always be   much of the work   content of a book
   in the environment   not according to facts

4. the lowest point

   bottom of the scale   cannot be helpful   given careful attention
   respect for   contribute to misunderstanding

5. an act of exercising

   newly decorated   training for an event   economical manner
   operate effectively   not a valid one

6. in terms of largeness

   more beautiful than   to make contacts   that which is immense
   form of publicity   very good reason

7. to impart knowledge

   lowered into the sea   simply lay limp   did not appear
   an act of teaching   love the out-of-doors

8. act of justifying

   state of excitement   to get an education   the village school
   await the results   prove to be right

9. set form of procedure

   an orderly arrangement   across the fields   the day before
   in a distant city   ask his advice

10. a division of the year

    a closely knit group   one of the seasons   under no obligation
    corn in the field   a short period

11. article of furniture

    a table in a room   in order to present   train of thought
    time to study   conscious effort to look

12. state of being near

    recreation is fun   in a close-by vicinity   it is apparent
    a sense of humor   give the keynote address

13. an affirmative reply

    concerning the role   prone to limit   to answer yes
    to change human nature   structure of society

14. be in opposition to

    to enhance the quality   groping for words   bit of conversation
    to be against   be frightened by

15. a gallant person

    assigned to work   more natural light   easily identified
    during slack period   one noble in spirit

16. state of inattention

    lack of attention   type of position   near the state line
    usually enough   something hard to believe

17. the inside of anything

    pleasant experience   that which is interior   compelled to study
    in the home   a great honor

18. keep possession of

    a brave life   good deal of expense   retain ownership of
    born in slavery   to live in a small town

(continued on next page)

19. to make an offer   almost immediately   almost like a dwarf   to show skill

                                       to present for acceptance   a great name

20. hesitant to answer   not at all pleased   an immediate appeal   type of occupation

                                       soon to be at home   to pause undecidedly

Time _____ Sec.   RATE (from table on page 299):   R. _____

No. Errors _____   COMPREHENSION (100 − 5% for each Error):   C. _____

III-12   EFFICIENCY (R × C):   E. _____

In the following drills, the answers appear in a vertical column beneath the key phrase. Read the key phrase and then let your eyes drop, trying to keep them centered on the line and trying to grasp the meaning of each phrase by a single glance. Place a check mark in front of the phrase most nearly the same as the key as in the previous exercises.

Exercise 13

1.   related to the newspaper

     a thirst for great fame
     a working compromise
     associated with the press
     dependence upon authority
     emphasis upon scholarship

2.   the general run of things

     a withdrawal from life
     a method of study
     the force of the spoken word
     to be determined about
     usual course of events

3.   quality of being sensitive

     wrote for publication
     learned men of the past
     very sensible activity
     capacity of receiving impressions
     the unlimited activity of

4.   a very robust person

     a comparison of translations
     an ideal preparation for
     to be greatly praised
     to study mathematics
     one who displays strength

5.   a person who is altruistic

     cultivation of the body
     the development of good citizens
     one who is not selfish
     a sense of danger
     material to be memorized

6.   a state of bewilderment

     overwhelming amazement
     soon to become a famous man
     as head of the school
     during the hot summer months
     a quality of good speech

7.   characterized by kindness

     a means of eloquence
     simplified method of study
     dynamic and aggressive
     cruel action
     an amiable person

8.   sufficient to satisfy

     the language of instruction
     a leader in public affairs
     service to the state
     an ample amount of anything
     a model of best style

9.   something which is distinct

     excellent skill in logic
     a liberal education
     to cover a large area
     one of the unstable elements
     set apart from others

10.   following a given course

     acquired fame as a teacher
     adhering to a set plan
     a method of discipline
     due to organization of
     close personal relations

11.   throughout the universe

     the aim of the school
     the most striking contrasts
     best for the purpose of
     all over everywhere
     a careful use of words

12.   be concerned with the result

     to make a new demand
     of the many studies made
     to anticipate the outcome
     a variety of accomplishments
     along new lines

(continued on next page)

13.   increasing in difficulty

becoming more complex
an occasional work of charity
to vary widely in capacity
conditions of the time
in their prime condition

14.   to be scattered abroad

to discover the nature of
the scientific method
that which is dispersed
rights of the individual
in the same way as before

15.   looked upon as important

to be equipped with pins
thought to be significant
on the part of others
training in manual skills
to delay the growth of

16.   according to the facts

related to the truth
to lack of facilities
no provision is made by
it is encouraging to note
should be considered now

17.   an official announcement

the administration of the plan
authorized by proclamation
a consensus of opinion
a successful program
a series of serious talks

18.   to be denied an opportunity

the most unusual feature
the plan in operation
to prove very helpful
to withhold a privilege
out of the picture

19.   a violation of the law

on a less extensive scale
an act which is illegal
social opportunity for all
suggested by tradition
forcing a rule upon men

20.   that which might be available

to be potentially obtainable
the proper thing to do
helps to limit cost
to fulfill their purpose
the best chance of success

Time _____ Sec.

No. Errors _____

III-13

RATE (from table on page 299):

COMPREHENSION (100 − 5% for each Error):

EFFICIENCY (R × C):

R. _____

C. _____

E. _____

Exercise 14

1. **at a marked disadvantage**

   possessed with a severe handicap
   a tendency to evasion
   an opportunity to learn
   included in this report
   unable to attend now

2. **process of becoming essential**

   does not rank very high
   soon to be indispensable
   a genius for memorization
   an active force
   the better choice

3. **as frequently as needed**

   to think through a problem
   to gain a great deal from it
   as often as necessary
   a conflict in the soul
   to sacrifice truth

4. **occurring once each year**

   welcoming the newcomer
   more than this number
   not upon a class basis
   an annual event or happening
   to be isolated from fear

5. **matter added to a book**

   helpful in this regard
   be adopted generally
   the appendix of a book
   less important than the other
   of like-minded friends

6. **to apply oneself to a task**

   to engage with close attention
   to work and play together
   necessary for the future
   is being done carefully
   take the part of

7. **approximate or nearly exact**

   in the attainment of
   close to correctness
   the sense of belonging to
   sharing in a common cause
   on the honor system

8. **to hear and then decide**

   a varied social program
   the most recurrent problem
   brief word of warning
   to submit to arbitration
   the poorest showing

9. **body of men armed for war**

   by those who instruct
   securing more cooperation
   a military organization
   far more recent origin
   about every two years

10. **that which is artless**

    validity of the argument
    the average length of time
    implied or stated power
    equip the new engine
    something made without skill

11. **a violent onset or attack**

    to assault another person
    a qualified worker
    more suited to serve
    a different view of the matter
    open to criticism

12. **act of taking for granted**

    found most effective
    the acceptance of an assumption
    to use up excess energy
    advantage in keeping open
    in their own planning

13. **outrageously cruel or wicked**

    resentment of authority
    a building program
    used for special occasions
    occur in another year
    quality of being atrocious

14. **to attempt to do something**

    the central part of
    a wholesome program
    the equalizing of cost
    to make trials or experiments
    social event of the year

(continued on next page)

15.   activities at an auction

cutting down the cost
a drain on the resources
the most vexing problem
a series of
sale of goods to highest bidder

16.   having a genuine origin

to better existing conditions
that which is authentic
on a less extensive scale
voluntary pay into a fund
opportunity for all

17.   to clothe with legal power

definite limitations
a philosophy of life
in an assured manner
to establish by authority
more difficult to attain

18.   manuscript of an author

widely adopted means
may not be included in it
that written by his own hand
three times each hour
to arrange a date

19.   a desire to turn away

feeling of aversion toward something
fairly well integrated
the most powerful force
a successful plan
noted by many

20.   strong conviction of truth

an artificial separation
it is quite obvious
one can learn to swim
all learning situations
a belief of some sort

Time _____ Sec.   RATE (from table on page 299):   R. _____

No. Errors _____   COMPREHENSION (100 − 5% for each Error):   C. _____

III-14   EFFICIENCY (R × C):   E. _____

Exercise 15

1. a radiant brightness

    considered to be brilliant
    in response to the question
    a change in personnel
    over a period of years
    to receive the benefits

2. to inflict a bruise on

    a surface injury to flesh
    a little more under control
    to be derived therefrom
    the extent to which
    included in the survey

3. to confer or bestow upon

    the value of democracy
    principles of sound health
    that which is awarded
    in the given order
    to decide a given policy

4. not adapted to its purpose

    opposing points of view
    belief on any matter
    something awkward or unhandy
    those elected to office
    learn by living

5. directed or turned backward

    rights of others
    in a contrary or reverse way
    social changes take place
    a mode of behavior
    must be so guided

6. a baffling situation

    wholesome way of life
    adapted to local conditions
    a major purpose
    a perplexing and frustrating experience
    it becomes true

7. barracks used by the army

    to select wise leaders
    the amount of power
    complete control of
    concerns itself with
    buildings for lodging soldiers

8. a tract of barren land

    has general oversight
    under this type of
    may lack knowledge
    be present at all times
    not capable of producing vegetation

9. combat between two persons

    a possible disadvantage
    serve to remind us
    a battle between two individuals
    important details
    eligible to vote

10. lives by asking alms

    be reduced to a state of beggary
    in terms of its needs
    in an advisory capacity
    a well-rounded opinion
    must be decided

11. rhythmical flow of language

    a fair representation
    rise and fall of the voice
    may safely be regarded
    a negligible role
    in the drama of life

12. to strike or cross out

    on the highest level of thought
    cancel out the effects of
    a tenth of the total
    indicate the bases for
    the most emphasis

13. the seat of government

    a fair scholastic record
    rely on personal appeal
    for the best interest of
    the capital city of a state
    to compete for office

14. exercising or taking care

    an equal chance to
    the great majority of
    a position of dominance
    a state of being careful
    one most capable of working

(continued on next page)

15.   that which effects a result

can be considered good
by making such mistakes
will learn for the better
one can hardly say
the cause of an event

16.   a numbering of the people

certain other problems
taking a census of the population
merit specific attention
its primary purpose
to hold public office

17.   thoroughly established

in an unsatisfactory manner
with serious consequences
can solve the problem
to keep a diary about
that which is indisputable

18.   to be challenged to a duel

involved in the process
is to be arranged at once
a summons to fight
better than doing nothing
for the most part

19.   to gather into one body

suggested by the title
a valid philosophy
based on two categories
to assemble or accumulate together
may be expressed adequately

20.   a contest between rivals

to contend in rivalry
under what conditions
types of development
two principal aspects of the job
can be separated

Time _____ Sec.   RATE (from table on page 299):   R. _____

No. Errors _____   COMPREHENSION (100 − 5% for each Error):   C. _____

III-15   EFFICIENCY (R × C):   E. _____

Exercise 16

1. to maintain possession of

   learn to cooperate
   one's own behavior may be good
   product of his experience
   be limited to
   to have and to keep

2. causing acute suffering

   result in desired learnings
   effort should be made
   never takes place singly
   that which is tormenting
   purposive in nature

3. without the least delay

   in any given situation
   that which is done instantly
   must be borne in mind
   to win high marks
   means to desired ends

4. an embarrassing situation

   some sort of an award
   the joy of participating
   oriented at the time
   a chance to appreciate
   a confusing predicament

5. to beware of something

   be on your guard
   by which it may be achieved
   most vital to everyone
   covered by study last year
   from time to time

6. that which is deducted

   cuts across all activities
   a search for friends
   the part that is taken away
   represented to all
   be well aware of

7. to wander from direct course

   a brief description of
   the form of inquiry
   to designate all functions
   a degree of guidance
   having gone astray

8. a main division in a book

   to mold public opinion
   a somewhat greater degree
   to arrange into chapters
   to learn by doing
   keep in touch with

9. talk in an informal manner

   promote greater interest
   idle chat in a conversation
   a result of many requests
   to grant freedom
   to try to stop it

10. the chief of the group

    giving some trouble to
    a definite tendency
    to prevent for safety's sake
    the leader of the organization
    in a hurry to go

11. to make pure and clear

    to clarify the issue or report
    an intelligent outcome
    a radical group
    a difficult time existing
    to make a necessity

12. the act of classifying

    a chance to learn
    spent to good advantage
    the end of the year
    to group or segregate in classes
    not in itself harmful

13. a device for measuring time

    instrument such as a clock
    made for the sake of
    to be unbiased and fair
    to keep before them
    a period for study

14. a systematic body of law

    closely related to
    the one just discussed
    to find some way
    the wrong attitude toward
    any system of rules or principles

(continued on next page)

15.   of the farther side of

a distinct advantage
that which is beyond
in the graduate school
problems which arise daily
on various issues today

16.   land adjacent to a border

help to the committee
obviously of little value
that which lies next to
duplication of work
very easily accomplished

17.   that which is borrowed

at a later period
to receive with intention of returning
a primary advantage
chosen for their ability
only in one sense

18.   the lowest part of anything

that which is the bottom
a possible opportunity
to learn democracy
unable to practice
a higher standard of living

19.   a device used for stopping

not very probable
among the most important
in a very sincere sense
to apply a brake to
highest total number

20.   shortness of duration

to be circulated
combine to control members
characterized by brevity
change from previous form
true in many cases

Time _____ Sec.   RATE (from table on page 299):   R. _____

No. Errors _____   COMPREHENSION (100 − 5% for each Error):   C. _____

III-16   EFFICIENCY (R × C):   E. _____

Exercise 17

1.   a king who rules over a kingdom

    an act of binding up wounds
    extending to a great distance
    in the direction of the wind
    a group of related plants
    the monarch of a kingdom

2.   situated below the normal level

    all under one household
    to suffer extreme hunger
    that which is relatively low
    having intimate knowledge of
    may not be interfered with

3.   to magnify or to exaggerate

    quality of being impure
    not of any one style
    an act of impelling force
    an addition that improves land
    to enlarge either in fact or appearance

4.   anything suggestive of a map

    land used for crops
    conducted in a false manner
    a representation of the surface of the earth
    to affect the conscience
    printed for several issues

5.   one who voluntarily suffered death

    an approaching obstacle
    with excellent qualities
    along the sandy shore
    being of a very quiet nature
    a martyr for the sake of principle

6.   recalling what has been learned

    surrounded by fresh water
    using the faculty of remembering
    in some other place besides this
    an act of the legal officer
    precise indication of results

7.   represented on a small scale

    closely resembling someone
    as frequently as needed
    not knowing what to do now
    responding to the loud noise
    reproduced on a miniature level

8.   a time unit of one minute

    working in pleasant surroundings
    the sixtieth part of an hour
    commenting on the subject
    tend to produce sleep quickly
    allowed special privileges

9.   to be considered as moderate

    marked by serious crimes
    a resting place at night
    short pause in reading prose
    which is within reasonable limits
    a bell-shaped flower

10.   that which instills moral lessons

    a joint at this point
    a system of teaching morals
    open hearth of a furnace
    in place of military services
    pertaining to the feudalism

11.   to be classified as a moron

    no possible hope for the future
    a moderately feeble-minded person
    showing a liking for all
    a desire to conceal something
    realizing the real danger

12.   something difficult to explain

    planned according to specifications
    to go out and search for work
    qualified for some type of work
    a complex situation or mystery
    at a severe disadvantage

13.   have but a little margin

    to have very narrow limits
    a method of storing up energy
    including most of the past
    forgiving that which was done
    anticipate an approaching event

14.   not engaged on either side

    acquire a sense of belongingness
    part of the life at home
    being in the same situation
    quality or state of being neutral
    involved to such an extent

(continued on next page)

15.   to name as a candidate for office

        a state of being nominated
        usually not returned too soon
        serious and of sincere purpose
        forced to leave school
        to clarify their own thinking

16.   that which is counted normal

        various phases of the project
        go toward their new job
        of some value to others
        does not deviate from the average
        development in growth

17.   an obstacle or hindrance to

        that which stands in the way
        to be of some service
        having a large vocabulary
        one of the better opportunities
        act according to arrangements

18.   a type or fashion out of date

        necessary for successful learning
        instead of the other
        counted as obsolete in style
        being careful in what one does
        in the light of changed plans

19.   to prove or show to be just

        an object of special devotion
        decorations for festivals
        to vindicate or justify an act
        dapper hero of a great drama

20.   a cruel exercise of authority

        under the oppression of a tyrant
        one who usually does his best
        for those who understand
        before the opening performance
        the one who is never on time

Time _____ Sec.   RATE (from table on page 299):   R. _____

No. Errors _____   COMPREHENSION (100 — 5% for each Error):   C. _____

III-17   EFFICIENCY (R × C):   E. _____

Exercise 18

1. the act or process of explaining

   a salutation or greeting
   to combine in a group
   a network of pipes
   operated by gravity
   to make plain by means of interpretation

2. having an intimate knowledge of

   state of being unbleached
   a large citrus fruit
   a grainlike particle
   closely acquainted or familiar with
   to act or serve as a governess

3. conventional usage in dress

   for extinguishing a fire
   the gloom or melancholy
   that which is in fashion
   goal made by a drop kick
   to catch a glimpse of

4. that which is frail or flimsy

   any plant of a family
   that which is without strength or solidity
   divided into two equal parts
   often used in police work
   that which gathers

5. something that floats on water

   a kind of a watertight structure
   a tale of adventures
   the center of the earth
   an entire range or series
   a transaction involving risk

6. the terminal part of the leg

   the foot of an animal or a person
   an increase in profits
   to silence by authority
   the functions of a public office
   to hit a foul ball

7. valid or existing at all times

   a large amount of light
   to be eternal or infinite in duration
   to receive and retain
   any of the various weeds
   an opening through anything

8. the event which takes place

   to impose restraint upon
   a score made by playing
   that which happens or occurs
   the person in possession of
   the acts of one who hoards

9. one who acts as a witness

   a place of business
   a tight hold or grasp
   a narrative of events
   a person who gives evidence as to what happened
   a natural elevation of land

10. quality of being excellent

    to receive payment of
    deviating from the common rule
    in some future time or state
    to form or put into a herd
    extremely good of its kind

11. state of going beyond limits

    extent to which sound may be heard
    destitute of courage
    in a state of good health
    operated by the hand
    that which exceeds what is usual

12. suitable to the end in view

    sudden stroke of success
    to hit the right note
    a cart pushed by hand
    personal conduct motivated by expediency
    where prisoners are confined

13. contrary to natural instincts

    state of being important
    intensity of the stimulus
    something considered as abnormal
    careful denoting the action of
    occupy the same position

14. living in a state of disguise

    of the essence of mental concentration
    living under false pretenses
    to follow as a pattern
    quality of being immense
    not separated in time or space

(continued on next page)

15.   following in consecutive order

      sequence with no interval or break
      manage with frugality
      the flower of the plant
      pertaining to water power
      regards for the interests of others

16.   delightful in a high degree

      in the nature of an enchantment
      an uncertain state of mind
      marked by a lack of food
      turn in such a state or position
      to be held as hostage

17.   devoted to a sacred and holy cause

      found on old walls and roofs
      consecrated to a noble purpose
      become the head of a family
      passing through the earth
      the character of a person

18.   the customary thing to do

      the famous place of execution
      considered as promising too much
      a habitual course of action
      belonging to a larger order
      of some remote ancestor

19.   of the nature of an illusion

      a tank holding green liquid
      in order of arrangement
      avoid an embarrassing position
      that which has a deceptive appearance
      an exclamation of surprise

20.   near the beginning of a period

      so that all are included
      arising from bad character
      a restricted portion of space
      plants of related genera
      that which happens early

Time _____ Sec.

No. Errors _____

III-18

RATE (from table on page 299):   R. _____

COMPREHENSION (100 — 5% for each Error):   C. _____

EFFICIENCY (R × C):   E. _____

Exercise 19

1. the planet which we inhabit

    the earth upon which we live
    divisible by two or four
    what might not be expected
    in about the same place
    the period from sunset to darkness

2. the act or process of educating

    the melting or freezing point
    to develop and cultivate the mental processes
    triumph over a discovery
    a motor fuel
    to present on the stage

3. excessive love and thought of self

    the practice of referring overmuch to oneself
    in commendation of someone
    the science of moral duty
    a river current
    form an opinion of

4. to feel resentful toward another

    a literary composition
    to be envious of the other person
    one who writes essays
    to gain complete control
    ideally perfect or complete

5. exactly the same in measure

    a mode of behavior
    the fulfillment of the conditions
    to be equal in quantity or degree
    equivalent to a triangle
    with intent to deceive

6. belief in what is untrue

    an error in the way a person thinks
    state of being erected
    from some particular date
    an instant of time
    to complete the plan of the work

7. that which no longer exists

    due to external causes
    that which becomes extinct
    a way of winning the peace
    belongs to the newly formed group
    preceding the owner's name

8. that which is very convincing

    a case demanding action
    testing all possibilities
    to be supported by evidence based on facts
    for use as evidence
    to reveal by signs

9. to be in the nature of a formula

    a perceptible effort
    that which is exhaled
    be given off as a vapor
    to have a prescribed or set form
    to release from some liability

10. to throw into a state of alarm

    terror excited by sudden danger
    serving as a warning
    given in excess of actual loss
    a model or a pattern
    any person earning his living

11. holding all it can contain

    that which justifies a fault
    to be full or complete in quantity
    permission to practice
    an officer of the state
    extremely good of its kind

12. the act of gaining something

    a bill of exchange
    to go beyond the limits
    the accumulation or increasing of profits
    a testing of knowledge
    ascertaining the truth of

13. motion intended to express an idea

    condition of being fit
    a sending forth
    making an excursion
    a gesture used to enforce an opinion
    suitable for the end in view

14. the act of giving a present

    connected with an institution
    to evaporate moisture from
    sold under eminent domain
    that which is expected
    to give a gift to someone

(continued on next page)

15.   to move gently and smoothly

a laying out of money
a particular study or work
to unfold the meaning of
one who has special knowledge
the act or action of gliding

16.   the mark set to bound a race

that which is exported
by means of a probe
the goal to obtain in winning the race
to search for a discovery
the influences of climate

17.   in the nature of an interview

that which exemplifies
a common expression
usually followed by with
a meeting face to face with a client
a public exhibition or show

18.   act or process of irrigating

indicative of character
expected to do his duty
delusions of greatness
beyond the established limits
to supply water to the land by canals

19.   tract of land surrounded by water

seized to secure payment
to understand the void of space
commence or enter upon
unable to speak intelligibly
that which is regarded as an island

20.   the first month in the year

without a sense of fear
the embodiment of joy
cast light on a surface
January, named after the Latin deity, Janus
being in the first category

Time _____ Sec.

No. Errors _____

III-19

RATE (from table on page 299):

COMPREHENSION (100 − 5% for each Error):

EFFICIENCY (R × C):

R. _____

C. _____

E. _____

Exercise 20

1.   to grant or pay a pension to

    an allowance to one retired from service
    various points along the way
    soon after the movie
    seeking a helping hand
    those often in distress

2.   an involved state of affairs

    shortly after the rain
    absorbed in international affairs
    believed to be of sound mind
    that which is perplexed
    going inside the house

3.   related to the matter in hand

    as far as that goes
    pertinent to the present condition
    in many ways the best
    this is advisable to all
    not interested in stirring up doubt

4.   capable of being molded or modeled

    to return to something
    concerned with the truth
    formative in nature as clay or plastic
    should be removed at once
    in detailed reply

5.   suitable to the public in general

    quality or state of being popular
    a small decrease in enrollment
    recent influx of workers
    should not be tolerated
    for an hour or more

6.   one who carries luggage for hire

    many still stand in line
    a lack of responsible help
    wired for a public address system
    at the same time each day
    the duties of a porter

7.   the state of being possible

    to make better personal adjustment
    within the powers of performance
    on the part of the college
    within each building
    one of long standing

8.   an act of safety taken beforehand

    a feeling of security
    able to make the grade
    spoken of in various ways
    a precaution taken in advance
    who has learned to help others

9.   a question proposed for solution

    the prime purpose of
    in reaching this goal
    a query relative to a problem to be solved
    a set of new conditions
    satisfied with everyone

10.   under the protection of providence

    safeguarded by divine care and guidance
    an over-all plan
    seriously looking forward to
    it was evident to everyone
    his greatest error

11.   to solve or discover by ingenuity

    a state of being frozen
    combined with another element
    to puzzle out a mystery
    a railroad baggage car
    an inevitable conclusion

12.   a measure containing two pints

    expressed in algebraic symbols
    a glimpse of the future
    the first in time or in place
    a measure in music
    a vessel holding one quart

13.   to go from place to place

    an inflated ball to be kicked
    to ramble or wander with no set goal
    support for the feet
    to waste precious time
    one in charge of an office

14.   the purpose of a reservoir

    one who loads a ship
    prescribed manner of behaving
    a person who seeks a fight
    a place where anything is kept in store
    to make a defense

(continued on next page)

15.   made in the likeness of a robe

          to attempt to defeat
          the plot of a dramatic poem
          action which is extravagant
          that which is not expected
          a long loose outer garment

16.   a sample portion of the whole

          a sudden hostile movement
          the pupil of the eye
          one expert in penmanship
          a part presented for inspection
          to form a mental image of

17.   to scatter or distribute widely

          the orbit of the eye
          to separate in different directions
          a very poor person
          vessel with a narrow stern
          a thing to be regretted

18.   preceding in the order of time

          coming first in logical order
          a contest for a reward
          of standard quality
          to translate or paraphrase
          prompt in action or thought

19.   not ready or prompt in moving

          wreck due to a collision
          a thickly populated street
          to be slow or tardy in action
          water pent up behind a floodgate
          part of a railroad

20.   to patrol a given territory

          his first voyage to Europe
          should arrive any day now
          please come whenever possible
          he never will do that again
          the guard going the rounds

Time _____ Sec.   RATE (from table on page 299):   R. _____

No. Errors _____   COMPREHENSION (100 — 5% for each Error):   C. _____

III-20   EFFICIENCY (R × C):   E. _____

SERIES IV
Sentence Meaning Drills

These exercises are designed to develop still further your eye span and ability to recognize similar ideas. This ability is of great importance in being able to read for meaning, or in reading to find the answers to questions.

In these exercises you are given a key statement which expresses a certain idea as the basic part of that sentence. Read this statement carefully and think about its meaning. Ten statements follow this key statement. With each of these ten you are to read quickly and decide whether the basic idea is about the same as the key sentence or whether it is basically different. If the idea is the same, place the letter "S" in the space after the number. If the idea is different, place the letter "D" after the number of the sentence. As soon as you have completed the last sentence call for your time and look up your rate in the table on page 301. Then correct your answers by using the keys on pages 311 or 317 and compute comprehension and efficiency as indicated. Then record rate and efficiency on the Progress Chart.

These exercises begin on page 109; tables are on page 301; progress charts are on page 289. Keys are on pages 311 and 317.

EXAMPLE

It is difficult for a president to be a great man unless some crisis occurs in his administration.

. . . .

7. Unless a crisis occurs during his administration, a president seems to have little chance of becoming famous.

8. The difficulty of becoming president is great.

9. A man may become president who is not destined for greatness during his term.

10. It is easier for a man to be a great president in time of crisis.

7.	S
8.	D
X 9.	D
10.	S

Time __54__ Sec.	RATE (from table on page 301):	R.	200
No. Errors __1__	COMPREHENSION (100 — 10% for each Error):	C.	90
IV-15	EFFICIENCY (R × C): (200 × .90) — 180.00	E.	180

Exercise 1

Some statistics, startling as they may sound, are not unusual.

1. Startling statistics are not always as unusual as one might think.   1. _____
2. Unusual statistics are usually startling to the reader.   2. _____
3. Some compiled data may sound arresting and yet, in reality, be rather commonplace.   3. _____
4. Statistics are unusual to a person engaged in research.   4. _____
5. Students interested in studying many of the college subjects will find a course in statistics mandatory.   5. _____
6. The statistics which we have here may sound startling, but they are really quite usual.   6. _____
7. Unusual facts are more interesting than common ones.   7. _____
8. A table of statistics is very useful in many fields of study.   8. _____
9. Startling facts make startling statistics as a rule.   9. _____
10. Statistics are not unusual just because they attract considerable attention.   10. _____

Time _____ Sec.   RATE (from table on page 301):   R. _____

No. Errors _____   COMPREHENSION (100 − 10% for each Error):   C. _____

IV-1   EFFICIENCY (R × C):   E. _____

Exercise 2

There are no special tricks for concentrating and none are necessary.

1. One of the first things that a college student must learn is the knack necessary for concentrating.   1. _____
2. Concentration is an art which college students will find very necessary in their studying.   2. _____
3. Special tricks for concentrating are not especially needed.   3. _____
4. Concentration, although difficult, does not require the use of particular tricks.   4. _____
5. Necessary tricks for concentration are special ones and not easily learned.   5. _____
6. It is necessary to learn to concentrate quickly.   6. _____
7. There are tricks necessary in learning to concentrate well.   7. _____
8. There are tricks to all trades.   8. _____
9. Special tricks are not necessary in developing an ability to concentrate.   9. _____
10. Concentration is a result of a series of special studies by a student.   10. _____

Time _____ Sec.   RATE (from table on page 301):   R. _____

No. Errors _____   COMPREHENSION (100 − 10% for each Error):   C. _____

IV-2   EFFICIENCY (R × C):   E. _____

Exercise 3

Spaced reviewing develops better understanding of material.

1. Spaced reviewing is another name for rote reviewing.   1. _____
2. The best way to understand a lesson is to read it and reread it frequently.   2. _____
3. Review is necessary in order to pass the course.   3. _____
4. Reviewing once each week or at regular intervals is a good way to improve one's comprehension of a subject.   4. _____
5. Reviewing at intervals brings about better understanding.   5. _____
6. Teachers use rote learning as a principal method to help students understand material.   6. _____
7. Better understanding is developed by frequent reviewing at regular intervals.   7. _____
8. The time of the reviewing of material is an important factor.   8. _____
9. To better understand material, one should read it carefully at least twice.   9. _____
10. Better understanding is a goal of all good teachers.   10. _____

Time _____ Sec.   RATE (from table on page 301):   R. _____

No. Errors _____   COMPREHENSION (100 − 10% for each Error):   C. _____

IV-3   EFFICIENCY (R × C):   E. _____

Exercise 4

Power equipment is not essential to productive activity on a farm.

1. Modern farming methods require mechanization on the farm.   1. _____
2. A farm may be able to produce quite well without power machines.   2. _____
3. Productive activity on farms can be accomplished without the use of tractors or similar equipment.   3. _____
4. Power equipment is not essential for production on a farm.   4. _____
5. Horses were once used for farming purposes, but since the widespread use of electricity they have become obsolete.   5. _____
6. Marginal farms are those which have no power equipment.   6. _____
7. Farms may become quite productive without the use of power equipment.   7. _____
8. Most farms in the United States are not self sustaining.   8. _____
9. The high cost of modern farming machinery has kept many farmers from developing their farms into productive units.   9. _____
10. Good lighting is not necessary on a farm.   10. _____

Time _____ Sec.   RATE (from table on page 301):   R. _____

No. Errors _____   COMPREHENSION (100 − 10% for each Error):   C. _____

IV-4   EFFICIENCY (R × C):   E. _____

Exercise 5

Geographical factors have something to do with the mode of living.

1. The way we live depends on where we live.   1. _____
2. There is no connection between geography and living habits.   2. _____
3. Man's living is modified by physiographic influences.   3. _____
4. The geography of a country will tell a great deal about the people residing in that country.   4. _____
5. Climatic influences are quite apparent in weather maps.   5. _____
6. Geographical environment may affect society indirectly by changing the human physique.   6. _____
7. Geographical environment is one of the factors in determining one's standard of living.   7. _____
8. Religious faith is a result of geographical location.   8. _____
9. Human behavior varies according to the weather.   9. _____
10. The cultural developments that affect one's way of living are often determined by the topographical conditions in any given locality.   10. _____

Time _____ Sec.   RATE (from table on page 301):   R. _____

No. Errors _____   COMPREHENSION (100 − 10% for each Error):   C. _____

IV-5   EFFICIENCY (R × C):   E. _____

Exercise 6

Contrary to popular opinion, forgetting is not simply a weathering away of once known impressions.

1. Forgetting is a loss of memory.   1. _____
2. Many people seem to have the mistaken idea that forgetting is merely a gradual loss of impressions once held.   2. _____
3. The process of remembering is complicated.   3. _____
4. Forgetting is not as simple a process as many people think.   4. _____
5. Popular opinion is often the incorrect opinion.   5. _____
6. Psychology is a subject in which one studies many things.   6. _____
7. Impressions which are gained during life make up what we call memory.   7. _____
8. Popular opinion on a subject shapes our opinions on that same subject.   8. _____
9. Impressions of a thing are the same as opinions about that same thing.   9. _____
10. Forgetting consists of more than just losing impressions once held.   10. _____

Time _____ Sec.   RATE (from table on page 301):   R. _____

No. Errors _____   COMPREHENSION (100 − 10% for each Error):   C. _____

IV-6   EFFICIENCY (R × C):   E. _____

Exercise 7

The process of change is one in which the invention comes before we anticipate its social effects.

1. The social effects of the inventions that occur are relatively unimportant.   1. _____

2. Instead of creating stability, inventions force us to unanticipated adjustments to the effects they create in our society.   2. _____

3. Technological developments always precede the social processes of adjustment which they cause.   3. _____

4. A moratorium should be declared on invention and scientific discovery until the social institutions of man catch up.   4. _____

5. The inventions already in existence have exerted little influence on our social order.   5. _____

6. We seldom know what social effect will take place due to an invention.   6. _____

7. Before this process of change can be controlled, it must first be anticipated.   7. _____

8. Social effects are generally not only not anticipated; they are not recognized.   8. _____

9. The problem of the control of social change resolves itself largely into the problem of the control of the effects of the environment. 9. _____

10. Inventions come before the social effects which they inevitably cause.   10. _____

Time _____ Sec.   RATE (from table on page 301):   R. _____

No. Errors _____   COMPREHENSION (100 − 10% for each Error):   C. _____

IV-7   EFFICIENCY (R × C):   E. _____

Exercise 8

Biological man is fortunately very adaptable, more so than most other animals.

1. Man is capable of making physiological adjustments to environment more readily than most animals.   1. _____

2. Biological man's adaptability is not infinite.   2. _____

3. Famine is one of the adjustments that man finds very difficult to meet.   3. _____

4. For thousands of years man was adjusted to an environment which called for muscular activity in the open air.   4. _____

5. Cities are a radically different type of environment from the country.   5. _____

6. Few animals could become adjusted to a variety of living conditions as easily as man.   6. _____

7. Adjustment between man and his culture always will exist as a very serious problem.   7. _____

8. Laborers are able to become better adjusted to factory machines than animals such as the saber-tooth tiger were able to adjust to changing conditions.   8. _____

9. Down through the ages it has been seen that the human animal is the most adaptable of the animal kingdom.   9. _____

10. It is fortunate that all animals have learned to adapt themselves quickly.   10. _____

Time _____ Sec.   RATE (from table on page 301):   R. _____

No. Errors _____   COMPREHENSION (100 − 10% for each Error):   C. _____

IV-8   EFFICIENCY (R × C):   E. _____

Exercise 9

Man's inherited nature changes via the germ plasm exceedingly slowly, while culture changes more rapidly.

1. Heredity plays a big part in shaping our nature, but environment plays an equally important part.

    1. _____

2. Our culture changes radically and rapidly, whereas the genes mutate slowly in individual reproduction.

    2. _____

3. Innate personal changes do not come about rapidly, while cultural changes may take very little time.

    3. _____

4. Social and cultural changes come about more quickly than changes in human beings.

    4. _____

5. We find that man's nature is inherited from both parents and is modified by his culture.

    5. _____

6. Man is a creature of habit, which in turn affects society's actions.

    6. _____

7. Studies show that man can change his inherited personality but very little solely by his own efforts.

    7. _____

8. A cause of social disorganization is the lack of adaptation of man's inherited nature to the environment of group and culture.

    8. _____

9. The changes in man's nature are difficult to understand.

    9. _____

10. Changes via the germ plasm are difficult to understand and explain.

    10. _____

Time _____ Sec.   RATE (from table on page 301):   R. _____

No. Errors _____   COMPREHENSION (100 − 10% for each Error):   C. _____

IV-9   EFFICIENCY (R × C):   E. _____

Exercise 10

Careful selection in the breeding of dairy stock will pay dividends in increased milk production.

1. The mating of good bulls and good cows will result in more milk from their offspring.

    1. _____

2. Farmers should be more careful in selecting their dairy breeding stock if they wish higher milk records.

    2. _____

3. It is necessary to have good dairy livestock for breeding if one expects a good milk production record.

    3. _____

4. Dairy farmers find it financially advantageous to invest in high quality stock for breeding purposes.

    4. _____

5. Increased milk production is the aim of every dairy owner.

    5. _____

6. Adequate food is required for all breeds of dairy stock.

    6. _____

7. Certain types of cattle are better for dairy stock than some other breeds.

    7. _____

8. Breeding of dairy stock must be done carefully to increase milk production.

    8. _____

9. It is no wonder that many farmers have low milk production from their dairy stock since the quality is so poor.

    9. _____

10. Careful selection in breeding of all livestock will pay dividends in increased production.

    10. _____

Time _____ Sec.   RATE (from table on page 301):   R. _____

No. Errors _____   COMPREHENSION (100 − 10% for each Error):   C. _____

IV-10   EFFICIENCY (R × C):   E. _____

Exercise 11

Although imbeciles learn to talk, there is great lack of ideas among them.

1. Imbeciles can be taught to talk, but we find that they have relatively few ideas.   1. _____

2. All that a true imbecile can learn to do is to talk and not to think.   2. _____

3. Although talking, imbeciles have few ideas.   3. _____

4. Most people think that because imbeciles learn to talk it is a sign that they can have a great many ideas.   4. _____

5. Ideas are relatively foreign to imbeciles, but speech is not.   5. _____

6. The study of imbeciles is to be found in abnormal psychology.   6. _____

7. Although imbeciles learn to talk, there is great variety of ideas among them.   7. _____

8. It is little use to teach imbeciles to talk since after they learn the language they find it difficult to express ideas.   8. _____

9. The lack of ideas is one mark of an imbecile although he may have a working knowledge of the language.   9. _____

10. Imbeciles may learn to use the language but find few ideas to express.   10. _____

Time _____ Sec.   RATE (from table on page 301):   R. _____

No. Errors _____   COMPREHENSION (100 — 10% for each Error):   C. _____

IV-11   EFFICIENCY (R × C):   E. _____

Exercise 12

The blue prints for the new school house are deficient in that they fail to provide for adequate fire protection.

1. The new school building is a fire trap.   1. _____

2. Blue prints for buildings are difficult to read without training.   2. _____

3. In making the school plans provision of minimum safety facilities to be used in case of fire apparently was overlooked.   3. _____

4. Adequate fire protection has not been provided for in the plans for the new school.   4. _____

5. The architect did not provide adequate safety plans for the new school house.   5. _____

6. The blue prints for the new school house are inadequate.   6. _____

7. In general, good blue prints for buildings provide adequate fire protection.   7. _____

8. The blue prints as drawn by the architect for the new school building are not adequate in that they fail to provide for protection from fire in some cases.   8. _____

9. The city law states that all schools must be fire proof.   9. _____

10. Adequate fire protection for the blue prints of the new school house has been neglected.   10. _____

Time _____ Sec.   RATE (from table on page 301):   R. _____

No. Errors _____   COMPREHENSION (100 — 10% for each Error):   C. _____

IV-12   EFFICIENCY (R × C):   E. _____

Exercise 13

The assets of the business have increased threefold within the last decade.

1. Business has been unusually good in the last three years.   1. _____

2. By studying records of the business we find that its assets have grown three times greater in the last ten years.   2. _____

3. Successful businesses must have assets greater than their liabilities.   3. _____

4. In a boom, business does well whereas in a depression, business does poorly.   4. _____

5. Increases in assets over a span of years are indications that the business is prospering.   5. _____

6. During the last decade the business has increased its assets 300 per cent.   6. _____

7. The increase in the assets of a business is a good indication of how well the business is doing.   7. _____

8. Careful records must be kept for a business so that the owner can tell how much his assets have increased.   8. _____

9. A threefold increase of assets of the business is shown in the last ten years.   9. _____

10. The balance sheet for the business shows that the assets have tripled within ten years.   10. _____

Time _____ Sec.   RATE (from table on page 301):   R. _____

No. Errors _____   COMPREHENSION (100 — 10% for each Error):   C. _____

IV-13   EFFICIENCY (R × C):   E. _____

Exercise 14

Horseback riding is beneficial to the physique in general, but may have detrimental effects on the leg bones.

1. When we ride horseback, the horse buffets the rider violently.   1. _____

2. A number of horses make up a herd.   2. _____

3. Horseback riding is good for one in spite of the fact that one's legs may be adversely affected.   3. _____

4. We receive some benefits from horseback riding, but may become bowlegged.   4. _____

5. Riding horseback is healthful exercise, but has a tendency to cause curvature of the legs.   5. _____

6. Dancing requires a certain amount of work plus natural talent in timing and balance.   6. _____

7. Horseback riding is good exercise, but it may develop undesirable changes in the lower appendages.   7. _____

8. "A donkey can walk between his legs without its ears being touched" is frequently said of the people who ride horseback a great deal.   8. _____

9. When one approaches the horse, the rider is expecting to indulge in an enjoyable exercise.   9. _____

10. Riding generally is unhealthy from the standpoint of general physical condition.   10. _____

Time _____ Sec.   RATE (from table on page 301):   R. _____

No. Errors _____   COMPREHENSION (100 — 10% for each Error):   C. _____

IV-14   EFFICIENCY (R × C):   E. _____

Exercise 15

History has shown that it is difficult for a president to be a great man unless some crisis occurs in his administration.

1. Presidents usually do not secure lasting prominence unless there has been a serious crisis during their administrations. 1. _____

2. Social and economic control is generally exercised by or through the president in time of crisis. 2. _____

3. The history of many a country shows a period of particularly great prestige which is usually associated with the administration of an outstanding president. 3. _____

4. We tend to overestimate the originality, initiative, and even the ability of the president in times of stress. 4. _____

5. Presidents of the United States have often taken credit for prosperity when it was due to favorable rainfall or to the discovery of gold mines. 5. _____

6. It is natural that presidents are blamed for business depressions which they play little part in making. 6. _____

7. Unless a crisis occurs during his administration, a president seems to have little chance of becoming famous. 7. _____

8. The difficulty of becoming president prevents many great men from securing the office. 8. _____

9. A man may become president who is not destined for greatness during his term. 9. _____

10. It is easier for the man in office to be a great president in time of crisis. 10. _____

Time _____ Sec. RATE (from table on page 301): R. _____

No. Errors _____ COMPREHENSION (100 − 10% for each Error): C. _____

IV-15 EFFICIENCY (R × C): E. _____

Exercise 16

It has been pointed out that it is sometimes necessary to adjust yourself to those who fail to adjust to you.

1. People often find it necessary to make adjustments in their lives in order to satisfy other peoples' idiosyncrasies. 1. _____

2. It is sometimes necessary to force all others to adjust to one's desires for certain periods of time. 2. _____

3. We have learned in various life situations that sometimes we must follow other people's ways since they can't seem to follow our ways. 3. _____

4. International tension could be lowered if each nation could learn to adjust itself to other nations. 4. _____

5. Adjustment is a constant problem to the spider monkey. 5. _____

6. Imitation is one way of adjusting one's life to that of others with whom one wishes to live happily. 6. _____

7. Other people in order to get along well with a certain individual may have to learn to adjust to him. 7. _____

8. It has been pointed out that there are always two sides to every problem which must be considered. 8. _____

9. Instead of going our own way when someone does not agree with us, it may be necessary to learn to make adjustments to his wishes. 9. _____

10. It has been pointed out that people like to have their own way. 10. _____

Time _____ Sec. RATE (from table on page 301): R. _____

No. Errors _____ COMPREHENSION (100 − 10% for each Error): C. _____

IV-16 EFFICIENCY (R × C): E. _____

Exercise 17

Surveying the site for the new highway was very difficult because of the rugged terrain.

1. The presence of surface irregularities made mapping out the new highway very difficult. 1. _____
2. Surveying for the new highway took almost three months due to the moisture in the soil. 2. _____
3. George Washington when a young man went on a surveying party for the site of the new Cumberland Road over difficult and rugged terrain. 3. _____
4. The new highway would have been relocated to go through a certain section of the country if the terrain had been smoother. 4. _____
5. Many severe eroded gulleys and prominent outcroppings of rock provided extreme obstacles in the preliminary work on the new highway. 5. _____
6. The final location of the new highway is always of vital interest to the people through whose land it might go. 6. _____
7. The rugged terrain made difficulties in surveying the site for the new highway. 7. _____
8. Engineers had great difficulty in surveying the land for the new highway because of the very rugged terrain over which they worked. 8. _____
9. Surveying is not a difficult thing to do if the land is smooth and the landowners are cooperative. 9. _____
10. Broken and irregular topography caused the engineers a great deal of trouble in surveying for the new highway. 10. _____

Time _____ Sec.   RATE (from table on page 301):   R. _____

No. Errors _____   COMPREHENSION (100 − 10% for each Error):   C. _____

IV-17   EFFICIENCY (R × C):   E. _____

Exercise 18

The home economics courses taught in our high schools can be of great use to the boys and girls who take them.

1. Boys and girls who take courses in home economics probably will find them useful. 1. _____
2. The home economics courses taught in high schools are too impractical to be of real use. 2. _____
3. The boys and girls who take home economics in high school learn many things that will be of value to them. 3. _____
4. The equipment found in the high school for the home economics course is so different from what the students have at home that they gain no real value from using it. 4. _____
5. One of the most difficult courses offered in high school is economics. 5. _____
6. Since most girls marry, home economics should be taken by them. 6. _____
7. Students in high school will find that home economics can be a very useful subject. 7. _____
8. Throughout the years of high school life the students should take those subjects which will be of the most use to them after they graduate. 8. _____
9. The boys and girls will find that the things they learn in home economics can aid them greatly. 9. _____
10. Home economics as taught in present day schools is of little practical value to boys. 10. _____

Time _____ Sec.   RATE (from table on page 301):   R. _____

No. Errors _____   COMPREHENSION (100 − 10% for each Error):   C. _____

IV-18   EFFICIENCY (R × C):   E. _____

Exercise 19

One of the student's problems is recognizing what should be known and then fixing it in memory so that it will be there when wanted.

1. One student problem is knowing what facts are important and then being able to remember them.   1. _____

2. The success of an individual depends on how well he adjusts to the new school environment.   2. _____

3. Rote learning is highly desirable for students so that they may have the facts needed always in mind.   3. _____

4. Learning the important things is a problem and remembering them in order to use them is a part of that problem.   4. _____

5. A good way to study is to read the lesson at least twice, and then listen closely to the instructor in class.   5. _____

6. Recognizing key ideas and establishing systems for retaining them are two important problems in learning how to study.   6. _____

7. Many students find that one difficulty in studying is their inability to recognize what is important and to apply effective techniques for remembering ideas.   7. _____

8. Students find that it is important to analyze the salient facts and keep them in mind for later use.   8. _____

9. Universities are good places to learn what is important.   9. _____

10. The solving of problems is the best way to learn important facts.   10. _____

Time _____ Sec.   RATE (from table on page 301):   R. _____

No. Errors _____   COMPREHENSION (100 — 10% for each Error):   C. _____

IV-19   EFFICIENCY (R × C):   E. _____

Exercise 20

To look upon the faces of high school seniors, one would never guess that at least one out of twenty eventually will be found in a hospital for the insane.

1. The chances of a child being placed in a mental hospital sometime during his life are about 1 in 20.   1. _____

2. Insanity is just another form of illness, no more reprehensible than physical disease.   2. _____

3. High school students are very inclined to become mentally ill.   3. _____

4. Sentiment seems to prevail that insanity is increasing in our society.   4. _____

5. Every individual who shares group life with others develops a personality.   5. _____

6. By looking at the faces of the high school seniors one can tell that at least one belongs in a hospital.   6. _____

7. Hospital space should be enlarged to meet the heavy demands now being made on it.   7. _____

8. The tragic fact that five out of a hundred of the high school seniors will eventually find their way to a mental hospital is hard to realize.   8. _____

9. The high school seniors should face the fact that of their group half of them will become mentally ill.   9. _____

10. One can't tell by looking at high school seniors that a certain ratio of them will enter a hospital for the mentally disturbed.   10. _____

Time _____ Sec.   RATE (from table on page 301):   R. _____

No. Errors _____   COMPREHENSION (100 — 10% for each Error):   C. _____

IV-20   EFFICIENCY (R × C):   E. _____

SERIES V
Idea Reading Drills

These exercises are designed to train you in reading for ideas in short selections of material. These articles range from 500 to 800 words in length and should be read as rapidly as possible — at most in three minutes, preferably in less time. In reading you should try to grasp the main ideas, the recurrent theme, and the purpose for which the author seems to have written the article. Remember that headings frequently provide clues to this.

At the beginning of each article you will find the length of the article and the readability scores as computed by the Flesch Formula (15). The higher this score is, the easier the material is to read. General levels of readability are as follows:

Readability Score	Grade level of reading difficulty
0-30	College Graduates
30-40	College Juniors and Seniors
40-50	College Freshmen and Sophomores
50-60	High School Students
60-70	Junior High Students

Exercises are arranged so that each successive exercise will be a little more difficult than the one preceding it. Therefore you will be striving to increase both your reading speed and your reading level. Spaced at intervals down the left hand margin are numbers indicating the number of words read to that point. As the instructor calls time intervals you can glance quickly at these numbers and note your approximate speed.

Read each article as rapidly as possible and ask for your time when you have finished. This time will be given in seconds, and you then can find your rate of reading by using the table on page 303 which will give you your *rate of reading in words per minute*.

Then answer the two questions which deal with the main ideas of the article. You should have no difficulty in answering these correctly. In the Multiple Choice (M. C.) questions, select the answer which seems most appropriate and place a check on the line before that answer. On the True - False (T - F) questions, circle either the "T" or the "F" to indicate your understanding of the accuracy of the statement. If you answer both of the questions correctly according to the key, your comprehension will be 100 percent and your *efficiency* score will be the same as your rate. Missing one question cuts your efficiency to one half of your rate, so you should concentrate on the main ideas you read.

When you have computed your efficiency, turn to page 291 and record this score on your progress chart. If you have missed a question, you should record both rate and efficiency to show the comparison. Keys are on pages 311 and 317.

Number V-1

Man's Conquest of Lightning

(Reprinted from the pamphlet *Thunderbolts in Harness*,
by permission of the General Electric Co.)

──────────── WAIT FOR SIGNAL TO BEGIN READING ────────────

You're in the picture

What of lightning and you? Though scientists and engineers in such places as General Electric's High-Voltage Engineering Laboratory have developed protective devices for building and electric equipment, people can't be wired and grounded at will. There are, however, a few precautions which individuals may follow for their own safety.

There are two places in the home that afford absolute protection against any lightning bolt; the refrigerator and the furnace. Of course, you may freeze or roast, but you won't get struck by lightning. For practical purposes, however, just carry on ordinary routine during a thunderstorm, with these exceptions: **100** (1) avoid overhead wires, (2) don't use the telephone unless it's necessary, and (3) stay out of the bathtub. Actually there is very little danger of being killed or injured by lightning in the modern home, but there's no sense in asking for trouble. (Radio antennae, incidentally, should be properly grounded.)

Do not swim during a storm. One of the most dangerous places for a person to be is in or on the water when lightning is flashing nearby. Despite the low target presented by a lake, for instance, water is often struck by lightning. The chances for being hit **200** directly are slim, but the flow of current through water in which you are swimming is very dangerous.

Things to watch

A golf course is not the best place to be during a lightning storm, though it's no more dangerous than any other open field. It isn't advisable to carry a metal club on your shoulder if you do happen to be caught on the links by a storm.

Also, it's not healthy to stand under a tree while lightning and thunder blast away from above, especially an isolated tree. You might argue that the tree would act as a natural lightning rod, affording a **300** cone of protection. This is not the case. A tree can't carry large volumes of current; the lightning bolt may jump away from it at any point, toward a more desirable conductor. Thus, a person standing under a tree that's struck by lightning may be hit by a side-flash. Also, flying branches and splinters are dangerous.

One of the best places to be during a thunderstorm is in an automobile, where you are nearly surrounded by a metal body. Also, steel-frame buildings are usually quite safe, because the framework carries the **400** charges off to the ground harmlessly.

Dr. McEachron, the noted General Electric lightning expert, offers a bit of philosophy about lightning. He says:

"If you heard the thunder, the lightning did not strike you; if you saw the lightning, it missed you; and if it did strike you, you would not have known it."

Lightning rods

Probably one of the oldest, simplest, and at the same time, most useful electrical appliances known to man is the lightning rod. Its principal use is in rural areas, where isolated farm buildings are much **500** more apt to be struck, and when struck, the damage may be much greater because good fire protection is lacking. Nine-tenths of the annual 2000 American lightning casualties occur in the country or in small towns. The city dweller and his home are protected by tall steel-frame buildings which are themselves lightning rods.

The duty of the lightning rod and its ground connections is plain. Projecting a few feet above the building it guards, the rod offers to the normally destructive bolt of lightning an unobstructed and easy pathway to the ground. By properly installing lightning rods, one may often save many times their **600** cost in fire prevention alone.

──────STOP — ASK FOR YOUR TIME──────

Record time immediately on next page
and answer the questions on content.

Time _____ Sec.   RATE (from column 2 of table on page 303):   R. _____

No. Errors _____   COMPREHENSION (100 — 50% for each Error):   C. _____

V-1   EFFICIENCY (R × C):   E. _____

ANSWER THESE QUESTIONS IMMEDIATELY (V-1)

1. (M. C.)   The main idea the writer is interested in getting across to the reader is:

____(1)   If you saw the lightning, it is evident you were not struck by it.

____(2)   There is a very slim chance of being killed by lightning; however, a person should exercise reasonable precaution to avoid the danger.

____(3)   In case of a severe lightning storm, a person would be wise to stay away from water.

____(4)   The refrigerator and the furnace are two places in the homes that are absolutely safe against any lightning bolts.

2. (T — F)   Any steel-frame building or enclosure will serve as an excellent place for safety during an electrical storm.

Number V-2

Research Is a State of Mind

BY CHARLES F. KETTERING

(Reprinted from the pamphlet *Short Stories of Science and Invention*,
by permission of General Motors Corporation)

──────── WAIT FOR SIGNAL TO BEGIN READING ────────

Research is a State of Mind

Every time I have been in the studio audience at Radio City I've been impressed with the fact that it takes much less energy to *listen* to music than to *direct* or *play* it. So I will give you a very simple comparison between Music and Research that we have used many times.

This afternoon we listened to the compositions of Mozart. He was one of those rare and talented individuals who had the natural gifts of both composition and execution. He was a child prodigy. This type of individual is rare but each generation may produce one or more — they occur not only in the musical field but also in art, medicine and science, and their contributions are of great importance! Most of our work, however, must be done by people with just ordinary abilities in the beginning who reach positions of skill or responsibility by practice, study and plain persistence.

Now, I don't know the individual histories of the men in the orchestra, but I suspect the majority of them are there as the result of arduous practice, much hard work, and sacrifices of many kinds. The Symphony Orchestra is a body of men, who, in order to perform superbly as a group, must first be able to perform equally well as individuals. Just organizing a group of poor musicians doesn't make a good orchestra.

Research is done in much the same way. Our work can either be the effort of a group or of individual specialists. In fact, just like a good orchestra, each man must be a skilled and talented individual. There is one outstanding difference, when we compare Orchestras with Research — Research has no Mozart score to follow — we are working with unwritten scores. The procedure must be different in nearly every case. It is more like composition and performance at the same time.

For many years there has been much misunderstanding as to just what Research is. The popular conception seems to be that there is something mysterious about it, and before any Research can be done it is necessary to have expensive scientific apparatus and large, elaborately equipped buildings. Actually, this is not so. Research isn't a physical thing at all but just a state of mind. It is a simple organized way of trying to accomplish something you wish to do — so simple that anyone can do Research anywhere at any time.

First, you select the problem you would like to solve, then you list at least ten reasons why this has not been solved. But in picking that problem be sure to analyze it carefully to see that it is worth the effort. It takes just as much effort to solve a useless problem as a useful one.

After *carefully* — and I want to emphasize that word "carefully" — selecting the problem and the ten things between you and the solution, you then use the same procedure as in solving a cross-word puzzle. You take the easy obstacles first and by a process of elimination you arrive at last at the one or two major ones. In the solution of the remaining obstacles you may need some simple apparatus, but the things you will probably need most are infinite *patience* and *persistence*. Few people realize the difficulties of doing any new thing.

Maybe one of the reasons people become discouraged is because of their education. During all of our years at school we were examined two or three times a year. If we failed once we were *out*. In contrast, all Research work is 99.9 per cent failure and if you succeed once you are *in*. If we are going to progress in any line we must learn to fail intelligently so we won't become discouraged at the 99.9 per cent failure.

As we approach the end of the War and make plans to go back to our normal ways of living we are going to be faced with unlimited problems. I am talking about Research because it is just a method of intelligent planning. As you probably know, some four or five hundred postwar planning groups have been organized to take care of some of these problems for us. $\underset{\leftarrow}{700}$

That is a step in the right direction, but I don't believe that is enough — we ought to have 135,000,000 planners. Each individual in this country should be doing his or her own planning — should be forming

a one man or woman research project. We should not be looking outside for this help. We should be doing it for ourselves — as individuals.

But as we face tomorrow let us pick our problems very carefully and separate clearly in our minds the great difference between constructive postwar planning and very unproductive postwar wishing. $\underset{\rightarrow}{800}$

———STOP — ASK FOR YOUR TIME———

Record time immediately and answer the questions on content.

Time _____ Sec.   RATE (from column 4 of table on page 303):   R. _____

No. Errors _____   COMPREHENSION (100 — 50% for each Error):   C. _____

V-2   EFFICIENCY (R × C):   E. _____

ANSWER THESE QUESTIONS IMMEDIATELY (V-2)

1. (M. C.) In this article, the author wants the reader to get the point of view:

    ____(1) that research is not a difficult job, and very little effort is required to do research work.

    ____(2) that most everyone possesses the natural gift of intelligence to achieve greatness if one would only work hard enough.

    ____(3) that research doesn't necessarily require expensive equipment; however, it does require a high degree of orderly thinking, patience, and persistence.

    ____(4) that music and research have much in common.

2. (T — F) The author maintains that men in research encounter failure much more often than success and that therefore they have to learn to fail intelligently.

Terrible Turbidity

(Reprinted from the January 26, 1953, issue of *Time*, courtesy *Time Magazine*,
copyright *Time*, Inc., 1953)

———————— WAIT FOR SIGNAL TO BEGIN READING ————————

One of the great mysteries of the ocean is the series of long, deep, gorges that wind across the continental shelves like submerged river valleys. Oceanographers thought at first that they were really valleys cut by ancient rivers when sea level was lower, and flooded by the rising water when ice age glaciers melted. This theory went out of fashion when improved sounding methods showed that some of the streamlike channels lead down to the ocean floor itself three miles below the surface. The level of the ocean could never have fallen as low as that.

A more recent theory has it that the gorges were 100 cut by "turbidity currents," i.e., rivers of mud on the bottom. When a slope of loose material is disturbed — by an earthquake, for example — mud and sand get mixed with water. Since the turbid mixture is heavier than clear water, it flows down the slope, eroding a valley just as a river does on land. This was known to happen in lakes, and many oceanographers believed that the same thing happened deep under the ocean.

Cable trouble

In an issue of *American Journal of Science*, Bruce C. Heezen and Maurice Ewing of Columbia University 200 buttress this theory with a neat bit of historical research. In 1929 a strong earthquake shook the continental shelf 450 miles east of Nova Scotia. It cut a whole shelf of telegraph cables in a peculiar way. Six cables went out at the same time, but others did not fail until many hours later.

Heezen and Ewing appealed to Western Union and other cable companies. Just as they hoped, the companies had made careful studies of the costly disaster 24 years ago and had kept all the records. As each cable had failed, the exact second of its failure was carefully recorded by instruments on land. Other 300 instruments had determined accurately the position of each break and more information had come from the repair crews. Long sections of some of the cables had been carried away and lost, but other cables had been buried deep under mud and sand.

Bit by bit, Heezen and Ewing reconstructed what must have happened on that day of undersea commotion in 1929. The sea bottom near the epicenter of the quake is rather irregular with many comparatively steep slopes of loose material. The quake must have jolted this detachable stuff loose starting 400 slumps and landslides that cut the nearest cables at about the same time.

Racing mud

The trouble did not stop there. The stirred-up mud and sand got mixed with water, and the heavy turbid fluid raced down the continental slope like an enormous river more than 100 miles wide, cutting cable after cable. By plotting the exact time and place of each cable break, the oceanographers could estimate closely how fast the turbidity current flowed. On the sloping continental rise (at the foot of the continental slope), it raced at 50 knots (57.6 m.p.h.). 500 More than 13 hours later, when it cut the last cable 300 miles to the southeast, the mud was still flowing at 12 knots. It must have spread for hundreds of miles over the flat ocean floor.

This reasoning is supported by the fact that many cables were not merely broken but buried by the mud flow. Heezen and Ewing believe that many such flows, racing for hundreds of miles through the still depths of the ocean, have carved the gorges on their slopes. They believe that the "deltas," where their finest material finally settles down, are the flat plains that form the floors of many deep 600 ocean basins.

————STOP — ASK FOR YOUR TIME————

Record time immediately on next page and answer the questions on content.

125

Time _____ Sec.   RATE (from column 2 of table on page 303):   R. _____

No. Errors _____   COMPREHENSION (100 − 50% for each Error):   C. _____

V-3   EFFICIENCY (R × C):   E. _____

ANSWER THESE QUESTIONS IMMEDIATELY (V-3)

1. (M. C.)   The long deep gorges winding across the sloping floor of the ocean are caused by:

   ____(1)   Cracks opened by earthquakes.

   ____(2)   Channels cut by racing mud along the ocean floor.

   ____(3)   Ancient rivers.

   ____(4)   Channels cut by glacial ice.

2. (T — F)   In 1929 the earthquake broke all of the undersea cables at the same time.

Number V-4

Why I Volunteered

By James Scales

(Reprinted from the March, 1962, issue of *Health*, by permission of the editor)

———————————— WAIT FOR SIGNAL TO BEGIN READING ————————————

C-Day at the Ohio Penitentiary!

A small vial filled with live cancer cells, waiting hypodermic needles, and thirty-three men ready to present their arms for injections — this was the setting last July 19 in a program of cancer research being conducted in a state penitentiary in Ohio.

This experiment was part of a cancer study that has been characterized by Dr. Chester M. Southam, of the Sloan-Kettering Institute for Cancer Research, New York City, as a contribution to the fight against cancer that can be matched nowhere else in the world.

The thirty-three men who were injected with live cancer cells last July are all serving sentences at the penitentiary. Among them are two who are "doing the book" for murder, a number for armed robbery, a burglar or two, some forgers, a safe-cracker and an automobile thief. In all, 204 men have participated in the research program since it was instituted at the penitentiary in 1956, and for seven of the 33, this was the second time around, having taken part in another phase of the program in 1959.

One man's story

One is led to wonder why a man, particularly one who is in a penitentiary, volunteers to become involved in such a project as this one. I questioned one of the C-Day volunteers, and here is his explanation:

Early in July, I requested that my name be added to the list of volunteers for the cancer project, and on the nineteenth, I was one of the thirty-three who served on phase seven. When a doctor injected live cancer cells into my forearm, I became a person who, if things go as planned, may be partly responsible for a significant advancement towards the prevention and cure of a terrible disease. I am confronted now with the remote possibility that, should something go wrong, I will develop cancer.

I am no hero, nor am I a moron. Since my minimum sentence has been completed I am at present serving assessed time, and judging by the past actions of the parole board, I may be paroled at my next hearing.

Above all, I am not seeking publicity. Why then do I volunteer? If this undertaking involves no personal reward, why do I take such a chance? I will try to tell you:

Since the beginning of time, countless numbers of men who have been willing to become involved in medical progress must have asked themselves, and been asked by others the same question: Why?

We cannot know their reasons, but I believe they would for the most part add up to this: If we are to progress in any field, some of us must be willing to take the first steps. History has recorded time after time that each of us has to sacrifice something in order to make this a better world today, tomorrow, and for the years to come. To date, I have offered nothing constructive, but now I have my opportunity to contribute.

One thing for certain. I will not inform my loved ones of my participation in this project, because families have a habit of worrying unnecessarily. So my family will never know about this, but I will know! Every time I look in the mirror, or have that conversation with my conscience, I will know that I have tried to help.

"I am proud of me!"

Should this latest experiment prove conclusive, it will be the most exciting experience I have ever known. Now I can say, "I am proud of me!"

What have these volunteers accomplished? So far, the project has revealed that within man's body there is a mysterious power that springs into action when cancer cells are implanted, and manufactures antibodies to protect the body against the invasion.

Answers — And questions

These results determined by the cancer project tests have created new and puzzling questions. Are these men who have been injected with cancer cells now immune to the disease? Will the one out of four who, according to statistics, would have been likely to contract cancer in later years, be spared? Will the antibodies that have been produced continue to spring to the defense?

700 ←

These answers will evolve only as time spells out the contribution of the prisoners of the Ohio penitentiary who took part in the series of C-Days there.

One volunteer, who frankly admits to no knowledge of the science of medicine, summed it up in this manner:

"We fight fire with fire, poison with poison. We heal bee sting with the venom from a bee and we use cobra poison to cure the man bitten by a cobra. Why is it unusual to think that cancer can be cured by cancer?"

800 →

In that we have food for thought!

———STOP — ASK FOR YOUR TIME———

Record time immediately and answer the questions on content.

Time _____ Sec.   RATE (from column 4 of table on page 303):   R. _____

No. Errors _____   COMPREHENSION (100 — 50% for each Error):   C. _____

V-4   EFFICIENCY (R × C):   E. _____

ANSWER THESE QUESTIONS IMMEDIATELY (V-4)

1. (M. C.)   The prisoner in this story was willing to have live cancer cells injected into his body because:

_____(1)   With low intelligence, he did not understand what he was doing.

_____(2)   He was serving a life sentence, and had nothing to lose.

_____(3)   He wanted the publicity that resulted from his action.

_____(4)   He wanted to contribute to medical progress and to help others.

2. (T — F)   So far, the cancer research problem has proved that man's body can manufacture antibodies to cancer cells when they are injected.

Number V-5

The Burning Rivers

PART I

(Reprinted from the pamphlet of the same name, by permission of the American Petroleum Institute)

───────── WAIT FOR SIGNAL TO BEGIN READING ─────────

As old as the hills

Very ancient indeed is the use of petroleum. Pitch was the mortar for the walls of Babylon and the sealer for the round boats of woven reed that still ply the Euphrates as they did before the Christian era. Egypt's ancient kings rode in chariots that used pitch for axle grease. The Chinese were using natural gas through bamboo pipe lines to heat and light their houses 2,000 years ago. History is filled with references to uses of petroleum in one or another of the many forms found naturally.

Less well-known is the fact that petroleum had 100 been collected and used in this country many hundreds of years before the Drake well was drilled in 1859 — for hundreds of years, in fact, before the first white man set foot on the American continent. There is no written evidence of this, of course; nevertheless, the remains of ancient workings in the oil regions of Pennsylvania, Kentucky, and Ohio are indisputably hundreds of years old, and they were used to collect oil.

Indians collected oil

When first visited by white men, the Indians were collecting surface oil from some of these old sumps and pits; but early oil historians who saw the work- 200 ings pretty generally agreed they did not appear to be the work of the Indians. The eastern Indian was a man of parts, but he was not a digger of wells. And these old oil pits were carefully prepared, frequently lined with timbers, and resemble the work of the people, whoever they were, who mined copper near Lake Superior. Many of the sumps were covered by trees several feet in diameter when they first were seen by white men — which testifies to their antiquity. The Indians were more inclined to depend on oil springs and surface seepages. We have no idea 300 now who these ancient people were, but we have strong evidence that the eastern oil fields were yielding of their product hundreds of years ago, and on a more extensive scale than they were when the whites first penetrated the region. The first actual record of the use of petroleum product on this continent comes from . . . well, take your choice!

Stopped in California

In 1542, Juan Rodrequez Cabrillo, a Portu- 400 guese navigator in the service of Spain, made a voyage in two vessels up the coast of California. The somewhat sketchy accounts of his voyage lead to the conclusion that he stopped at a pitch deposit at Carpenteria, Calif., below Santa Barbara, and repaired his ships. The Indians of the region were using the deposits there to waterproof their dugout canoes, and it is logical that Cabrillo would have taken advantage of the opportunity. Cabrillo died on the voyage, and was buried on San Miguel Island, although his grave never has been found.

Used Sabine Pass pitch

In 1543 a group of the survivors of the De Soto expedition, attempting to sail from the mouth of the Mississippi back to Mexico, were blown ashore 500 near Sabine Pass, and there stopped and repaired their boats with pitch from a surface deposit.

In 1627 a French missionary, Joseph de la Roche D'Allion, visited a famous Indian oil spring near Cuba, N. Y. He wrote a letter, dated July 18, 1627, back to France about it, in which he said, "these Indians collect a good kind of oil called Atouronton, which is translated to mean 'oh how much there is of it!' " When other French missionaries visited the same area, they reported visits to the spring; so that by 1670 it was marked on a map of the French 600 colonies.

─────STOP — ASK FOR YOUR TIME─────

Record time immediately on next page
and answer the questions on content.

Time _____ Sec.	RATE (from column 2 of table on page 303):	R. _____
No. Errors _____	COMPREHENSION (100 − 50% for each Error):	C. _____
V-5	EFFICIENCY (R × C):	E. _____

ANSWER THESE QUESTIONS IMMEDIATELY (V-5)

1. (M. C.)   The author of this article is interested in the reader getting the idea:

    _____(1)   that petroleum has been in use in one form or another for a long time.

    _____(2)   that it is difficult to tell from the records who first made use of petroleum products.

    _____(3)   that Indians made use of petroleum products before the white man came to America.

    _____(4)   that a petroleum product can be used for a variety of things.

2. (T — F)   There are several records, written prior to the time the first white man set foot on the American continent, telling how petroleum was used by the natives.

Number V-6

The Burning Rivers

PART II

(Reprinted from the pamphlet of the same name, by permission of the American Petroleum Institute)

———— WAIT FOR SIGNAL TO BEGIN READING ————

Burning spring

Little is recorded about petroleum for the next 80-odd years, although William Byrd III visited two "burning springs" southwest of Richmond, Va., in 1705. In 1753 George Washington and General Andrew Lewis received a patent on a section of land near the present city of Charleston, W. Va., that contained a "burning spring." There is no evidence that the Father of His Country realized what he had, but his voluminous correspondence on the subject evinces a keen desire to hold onto the land, and his will says: "The tract was taken up by General Andrew Lewis and myself for and on account of a bituminous spring 100 which it contains, of so inflammable a nature as to burn as freely as spirits, and is as nearly difficult to extinguish."

Used as medicine

At about the same time the early traders and explorers penetrated across the Alleghenies and followed the Indian trail down what is now Oil Creek, in Venango County, Pennsylvania, scene of the first oil well and its first boom. Oil then flowed as a scum over the surface of Oil Creek, and was collected by the Indians for use as a medicine, for mixture with war paint, and for burning. The early travelers and 200 settlers followed their example and collected oil from the Cuba spring, from Oil Creek, from the area of George Washington's spring in West Virginia, and from Johnson County, Kentucky. It was skimmed like cream from milk and with a broad flat board thinned at one edge. The oil, removed by scraping the instrument upon the lip of a cup, then had a very foul appearance like very dirty tar or molasses but it was purified by heating it and straining it through flannel or other woolen stuff. It was used by the people of the vicinity for sprains and rheu- 300 matism and for sores upon their horses. It was

widely admired for both purposes. Undoubtedly other springs were known and visited, but frontier records were sketchy, to say the least, in those days.

Peace and war trails

The Indians had an unusual custom of "peace trails" and "war trails". On the peace trails were such common necessities as salt deposits, oil springs, and the like. Thus a party of Indians traveling the "peace trail" could traverse hostile territory to obtain supplies of necessities. The early French noted one 400 such area around the Cuba, N. Y., oil spring. It was neutral ground, to which all had access; and the Indians who lived there were called by the French; the "Neutral Indians."

The trail down Oil Creek in Pennsylvania was another such area, as was the seepage area in Nacogdoches County, Texas. The same is true of the Kentucky and West Virginia seeps and springs. Early travelers, learning of this, stuck to the peace trails, and soon discovered and used oil for a variety of purposes. Travelers up the Spanish Trail, as early as 1790, were using oil from springs for medicine 500 for themselves and their horses and to lubricate the axles of their wagons and carts.

Drill for salt

As permanent settlers came in, the peace trails disappeared, and war was permanent and savage; but meantime the whites had learned to use oil — and before 1800 it was being collected and sold for medicine. The trade naturally was small, and no effort was made to gather any more oil than could be skimmed off the surfaces of springs and creeks.

Although the first oil well was drilled in 1859, the method used to drill it appeared west of the Alle- 600 ghenies many years earlier. Salt was a highly prized commodity in the newly settled western country, and in 1806 the Ruffner brothers started a salt works at what is now Charleston, West Virginia. The method was to drill a well to salt water, which would flow to the surface in artesian fashion, then evaporate out the salt.

Hollow log was "pipe"

The Ruffners dug down to bed rock, and in the shaft fixed a "conductor" made of a hollow sycamore log. They then dug down to 58 ft., where a strong flow of salt water was found and used. While the Ruffner's encountered only a trifling amount of oil, they did get a small flow of natural gas which they used for fuel to evaporate the salt. Many of the later salt well drillers were not so lucky. They got little or no natural gas, but large quantities of oil for which they had not the slightest use whatever.

700 →

750 →

————STOP — ASK FOR YOUR TIME————

Record time immediately and answer the questions on content.

Time _____ Sec.

No. Errors _____

V-6

RATE (from column 3 of table on page 303):

COMPREHENSION (100 — 50% for each Error):

EFFICIENCY (R × C):

R. _____

C. _____

E. _____

ANSWER THESE QUESTIONS IMMEDIATELY (V-6)

1. (M. C.) As a central idea, the author suggests that:

_____(1) The early settlers in America recognized the great potential value in petroleum.

_____(2) The Indians collected oil by taking it off the surface of Oil Creek.

_____(3) The use of "peace trails" led to the discovery of valuable oil wells by the early travelers.

_____(4) The Indians and early settlers found petroleum of practical value when used for medicinal purposes.

2. (T — F) The evidence indicates that early settlers believed that petroleum would some day be in great demand as a fuel.

Number V-7

If Volunteers Quit!

BY DR. EDWARD A. LINDEMAN

(Reprinted from the January, 1954, issue of *Scouting*, by permission of the publishers)

WAIT FOR SIGNAL TO BEGIN READING

I dreamed one night that all the "volunteers" in all the various organizations quit and went home. While I mused, I imagined that on a certain hour of a certain day all of the volunteers in America went on strike. They all decided to quit, stay at home, and not even go to another committee meeting. I tried to estimate how many of them there would be. At that time, which was some four or five years ago, the estimate was about twenty million. There were then, I assumed, about twenty million citizens who day in and day out gave of their time and energy without 100 any financial recompense on behalf of the health, welfare and educational institutions of their community. And so they all went on strike. And then I allowed my imagination to wander. What would happen? What events would take place if all of the volunteers quit suddenly?

I don't know how your mind would work in this connection, but mine led me to the conclusion that within six months we would become a dictatorship. Within six months all of our free institutions would be gone. All of our activities would be now subsumed in some form of bureaucratic officialdom. 200 Nothing would be left for the uncoerced individual to do. He would have no task to perform.

I really believe that we would lose our democracy. Maybe not in six months, my time schedule was perhaps a little accelerated. But certainly, within a definite period of time, without any opportunity for the free choice of individuals, citizenship, democracy and freedom, I am sure, would disappear.

Never was it more important that we assume such obligations. We happen to have reached one of those periods in history when the complexity of the problem far outruns the available leadership. 300

When this sort of situation prevails, the problems and complexities seem to outrun the resources and you get a kind of negativism, in which nearly all of the descriptive phrases used about our society are couched in negative terms. Mr. Toynbee calls this the Age of Trouble. The psychiatrists call it the Age of Anxiety. Four recent books were published in New York, all of which have the word "fear" in the title. Some moralists describe it as the Age of Disbelief, or the more popular word now is the age of Secularism.

400 These are all negative terms, and obviously man cannot live by negation. If I were asked to give a recipe to people who want somehow or another to find a way out of negation, I would say "volunteer." Find something to do in relation to human welfare.

We expect people in a free society to engage in this kind of activity because they really care about what happens to people. That means they are responsible citizens. That is what the word "responsible" means. It means "capable of responding to need."

In a society where there were not a preponderant number of citizens who really cared about what 500 really happened to people there would be no sense in freedom. There would be no demand for freedom at all.

The second reason we expect people to volunteer to participate as citizens in the work of human welfare is because we want them to demonstrate their belief in the principles of voluntarism. I don't believe you can have a free society unless you have a large number of activities which are uncoerced and function outside of bureaucratic control.

Belief in voluntarism is not necessarily an indication that you disbelieve in government. But it does 600 mean that there must be, for all governmental activities, some voluntary counterpart. It was the French philosopher, de Tocqueville, who stated that the health of a democratic society may be measured in terms of the quality of functions performed by private association, not the quantity. The mass quantity problems are not going to be solved by private association. But the quality is measured by what is done by the uncoerced free people.

The third reason we ask for volunteers on a wider scale is that we must find some way of bringing about a coalescence between the two great forces — namely democracy on the one hand, and science on the 700 other. And how to do this, it seems to me, is the major task of democratic peoples.

If then, the volunteers were to disappear from American society, if men were to cease, either from necessity or from choice, to exercise their right to have active roles in the life of their community, then only the shell of democracy would remain. When free men have surrendered the right to give of themselves, their money and their time, generously and voluntarily, to the causes which are dear to them the heart 800 of a free society has ceased to beat.

————STOP — ASK FOR YOUR TIME————

Record time immediately and answer the questions on content.

Time _____ Sec.

No. Errors _____

V-7

RATE (from column 4 of table on page 303):

COMPREHENSION (100 — 50% for each Error):

EFFICIENCY (R × C):

R. _____

C. _____

E. _____

ANSWER THESE QUESTIONS IMMEDIATELY (V-7)

1. (M. C.) Dr. Linderman felt that if all volunteers quit, the work of maintaining our democracy would:

    ____(1) Be done by paid employees hired by the various private organizations.

    ____(2) Not be necessary as things would continue in a satisfactory level without volunteer work.

    ____(3) Be done more efficiently by the various states.

    ____(4) Fall into the hands of power-loving dictators.

2. (T — F) The author believes that voluntary activity in meeting societal needs is an essential part of the democratic process.

No Limits, No Seasons

BY ANDY RUSKANEN

(Reprinted from the December, 1962, issue of *Wyoming Wildlife*, by permission of the editor)

──────────── WAIT FOR SIGNAL TO BEGIN READING ────────────

It's December, and time for evergreens, Santa Claus, snow and staggering gift bills.

It's also time for Joe Sportsman to mope around the house, wishing it were June so he could land a trout, or September so he could bag an antelope.

The mere mention of a bird watching excursion brings a scornful smile, perhaps an uproar of laughter, from the hairy-chested sportsman who is developing a bad case of prison pallor from staying indoors, waiting for the arrival of fishing season.

But some sportsmen aren't content to stagnate for five months every year, because they've learned that bird-watching isn't the "sissy" pastime it's often 100 pictured. These sportsmen have found it takes more than a little stamina and ability to hike through a forest in hip-deep snow to watch a flock of winter birds or to sit on a barren, wind-swept hilltop at midnight observing the lunar migration of thousands of birds.

Birds are an integral part of everyday life. They are seen more by us than any living creature, except other humans. Everyone sees birds, but relatively few watch them. This is the difference between a "bird-seer" and a bird watcher.

It is easy to become a bird watcher, because 200 elaborate preparations aren't necessary. A walk to the backyard for the sole purpose of studying birds is all that's required to begin. Of course, more preparation is necessary if the individual is to begin watching birds seriously, but they aren't nearly as complicated or expensive as those required for hunting and fishing.

Adequate clothing is the most important part of a bird watcher's gear, especially in winter. Nothing can dampen a budding bird watcher's enthusiasm more than sitting in skimpy clothing for a couple hours on a snow-covered rock, waiting for a flock of 300 winter birds to appear. A heavy coat, a cap with warm ear flaps, and high-topped, rubber-soled boots over a pair of heavy woolen socks are necessary for the winter bird watcher. Khaki or green-colored clothing blends well with most surroundings and helps camouflage the observer.

400 A good bird identification book is a must for the beginning bird watcher. There are a number of excellent books, among them *A Field Guide to Western Birds* by Roger Tory Peterson, and *Audubon Bird Guide* by Richard H. Paugh.

Anyone planning to take up bird watching will want to keep a record book. A loose-leaf notebook and filler paper is well suited to this purpose, since pages can easily be added, removed or rearranged. The book may also be used to record other natural phenomena — the appearance of the first flowers in spring, and types of animals and insects seen on trips.

Photography is a favorite sideline of the bird watching fraternity and, contrary to common belief, isn't limited to professionals. Anyone, even a beginner, can take pictures of birds. He will probably want a good camera as he gains experience in bird 500 photography but, while he experiments, the old "brownie" lying on the cupboard shelf does the job fine.

Among other activities connected with bird watching is the building of bird feeding stations. If done properly, the operation of a bird feed box can provide hours of interesting watching and a valuable service to the birds. There are any number of plans available for the construction of bird feed stations.

Another activity that has become a favorite of bird watchers in recent years is lunar migration observations. The purpose of the observations is to 600 count the number of birds that pass the full moon on their way south on a given night.

Bird banding is an activity enjoyed only by the most expert bird watchers. To become a bird bander, a permit from the federal government is required and, to secure the permit, three recognized ornithologists must vouch for the applicant.

Besides providing hours of pleasure for the bird watcher, banding yields scientific data on migration times, dispersals, ages of birds and individual bird behavior.

One activity not limited to experts is the annual Christmas count which is an Audubon Society custom instituted more than fifty years ago. It is conducted ⤆700 each year on a designated day between Christmas and New Year's in all parts of the nation when watchers are organized into groups and assigned to count all birds seen in specific areas, fifteen miles in diameter. The information gathered is used to determine the number and condition of birds in specific areas.

Bird watchers never have a closed season. They can enjoy their sport anytime, anywhere and with little expense. If a few more sportsmen would try bird watching, perhaps the five-month lag between ⤇800 hunting and fishing seasons wouldn't seem so long.

————STOP — ASK FOR YOUR TIME————

Record time immediately and answer
the questions on content.

Time _____ Sec.	RATE (from column 4 of table on page 303):	R. _____
No. Errors _____	COMPREHENSION (100 — 50% for each Error):	C. _____
V-8	EFFICIENCY (R × C):	E. _____

ANSWER THESE QUESTIONS IMMEDIATELY (V-8)

1. (M. C.)   The main point that the author makes in this article is:

   _____(1)   Most sportsmen think that bird-watching is a "sissy" pastime.

   _____(2)   Bird-watching is a favorable sport because it is interesting, inexpensive, and unlimited by season.

   _____(3)   Many people take up bird-watching because they do not have the stamina or ability to hunt or fish.

   _____(4)   The steps necessary for bird-watching activities are complicated.

2. (T — F)   The author believes that bird-watching should not be open during hunting season.

Number V-9

The Turning Wheel

By Charles F. Kettering

(Reprinted from the pamphlet *Short Stories of Science and Invention*,
by permission of General Motors Corporation)

—— WAIT FOR SIGNAL TO BEGIN READING ——

When we think of our modern civilization — both in Peace and War, we must marvel at the ingenuity and complexity of the many things that make up our World of today. We hear about such things as the Electron Microscope — Radar — jet propulsion and the atom smasher, and we know of the marvelous devices that helped us win the war — the tanks, the huge bombers, submarines, and amphibious vehicles.

While we may think of the complicated nature of all this, in my judgment if we took away just one simple invention, an idea now over 4,000 years old, warfare on all fronts and a good part of the activity of our 100 present civilization would cease almost instantly. That invention, as you may have guessed, is the wheel. You might suggest other elements such as bearings, lubrication, steel and wood, which may be equally important. Just who invented the wheel is not known as it is one of those natural evolutions that has come about as the result of men contributing their ideas throughout thousands of years.

This useful idea probably started when some prehistoric ancestor of ours tried to move a heavy object. He might have first put runners or skids under it and 200 tried to drag it over the ground. And one day as he pulled it through the forest, it passed over a log which began to roll and the whole thing moved much easier. So he began to use runners and rollers together and gradually he used larger and larger rollers, and then sections of rollers and at last he put these on axles.

But the time interval between the prehistoric rolling log and the Egyptian chariot wheel must have been thousands of years. With the coming of the new method of moving things, various types of 300 problems put in their appearance. The discs wore badly on the edges so some ingenious man split a sapling and wrapped the thin, flexible strips around the rim — this was the first tire. The axle shafts would wear so the development of lubricants and bearings started. And when people began to ride in the carts, the question of comfort arose and the spring was born. All of these inventions improved the various pieces of apparatus and great progress started, particularly when the railroad and automobile came along. But, up to the time of the bicycle and the 400 pneumatic tire, the Egyptian chariot and the wagon wheel of today were basically the same.

But the use of rolling vehicles had a powerful influence on civilization — distances were shortened — commerce and communication moved ahead. The people gave up walking and began to ride. Whether it was a Roman cart rolling into Gaul or a prairie schooner crossing our western plains, they both did their share in expanding the frontiers.

But the principle of the wheel has served man in other ways besides transportation. Centuries ago men learned to add teeth and called them gears thereby 500 discovering a new means of transmitting power and increasing leverage. He put them in watches and clocks and later these gears made the gasoline automobile and thousands of other things possible.

Practically all land transportation and many of our everyday jobs are made possible by the use of wheeled devices. Our factories are mazes of rotating pulleys and belts as they produce weapons for our armies — the turning wheel is the symbol of the mechanical age.

It may seem a far cry from the rolling log of our prehistoric ancestors to the tremendous rubber tired wheels of a B-29 bomber, but the principle is the 600 same. Dunlop, with the pneumatic tire, and hundreds of other men have contributed in many ways to its development, and it is interesting to note that even today many constructive inventions are being made to improve this simple device.

If we are still finding ways and means of improving

an invention made over 4,000 years ago, we must realize the tremendous field that lies ahead in improving more recent inventions. And what is still more important, think of the opportunities in the field of principles yet undiscovered. Although man may be very dependent upon this invention, the fact remains that Nature found other means of travel, ⇄⁷⁰⁰ because the animals, the fish, and the birds have been moving on the land, and in the water and in the air for millions of years. Yet, in all her myriad of living creatures, Nature has never used our very necessary ⇄⁷⁵⁰ principle of the wheel.

—————STOP — ASK FOR YOUR TIME———————

Record time immediately and answer the questions on content.

Time _____ Sec.

No. Errors _____

V-9

RATE (from column 3 of table on page 303):   R. _____

COMPREHENSION (100 — 50% for each Error):   C. _____

EFFICIENCY (R × C):   E. _____

ANSWER THESE QUESTIONS IMMEDIATELY (V-9)

1. (M. C.)   The most prevalent idea in this article is:

    ____(1)   the belief that the man who invented the wheel made the most important single discovery in history.

    ____(2)   the difference between the wheel used by prehistoric man and the wheel used by modern industry.

    ____(3)   that the improvements of the wheel with its increasingly larger number of usages have taken many centuries to develop.

    ____(4)   the principle of the wheel has served man in other ways besides transportation.

2. (T — F)   The author believes that as men developed the idea of the wheel he made a major improvement over nature since the use of wheels does not occur naturally in plant or animal life.

Number V-10

Push-Button Hospital

(Reprinted from the June 29, 1953, issue of *Time*, courtesy *Time Magazine*, copyright *Time*, Inc., 1953)

——————————— WAIT FOR SIGNAL TO BEGIN READING ———————————

Mrs. Lois Harris leaned back luxuriously in her bed, which could be raised or lowered simply by pressing a button, and declared: "This is really living. Modern homes have nothing on this." Her roommate, Mrs. Helen Sigmund, agreed. Tired of looking through the plate-glass sliding doors at the shrub-covered hillside above Los Angeles' famed Sunset Boulevard, she simply reached up and pulled a switch. Automatically, yellow cloth curtains rippled across, closing in the room. Said Mrs. Sigmund: "We'll be spoiled rotten by the time they take us home."

The setting was no luxury hotel, though it looked like one from the outside. It was the new Kaiser 100 Foundation Hospital, opened in 1953, for the 95,000 area subscribers to Henry J. Kaiser's prepaid medical and hospital care plan. To shy, freckled, Dr. Sidney Garfield, head of the eleven-hospital Kaiser chain, the ultra-modern Los Angeles unit comes near to fulfilling a 20-year dream: the perfect hospital from the point of view of patients, visitors, nurses and doctors.

Three corridors

Instead of a single central corridor for patients and visitors, corpses and dinner wagons, there are three corridors. The central one is used by doctors, nurses and patients. Balconies on each side of the building 200 serve as corridors for visitors, who thus cannot get in the way or see what they should not see. At intervals along the work corridor are stations for nurses, who serve only four rooms each, thus saving countless steps and precious time. Surgeon Garfield has arranged the four operating rooms in a clover-leaf pattern around a central instrument room. The hospital's five lower floors are for regular medical, surgical and obstetrical cases, the two top floors for convalescent patients, who can lounge and walk around at will. They enjoy this extra freedom, and 300 can be waited on by maids, thus saving nurses' time.

Babies in the drawer

Another boon is the modified "rooming-in" for babies. Alongside the head of each mother's bed is a drawer-like arrangement with a plateglass front. Last week, Mrs. Harris reached over, pulled out the drawer, and there in a bassinet snuggled Cynthia, three days old. When she had finished cooing at the baby, Mrs. Harris pushed the drawer back and Cynthia was again in the semiprivate nursery which she shared with Mrs. Sigmund's baby. When Mrs. Harris closed the drawer, a light flashed on in the central 400 corridor, showing the nurse on duty that Cynthia was once again in her charge.

For all its gadgets, the Kaiser hospital costs no more than the current big-city average: $3,000,000 for 210 beds in private and semiprivate rooms. Its charges for those who are not members of the Kaiser plan are not out of line — $15 a day in a double room and $22 in a single, and members seldom pay more than their monthly dues. But to the patients the money means less than the atmosphere. Said Mrs. Sigmund: "It's really nice to be in a hospital 500 that's so pleasant instead of like a jail."

——————STOP — ASK FOR YOUR TIME——————

Record time immediately on next page
and answer the questions on content.

Time _____ Sec. RATE (from column 1 of table on page 303): R. _____

No. Errors _____ COMPREHENSION (100 — 50% for each Error): C. _____

V-10 EFFICIENCY (R × C): E. _____

ANSWER THESE QUESTIONS IMMEDIATELY (V-10)

1. (M. C.) According to this article the thing the patients enjoyed most about the new hospital was:

    ____(1) The low cost.

    ____(2) The picture windows.

    ____(3) The adjustable beds.

    ____(4) The pleasant atmosphere.

2. (T — F) Costs of this new hospital are prohibitive for those who are not members of the Kaiser hospital plan.

Number V-11

The Burning Rivers

PART III

(Reprinted from the pamphlet of the same name, by permission of the American Petroleum Institute)

────── WAIT FOR SIGNAL TO BEGIN READING ──────

Spring-pole drilling

It's interesting to note the Ruffners' drilling method — not only because it was widely used in the early oil wells, but also because it was adapted from the Chinese method used 2,000 years before.

The chief feature was the spring pole, a long green pole with one end firmly imbedded in the ground or attached to the butt of a tree. This then passed over a post near the well location, which was higher than the far end of the pole. To the spring pole were attached the drilling tools, consisting mainly of a heavy length of iron, slightly sharpened on the end, [100] and chained to the spring pole. At the far end of the spring pole, a couple of men would throw their weight on it, thus dashing the iron bit against the bottom of the hole. There were a number of variations of this primitive method in the Ruffner and later wells, but the spring-pole rig remained in use for a long time.

The "burning rivers"

For more than half a century after the Ruffner well, oil's history consisted largely of "burning rivers." Somebody drilled a salt well, got oil; the oil flowed over the surface of the nearest stream, caught fire, [200] and moved majestically downstream to give the pioneer countryside a topic of conversation for years to come.

This occurred on Duck Creek, 30 miles north of Marietta, Ohio, in 1814; on the Big South Fork of the Cumberland in Wayne County, Kentucky, in 1818; on the Muskingum, the Little Kanawha, and other streams in the region. All of which brings us to 1829 and the story of the oil well that was born 30 years too soon.

Lemuel Stockton, that year, decided to drill a salt well on his farm, located 2 miles north of Burkesville, [300] in Cumberland County, Kentucky, and some quarter-mile from the banks of the Cumberland River. Steam power was employed, its first recorded use in drilling operations.

Oil pours on ground

At the depth of 180 ft., the bit hit oil sand, and crude poured out of the well and onto the ground. It flowed by heads for several weeks; then settled down to steady production — all of which was allowed to pour into the Cumberland River. The flow covered the whole surface of the river, caught fire and traces [400] of it were found on the Cumberland as far as Gallatin, Tennessee, 100 miles away.

Why this oil was not captured and used remains a mystery. The use of "rock oil" as a lubricant was known, and had been known for a number of years. Burned for lighting purposes, crude oil gave off an unpleasant odor; but for a decade or more a number of suggestions for simple purification had been made. The best explanation probably is that the world simply wasn't ready for oil yet, and men's imaginations needed more time to "jell" before petroleum could become a commodity. Another consideration [500] is that Kentucky in 1829 was far from being a settled commonwealth, and the gropings toward an understanding of petroleum that were going on in the world had no chance to penetrate to the remote banks of the Cumberland. Oil from "The American Well, Burkesville, Kentucky," eventually was bottled and sold as medicine, however, and played its part in the chain of circumstances that led to the founding of the American petroleum industry in 1859.

Light was needed

The crying need of the day was for a new source

of light, and all over Europe men were experimenting with the distillation of flammable liquids — suitable for use in lamps — from oil shales, tars, and coal. $\overset{600}{\rightleftarrows}$ James Young of Scotland distilled "paraffin oil" from coal as early as 1848, and Abraham Gesner, a Canadian, started the manufacture of illuminating oil from coal 2 years earlier. Gesner called his product "kerosine"; but "coal oil," which was being made in a number of tiny refineries, was the more popular name for many years to come.

Kerosine from oil

Thus it was that, when Professor Benjamin Silliman,

Jr., of Yale, in 1854 issued his now famous report that kerosine and a number of other products could $\underset{700}{\rightarrow}$ readily be made from petroleum, the gropings of a century toward an understanding of this great mineral resource reached fruition.

The stage was thus set for Colonel Edwin L. Drake to drill the world's first oil well on the banks of Oil Creek, near Titusville, Pa., and usher in the "Petro- $\overset{750}{\rightarrow}$ leum Age" on August 27, 1859.

————STOP — ASK FOR YOUR TIME————

Record time immediately and answer the questions on content.

Time _____ Sec.	RATE (from column 3 of table on page 303):	R. _____
No. Errors _____	COMPREHENSION (100 — 50% for each Error):	C. _____
V-11	EFFICIENCY (R × C):	E. _____

ANSWER THESE QUESTIONS IMMEDIATELY (V-11)

1. (M. C.)   The major point stressed by the author is:

   _____(1)   It was a tragic shame to let so much petroleum go to waste.

   _____(2)   The early settlers readily recognized petroleum as a source for many valuable usages.

   _____(3)   The failure to recognize the value of petroleum by the early settlers resulted in almost a complete loss of the oil found during that period.

   _____(4)   The report of Benjamin Silliman, Jr., informed the world that kerosene and other products could be made from petroleum.

2. (T — F)   The Ruffners' drilling method was an original invention of the Ruffner brothers.

Number V-12

Futures Unlimited

(Reprinted from the pamphlet "Electronics," by permission of the Executive Vice-President of Electronics Industries Association)

────────── WAIT FOR SIGNAL TO BEGIN READING ──────────

The universe can be your oyster. Pry it open!

Electronics and other fields of science and technology offer personally rewarding careers which also contribute significantly to our national security and welfare. Yet there are so many subdivisions of the broad field expressed in that simple word "electronics" that a choice of where to start is bewildering. Fame and fortune usually come to those who know what they are doing — and do it. To know what you are doing means basically that you are interested enough to find out. It doesn't matter what branch of electronics you decide to enter. If you're truly interest- 100 ⟵ ed in that branch, you'll almost certainly find working in it a fascinating and profitable experience all your life. But to find the pearl in an oyster, you must first know where to search for pearl-bearing oysters.

Your search for knowledge

One important way to begin your search is by reading books about electronics and allied fields. This will not only sharpen your curiosity to discover more and more in one of the most intriguing fields of engineering devised by man, but it will suggest your ultimate choice of interest. You'll soon be knee-deep in "pearl-bearing oysters." The treasures 200 ⟵ you select will depend on your own personality. In order to get you started, see your counselor for a suggested reading list. Choose the titles most appealing to you in terms of their categories. Some of the greatest scientists, experimentalists, engineers, and inventors that the world has ever known became interested in their field because they were inspired by reading a book on the subject while they were still in high school. This was equally true of many of the world's foremost teachers and craftsmen.

Complexity behind simplicity

As you read about electronics, you're sure to begin 300 → noticing things in the everyday world that are not as commonplace as they seem. Television receiving antennas, for example, may be seen everywhere. It's hard to avoid seeing them. Yet as you start to understand how radio waves are polarized, you'll begin to marvel at the ingenuity and knowledge that went into their design. If you're at all curious, you'll probably also wonder about the wire fences and screened windows or doors that you pass. Each one of these is continuously absorbing radio signals, not only from the Earth's broadcasting stations but from 400 → the entire Universe of stars! Each is a potential radio telescope. All it takes is that it be shaped to focus these radio signals into a receiving system.

As a matter of fact, Karl Jansky, a young radio engineer, discovered in the early 1930's that radio signals were reaching the Earth from outer space. Another young engineer discovered, a few years later, that such signals were really flooding the Earth. He achieved this monumental discovery in his own backyard. He used what amounted to a modified wire-screen door as an antenna. Thus was radio astronomy born, a vitally significant new science, made possible 500 → by electronics. The young man's name was Grote Reber. His knowledge and curiosity stimulated one further breakthrough in man's endless struggle to understand and remake his world as a better place to live.

New ideas behind breakthroughs

Another prominent electronics specialist, L. A. Kilgore, summed up very beautifully the one thing behind all breakthroughs. He was referring to the field of electrical engineering. What he said applies to the entire sweep of occupations — from theorist to salesman, from research assistant to laboratory bench-technician. This is what he said. "The creative person is usually the type who tries to assign a cause for every observed fact. There is a direct benefit in the ⁶⁰⁰⟵ habit of digging into unexplained observations, because here we often turn up some fact — that others have overlooked — which may be the key to a new theory or a new device.

". . . New ideas in their original form are often crude, unfinished, even messy. Our training may have taught us to tolerate only the accurate, complete, and neat solution. One reason junior experimenters who later study engineering often turn out to be creative may be that they learned quite early the habit of seeing new uses for discarded objects."

This is a stimulating statement. It certainly sums ⁷⁰⁰⟵

up the reason why Karl Jansky and Grote Reber could discover an ultra-important new science like radio astronomy. This led to a whole series of new electronics technologies, such as radio tracking and telemetry. All are invaluable to the exploration of the space frontier. Radio-telescope antennas have also been used to transmit powerful radar pulses across millions of miles in an attempt to analyze the atmosphere and surface of the planet Venus. So the Universe *can* be your oyster. If you are curious enough to pry it open, you will find the pearl par- ⁸⁰⁰⟶ ticularly suited to you.

————STOP — ASK FOR YOUR TIME————

Record time immediately and answer the questions on content.

Time _____ Sec.	RATE (from column 4 of table on page 303):	R. _____
No. Errors _____	COMPREHENSION (100 — 50% for each Error):	C. _____
V-12	EFFICIENCY (R × C):	E. _____

ANSWER THESE QUESTIONS IMMEDIATELY (V-12)

1. (M. C.) In this article the phrase, "The universe can be your oyster" means:

    _____(1) There are many subdivisions in the field of electronics.

    _____(2) Those who reach fame and fortune know what they are doing.

    _____(3) One may find his life's work in electronics if he has sufficient interest and curiosity to explore the career opportunities in that field.

    _____(4) Many of the world's foremost teachers and craftsmen became interested in their field because they were inspired by reading a book on the subject while still in high school.

2. (T — F) According to L. A. Kilgore, breakthroughs often may be stimulated by rediscovering facts previously overlooked or by finding new uses for discarded objects.

Bell's Legacy to the World

(Reprinted from the pamphlet *Alexander Graham Bell*,
by permission from the Bell Telephone System)

─── WAIT FOR SIGNAL TO BEGIN READING ───

Citizen

Alexander Graham Bell became a United States citizen in 1882 — a fact of which he was very proud. The Government and Constitution of the United States he once described as one of the most remarkable inventions in the history of man. He died in August 1922 and was buried in Nova Scotia. During the funeral service on August 4, all telephones served by the Bell System were silent for two minutes. At his request, his epitaph on the grave near his Beinn Bhreagh home reads, "Born in Edinburg . . . died a citizen of the U. S. A."

He was, however, something more than this — a $\underset{\leftarrow}{100}$ citizen of the world, who left a legacy for all men.

Enthusiastic and tireless, he was apt in his younger days to wake others in the middle of the night to share with him the excitement and adventure of progress on some experiment. And teachers of the deaf tell of watching Bell communicate to large audiences his own enthusiasm for the teaching methods he advocated.

Bell was impulsive and generous too. Soon after he had invented the telephone, when he had very little money, his first public lecture brought him $85. He spent it all on a silver model of the telephone $\underset{\leftarrow}{200}$ for his fiancee. And though it was he who had founded the telephone art, as the father of Bell Telephone Laboratories, he was the first to give credit to those who came after him. In the last year of his life he said, "The telephone system as we know it, is the product of many, many minds, to whom honor should now be given for the wonderful and beneficial work it has accomplished."

Genius

To telephone people everywhere, engaged as they are in rendering public service on which the lives

$\underset{\rightarrow}{300}$ and happiness of other men and women so often depend, Alexander Graham Bell's career of service to humanity offers special inspiration. And with them, others will write his name high on the roll of versatile American geniuses who have contributed to the welfare of mankind. Bell's work for the deaf hastened the development of enlightened methods for their education, and inspired improvement of institutions devoted to their care. His support of aviation led to the invention of the aileron stabilizer which continues in use today. His telephone has had incalculable influence upon the world and has largely $\underset{\leftarrow}{400}$ shaped the whole pattern of modern life. It has given employment directly to hundreds of thousands more who supply raw materials and finished goods for use in the telephone industry.

For countless millions of others, in cities and on farms, the telephone is an indispensable tool of living — in the hour-to-hour conduct of business, in the administration of government, in minor emergencies and great ones, and in maintaining family and community ties. To make telephone service what it is today — and what it will be tomorrow — many people and many inventions have contributed and are contributing through a con- $\underset{\rightarrow}{500}$ tinuous succession of work and ideas. But it is not to be forgotten that this progress began with the achievement of Alexander Graham Bell.

All his life Bell was interested in flight. He helped finance S. P. Langley's experiments with heavier-than-air machines. His vision as to the future of aviation was remarkable. He urged establishment, by the Smithsonian Institution, of the Langley Medal for aviation progress, the first award of which was made to the Wright Brothers. He predicted that it would not be many years before "a man can take dinner in New York and breakfast the next morning $\underset{\rightarrow}{600}$ in Liverpool." And in a magazine article in 1908 he wrote "The nation that secures control of the air will ultimately rule the world."

With the airplane, Bell's telephone has made the world smaller. Swift communication and transport have already had a vast effect on human relations, and will have more. They are, of course, only agencies in the hands of man; but both, because it is their function to bring people together, promise to be mankind's chief physical aids in achieving better understanding among the peoples of the earth.

Benefactor

In his thinking, as well as in his works, Bell left much for others. We may well conclude this tribute ⟵700 with words in which, speaking to children, he spoke to us all:

"Don't keep forever on the public road, going only where others have gone. Leave the beaten track occasionally and dive into the woods. You will be certain to find something you have never seen before. Of course, it will be a little thing, but do not ignore it. Follow it up, explore all around it; one discovery will lead to another, and before you know it you will have something worth thinking about to occupy your mind. All really big discoveries are the results 800⟶ of thought."

———STOP — ASK FOR YOUR TIME———

Record time immediately and answer the questions on content.

Time _____ Sec.	RATE (from column 4 of table on page 303):	R. _____
No. Errors _____	COMPREHENSION (100 — 50% for each Error):	C. _____
V-13	EFFICIENCY (R × C):	E. _____

ANSWER THESE QUESTIONS IMMEDIATELY (V-13)

1. (M. C.)   The writer wants the reader to recognize Bell's legacy to the world as:

    ____(1)   a genuine spirit of service to humanity.

    ____(2)   his sincere appreciation of the fact that he was an American citizen.

    ____(3)   his development of improved methods for the education of the deaf.

    ____(4)   the philosophical thought which he often conveyed as he spoke to children.

2. (T — F)   Alexander Graham Bell concentrated his interests and efforts entirely on the telephone and its improvements.

Thunderbolts In Harness

(Reprinted from pamphlet of the same name, by permission of the General Electric Company)

─────────── WAIT FOR SIGNAL TO BEGIN READING ───────────

A vigil in the clouds

Each summer, in the "thunderstorm season," a man, who has to be part electrical engineer, part photographer, and part night watchman, takes up his vigil watching for lightning bolts to strike the mooring mast atop New York's loftiest skyscraper. Most of his work consists of sitting around waiting for thunderstorms, but when one comes he has to go into action fast.

Special high-speed rotating cameras focused on the top of the Empire State building are located in another skyscraper eight blocks away. Oscillographs and recorders are atop the Empire State Building. When a storm is building up sufficient intensity to $\overset{100}{\leftarrow}$ produce a stroke, these devices are automatically turned on by an electrical corona device. When the building is struck, the oscillographs automatically measure the stroke's characteristics.

A phone call warns the lightning watcher that a storm is approaching. No matter what time of night, he grabs a cab and rushes to the camera location and waits. Many times nothing happens except at distances too far to obtain good records. Frequently, however, the watch is rewarded by obtaining good lightning photographs.

A youngster's theory

When a bolt does strike, though, the lightning watcher is busy taking pictures and speaking into a $\overset{200}{\leftarrow}$ voice recorder, describing what he sees as it happens.

Similar photographic research is carried on during the summer months in Pittsfield, from an observatory located on the roof of one of the city's tallest factory buildings. There, too, lightning watchers make the mad dash to the camera when a thunderstorm approaches.

One scientist's five-year-old daughter was slightly confused by the procedure. Many times at night, when the best lightning pictures are taken, she would hear her father get up to answer the telephone, then dress quickly and hurry out. Soon it would rain $\overset{300}{\rightarrow}$ and there would be thunder and lightning. Convinced that her father had something to do with the storm, the little girl begged her mother to "tell daddy to turn it off."

Like a pilot house

The setup and operation at the Pittsfield Observatory is somewhat different from that of the watching post in New York. From the Pittsfield observatory one can view the surrounding countryside for several miles in all directions. The lookout itself resembles a pilot house of an old-time Mississippi River boat. It is round and constructed almost entirely of glass $\overset{400}{\rightarrow}$ and steel. The observer stands on an upper platform, where he views the heavens through a periscope which can be turned to cover the entire sky. Below him is a multiple-lens camera, set so that it will photograph all points on the horizon.

Suspense

Though lightning research was rewarding John Q. Public with better and more dependable electric power all the time, he knew little about it until the New York World's Fair of 1939 and 1940. Literally millions of visitors to the man-made lightning "show" were thrilled or frightened as the 10,000,000-volt charge leaped the 30-foot gap between two generators, and artificial thunder crashed against the $\overset{500}{\rightarrow}$ walls of the room and echoed back. The reactions of the audience range from nervous, self-imposed calm to downright uneasiness. The appearance of the darkened room with red signal lights glowing, the tall stacks of black and chromium, the shiny sphere-capped rods, the smell of ozone from previous "shows," and the ominous 15-second hum as the electric charge built up heightened the spell of tension. This spell was climaxed by the gigantic bolt of lightning and its thunderous crash. One of the most interesting demonstrations at the Fair was striking a hard maple post, which was blown violently 600 apart by the lightning.

————STOP — ASK FOR YOUR TIME————

Record time immediately and answer the questions on content.

Time _____ Sec.	RATE (from column 2 of table on page 303):	R. _____
No. Errors _____	COMPREHENSION (100 — 50% for each Error):	C. _____
V-14	EFFICIENCY (R × C):	E. _____

ANSWER THESE QUESTIONS IMMEDIATELY (V-14)

1. (M. C.)   The main idea expressed in this article is:

    ____(1) a lightning watcher has a very dangerous job.

    ____(2) it is important for the lightning watcher to be present at his post at all times.

    ____(3) the research experiments with lightning have been rewarding in that they have provided a better understanding of the natural powers of electricity.

    ____(4) one scientist's daughter believed her father was the cause of the electrical storms.

2. (T — F)   The primary function of a lightning watcher is to observe the activity of the lightning during a storm and to secure objective records of that activity.

Number V-15

Sunshine In the Rockies

(Reprinted from the pamphlet of the same name, by permission of the American Petroleum Institute)

───────────── WAIT FOR SIGNAL TO BEGIN READING ─────────────

Oil boom

Undoubtedly, oil in the Rockies has as ancient a history as it has anywhere in America. Traveling bands of Indians bathed themselves in Wyoming's oil seeps just as they did in those in Pennsylvania. The earliest explorers used oil to bathe sores on their horses and on themselves.

In 1862, just 3 years after the Drake well, some shallow wells were drilled in a seep near Cannon City, Colorado, and in 1876 the first successful oil well in the Rockies was drilled at nearby Florence, a field that is still producing.

And here is an interesting — and formerly typical **100** — oil-field story about DeBeque, Mesa County, Colorado, related in the *Denver Republican* of January 18, 1902:

"I did not attend the opening of Creede or Cripple Creek," said Charles M. Hicklin, one of the promoters of the successful DeBeque Oil Company and a well-known railroad man, "but I will bet there were no more picturesque features connected with the birth of those mining camps than was the case at DeBeque when the outside world heard of the oil strike.

"Within 24 hours DeBeque became metropolitan. The one hostelry, the Hotel DeLano, was packed with visitors; and the proprietor, entering into the **200** spirit of the scene of the occasion, had a large blackboard placed in the bar room on which was placed the latest intelligence from the scene of the strike, half a mile away, mind you!

"One of the first to drift into town was a gambler from Grand Junction who selected a corner lot that ordinarily was held at $200 with no takers, which he purchased for $1,000. 'What possessed you to pay such a price as that?' I asked him. 'That's the place I want,' he responded. 'I'm a gambler, and I know what I want.'

300 "Anyhow, that set the now metropolitan town crazy. The price was in keeping with the suddenly acquired dignity of the town, and the figure fixed by the Grand Junction gambler is now the standard."

As is often the case in such exciting "discoveries," the DeBeque strike of 1902 produced 8 barrels a day for 8 days, and it was not until 1913 that commercial production began in the DeBeque Field.

Long distances

Salt Creek, Wyoming, however, was a different story. Brought in in 1908, the field was assured of production from the start, and has been a constant producer since.

400 The vast distances and the lack of adequate transportation hampered oil development in these rugged mountains. Salt Creek, for instance, in the early days was 50 miles from the nearest railroad, and everything had to be hauled into the field and production taken to Casper in improvised tank wagons.

When P. M. Shannon, about 1900, moved his tools from Pennsylvania to take a try at the Salt Creek area and drilled the first wells there — north of the present field — they were dropped off the railroad at Laramie and hauled overland 200 miles by team.

500 There was oil at Salt Creek, lots of it! It was developed, however, by enterprising Americans, rather than experienced oil men. They knew they had a great oil field in an undeveloped area.

No market

From that day forward, however, the story of oil in the Rockies assumes a monotonous regularity. Sure there was oil, plenty of it! But there was no market. The Rockies were sparsely populated, and the local market easily supplied. Rocky Mountain oil could not compete with crude from Oklahoma,

Texas, Louisiana, Illinois, Kansas, and the other producing states closer to the centers of population. Oil production languished in the mountains. Thomas ⁶⁰⁰⇆ S. Harrison, Denver consulting geologist, reports in his admirable historical article that at one time there were 20 million barrels of Salt Creek crude in storage. Rangely, the new great Colorado field, was discovered in 1933 — and the discovery well capped for lack of market.

Then along come World War II with its insatiable demands for oil. The industry, aware of the potentialities of the Rocky Mountain states, moved in, and large-scale production resulted. When 1946 came with an even greater demand for oil than in the war years, the future of oil production in the Rockies was assured. No matter how high the mountains ⁷⁰⁰⇆

nor how deep the valleys, oil is coming out of the Rockies in ever-increasing quantities. No real estimate is possible today of the extent of reserves in the Rocky Mountain states. It is conceded that there are great unexplored areas of oil promise. The influx of residents to the Pacific Northwest, the increasing national demand, and the realization that Rocky Mountain oil can be produced profitably mark the end of the days of stalled production.

So there is sunshine in the Rockies, and the faith and indomitable courage of oil's Mountain men has ⁸⁰⁰⇉ been justified.

————STOP — ASK FOR YOUR TIME————

Record time immediately and answer the questions on content.

Time _____ Sec.	RATE (from column 4 of table on page 303):	R. _____
No. Errors _____	COMPREHENSION (100 − 50% for each Error):	C. _____
V-15	EFFICIENCY (R × C):	E. _____

ANSWER THESE QUESTIONS IMMEDIATELY (V-15)

1. (M. C.)   The *primary* purpose of this article is to get the idea across to the reader that:

   ____(1)   the history of oil in the Rockies is as ancient as anywhere in America.

   ____(2)   wherever oil was discovered, there was generally a great increase in the price of property.

   ____(3)   the limited amount of oil discovered in the Rocky Mountain area handicapped the development of the oil industries.

   ____(4)   the Rocky Mountain section has been rich in oil reserves for many years but until recently there was no sure market to encourage quantity production.

2. (T — F)   Real production in large quantities of Rocky Mountain oil was brought about by World War II.

Number V-16

Forests and Water

(Reprinted from the pamphlet of same name, by permission of the U. S. Department of Agriculture)

─────────── WAIT FOR SIGNAL TO BEGIN READING ───────────

Water — The lifeblood of civilization

Water is the priceless resource on which all growing things depend. It is the lifeblood of civilization.

Where there are ample supplies of good water, vigorous nations can flourish. Farms thrive, cities prosper. When the supply of water fails farms are abandoned, communities are imperiled, and cities and cultures die, leaving crumbling ruins to mark their past glory.

The city dweller of the humid East, accustomed to unstinted quantities of water for drinking and cooking, bathing and washing, and sprinkling lawns and gardens, encounters few of the difficulties that beset the inhabitants of western plains and semidesert 100 communities. Yet even he is sometimes brought face to face with local water shortages, resulting from low supplies in reservoirs or in streams that feed his water mains. Year in and year out, the eastern farmer confidently expects enough rain to bring through his crops. Only during the most severe droughts does he worry about parched crops and seared pasture.

How different it is in the arid portions of the West. Here, where Nature is lavish with sunshine but niggardly with moisture, the struggle for existence is to a large extent a struggle for water. Here men once were 200 killed in disputes over water rights. Throughout the Southwest, the farmer or rancher knows that until water, can be brought to his land it is worthless for cultivated crops. Perhaps 20 to 30 unirrigated acres will feed a cow for a month or two during the year. Undeveloped, his land may be worth 50 cents per acre. Bring water to it, and its value jumps fiftyfold, a hundredfold, sometimes a thousandfold.

Sometimes we have too much water

Newspapers often tell us of floods in some parts of the United States. Nearly every year, on the great central drainages, heavy rains and melting snow cause 300 the waters to pour out of mountains and plains, to turn brooks into torrents, and to swell quiet streams into wild turbulent rivers. From Cairo to New Orleans, and from Pittsburgh to Paducah, the cry "River rising. River rising" is a familiar yet fearful refrain . . . . When the rivers sometimes become too high or too swift to be restrained, communities are inundated, families flee from their homes, croplands are washed out, and transportation comes to a halt. Hunger, disease, and death stalk the raging waters.

Although given less publicity, the agricultural 400 damage done by the many smaller, more frequent floods usually far exceeds the losses caused by the spectacular ones. In the Central States, ditches and drains cause the flows from spring rains and melting snow to run far more rapidly than in the days before white men settled on the land. Once, excess spring flood waters emptied into lakes and swampy lands, there to be detained for slow release into streams and rivers. Now, systematic drainage has virtually eliminated these natural reservoirs.

In the more rolling sections of the East, spring run-off was formerly absorbed and held temporarily in the 500 porous soils beneath the unbroken expanses of forest. When large areas were converted to farm use, removal of the forest and practice of up-and-down hill plowing deprived the soils of much of their ability to catch — and store — water.

The effects of eliminating the natural forest cover are shown in the gullied farm lands and widened stream channels found in some densely settled areas. Partly because the stream channels are more or less filled with material washed down from the uplands, and partly because storm runoff has increased, the channels are today no longer able to carry all the 600 flow from heavy precipitation. This explains why the streams overtop their banks far more often than in the days before settlement.

Sometimes we have too little water

The same misuse of our land that helps to induce floods is also partly responsible for serious and costly shortages. When water from rain and snow is not stored in the soil but runs off quickly, there is no reserve to keep streams, lakes, and natural underground reservoirs supplied during the drier months of the year. Many of the 80 million Americans who depend on public water-supply systems have a vital interest in preventing water shortages.

Lack of water sometimes causes serious crop **700** failures on irrigated farms. It has actually forced an exodus of people from some regions — for example, parts of the Great Plains where recurrent dust storms and depleted soils have made farming difficult. It has imperiled California's Central Valley, one of our great farming regions. It is generally believed, also, that underground supplies in the Mississippi and Ohio River Valleys, as well as in the Piedmont, are being drained faster than they are replenished. On many farms, wells go dry during summer heat and farmers have to fetch water long distances to **800** keep thirsty cattle alive.

———STOP — ASK FOR YOUR TIME———

Record time immediately and answer the questions on content.

Time _____ Sec.	RATE (from column 4 of table on page 303):	R. _____
No. Errors _____	COMPREHENSION (100 — 50% for each Error):	C. _____
V-16	EFFICIENCY (R × C):	E. _____

ANSWER THESE QUESTIONS IMMEDIATELY (V-16)

1. (M. C.) The author's central theme is:

   ____(1) floods are the result of modern farming methods.

   ____(2) better social planning concerning the use of water supplies would prevent floods and droughts.

   ____(3) people who live in the East do not appreciate the real value of water as Westerners do.

   ____(4) either too much or too little water may cause serious damage to the land, and severe loss to man.

2. (T — F) The same basic factors of land cultivation and land misuse contribute greatly both to floods at one time and to water shortage at another.

Number V-17

Fable of the Meadow Larks

By Lester W. Ristow

(Reprinted from the Phi Delta Kappa magazine, by permission of the editor)

———— WAIT FOR SIGNAL TO BEGIN READING ————

Once upon a time the people of a little town quite like that in which I live decided that it would add greatly to the beauty and pleasure of their lives if there were a great many meadow larks living in their midst. Besides the cheerful songs to delight both young and old, there would be the happy, busy fluttering of wings, and the flashing of brilliant yellow breasts — a very ecstasy of beauty to enchant the visitor and gratify the native.

Having thus decided upon a means of adorning their village, the people elected a Board of Beautification to take the proper measures to induce the ⟵100 meadow larks to come, and to provide adequate facilities for them. After long and sagacious deliberation the Board of Beautification submitted a plan. They would set up hundreds of neat attractive little bird houses for the meadow larks and they would provide nutritious bread crumbs for them to eat.

By means of a tax-rate increase and a bond issue sufficient funds were raised to pay for the construction of the attractive little bird houses with enough left over to provide a meager ration of crumbs. When all this was done the people waited in happy ⟵200 anticipation for the coming of the meadow larks, but very few meadow larks came and those who did come stayed only a brief time.

For a while the meadow larks found it interesting to flutter about prettily and to sing gaily for these townspeople who were so appreciative. The meadow larks felt proud and important when the people praised their performances in glowing terms, and the attractive little bird houses did offer security — but who could live on crumbs?

After a time the people began to look at the attractive little bird houses in wondering disappointment and to question each other about why there were ⟵300 no meadow larks therein. The Board of Beautification deliberated again and presented the people with an answer — there was a serious shortage of meadow larks! The people became so concerned that nearly every club, lodge, and organization of whatever kind appointed a committee to work upon the problem of the meadow lark shortage. The committees all agreed that the solution to the problem was to produce more meadow larks. Committees were appointed to gather all the meadow lark eggs they could find and ⟵400 to hatch them by the most rapid and scientific means. However, the ungrateful meadow larks would not stay in the attractive little bird houses. They preferred to go out into the fields and eat fat worms.

Perceiving this, the people voted higher taxes which made possible a small increase in the quantity of crumbs, but the meadow larks still would not stay in the attractive little bird houses. Finally, the meadow lark shortage became so acute that it was necessary for the Board of Beautification to permit sparrows, swallows, and even a few crows to substitute for the meadow larks on an emergency basis.

500⟶ Everyone knew that these substitutes could not sing and that their breasts were not yellow — in short they were not meadow larks. But at least the attractive little bird houses were occupied, and in the meantime the people worked hard on the problem of the meadow lark shortage. Every means was tried to produce more and more meadow larks in order to overcome the shortage, but no matter how many meadow larks were produced, few ever remained to live in the attractive little bird houses — it was so easy to find plenty of fat worms out in the fields. 600⟶ And so the meadow lark shortage continued.

————STOP — ASK FOR YOUR TIME————

Record time immediately on next page
and answer the questions on content.

Time _____ Sec.   RATE (from column 2 of table on page 303):   R. _____

No. Errors _____   COMPREHENSION (100 − 50% for each Error):   C. _____

V-17   EFFICIENCY (R × C):   E. _____

ANSWER THESE QUESTIONS IMMEDIATELY (V-17)

1. (M. C.) Being an educator, the author has used this fable to try to convey which of the following ideas about the reasons for a shortage of teachers.

_____(1) They like to live in the country rather than in the city.

_____(2) Despite all other things, teachers must have the respect of the community to be satisfied.

_____(3) Many teachers are ungrateful for all the things done for them and will leave teaching no matter how much is done for them.

_____(4) Schools will be unable to keep teachers until wages are raised to meet the competition of outside employment possibilities.

2. (T — F) One of the reasons the author wrote this was that he felt that people should take a greater interest in the raising of meadow larks as a means of beautifying their cities.

Number V-18

Jungle Marauders

(Reprinted from the July 28, 1952, issue of *Time*, courtesy *Time Magazine*, copyright *Time*, Inc., 1952)

—————— WAIT FOR SIGNAL TO BEGIN READING ——————

The queen's army

On display in Manhattan's American Museum of Natural History are some of the earth's fiercest creatures: a colony of army ants (Ection hamatum) from Barro Colorado Island, C. Z. In the museum's exhibit, the ants seem harmless enough. But in their native country, they sweep through the jungle like Mongol hordes, killing every living thing that cannot run, leap or fly fast enough to escape them. They have even been known to kill disabled men who lay helpless in their path.

These ferocious marauders were brought to the U. S. by Dr. Theodore Christian Schneirla, the world's leading expert on army ant behavior. For many years, 100 Dr. Schneirla has followed the campaigns of army ants on Barro Colorado Island, and gradually he is untangling the knot of mysterious biological laws that govern their society. During his latest stay on the island, he made some new discoveries about the life and reign of the army ants' queens.

Expendable workers

Like all social insects (bees, ants, termites, etc.), army ants pass through a two-stage system of reproduction. First stage is the queen's fabulous egg-laying. Once fertilized, she produces hundreds of thousands of eggs, most of which develop into female workers. These fierce, frustrated virgins form 200 the bulk of the colony and do all of its working and fighting. Since the queen is protected while the workers are expendable (casualties are heavy, for instance, in attacking a wasp nest), the queen eventually becomes the mother of all her followers.

During the second stage, the colony itself reproduces, dividing into two sections like a fissioning amoeba. Once each year, in the dry season, about 1,500 of the eggs develop into winged males; a crucial six turn into nubile females. As the males begin to emerge from their pupa cases, the throngs of stinging virgins seem to sense a coming event in 300 which they cannot participate except by vicarious action. They get wildly excited and overly active. Amid scenes of more-than-antlike activity, the colony begins to divide, each part gathering around a queen that has more attractiveness (apparently a chemical odor) than her rivals.

During this recurring crisis of ant society, the winged males function as a sort of cross-fertilizing pollen. Like drone bees they are sexually impotent until they have flown for a while. Therefore they are not likely to form incestuous unions with the 400 young queens (their sisters) in their own colony. Instead they fly to other colonies, where a few find unrelated young queens that are ripe for fertilization.

Doughty queen

Sometimes a reigning queen, four times as long and many times as heavy as the half-inch workers, has unusual attractiveness, and makes off year after year with part of the colony. Zoologist Schneirla marked many queens by cutting delicate notches in the edges of their abdominal armor. On his latest trip, he found one doughty old queen still marching with her army after 4½ years.

What happens to the rejected queens, either old 500 or newborn? Many times Dr. Schneirla has watched their pathetic end. As the sections of the divided colony move off separately, the rejected queens are left behind, each surrounded by a doughnut-shaped pile of imprisoning workers.

Death of a monarch

Dr. Schneirla grew fond of a feeble old queen that he had followed for months of wanderings through the jungle. One day, while her people moved off in two sections, each headed by a young queen, she was left on a tree trunk in a prison of her daughters' bodies. Soon they would follow one of the armies, 600 leaving her to be devoured by some sharp-eyed bird.

————STOP — ASK FOR YOUR TIME————

Record time immediately on next page
and answer the questions on content.

Time _____ Sec.	RATE (from column 2 of table on page 303):	R. _____
No. Errors _____	COMPREHENSION (100 — 50% for each Error):	C. _____
V-18	EFFICIENCY (R × C):	E. _____

ANSWER THESE QUESTIONS IMMEDIATELY (V-18)

1. (M. C.) The author's major emphasis throughout the article is about:

     _____(1) the ferocious nature of the army ants.

     _____(2) the role of a queen in a colony of army ants.

     _____(3) the detailed research equipment necessary for an understanding of biological laws that govern the society of army ants.

     _____(4) the close comparisons between the social life of bees and that of the army ants.

2. (T — F) Queens always play a prominent part in the life of the colony until they die from old age.

Number V-19

Conquest of a Mountain

(Reprinted from the July 28, 1952, issue of *Time*, courtesy *Time Magazine*,
copyright *Time*, Inc., 1952)

WAIT FOR SIGNAL TO BEGIN READING

A towering challenge

Mountaineering veterans of some of the toughest climbs of the Alps, the Rockies and the Himalayas are currently flocking to Peru, drawn by the country's cluster of virgin (i.e., unclimbed) peaks ranging up to 20,000 ft. or more. In recent months, two major expeditions have been preparing assaults on the spectacular snowcrest of Salcantay, 20,551 ft. above sea level. One, an American-French group, has been reconnoitering the peak in an airplane; the other, a Swedish-Italian group, has been warming up by scaling other Peruvian slopes.

Last week, while the big parties were still flexing their muscles, Lima learned that two Swiss moun- **100** taineers, traveling light, had grabbed off the honors for the first ascent of Salcantay.

A dash up

Getting ready for Salcantay, blond Marcus Broennimann, 28, a mining engineer, and leathery Felix Marx, 48, a foundry technician, bought 1,600 ft. of rope, feather-lined suits, three tents, sleeping bags, canned milk, chocolate, dried fruit and special concentrated food. At the mountain city of Huancayo, they loaded the gear and Broennimann's plump bride Susan into a pickup truck, and drove 530 miles to ancient Cusco.

It took two days of climbing to reach the 15,000-ft. level of Salcantay's eastern face — and they were **200** immediately snowed in for three days. Six days later, they built a base camp of snowblocks at 17,220 ft. Susan stayed there; the bearded Swiss slogged on for three days to 18,500 ft. and pitched a tent for their high camp. At that rarefied height, the temperature, in the bright sunlight, was 122° F.; twelve hours later it fell to −15°. Nevertheless, the climbers toiled on next day, up another 1,300 ft. to a cave. The following morning, as the sun rose out of steaming Amazonian jungles far to the east, they moved on to the top.

300 It was an exhausting scramble. Dry snow, fine as sand, and rock, crumbled by the unending freeze-and-thaw, gave no foothold. But at 11:55 a.m., sucking at the thin, cold air, they were at the center of the long, narrow summit, where they firmly planted a Peruvian flag.

A tumble down

Ninety minutes later, in high elation, they started down. Nightfall pinned them on an icy hogback. Broennimann slipped, the rope which tied him to Marx spun out and then broke, and he tumbled 100 ft. to fetch up in soft snow with a broken rib. In **400** darkness, his feet beginning to freeze, he got back to high camp, where Marx rejoined him a little later.

They dropped cautiously downward next day, picking up Susan at Base camp, and continuing until Broennimann's pain-racked feet would take him no farther. Then Marx rushed on for help, leaving the Broennimanns huddled together for four days and nights through a raging blizzard. Marcus had a growing fear that his feet might have to be cut off. But last week, carried to a small hacienda at the foot of Salcantay, Broennimann was resting with the comforting assurance from a local doctor that amputa- **500** tion would not be necessary.

———STOP — ASK FOR YOUR TIME———

Record time immediately on next page
and answer the questions on content.

Time _____ Sec.   RATE (from column 1 of table on page 303):   R. _____

No. Errors _____   COMPREHENSION (100 — 50% for each Error):   C. _____

V-19   EFFICIENCY (R × C):   E. _____

ANSWER THESE QUESTIONS IMMEDIATELY (V-19)

1. (M. C.)   The major idea conveyed in this article is:

_____(1)   Swiss are better climbers than American or French climbers.

_____(2)   High mountain climbing is hazardous in many ways.

_____(3)   Peruvian Mountains are the highest in the World.

_____(4)   Many men wanted to secure the reward for climbing Mt. Salcantay first.

2. (T — F)   The two mountaineers were able to descend the mountains quite rapidly.

Number V-20

Conservation the Indian Way

By James Hull

(Reprinted from the November-December, 1962 issue of the *Conservation Volunteer*, by permission of the editor)

───────── WAIT FOR SIGNAL TO BEGIN READING ─────────

The early American Indian has been called "the first conservationist." In his simple and uncomplicated way, he believed that God's creation was provided as a source of food, clothing, and enjoyment for man, and that man, in his appreciation, should take only what he needed and use, frugally, that which was taken. Skill in the hunt was admired, but killing for sport was unknown.

With the arrival of the fur trader and the market hunter, the game resources of the Indian became legal tender for the perishable luxuries of the white frontier. The Indian no longer hunted for food alone. 100 His needs and appetites now included rum, tobacco, calico, the cheap gew-gaws and jewelry of the fur trade, and guns, ammunition and traps with which to secure ever greater quantities of pelts for barter with the traders. The Indian had forgotten the unwritten laws and principles of his race and had become, in the process, the instrument of his own swift descent to poverty.

As the vast hunting grounds of the Red Man became ever smaller and were finally compressed into the tiny areas set aside as reservations, game and fish ceased to be a dominant factor in the Indian 200 way of life. The dollar became the only barrier to starvation and the trading post the only source of food and the necessities of life. Many of these reservations were opened to white settlers which further depleted the game resources and removed the last remaining vestige of dependence which the Indians may have felt toward hunting and fishing as a means of securing a livelihood.

This revolution in the economics of the Indian progressed with less speed on those few reservations which were established in remote areas far from later industrial development. Here, the Indian continued, until recent times, to take a part of his subsistence 300 from the forests and waters of his environment, and to practice, voluntarily, the simple principles of conservation followed by his ancestors.

Perhaps the best example of this lingering consciousness of the values inherent in Nature is to be found on Minnesota's Grand Portage Reservation, the wedge which forms the State's northeastern extremity and the very tip of the Arrowhead Country. Nearly all of this Reservation remains in Indian ownership, a circumstance which permits the Indian Council to establish and administer its own game 400 laws. These laws allow the taking of moose and deer, by the Grand Portage Indians, during nine months of the year. Equally liberal laws govern the taking of fish and furbearers.

It is not difficult to visualize the speed with which game would be eradicated in a non-Indian area of like size under this kind of system. Deer, moose, bear, beaver, otter, fisher, bobcat, and other furbearers remain quite plentiful on the Grand Portage Reservation in spite of the fact that there has been a continuing and growing need for the food and income which this game could have provided and in spite of 500 the constant depredations of non-Indian poachers.

With this background of preservation of the natural charm and resources of their Reservation, the Grand Portage Indians are setting aside a large portion of their Reservation as a wilderness park for the use and enjoyment of the public. This park embraces the entire shoreline of the Reservation and encompasses the most spectacular scenery to be found anywhere in the Middle West. The hitherto hidden beauty of Pigeon Falls, Pigeon Point, the Susie Islands, the Waus-waug-oning Bay will be exposed and preserved in its original state, unmarred by commercialization.

In this unselfish planning, the Grand Portage 600 Indians did not forget the tourist who prefers modern comforts and accommodations. Careful zoning has provided locations, outside the wilderness area, for motels, dining rooms, and such other conveniences as shall be needed. Location, design, and decor of all buildings will be handled with painstaking care and in a manner which will detract, as little as possible, from the native charm.

In planning for the Park development, the Grand Portage Council has not overlooked continued conservation of game and fish on the Reservation. These values have acquired added significance as potent attractions to the tourist, the Nature lover, and the photographer.

Conferences with State and Federal officials promise ⇄700 the kind of help and cooperation which can hardly fail to enhance the wildlife resources of the Reservation. Hunting will continue to be regulated by the Grand Portage Grand Council.

This is a big program, and one which has no precedent in the history of the Minnesota Chippewas. It offers the people of Grand Portage the only chance for progress and improvement which has come their way since the days of the fur trade. If offers them, also, an opportunity to prove to the world that the →800 Indian is not only the first but the best conservationist.

STOP — ASK FOR YOUR TIME————

Record time immediately and answer the questions on content.

Time _____ Sec.

No. Errors _____

V-20

RATE (from column 4 of table on page 303):

COMPREHENSION (100 — 50% for each Error):

EFFICIENCY (R × C):

R. _____

C. _____

E. _____

ANSWER THESE QUESTIONS IMMEDIATELY (V-20)

1. (M. C.) Minnesota's Grand Portage Indians are an example of:

    ____(1) A group of people keeping alive the simple principles of conservation practiced by their ancestors.

    ____(2) A tribe who depleted their game resources in order to purchase the luxuries carried to them by the early fur traders.

    ____(3) Reservation dwellers who foolishly opened their hunting areas to white settlers.

    ____(4) A simple people who have gained significance mainly by attracting nature lovers, tourists, and photographers to their area.

2. (T — F) The Grand Portage program offers the Indian opportunities for progress and a chance to prove that he is the best as well as the first conservationist.

SERIES VI
Exploratory Reading Drills

These exercises are designed to measure your ability to read continuously one long article and then to recite on the material at the end. This type of reading will be contrasted with that of the exercise in Series VII where you read in smaller units and do a spaced recitation. Many students argue that they do not have time for the SQ4R method of study or for self-recitation. A comparison of your efficiency scores between these two types of exercises is one of the best objective answers to your own possible hesitancy to try these study techniques.

As in Series V exercises, you will find the length and the readability scores at the top of each article and you will find the numbers in the left hand margin which will help you to estimate your speed. Articles become progressively more difficult as you proceed through the series and here again you are working toward increasing reading speed and reading level. In this case, however, you have more material and more ideas to retain and you will be tested more thoroughly on the material read.

When given the signal to begin an article you should read as rapidly as possible, concentrating on main ideas and watching for any clues to those ideas. When you finish reading, ask for your time immediately and compute your rate in the same manner as in Series V.

Then go on to the ten questions on the material and answer them as accurately as possible. Answer the (M. C.) and the (T — F) questions as instructed before. In the Completion questions (C), you are to fill in the word or words which will best complete the meaning of the sentence. After these are scored according to the key, you compute your comprehension by deducting (from 100) 10 points for each question missed. You may then compute your *efficiency* by multiplying the *rate* by the *comprehension* and record the efficiency score on the graph on page 291. Keys are on pages 312 and 318.

Happy Land of Sky-Blue Waters

BY HENRY BRADSHAW

(Reprinted from the April, 1952, issue of *American Magazine*,
with the permission of the editor)

─────────── **WAIT FOR SIGNAL TO BEGIN READING** ───────────

My fishing rod must be a water wand. I set it in my closet at home in Iowa, and the tip tips. It bends toward the north woods of Minnesota and Wisconsin. There *is* water up there — over 18,500 lakes and a multitude of rivers. Fishing water, swimming water, boating water, and of course that good old stand-by of Wisconsin, Waukesha Water — the famous mineralized drinking fluid guaranteed to cure everything but vacation fever.

But water isn't all we have found there. Cool woods, good highways, grassy airports, sand and rock beaches, sculptured scenery — these, too, are ← 100 added stars in the crown of Minnesota and Wisconsin. It's a northland vacation paradise — a happy land of waters — available to all.

And wherever my wife, Vera, and I have gone — from the Canadian border south to Madison, Minneapolis, and St. Paul; from Alexandria east to Lake Michigan — our vacations have been flavored with the folklore aura of a giant lumberjack, Paul Bunyan, that mythical, humorous hippodrome star who dusted his cap with a strawstack, whose every footstep created a lake, and who is idolized by tourists and woodsy chambers of commerce, alike. This country they told us everywhere we went, was Paul's favorite ← 200 bailiwick.

The Red Lake region

We fell in love with the remote, rustic Red Lake region, with its sincere, intelligent people, and with its bountiful wildlife. In the evenings every clearing carried a promise that we'd spot a deer, far back, nibbling at the short, green grass. We knew right where to find one love-making mallard duck and his sweetie — in a brush-shaded nook in the roadside drainage ditch. On a day when the wind blew gently from the south the red-winged blackbirds, like

aerialists, swayed from their frail perches on golden, 300 → bowing reeds along the banks of the Tamarac River, and in the evening the bullfrogs put on one of the mightiest croaking confabs we'd ever heard.

We toured one day to the Red Lake Indian Reservation, about an hour's drive to the southwest from Waskisk, and were intrigued by the primitive Chippewa village of Ponemah, in the dark, heavy forests. Around Ponemah we discovered older Chippewas who speak no English, hut dwellings with sod foundations, a mystical off-the-road strange ceremonial rite, and we saw the pagan graves.

These graves are above ground: gaily painted wooden boxes, hung with treasures of the spirit 400 → occupant — bells for the dancing braves, rhinestone earings for the proud old woman, beads for the young girl. They lent an air of weirdness and suspense to this spacious area.

A visit to the icebox

Another day we drove 63 miles south from Waskish to the town of Bemidji, nicknamed "the icebox," which claims to be the coldest spot in the nation. Just let winter come, and thermometers nosedive to 50 below. It's an invigorating town, built on both Lake Bemidji and the Mississippi and is the hub of activity for hundreds of hide-away lakes.

500 → There's one thing Vera invariably wants to do when we get to Bemidji, one thing other than whiz through a speedboat ride on the lake. She wants to snap a picture of the red-and-blue statues of Paul Bunyan and his Blue Ox, Babe, who drank a lake dry every day. Not only are these statues of Paul and Babe the largest in the world, they're also among the most photographed.

From Bemidji, we drove southwest to Itasca State Park, where stands the greatest area of virgin Norway pines left in the United States — enormous, towering poles topped at 100 feet with umbrella-shaped greenery. When I looked up at those spires all the ego ⇆ 600 flowed out of my system. It swelled back, though, when I jumped across the Mississippi River. That trick isn't as formidable as it sounds. For here, where the mightiest river in America begins (by flowing north), it is only a miniature stream born from an insignificant bubbling spring. It started, a native told us, when one of Paul Bunyan's water wagons sprung a leak.

At Itasca we were only a skip and a holler from more gateways to resort areas than we could shake a stick at. To the southwest, we went to Detroit ⇆ 700 Lakes, where there's a July water carnival and an August golf tournament; then to Fergus Falls, with 1,000 lakes in its county; Park Rapids, a bubbling inferno of humanity from the time school lets out until it begins again, and with most of the inferno in shorts.

Tame fish

Lakes around all of these towns are famous not only for northern pike and walleyes, like Red Lake, but also for largemouthed bass (the plug smasher) and pan fish — those small varieties that bite ravenously on worms for folks who fish family-style: straight down. Nearly everywhere we went in Minnesota and Wisconsin we found these four types ⇆ 800 leading the league.

From Fergus Falls we wandered southeast for about 50 miles, enjoying the scenery and the busy portable lumber mills that dotted the way to Alexandria, the pulse of another lake region.

From this well-settled locality we drove northeast into eastern Minnesota, to Tame Fish Lake, near Aitkin on the Mississippi. We wheeled up beside a flowery park adjacent to the little lake, which is half wildlife refuge — a park built by the Vogt brothers, retired, from Omaha. From them, Vera bought a couple of frogs, waited while Hugo Vogt jangled a big dinner bell erected on the dock. Then she bravely ⇆ 900 leaned over the water and dangled a frog in her fingers. She jumped like she'd been hit with a rock when Amos, himself — a big black bass — swirled out, snatched the frog, and disappeared with a frightful splash. The next frog, I held. I guess I gripped it too tightly, for when Amos's twin, Andy swooped up to tear away the frog, he almost pulled my arm off. He got the bait, and didn't nick a finger.

From another angle, a whole army of bass that had 1000 → answered the bell became visible, lying below the surface, just waiting for some unbeliever to give 'em an inch on a frog.

Wilderness Airport

From Tame Fish Lake we swung northward, and that night we stayed at Arthur Otis's luxury lodge on Lake Siseebakwet, in a remote woods at the end of a sandy trail a few miles southwest of the Minnesota town of Grand Rapids. It's a unique resort in that Arthur has carved out of the timber a whopping big combination airport and golf course. At dinnertime two planes from Houston dropped in, and another 1100 → from Chicago came up for the night fishing. Fliers have been doing this for years, and they meet each spring at the "Wilderness Airport" for a special breakfast to inaugurate both flying and fishing seasons.

The open pits

Only 32 miles northeast of Otis's lodge the green forests changed to brown rocks; we were driving through the territory of the open-pit iron mines of the Mesabi Range near Lake Superior. We saw the mines all along U. S. 169, as far as Virginia. Especially we got a bang out of the mine in Hibbing, which is 1200 → the largest on this old globe. As I stood at its rim my head reeled, and I thought, "This is as bad as looking down from a thirty-five-story building."

That rusty hole is 370 feet deep, besides being 2½ miles long and ¾ of a mile wide. More dirt came out of it than out of the Panama Canal — no wonder the draglines, locomotives, and trucks in its bowels looked like toys and moved like snails.

From Virginia we headed northeast again, and on the way, Vera (a fiend for road signs) insisted we stop to read a plaque on a big stone. It informed us 1300 → that we were at the peak of the Laurentian Highland Divide, where a split raindrop flows two ways, part traveling north through the Red River to the Arctic, part rolling east via the Great Lakes and the St. Lawrence to the Atlantic. The sign forgot about the 1350 → part that washes to the Gulf with the Mississippi.

———STOP — ASK FOR YOUR TIME———

Record time immediately on next page
and answer the questions on content.

Time _____ Sec.

No. Errors_____

VI- 1

RATE (from table on page 305):

COMPREHENSION (100 — 10% for each Error):

EFFICIENCY (R × C):

R. _____

C. _____

E. _____

ANSWER THESE QUESTIONS IMMEDIATELY (VI-1)

1. (T — F) The water and lakes of Minnesota and Wisconsin are the only things that attracted the Bradshaws.

2. (C) The favorite folklore figure of this region is_____.

3. (M. C.) The most interesting thing the Bradshaws found in the Red Lake Indian Reservation was the:

____(1) Old Indian Chiefs.

____(2) Indian Graves.

____(3) Hand carved Indian jewelry.

____(4) Ceremonial dances.

4. (T — F) Temperatures never drop below zero at Bemidji.

5. (T — F) The much photographed "Paul and Babe" are found in Bemidji.

6. (T — F) In Itasca State Park, Mr. Bradshaw jumped across the Mississippi River.

7. (T — F) The most common fish in the Red Lake area is the brook trout.

8. (T — F) At Tame Fish Lake, the bass took food from the hands of the visitors.

9. (M. C.) Arthur Otis's luxury lodge on Lake Siseebakwet is a:

____(1) Modern country club.

____(2) Remote hunting camp.

____(3) Combination airport and golf course.

____(4) Popular motor-boat race course.

10. (C) The Mesabi Range area is well known for its_____ iron mines, of which the one in Hibbing is the largest in the world.

Number VI-2

Steinmetz: Latter-Day Vulcan

(Reprinted from pamphlet of same name, by permission of the General Electric Company)

——————————— **WAIT FOR SIGNAL TO BEGIN READING** ———————————

When Charles Proteus Steinmetz moved to Schenectady, New York, in January of 1894, he was entering a completely new phase of his life. He was leaving behind him social bitterness, poverty, and relative obscurity. The future would bring its reward for perseverance in the form of fame, accomplishment, and a generous measure of real happiness.

However, it wasn't all a bed of roses. There *were* mishaps along the way, but none so serious that Steinmetz couldn't later tell them as jokes on himself that would leave him and his listener shaking with laughter.

Fire causes temper

For instance, there was the time, soon after his <u>100</u> arrival in Schenectady, that the rented stable in which he had constructed a laboratory burned to the ground. It was definitely Steinmetz' fault. His landlord was enraged. The little scientist didn't improve the owner's temper when he exclaimed that he didn't mind the stable burning — it was the *laboratory equipment in it* that he hated to lose. For some time tempers were strained, but after the General Electric Company made up the joint loss, both Steinmetz and his land-lord came to speaking terms again. Steinmetz later regarded the incident of the fire as a big joke, but he <u>200</u> decided that he'd do best to build his own home and laboratory, then if he had to burn it down in the interests of science, he could!

Steinmetz was appointed head of the calculating department at the Schenectady plant. But office management and routine paper work weren't to his liking. He just wasn't cut out to sit behind a desk and tell other people what to do, and General Electric directors weren't long in finding it out. Little by little, they relieved him of his duties, taking great care that he wouldn't realize any change was being made. <u>300</u> Soon he was able to devote all his time to research, but still under the title "Head of the Calculating Department." He was perfectly happy, and so was the Company, for the department began to run more smoothly. To General Electric engineers, Steinmetz now became known, secretly, as the "Supreme Court."

Mental mathematics

One day a group of engineers found themselves completely stumped by a mathematical problem, so they decided to take their troubles to Steinmetz. If anyone could solve the problem, he could. They confronted him in his laboratory and outlined their <u>400</u> question to him, "Mr. Steinmetz, what is the cubic content of the metal which is removed from a cyl-indrical rod two inches in diameter when a two-inch hole is bored through the rod, separating it into two pieces?"

That *was* a problem! The scientist's brow furrowed as he became lost in deep concentration, then his face brightened, and with a smile, he exclaimed, "Why of course, gentlemen, the answer is 5.33 cubic inches." Needless to say, the engineers were dumbfounded, for Stienmetz had worked the entire problem out in his head!

Potatoes and beefsteak

Work on Steinmetz' home progressed very slowly, <u>500</u> indeed. The laboratory, a separate building on the same property, was soon finished, however, and he moved into it to take up temporary housekeeping there. What started out as a temporary proposition almost became a permanent one, for Steinmetz formed a strong attachment to his new living quarters.

However, he was lonely in his laboratory-home, and consequently invited a young engineer, Joseph LeRoy Hayden, to come live with him. Hayden accepted immediately; any engineer at the plant would have given his right arm for the privilege of living and working with Steinmetz. So, the two took up housekeeping together, eating and sleeping but little, and working long hours with experiments in ⁶⁰⁰ the laboratory.

There's some question as to *how* either Steinmetz or young Hayden survived this joint-housekeeping, for the similarity of meals from day to day was astounding. Steinmetz provided nothing but potatoes and beefsteak, day after day. The potatoes, he explained provided the carbohydrates, steak the proteins, and butter, which he put on steak in generous amounts, the fat — and fat, carbohydrate, and protein were all a man needed to stay alive. Hayden sometimes wondered.

At another time Stienmetz was convinced that the food value of vegetables was directly proportional to their color. Consequently Hayden was forced to ⁷⁰⁰ subsist for a time on a steady diet of bright yellow carrots.

Gaining new honors

As a result of his outstanding research in the electrical field, Charles Steinmetz was elected president of the American Institute of Electrical Engineers in 1901. In 1903, he was further honored by being invited to teach at Union College in Schenectady as professor of electrical engineering. He was also given the degree of Doctor of Philosophy. This meant a great deal to him, for because of his untimely escape from Breslau, he had never received his degree in Germany.

Students in Steinmetz' classes at Union needed ⁸⁰⁰ extreme patience to sit through his hour-long lectures, for the subject was often beyond their powers to comprehend. Steinmetz just didn't realize that nothing short of an Albert Einstein could understand him, even when he spoke in the simplest words he could muster. His thinking was on a level too high for the ordinary man.

But there were lighter moments in class which the sleepier boys would often miss. One day a student asked the Doctor, "Is it true that lightning never strikes twice in the same place?"

"Yes, I may say it is true in a great many instances." ⁹⁰⁰

"But, why is that?" queried the student.

"Because," answered the Doctor with a smile, "there is usually nothing there for lightning to strike a second time."

The doctor becomes a family man

When his new home had been completed, Steinmetz wandered alone about the vacant rooms. It was going to be a lonely place now, he thought. Young Hayden had left not long before to be married, and he and his wife had taken up housekeeping in another part of town. The bachelor scientist couldn't face living in such a large home by himself.

¹⁰⁰⁰ One night the Haydens heard a knock at their door, and, when it was opened, in walked Steinmetz. You can guess what he wanted. Would the Haydens *do him the favor* of coming to live with him in his new house? They certainly would. And there began one of the most charming *family* relationships possible. In fact, to make things complete, Steinmetz made Hayden his legally adopted son.

Connected to the Steinmetz family home was a large glass conservatory, and there Steinmetz pursued his hobbies, raising exotic plants and animals. There were literally hundreds of cacti and desert plants, ¹¹⁰⁰ bristling with prickles and thorns; and there were lizards, crocodiles, two crows, a number of stray cats, a dog, and other creatures in his collection of animals. One characteristic of this assortment of plants and animals is extremely interesting: they were *all* outcasts from society in their own right — things that other people would not or did not want. Steinmetz was their friend.

He did it with lights

The conservatory was very brilliantly lighted with mercury lamps which gave off a ghastly blue glow. And Steinmetz wasn't one to pass up a chance to play a practical joke. Therefore he had a full-length ¹²⁰⁰ mirror installed near the door of the conservatory. Not long afterward his motives became perfectly clear: A beautiful, blond-haired girl came to call on him one day. Like a spider enticing a fly into his web, the elfish Steinmetz invited the girl to come into his conservatory to see something. Quietly, and without explanation, he arranged for her to stand before the mirror. Then he switched on the mercury lights. The girl was very horrified by what she saw reflected in the mirror — the image obviously was her own, ¹³⁰⁰ but she had green skin, and dark purple lips. Whether the girl ever thought the trick was funny is not known, but each time the sly Doctor would tell the story thereafter, he would conclude with the dry comment, "That proves that beauty is only relative." Then he would laugh his croaking laugh until he ¹³⁵⁰ had to gasp for breath.

————STOP — ASK FOR YOUR TIME————

Record time immediately on next page
and answer the questions on content.

Time_____Sec.	RATE (from table on page 305):	R. _____
No. Errors_____	COMPREHENSION (100 — 10% for each error):	C. _____
VI- 2	EFFICIENCY (R × C):	E. _____

ANSWER THESE QUESTIONS IMMEDIATELY (VI-2)

1. (T — F) Steinmetz was a recognized scientist of great repute when he came to Schenectady, New York.

2. (M. C.) Steinmetz and his landlord had a big argument over:

   ____(1) The nature of his research.

   ____(2) His irregular hours.

   ____(3) His starting a serious fire.

   ____(4) His decision to build his own house.

3. (M. C.) Steinmetz often surprised his co-workers by his ability in the field of:

   ____(1) Abstract reasoning.

   ____(2) Mental mathematics.

   ____(3) Facial contortions.

   ____(4) Abnormal psychology.

4. (C) The man Steinmetz asked to share his laboratory work was_____.

5. (T — F) Steinmetz showed a thorough knowledge of nutrition in his selection of food.

6. (T — F) Steinmetz was given an Honorary Ph. D. Degree from Union College in Schenectady.

7. (T — F) Steinmetz usually talked over the heads of the students in his classes.

8. (C) Steinmetz legally acquired a family through the _____ of his laboratory assistant.

9. (T — F) His hobby of collecting plants and animals was characterized by his tendency to take those that were outcasts of society.

10. (T — F) Steinmetz was almost entirely lacking in a sense of humor.

Number VI-3

Let's Go Dutch

By Wayne Amos

(Reprinted from the March, 1953, issue of the *American Magazine*, with the permission of the editor)

───────────── WAIT FOR SIGNAL TO BEGIN READING ─────────────

Do you want a simple formula for discovering hidden wonders in our America? All you have to do is turn off the main highway and drift down any good side road, lazing through the countryside and loafing on the porch of a country store. I've tried this many times and something wonderful always happens, whether you're in California or Colorado or Massachusetts.

Traveling on a Pennsylvania byway

Just recently I was speeding down the 70 miles-per-hour Pennsylvania Turnpike between Philadelphia and Harrisburg, when suddenly I decided I wasn't in such a hurry and had time to apply my 100 favorite travel formula. This time I really hit the jackpot. I discovered the Pennsylvania Dutch country and roamed it for two days.

It's a world apart, drenched with history and tradition and almost as glowing with local color today as it was in the early 18th century when it was settled — mainly by Germans from the Upper Rhineland, but also by immigrants from Holland, Switzerland, Alsace-Lorraine, and Moravia. The local "Pennsylvania Dutch language" developed out of a hodgepodge of dialects and a sprinkling of English. It is still spoken in many sections and is even taught in adult-education classes. 200

This country of rolling hills and woods, rich farms, and wonderful food (which is one of the main attractions) covers the southeastern corner of the state below the Blue Ridge Mountains. The city of Lancaster is in the heart of it. On the eastern edge is George Washington's Valley Forge, symbol of American endurance, and on the western fringe is Gettysburg, where, on the quiet battlefield, you can easily imagine you are hearing Abraham Lincoln beginning his famous address: "Fourscore and seven years ago . . .." Near Gettysburg is the farm home of another president — Dwight D. Eisenhower.

300 In the center are the Welch Mountains, the end of the line for the "underground railway" used by escaping slaves before the Civil War. Near the village of Cornwall you can still see Peter Grubb's cannon foundry, where Washington and Lafayette came to inspect new firearms. These were test-fired into nearby fields, and now and then one of the old cannon balls is still turned up by a farmer's plow. "Hex signs," painted in geometric designs to frighten witches away, still adorn the rich, bulging barns, especially along Route 22 between Allentown and Harrisburg. Hex means witch in Pennsylvania Dutch. 400 No one admits he believes in witches, but the hex signs are there.

The life of the Amish

Most unusual of all the inhabitants of the Pennsylvania Dutch country, and perhaps the least understood, are the Amish farmers who live today much as their forefathers did more than 200 years ago, wearing odd clothes, and coming to town only by horse and buggy.

I sat on a bench in front of a general store in the tiny village of New Holland, a few miles east of Lancaster, and watched them pass by — the men wearing full beards (except for clean-shaven cheeks 500 and upper lips), wide-brimmed black hats, black coats without collars or buttons, tight-fitting black trousers, and high-top shoes, and the women in full black coats. The children were dressed exactly as their elders were.

I talked at length with one of these bearded figures who sat down on the bench and told me all about the Amish, pronouncing it "Ahmish." He was not stern, as I had anticipated, but affable and quite at ease. The Amish renounce all things of vanity, he said, and live "plain." In their homes are no mirrors except small ones for shaving, no curtains, no pictures, because they do not believe in making images for 600 adulation (even children's dolls have no faces), no musical instruments, no radios, no phonographs, no electricity, and few of them use trucks or automobiles.

The only power they permit comes from nature — from the wind or the water. Windmills pump their water, and water wheels — homemade paddle wheels placed in creeks and rivers and turning long rods leading to the house — power their washing machines and churns. Flowers they have in abundance, because these come from God's nature, too. So do the gasoline and oil that light their lamps, and the tobacco which 700 they grow and enjoy smoking in the form of cigars. Their major occupation is farming at which they work from 4 in the morning until after dark at night.

And what do they get in return? Peace and contentment, satisfaction in life. I couldn't help but believe my Amish friend for he was the most contented man I ever saw.

Life with the Mennonites

The Mennonites, who live nearby, are not quite so strict in their dress. They even own and drive automobiles, after carefully painting out all chrome decorations with black paint! But these two sects together make up only about 7 per cent of the Pennsylvania Dutch population. The rest of the people belong to Lutheran, Brethren, Reformed, and other Protestant churches.

Not far from New Holland I saw — as you would expect in this world of horses — a blacksmith shop. The smithy was a big man with long red hair, merry eyes and red chin whiskers. He greeted me pleasantly, and again I sensed that happy feeling toward the world. He was shoeing a horse, and showed me how he trimmed the hoofs, "just as people trim their toe- and finger-nails." Horses have to be reshod 900 every 6 or 7 weeks, he said.

I drove on across the hills, finding the neat countryside delightful. It's fine even in winter, and is more glorious in the spring and summer, when the laurel, rhododendron, and wild azaleas brighten the woods, and the markets in every town burst with produce from these farms which are said to have the richest nonirrigated land in the world. It's typical of Pennsylvania Dutch farmers, townspeople told me, that their apples are polished, not just on the top layer of the basket, but all the way to the bottom.

Having holiday fun

There are laurel festivals every June, and later in 1000

the season you may come upon an apple-butter-boiling party in the yard of a farm home, where you can see the "natives" in Dutch costumes, dancing Dutch dances and singing Dutch songs.

Also in June Gettysburg stages its annual Pennsylvania Dutch celebration with quilting parties in the streets, German bands, butter churning, square dancing, and all the girls in sunbonnets.

At Hershey, Pa., where you breathe a pleasant aroma of chocolate in the air, I was urged to come back in August for the Dutch Days celebration. There 1100 I could see the Pennyslvania Dutch at their games, dances and songfests, performing their handicraft skills in cloth weaving, quilting, and carpet making, and best of all — I could get my fill of real Pennsylvania Dutch cooking.

Several medium-priced hotels, such as the Brunswick in Lancaster, feature Pennyslvania Dutch menus, including favorite dishes like "Sowergabraten" (pickled pot roast with gingersnap gravy) and shoo-fly pie, a delicacy made of molasses and crumbs.

Conducted tours

There is a weekend all-expense bus tour of the Pennsylvania Dutch country operating out of Lancaster from Memorial Day through October 1200 that's lots of fun and very reasonable in price. It begins with dinner in your hotel in Lancaster Friday evening, and ends after dinner there Sunday night. Saturday you tour the countryside, returning to the hotel Saturday night, and Sunday you make another and different tour for a total of some 200 miles.

With a Pennsylvania Dutchman as an escort you stop off to visit such attractions as an Amish farm, where you have "dinner" at noon, an Amish blacksmith shop, the Ephrata Cloister, where you see how ascetics lived in the 18th century, Baron Stiegel's pre-Revolutionary iron foundry and glass works, a Mennonite settlement founded in 1710, and a 1300 modern pretzel factory. Saturday nights a Dutchman explains the local folklore and tells Pennsylvania Dutch stories.

My own visit to this treasury of Americana was just a taster and I'm going back "soon already," as the Dutch would say, for a longer look around and get fattened up on that wonderful Pennsylvania 1350 Dutch cooking.

————STOP — ASK FOR YOUR TIME————

Record time immediately on next page
and answer the questions on content.

Time _____ Sec.	RATE (from table on page 305):	R. _____
No. Errors _____	COMPREHENSION (100 — 10% for each Error):	C. _____
VI- 3	EFFICIENCY (R × C):	E. _____

ANSWER THESE QUESTIONS IMMEDIATELY (VI-3)

1. (C) The Pennsylvania Dutch country was settled mainly by_____.

2. (T — F) The local "language" can be traced directly to its European origin.

3. (T — F) There is evidence that the people still believe in witches.

4. (T — F) The people who proved most interesting to this writer were the Amish farmers.

5. (M. C.) Which of the following would you find in an Amish home:

    ____(1) Flowers.

    ____(2) Curtains.

    ____(3) Pictures.

    ____(4) Musical instruments.

6. (T — F) The only power the Amish permit must come directly from nature.

7. (T — F) The Mennonites are more strict in their dress than the Amish.

8. (T — F) The majority of the residents in this area are either Amish or Mennonites.

9. (C) The city of _____ seems to be the center of this Pennsylvania Dutch section as it is mentioned most frequently in the article.

10. (M. C.) One of the main attractions which the author mentioned several times was the:

    ____(1) Many celebrations and festivals.

    ____(2) Amish farmers.

    ____(3) Pennsylvania Dutch cooking.

    ____(4) Many historical spots.

Number VI-4

Sand-Painting Doctor

By Phyllis J. Boyd

(Reprinted from the July, 1953, issue of *Family Circle*, by permission of the editor)

——————— WAIT FOR SIGNAL TO BEGIN READING ———————

"Beware! Mother-in-law approaching. All sons-in-law hit the dirt!"

If you could imagine a radio transmitter operating on a Navaho Indian reservation, you might well hear this message come through to any married man of the tribe. But the Navahos don't need a transmitter, for all the women carry their own walkie-talkies — little silver bells attached to their dresses. And they ring the bells in plenty of time for the men of the tribe to get out of the way.

There's good reason for this precaution, for if a Navaho man sees or speaks to his wife's mother, he's breaking one of the many taboos of his people 100 and is in danger of visits from evil spirits. If he fails to heed his mother-in-law's warning, he will surely become ill. Then there's only one thing for him to do. He must consult a medicine man, who arranges an elaborate ceremony, or "sing," of prayer and chanting and painting with sand.

What may seem like a lot of hocus-pocus to the modern white man with his specialists and well equipped hospitals is one of the most sacred religious ceremonies of the Navaho people, for illness means only one thing to them: A taboo has been broken and 200 the spirits are angry. The offender may have eaten fish, or an animal living in water, or he may have played the old string game of cat's cradle during the summer months when spiders are not at rest. Nor is whistling after dark recommended; and you're asking for trouble if you kill an eagle, or walk where a bear or mountain lion has walked. There are no such words as "germ" or "bacteria" in the Navaho language.

When a Navaho becomes ill, he goes to see a medicine man (diagnostician). It is this specialist's job to discover the identity of the spirits causing 300 the trouble. This can be done in many ways — by reading the stars, by listening to the wind, or by "trembling hands." (The medicine man holds his hands outspread before him and thinks of all the yeis (deities) who may be angry. When he arrives at the right one, his hands will begin to tremble.)

Being one of the shrewdest men of the tribe, the medicine man keeps a mental black book of all the gossip in the village. He knows where villagers have 400 been, and when, and what they did, so he can often make a fairly accurate guess about the patient's trouble.

The cure begins as soon as the cause of the illness has been discovered. Although the sing is a solemn religious occasion, it is also a festive one for attendant friends and relatives, who gather for it dressed in their finest. Sometimes these visitors travel many miles across the rugged terrain of the reservation. The sing is a sort of open house, with the patient footing the food bill for everyone who attends. No one goes away hungry, but the patient himself fasts during the sing.

500 In the midst of the hustle and bustle of assembled well-wishers, a respectful quiet descends suddenly. Like a surgeon entering the bench, the singer, or sand painter, followed by his staff of apprentices, approaches the hogan (dwelling) of the one who is ill. The singer is no sleight-of-hand magician or fraud but a highly trained and amazingly skillful artist. He has years of apprenticeship behind him, a mastery of his ancient and honored profession in his mind and fingers, and a thorough understanding of human nature. He holds a place of reverence and dignity 600 unequaled in the tribe, and he is also respected by many white men. He is often consulted by white doctors and nurses who work on the Navaho reservation.

The medicine man brings with him his sacred pouch of tools which include rattles to frighten away evil, the prayer stick that is tied in the patient's hair, pouches of precious stones, dust gathered from a sacred place and offered to the gods as a sacrifice during the ceremony, pollen dust (usually from corn) used to purify the hogan and the patient, the medicine cup made of tortoise shell, earthenware, or gourd, special herbs that are mixed with water, then [700] tasted by the patient and rubbed on his body, and paints that are ground to fine powders by the apprentices under the singer's direction.

Eager helpers carry in a blanket filled with fresh clean drift sand that has been gathered from a wind-swept spot — never from the bottom of a waterway. At one point in their history the Navahos had flood trouble with the river-gods, so the Indians take no chances of angering the water people who live in rivers or lakes or the bottoms of arroyos.

With a skilled bedside manner the singer may engage in small talk with the patient or with family and [800] friends present in the hogan; but when the sing begins, the joking and chatting stop as the sand painter begins his chants and prayers to summon the spirts. Sometimes in a natural but low voice, sometimes in a shrill falsetto, the singer tells the legend of the sand painting and entreats the gods to cure the sufferer, while the patient sits quietly on a buckskin robe facing the east.

Artist-doctor at work

Spilling out his colors on bark palettes, the singer prepares to weave the intricate sand pattern that will "heal". He uses white from gypsum to signify the [900] east, or dawn; blue from charcoal and gypsum for the south, or sky; yellow ground from yellow ocher to picture the west, or twilight; black from charcoal of burned scrub oak (or from dry cedar mixed with sand or dirt) to represent the north, or darkness; and from pulverized sandstone, red — the color of the people of the night.

The sand painter then begins the art that has been passed down from generation to generation since the original five paintings were made by the gods themselves. With a steadiness that almost hypnotizes onlookers he allows the colored grains of sand to [1000] flow between his thumb and forefinger, creating symmetrical patterns and designs as perfect as any draftsman ever drew with precision instruments.

The yeis, with their elongated bodies and distinctive decorations, gradually materialize.

If the thunder-gods have struck the patient with lightning, the doctor begins by painting the dark circle of the universe; then, moving always from the east as the sun moves through the heavens, he adds the rainbows, and the white east bar, the blue south bar, the yellow west bar, and the black north bar. [1100] At each of these points of the compass he paints the female lightning gods, the thunderbirds — women with long bodies, rectangular heads, and outspread wings.

Chanting the ritual word for word as his ancestors did, the singer may work for hours on a single painting, which may be as large as 15 feet in diameter. When the painting is finally completed and pollen has been carefully scattered over it, the patient, with reassurance shining in his eyes, is seated on the design.

The painting is then carefully gathered up in blankets and taken out to be buried or thrown to the [1200] winds. This must be done before sundown, for the sand paintings tell the story of the Navahos and must not be left so that the evil people of the night may learn anything about them. If the sing is a long one like the yei-be-chai ("grandfather of the world," sometimes used to cure deafness), which lasts for nine days and nights, a new sand painting is begun each day.

Is the patient cured?

You may be thinking, "Well, this is all very fine — skill, art, and so on — but they don't actually cure anyone, do they?"

Clay Lockett, an authority and lecturer on Indian [1300] customs who has traded with the Navahos for many years to secure goods for his Indian arts-and-crafts shop in Tucson, Arizona, answered the question of sand-painting doctors' effectiveness by saying, "Yes, there must be hundreds of cases that have been cured. Whatever else the sings may be, they are good psy-[1350] chosomatic medicine.

————STOP — ASK FOR YOUR TIME————

Record time immediately on next page and answer the questions on content.

Sand Painting Doctor—continued

Time _____ Sec.

No. Errors _____

VI-4

RATE (from table on page 305):

COMPREHENSION (100 — 10% for each Error):

EFFICIENCY (R × C):

R. _____

C. _____

E. _____

ANSWER THESE QUESTIONS IMMEDIATELY (VI-4)

1. (T — F) If a Navaho man fails to heed his mother-in-law's warning, he will be punished by the council.

2. (T — F) To the Navaho people illness means the spirits are angry.

3. (C) When a Navaho becomes ill, he must go to see a _____.

4. (M. C.) Which of the following was not one of the ways mentioned to discover the identity of the spirits causing the trouble.

    ____(1) Trembling hands.

    ____(2) Going into a trance.

    ____(3) Reading the stars.

    ____(4) Listening to the wind.

5. (T — F) The patient must foot the food bill for the sing though he himself fasts.

6. (T — F) The singer must be a sort of magician.

7. (T — F) White doctors and nurses working on the reservation scoff at the singer.

8. (T — F) Clean drift sand gathered from a wind-swept spot is used in the ceremony.

9. (C) When the painting is completed and pollen scattered over it, the _____ is seated on the design.

10. (M. C.) The painting is then gathered up and thrown to the winds, for the Navahos do not want

    ____(1) The grandfather of the world

    ____(2) The night people

    ____(3) The enemy

    ____(4) Strangers

    to learn anything about them.

177

Number VI-5

Who Is to Blame for Juvenile Delinquency?

BY J. EDGAR HOOVER

(Reprinted from the January, 1954, issue of *Scouting*, with the permission of the publishers)

──────────────── WAIT FOR SIGNAL TO BEGIN READING ────────────────

Juvenile delinquency in America has grown to alarming proportions in comparison with the adult crime rate. Only last year 8% of all those arrested had not reached 18 while 13% were under 21.

Of no small concern is the magnitude of the offenses of the juvenile offenders. The crimes of youth have been by no means petty. Witness the fact that while 8% of all persons arrested were 17 years of age or less, this group accounted for 19% of the arrests for robbery, 37% of the arrests for larceny, 48% of the arrests for burglary and 53% of all auto theft arrests. 100

Not a joke

These are not the offenses of the pranksters or practical jokers; not the offenses of an occasional pilfering of an apple or orange from the neighborhood fruit store. The crimes of youth indicate an aping of not only the dereliction of the hardened criminal but also the viciousness and seriousness of his nefarious deeds.

The lamentable record of juvenile delinquents in the past is reflected today in the increasing crime rate among adults. This is only a logical aftermath, for today's criminal was yesterday's delinquent. As you sow, so shall you reap. The full meaning of 200 these Biblical words is exemplified in the case of Kenneth Allen Kitts who was recently apprehended by the FBI as a notorious bank robber and burglar. Kitts first came into the custody of prison authorities in July, 1929, when he was placed in the South Dakota Training School for Boys as an "unmanageable and incorrigible" youth.

At the time he was placed in this institution, Kitts was 12 years old. By the time he was 18 he had made two attempted escapes from this school. On being released, he set out on a series of burglaries and auto- 300 mobile thefts. Intermittent penitentiary sentences followed; his periods of freedom were devoted to more serious crimes. He soon began to hold up banks.

It was then that the FBI sought the apprehension of Kitts.

Need for action

The picture of juvenile crime is not a pleasant one. No doubt all of you reading this article have had your attention called to the juvenile problem on many occasions. The important question, however, is whether you did anything or are doing anything to alleviate this deplorable condition. Only when every civic-minded adult begins to take action will 400 the nation's crime rate among these delinquents decrease. All too often the youth of our nation have been pawns in the "buck-passing" tactics of those adult citizens who shirk their responsibilities to the country's youth.

What is needed to combat the rising tide of delinquency is a positive program of action by those responsible citizens who want to be a part of the crusade for youth; a crusade dedicated to molding youth into respectable God-fearing adult citizens. Any such program must have as its foundation the home, school, church, civic and social agencies, law enforcement authorities and recreational facilities.

500 During my 29 years as Director of the Federal Bureau of Investigations, I have found the basic cause of the high rate of juvenile crime to be a lack of moral responsibility among youth. A youth trained in moral responsibility recognizes his duties to god, his country, and his fellow man. He learns that the natural and moral law is the basis for a peaceful and well-ordered society. He develops respect for the laws.

Home

Instilling moral responsibility in a youth must begin at home. It is the parent who is the child's first teacher. The parent must teach the child the lessons of moral responsibility. He must be taught that ₆₀₀ ⟵ his desires should be guided by the laws of God and the laws of society. He must realize that many times his desires must be subjugated to the common good. It is the "selfish I" that has been the downfall of our youth. Failure to respect the rights of others — both personal and property rights — has led to notorious crimes. The commission by juveniles of over 50% of the auto thefts in 1952 shows a total disregard of the property rights of others. It shows a selfish desire, satiated only by stealing.

In all too many cases the parents have utterly ₇₀₀ ⟵ failed to carry out their responsibilities. They have failed by neglect, bad example, excessive drinking, quarreling and bickering in front of the children. It is little wonder that a child raised in such an environment loses all respect for law and decency. The natural result is too often a serious emotional disturbance in the child reflecting itself in delinquent behavior. The parent who does not take a sincere interest in his child's welfare is surely nudging him into the road leading to delinquency.

Church

The church has a dual purpose to perform in fighting delinquency. It must supplement the train- ₈₀₀ ⟵ ing of the youth who is receiving proper parental guidance. In addition, it may be the only source of guidance for the youth who is the victim of neglectful parents. Religious training teaches a child his primary duty in life, namely, obedience to the moral and natural law of God. The teachings are found in the Ten Commandments, familiar to children who receive religious training. No crime of burglary or larceny could be committed by a child who practices the Lord's command, "Thou shalt not steal."

Religious training also points out the home as a source of inspiration for the youth to honor his ⟵ father and mother. Great is the crime of the parents ₉₀₀ whose conduct prevents a child from honoring them.

The files of the FBI show that many delinquents have had no religious training whatsoever. They have never learned the value of prayer to solicit Divine help. In time of temptation they succumb, for they have never learned to rely upon God and to obey his teachings.

Boy Scouts

The Boy Scouts of America have been a leader in combating juvenile delinquency. It has translated a ₁₀₀₀ ⟶ boy's idle time into constructive channels. Boy Scouts cannot but be model citizens as they follow the ideals of the Scout Oath, to be good citizens, good men, and to fulfill their duty to God and their country. The Boy Scouts of America are taught respect for the laws of God and our country. They are taught devotion to their fellowmen.

Only recently I was present when the President of the United States awarded to a Boy Scout the Young American Medal for Bravery, a medal given annually by our government to youth selected for deserving acts of bravery. This Boy Scout rescued two brothers ₁₁₀₀ ⟶ from their burning home, then re-entered the house endeavoring to save others.

Many FBI Agents were members of the Boy Scouts of America. The ingrained ideals of love of God and country which they learned from their Boy Scout training are reflected in their work as Special Agents of the FBI. I am proud to be a member-at-large of the National Council of the Boy Scouts of America.

Youngsters learn the practical lessons of life in properly directed group activities. They are taught the value of team play, of cooperation, of clean living. They are taught to accept defeat in the spirit ₁₂₀₀ ⟶ of true sportsmanship. They learn that training and hard work are the secret of success in life as well as in play.

There is a job for all of us. Are our responsible citizens taking an adequate interest in juvenile activities? Are the parents of American youth raising their own children to be model American citizens? Are they aiding other boys to be just what they want their own children to be? Are the leaders of civic and social agencies making every effort to do good for all the youth of their communities? Have the ₁₃₀₀ ⟶ leaders of recreational activities a planned program for children of the community? Is there a community of interest in this community problem?

It is only when all Americans answer the challenge of delinquency that our nation will see a spiritual and moral resurgence among our youth, a resurgence ₁₃₅₀ ⟶ that will bring untold blessings for the future.

———STOP — ASK FOR YOUR TIME———

Record time immediately on next page and answer the questions on content.

Time _____ Sec.	RATE (from table on page 305):	R. _____
No. Errors _____	COMPREHENSION (100 — 10% for each Error):	C. _____
VI-5	EFFICIENCY (R × C):	E. _____

ANSWER THESE QUESTIONS IMMEDIATELY (VI-5)

1. (T — F)   Youths under 18 accounted for less than half of all auto theft arrests.

2. (C)   The author stresses the fact that today's criminal was yesterday's _____.

3. (M. C.)   The author has found the basic cause of the high rate of juvenile crime to be a:

   ____(1)   Disobedience of the natural laws of God.

   ____(2)   Lack of moral responsibility.

   ____(3)   Disregard for society's laws.

   ____(4)   Lack of religious training.

4. (M. C.)   The author stresses that we can expect a decrease in the crime rate among delinquents only when action is taken by:

   ____(1)   Every civic-minded adult.

   ____(2)   Churches.

   ____(3)   The FBI.

   ____(4)   Youth organizations.

5. (T — F)   Selfishness, uncorrected in the home, has been the downfall of our youth.

6. (T — F)   According to this author, a child's primary duty in life is to obey the natural and moral laws of God.

7. (T — F)   Many delinquents have had no religious training.

8. (T — F)   The author of this article stresses the value of his own boyhood experience as a Boy Scout.

9. (T — F)   The author believes that leaders of civic and social agencies are making every effort to do good for all the youth of their communities.

10. (C)   The name of the man who wrote this article is _____.

Number VI-6

Western National Parks

BY HORACE SUTTON

(Reprinted from the July, 1953, issue of *The Elks Magazine*, with the permission of the editor)

─── WAIT FOR SIGNAL TO BEGIN READING ───

For those who are searching for a space that is wide and open after spending a winter being confined, the Western parks offer nature in broad tracts virtually untamed and unspoiled. The southern circuit, in the first place, has Grand Canyon, a tremendous split in the earth's physiognomy that is 217 miles long, anywhere from 4 to 18 miles wide, and a mile deep. All this can be found in the northeast corner of Arizona.

Grand Canyon

Only 105 miles of the chasm are within the limits of the National Park, but still, that should give you plenty to look at. At Yavapai Point on the south $\overset{100}{\leftarrow}$ rim, it is ten miles across the ditch, and geologists from the National Park Service give daily lectures here about the wonders of nature. Among the wonders is the Colorado River which buzzes along through the canyon floor at anywhere from 2½ to 20 miles an hour chewing away a million tons of sand every day. This has been going on longer than I can quite comprehend, and it just shows you what persistence can accomplish.

For those who stand on the rim and look down, the Canyon is always changing. As the sun shifts the $\overset{200}{\leftarrow}$ vermilion shades become russet, the cerise becomes bronze, maroon blends into copper, the orange becomes tarnished, the white turns ashen gray. Those who view these proceedings from the south rim can make their headquarters at El Tovar Hotel. Paved footpaths run out from here and the morning drives of the motor coaches stop at Powell, Hopi, Mohave, Pima, and come to a halt at Hermit's Rest. An afternoon drive travels east through the Kaibab National Forest, skimming the Canyon's rim with stops at Yavapai, Yaki, Moran, and Lipan, terminating at the Indian Watchtower, which offers one of the finest $\overset{300}{\leftarrow}$ views of the Canyon, the Kaibab Forest, and the Navajo Indian country as well.

El Tovar Hotel, the Bright Angel Lodge and Grand Canyon Cabin Camp offer fine food and reasonable accommodations. The buses are operated by Fred Harvey, who also maintains a string of mules. The mules are for those who are less engaged by a long distance view than a close-up inspection. The penalty for this curiosity comes in the form of mule-back journeys into the Canyon itself. Guides lead the curious from the south rim down Bright Angel $\overset{400}{\rightarrow}$ Trail stopping at Indian Gardens and ending on the rocky banks of the Colorado exactly one mile below the rim. After lunch by the river, an afternoon's climb lands you back on the rim before dinner. Twenty thousand people make the trip every year. For those who would commune even closer to rock bottom, there is a two-day Phantom Ranch trip. The ranch, on the floor of the Canyon, has rustic cabins and even a swimming pool.

The numerous package tours of the Santa Fe Railroad ranging from two weeks to a month and priced from $200 up, cover not only the usual tourist $\overset{500}{\rightarrow}$ attractions of the western U. S., but also extend into Canada and Mexico. All 31 of the tours include stops at Grand Canyon.

Zion and Bryce

Travelers doing Grand Canyon can easily tie in visits to the Utah parks — Bryce Canyon and Zion. At Zion, the Virgin River is busy washing away a canyon from the Navajo sandstone beds. The Mount Carmel Tunnel at Zion has six windows cut out of the rock, giving magnificient views of the Canyon 1,000 feet below. Once out of the tunnel, the highway takes sightseers on a twisting trail to the $\overset{600}{\rightarrow}$ Canyon floor, a feat which took the river a million years to accomplish. There are trips to the floor by horseback too.

Bryce Canyon is something else again, possibly because it is not really a canyon at all but a sort of natural amphitheater formed out of the pink and white limestone. It is two miles wide, three miles long and 1,000 feet deep.

A variety of all-expense escorted tours are conducted through the southern Utah-Arizona parks by the Union Pacific Railroad. Figuring from Cedar City, Utah, and including all meals and lodging, there is a five-day Zion, Bryce and Grand Canyon trip for $78 and another over the same route with a shorter 700⤦ schedule for $71.75. Three days at Zion comes to $46 and two days of Zion and Grand Canyon is $40.75. There are convenient trains to Cedar City from Chicago and St. Louis and also from Los Angeles.

The Chicago Northwestern and Union Pacific tie up with a package tour of the Utah-Arizona National Parks covering all three from Chicago in twelve days for $238.50 in coaches, or about $50 more in sleeping cars. Another tour takes in the above areas and also Yellowstone, leaving Chicago every Sunday.

Yellowstone

Yellowstone was the great unbelievable phenome- 800⤦ non when it was first explored. New Englanders, who seem to have been more skeptical than most, simply refused to believe the existence of geysers bursting into the sky every few hours. Today, a million visitors come to see the wonders of Yellowstone. It is the largest and oldest of the national parks, comprising 3,500 square miles on which the black bear, the grizzly, the deer, the moose, the beaver, the antelope and the buffalo roam. The Giant geyser sends a jet of steam 240 feet in the air, which is 100 feet higher than Old Faithful.

The hotels at Yellowstone include Mammoth 900⤦ Springs, a full-fledged resort enterprise including cottages; Old Faithful Inn, a luxurious log cabin lodge with the geysers performing all but in the front yard; the Canyon Hotel near the rim of the canyon, and celebrated for its tremendous "lounge," one of the largest hotel rooms in captivity. There is a standard two-and-a-half-day hotel tour of Yellowstone pegged at $46.75, which includes all meals and lodging and transportation, but is based on two persons in a double room without bath.

The Northern Pacific Railway runs several "Yellowstone Vacation" tours, among them a four-day trip 1000⤦ based on a cost of $69.50, which begins at Gardiner, northern entrance to the Park area.

Glacier

Yellowstone occupies the northwest corner of the state of Wyoming but for those who are looking for lands even more northern, there are the Northern Rockies which form the Glacier National Park in the top of Montana. These mountains rise in an abrupt wall straight out of the Montana plain and appear higher than their average of about 10,000 feet. The range is covered by dense forests, glacial valleys and mountain meadows tossing with wildflowers all summer long. There are some sixty silver glacier 1100⤦ caps, 200 lakes, and cascades and waterfalls on which there is no census. If it's warm around your block, come to Iceberg Lake where small but cold bergs float on the surface in the middle of the summer.

There is no problem about where to rest one's head between sightseeing excursions. The Glacier Park Hotel commands the east entrance, Many Glacier sits on the edge of Swiftcurrent Lake, and the Lake McDonald Hotel rests by the shores of the largest lake on the west side of the park. Hotels are on the American plan, starting at $9.25 per day. There 1200⤦ also is lodging to be had at Alpine chalets at Granite Park and Sperry Glacier and at a number of camps with grocery stores nearby.

Glacier is the only national park on the main line of a transcontinental railway and is in easy reach from Chicago, St. Paul, or California and the west via Portland or Seattle. The Western Star, a Great Northern streamliner, stops at both the east and west entrances of the park every day during the summer season which on the railroad calendar runs from June 15 to September 10.

1300⤦ A good part of the Glacier Park area was bought from the Blackfeet Indians whose reservation adjoins the premises. The tribe sends a delegation to pitch a summer encampment near the Glacier Park Hotel and presents pow-wows each night. They wear beaded white buckskin, war bonnets of tossing eagle feathers and other raiment representative of the well-dressed 1350⤦ Indian.

————STOP — ASK FOR YOUR TIME————

Record time immediately on next page
and answer the questions on content.

Time _____ Sec.   RATE (from table on page 305):   R. _____

No. Errors _____   COMPREHENSION (100 − 10% for each error):   C. _____

VI-6   EFFICIENCY (R × C):   E. _____

ANSWER THESE QUESTIONS IMMEDIATELY (VI-6)

1. (T — F)   It is possible to motor down to the banks of the Colorado River in Grand Canyon Park.

2. (T — F)   It is possible to motor down to the banks of the Virgin River in Zion Park.

3. (C)   Bryce Canyon is sort of a natural_____.

4. (M. C.)   The largest and oldest of the national parks is:

     ____(1)   Yellowstone.

     ____(2)   Grand Canyon.

     ____(3)   Bryce Canyon.

     ____(4)   Zion.

5. (T — F)   Old Faithful is the highest geyser in Yellowstone Park.

6. (T — F)   One of the largest hotel rooms may be found in the Canyon Hotel in Zion.

7. (T — F)   Hotels in Glacier Park operate on the American Plan rather than on a fixed fee for the whole trip.

8. (T — F)   Glacier is the only national park on the main line of a transcontinental railway.

9. (C)   A good part of the _____ Park area was bought from the Blackfeet Indians.

10. (M. C.)   Which of the following was not mentioned as an attraction in Yellowstone Park:

     ____(1)   Spacious hotels and lodges.

     ____(2)   Beaver and other wild life.

     ____(3)   Indian pow-wows each night.

     ____(4)   Geysers of great beauty.

Number VI-7

Edison and Electricity

(Reprinted from pamphlet of same name, by permission of the General Electric Company)

─────── WAIT FOR SIGNAL TO BEGIN READING ───────

New Year's Eve in Menlo Park

It was New Year's Eve, 1879. A strange air of expectancy and exitement gripped the New Jersey village of Menlo Park. Nearly 3000 persons restlessly milled about the streets, and crowded close to the piazza of Mr. Edison's laboratory. Some had driven as far as 20 miles in carriages and wagons, but most had come by special trains run by the Pennsylvania Railroad for the occasion. They were there to witness the first public demonstration of Edison's wonderful new light.

As the early winter twilight deepened into darkness, the murmur of the throng was hushed in anticipation. 100 Inside the laboratory, a deft stroke of a finger made 60 lamps, placed on poles up and down the snow-covered street, spring to light among the bare branches of the trees. A ripple of involuntary applause ran through the audience. One old farmer was heard to remark, "We-ell sir, it's a pretty fair sight, but danged if I kin see how ye git the red-hot hairpin in the bottle!"

In the days and weeks that followed, Menlo Park became a kind of Mecca for the intelligently interested and the merely curious. Farm folk and city folk, scientists and businessmen, came nightly in 200 ever increasing numbers to see the "Edison lights."

An indifferent public

But widespread public acceptance of incandescent illumination was extremely slow — or so it seemed to the Edison group. For some time Menlo Park was the only place in the world where a complete incandescent system was on display. Relatively few, therefore, were able to see it in operation. Even the most glowing newspaper description could not arouse a general public interest in the new lighting.

Then too, there was opposition from gas and arc-light companies. As it became apparent that the new lamp threatened to displace the older illuminants 300

this opposition increased. On at least two occasions attempts were made to discredit the new system while it was being demonstrated before municipal officials. A member of one such visiting party managed to short-circuit a part of the system at Menlo by means of a piece of wire running up a sleeve, over his shoulder, and down the other sleeve. Special watchers, appointed by Edison, caught the erstwhile saboteur in the act. When the fact leaked out that the man had an interest in a gas company, public sentiment in 400 favor of the electric light was greatly enhanced.

Among the city officials who made the pilgrimage to Menlo Park was a delegation representing New York's Board of Aldermen. The outcome of their visit was an agreement by which Edison was to install a trial lighting system in an area on lower Manhattan — an area soon to become famous as Edison's "First District." The Edison Illuminating Company of New York was formed to do this job. The Wizard was now committed to making an historic step; his dream of "great cities alight from central stations" was coming ever closer to reality.

The task begins

Putting the project on a profitable commercial 500 footing proved to be a Herculean task — a far greater undertaking than the impatient New Yorkers realized. Plans for the installation were complete in essential detail, but devices had to be invented, developed, and built as the need for them arose. Necessity was the mother of these inventions — and Edison was the father.

Of necessity, Edison became a manufacturer. "There was nothing we could buy," he related, "or that anyone could make for us." So new companies were formed by Edison men to supply the new devices.

Since the Illuminating Company was reluctant to 600 manufacture them, Edison formed a lamp company and began producing lamps in one of his old Menlo Park buildings. Although the first lamps cost about $1.25 to make, Edison offered to supply all the lamps required by the Illuminating Company at 40c *apiece!* He was sure that he could produce them at a profit by effecting economies in production methods and by mass production.

The lamp factory was moved to larger quarters in Harrison, New Jersey, in 1880, when about 30,000 lamps were produced, at a cost of nearly $1.10 each. As production rose in the next few years, costs went 700 down. "The fourth year, I got the cost down to 37c," related the inventor, "and with a 3c profit per lamp, made up in one year all the money I'd lost previously. I finally got it down to 22c, sold them for 40c, and they were made by the millions. Whereupon the Illuminating Company thought it a very lucrative business and bought us out," he recalled.

Jumbo and the Mary Ann

One of Edison's greatest triumphs in dealing with electrification of the First District, was his development of a suitable generator. The project required electric current in undreamed of quantities. Existing 800 generators were far too small and inefficient.

The Wizard began by studing the design of dynamos then in use. Then he proceeded to fashion one unlike any of the others. It had two huge parallel magnets which made it resemble the Roman numeral II, and earned it the nickname *Long-Waisted Mary Ann.* Though the design violated accepted principles, it worked. What's more, it was nearly 90 per cent efficient.

The famous Jumbo dynamo was developed and exhibited at the Paris Electrical Exposition in 1881. The bipolar Mary Ann design was coupled with a huge 150-horsepower steam engine. Where previous 900 generators had been driven by complicated belting and shafting, the Jumbo's engine was linked directly to the dynamo. Its size alone caused people to gape. It weighed 27 tons and was capable of lighting 1200 incandescent lamps.

No one knew what to expect when the Jumbo was first tested one winter's night at Menlo Park. Heretofore the speed of stationary engines was rarely more than 60 revolutions per minute, but this machine was designed to turn up 700 rpm, and at a much higher steam pressure than most engines.

The shop in which the machine was set up stood on top of a shale hill. Edison amusingly recalled that 1000

at 300 revolutions "the whole hill shook under her," and at 700 rpm "you should have seen her run! Why, every time the connecting rod went up, she tried to lift the whole hill with her!"

After this harrowing experience, the Jumbos were not run at more than 250 rpm, which was really all that Edison had wanted anyway.

"65" becomes a mecca

Early in 1881, the Edison Electric Light Company leased an ornate brownstone mansion at 65 Fifth Avenue, New York, for an office. The house was an 1100 ideal place for showing off the lights in everyday operation, and also provided a headquarters from which Edison could closely supervise the many activities connected with the First District lighting installation.

For the next four years, "65" was a beehive of activity, day and night. Every day after dark, thousands of visitors came to see, to ask questions, and to marvel.

As they had at Menlo, Edison and his men worked with utter disregard of time. But all who worked at "65" remarked about the wonderful spirit of comradeship which existed there. They were all 1200 pioneers together, working for a common cause, all enthusiastic believers in the electric light. Edison himself was never closer to his men than during this period of their work together.

The year 1881 was one of tremendous strain and back-breaking toil for Edison. The host of new and important business interests had to be tended, and the First District installation demanded much of his time. Somehow he managed to keep up his research, taking out about 89 patents that year. In addition, he built experimentally the world's first fullsize electric railway at Menlo.

Success

By the end of the following year, the First District 1300 had become a profitable success. Edison had achieved his goal. He had subdivided electric current when others said it couldn't be done. He had invented a practical incandescent lamp where hundreds had failed and had made an efficient dynamo. He had planned, built and operated a complete electrical 1350 system powered from a central station.

————STOP — ASK FOR YOUR TIME————

Record time immediately on next page
and answer the questions on content.

Time _____ Sec.   RATE (from table on page 305):   R. _____

No. Errors _____   COMPREHENSION (100 — 10% for each Error):   C. _____

VI-7   EFFICIENCY (R × C):   E. _____

ANSWER THESE QUESTIONS IMMEDIATELY (VI-7)

1. (C) The occasion of all the excitement on New Year's Eve, 1879, at Menlo Park was the first public demonstration of Edison's new_____.

2. (T — F) The public accepted this new method of illumination very rapidly.

3. (C) Attempts to sabotage some of Edison's demonstrations were made by representatives of the _____ companies.

4. (T — F) The first installation of electric lights made necessary the invention of many additional control devices.

5. (T — F) Edison manufactured his first lamps at a great financial loss.

6. (M. C.) Edison did not develop a profit margin on the sale of his lamps until:

   ____(1)   the 2nd year of manufacture.

   ____(2)   the 4th year of manufacture.

   ____(3)   the 6th year of manufacture.

   ____(4)   the 10th year of manufacture.

7. (M. C.) The Jumbo dynamo was designed to operate at how many revolutions per minute?

   ____(1)   60

   ____(2)   350

   ____(3)   700

   ____(4)   1000

8. (T — F) The mansion at 65 Fifth Avenue was purchased as a home for Mr. Edison and his family.

9. (T — F) Edison was a rather autocratic supervisor and never got to know any of his men very well.

10. (T — F) By the end of 1882, Edison had achieved his goal of subdividing electric current.

Let's Go to the Finger Lakes

BY MARY ABBIE STURGEON

(Reprinted from the August, 1952, issue of *Family Circle*, by permission of the editor)

──────────── WAIT FOR SIGNAL TO BEGIN READING ────────────

Like slender turquoise stones the Finger Lakes are set side by side in the north-south valleys of central New York State. This is a land of great beauty all year round, especially in autumn when the hills, rising from the long lakes, are aflame with scarlet and yellow, when the air is crisp, loons and grebe are on the wing, and there is the pungent smell of harvest-ripe grapes and apples. A mystic quality pervades this unspoiled region, almost as if the moccasined feet of Red Jacket and Cornplanter still followed the trails that wind by lake shores and waterfalls, through forests and glens. 100

The Seneca Indians explained the Finger Lakes as ridges in the back of a gigantic turtle that had reared up out of the sea to form the earth. Later, white settlers said they were the imprint of the Creator's fingers when He laid his Hand in benediction on what was to be New York State. This legend is a popular one, but the fingers are not limited to five. There are at least 10 taperlike lakes in the area, the seven major ones (east to west) being Otisco, Skaneateles, Owasco, Cayuga, Seneca, Keuka, and Canandaigua. The 200 smaller lakes — Cayuta, Lamoka, and Waneta — are tucked away in the hills. Farther west are the "Fingerlings" — Honeoye, Canadice, Hemlock, and Conesus — divided from their big sisters by the rugged Bristol Hills. Beyond lies the great pastoral expanse of the Genesee Valley.

Geologists believe the Finger Lakes were once rivers, their flow arrested by dams of glacial debris left after ice masses had moved down from Canada. Moundlike deposits of sand, clay, and rock in the region are known today as "glacial drumlins." Myriad springs feed the lakes, and tributary streams cascade down hillsides, wind through glens, and fall from cliffs into the misty gorges below. 300

Although there's a faraway flavor to this quiet land, Syracuse is only a hill or so to the northeast, while Rochester and Buffalo are within a few hours' drive. Most of the Finger Lakes extend south from U. S. 20, a busy highway that streaks across the state from Albany to Buffalo. Good roads branch south to encircle the individual lakes, and by taking these tours (two to three hours each) you will discover for yourself the beauty of the region.

Explore as you please

You'll need your car because train and bus travel 400 are limited within the area and there are no conducted tours. You'll be on your own, free to wander over the countryside at your own pace. From Memorial Day until Labor Day the weather is warm enough for light clothing, and nights are cool enough for a blanket. This is considered the tourist season, though my favorite months are September and October.

There aren't any swanky resorts with planned social activities, but many lovely old houses along U. S. 20 have been turned into tourist homes with inviting names — Four Winds, Cobblestones, Candlewick House. There are modern tourist courts, many near the water, and most villages have at least one hotel. 500 For roughing it, state parks provide excellent camp sites, cabins, and trailer parks.

The Krebs restaurant in Skaneateles is noted for its enormous country-style meals. When you sit down to dinner there, you can expect to be eating for several hours. Fountainbleau on Cayuta Lake, Belhurst at Geneva on Seneca Lake, and Holloway House and Avon Inn to the west on U. S. 20 are popular with Sunday drivers, and though prices are higher than at the majority of local eating places, the delicious food and pleasant atmosphere make dining 600 an occasion.

As a rule advance reservations for overnight accommodations aren't necessary unless you want to stay in or near Geneva, which is crowded on week ends by people visiting boys stationed at Sampson, an Air Force indoctrination base on Seneca Lake.

(For further information about places to stay, public bathing beaches, fishing regulations, stream location, and so on, write for the current issue of *Finger Lakes Travel Guide*, published by the Finger Lakes Association, 200 Main St., Penn Yan, New York.)

Finger Lakes life

The Finger Lakes people are sturdy, friendly, proud, intelligent — not unlike their New England and Pennsylvania ancestors who came to the region in 700 ← the last years of the 18th century. White settlement began here after General George Washington sent the Sullivan-Clinton expedition, during the Revolutionary War, to wipe out the Iroquois tribes (primarily the Seneca) who remained loyal to the British. Coming up the Susquehanna River from Pennsylvania, Sullivan's forces marched up one lakeside and down another, burning cabins, plowing up beans, cutting down cornfields and apple trees. Indian resistance crumbled in 1779 at the Battle of Newton, near Elmira. The Indians fled, leaving a record that exists today in monuments, legends, and place names.

Among the farm products raised in the area are 800 ← grapes, wheat, potatoes, corn, beans, squash, pumpkins. Peach and apple orchards surround solid clapboard farmhouses with verandas and flanking wings. In spring, buckets hang from maple trees in dooryards, and children gather at backwoods sugarhouses to watch sap boiled down.

There may be fried perch or buckwheat cakes with maple syrup for breakfast, a clambake or ice-cream social at the close of day. Square dances are popular in the region, though the main event of the year (and the most fun, I think) is the county fair, where you can try your skill in a shooting gallery, eat cotton 900 ← candy, attend trotting races, or play judge at the exhibits.

The first crisp days of fall find the menfolk oiling their guns, with the family beagle at their heels; and village stores display bright plaid wool shirts, high boots, and fleece-lined caps. If you passed this way in midwinter, you would find the ponds, streams, and smaller lakes frozen (Seneca has frozen over only four times in the memory of white men) and transformed into miniature villages by men and boys fishing through the ice.

The towns you'll see

Towns are set at the ends of the lakes and, except 1000 ← for a scattering of tourist cabins, piers, boat liveries, and lakefront bathing parks, do not look like summer resorts. The towns are primarily farm-produce trading centers, and there is a solid Old World atmosphere about them.

The many colleges in the area extend culture to Finger Lakes towns. In Ithaca, Cornell really does stand "Far above Cayuga's waters," and the lake is streaked with the wakes of slender shells when the Cornell crew is out. Ithaca College is located here, too. Farther up Cayuga Lake is Wells College, a 1100 → girls' school founded by Henry Wells, who, with William Fargo (also a Finger Laker), established the firm of Wells, Fargo and Company, stagecoach operators in gold-rush days. There's a summer theater at Keuka College on the lake shore, while Hobart and William Smith Colleges are in Geneva, overlooking Seneca Lake. Elmira College (for women) in the city of Elmira, a southern entrance to the region, was founded in 1855 and was the first school in the United States to offer women the same courses and degrees offered in men's colleges.

Auburn, on Owasco Lake, is the largest community 1200 → in the area with a population of 36,772. The massive smokestacks and concrete walls you'll see there are part of Auburn State Prison, first built in 1816. Geneva, with its location on Seneca Lake and its cultural atmosphere suggests the Swiss city for which it was named, but to me it is also a reminder of Captain Charles Williamson, the dashing Scotsman whose story has been fictionized by Carl Carmer in his historical novel "Genesee Fever." Captain Williamson was sent to the Finger Lakes region after the Revolutionary War as an agent of the Poulteney Estate and laid out the town of Geneva in a grand 1300 → manner. The wide streets in Geneva and in Canandaigua slope up from the water to ridges where mellow old mansions are set back in spacious lawns. Painted in pastel shades or white, with columns and cupolas, these houses preserve the gracious atmosphere of 1350 → the lake villages in the early 19th century.

————STOP — ASK FOR YOUR TIME————

Record time immediately on next page and answer the questions on content.

Time _____ Sec.	RATE (from table on page 305):	R. _____
No. Errors _____	COMPREHENSION (100 — 10% for each Error):	C. _____
VI- 8	EFFICIENCY (R × C):	E. _____

ANSWER THESE QUESTIONS IMMEDIATELY (VI-8)

1. (C)   The author believes that this region is most attractive in the_____season.

2. (M. C.)   Geologists believe that the Finger Lakes were originally:

          ____(1)   rivers.

          ____(2)   glaciers.

          ____(3)   dry pits.

          ____(4)   subterranean despressions.

3. (T — F)   This region abounds in expensive summer houses and swanky resorts.

4. (T — F)   One can seldom find overnight accommodations unless one reserves them in advance.

5. (T — F)   There are many evidences of the Indian history in the legends and names of the Finger Lakes area.

6. (M. C.)   This area was the home of the Iroquois Indian tribes until:

          ____(1)   the Civil War.

          ____(2)   the French-Indian War.

          ____(3)   the Revolutionary War.

          ____(4)   the Spanish-American War.

7. (T — F)   A great variety of farm products is raised in this area.

8. (T — F)   All of the Finger Lakes freeze over in the winter season.

9. (C)   Ithaca, Wells, and Keuka are examples of the many _____ which are located in the Finger Lakes area.

10. (T — F)   The towns around the lakes are primarily farm-produce trading centers.

Number VI-9

Concepts of Communication

(Reprinted from Chapter IX, *Guidebook for Prospective Teachers*, Ohio State University Press, 1948, by permission of the authors, Lyle L. Miller and Alice Z. Seeman)

————————————— WAIT FOR SIGNAL TO BEGIN READING —————————————

Communication

You can get a hint concerning the higher purposes of communication by looking at the word itself. Communication is much more closely related to the word community than it is to any of the instruments of communication which man has created, such as language, radio, and pictorial or dramatic art. This point suggests that you will miss the deeper meaning of communication if you allow yourself to think only of the machinery of communication. You might get a further hint if you really examine the meaning of the word *community*.

What is a community?

You probably think of houses and streets full 100 of people at first, but as you think of modern means of transportation you remember that many teachers teach in consolidated schools and have to think of their community in a broader sense. We have come to think of community boundaries more in terms of "time of travel" than in terms of linear distance. Modern research in aeronautics makes it possible to travel to any part of the world within a few days' time. The major cities of the world are connected by many air lines that make them only a few hours' flying time apart. Whether we wish it or not, we find 200 ourselves drawn into a world community.

Breadth of community

Our means of communication today enable us to hear people in distant lands as they speak, and our recent progress in television, such as Telstar, enables us to see events in other parts of the world as they happen. All this makes us realize that linear boundaries no longer define a community. We need to look for a better definition. To have a community there must be something in common. Above all there must be some common values and some common ways of 300 living. One has a true community only to the degree that men enjoy common understandings and work together for common ends. A world community can be achieved only as men of different races and nationalities come to some common understandings, recognize some common problems, and work together for some common ends. The physical community must be supplemented by a community of mind and spirit. An insane asylum cannot become a community without becoming sane, for by community one always means a community of mind. One must have mind or spirit to build common understandings 400 with others. Unless one can communicate his meaningful experiences to others, he cannot enter a community of understanding with them.

Purpose of communication

The primary purpose of all communication, then, is to build increasingly more community of mind in the world. All the machinery of communication whose creation has been sponsored by a democratic state comes into its own, only when it is consciously employed to this end, namely, the end of building community of mind. It is in this enterprise that you must learn to take your central satisfactions. It is this purpose which must determine the quality of your 500 enjoyment. Perhaps it is desirable to take a more deliberate look at what all of this means.

All communication, if it is really communication, brings about some community of mind. Even when a man swears at you or threatens you, he establishes a temporary community of mind. You share the thought that he has expressed and you have had a momentary meeting of minds. But such a getting together is very much like a meeting of the match and powder keg. Communication moves between two extremes. Sometimes it is used primarily to inflate the ego, and the speaker indulges himself with the momentary sympathies of his audience; but 600 ← unless all that is said has been designed to benefit the hearers as well as the speaker, the delightful meeting will result in a delayed explosion. Language, therefore, when used in the wrong spirit, brings community of mind into being for a moment in such a way as to make subsequent understanding almost impossible.

Severing communication channels

Of course civilized people do not, as a rule, swear at one another. They have more refined and more subtle ways of cutting people down to such a size that they can more conveniently see over their heads. Probably some of the members of this class have 700 ← such smooth techniques along this line that they can combine a word, an inflection, and a look so artfully that no one but the person for whom the remark is intended will object, but that one person may want to die or commit murder. It is psychologically necessary for some people who become the victims of certain attitudes to go around setting themselves up by cutting other people down. Even the best persons are a little guilty of this kind of behavior at times. The extent to which a person allows himself to indulge in this pastime determines in large 800 ← measure the extent to which he can communicate with others. He soon finds that the doors at every entrance are being quietly shut in his face, and that day by day he is standing more and more alone. An invisible wall builts itself around such a person. The lines of communication leading into and from the world in which he lives mysteriously disintegrate. No loud talk, no cursing of his luck or of others, and no grant of power can enable him to penetrate this spiritually suffocating barrier to communication which he has brought into being by his attitude. 900 ←

What, then, is this quality which communication must have in order that it may serve the larger purposes of deepening sympathies and broadening understandings? Perhaps the problem can best be approached by recalling that every man is different from every other man. Since each person differs from everyone else, if people associate it is as inevitable as night following day that they will differ with one another. However inevitable this situation may be, it is true that when people differ they often make that fact cause for offense. When people "beg to differ with you" in a cocky or belittling way, you 1000 ← are almost sure to take offense. Some take offense when differences are expressed respectfully or even with humility.

Odd, is it not, that one should feel called upon to apologize for the fact that he is different from one, that he differs with another. If persons take offense, even polite offense, because one grew up with red hair, another with black skin, one as a Republican, and another as a Democrat, they are taking offense at differences rather than taking a sympathetic interest in differences with others. They are making 1100 → it difficult to communicate with one another.

Scientific attitudes

A look at the method and spirit of science also gives a feeling for the spirit of communication which builds community of mind. Regardless of race, creed, language, or nationality, the true scientist is interested in, sympathetic to, and open-minded about, the sincere and honest opinions of any other scientist whose thinking comes within his field of work. Differences of opinion are exchanged, cross-fertilization takes place, and new ideas spring up where only old ones grew before. They build an even broader community of mind, and science grows apace. Tolerance and openmindedness prevail in 1200 → order that conflicting opinions can be exchanged and men may grow in wisdom.

The spirit, therefore, of your personal and private conversations as well as of your public or professional exchange of ideas may or may not be marked by democratic qualities. If, as a consequence of attempts at communication, more community of mind, more common understandings, have been brought into being, then may you be assured that human communication is serving a purpose which justifies the invention of ingenious devices for extending the blessings of communication among men.

Communication — A two-way road

1300 → As time passes you must rate yourself in two different roles. As the actor playing the active role of communicating, how well can you call this spirit of ethical community into being? As audience, how well can you foster this spirit in the way you participate in any enterprise of which you may be a part? 1350 →

———STOP — ASK FOR YOUR TIME———

Record time immediately on next page
and answer the questions on content.

Time _____ Sec.   RATE (from table on page 305):   R. _____

No. Errors_____   COMPREHENSION (100 — 10% for each Error):   C. _____

VI- 9   EFFICIENCY (R × C):   E. _____

ANSWER THESE QUESTIONS IMMEDIATELY (VI-9)

1. (C)   This author believes that basic to understanding communication is the understanding of the word _____.

2. (T — F)   He states that community boundary lines today are thought of in terms of traveling time.

3. (T — F)   The idea is presented that a community implies common standards of speech, religion, money, and politics.

4. (C)   Basic to any community in the true sense, this author believes there must exist a community of _____.

5. (T — F)   The primary purpose of communication is economic.

6. (M. C.)   The author believes that civilized people put other people "in their place" by:

    _____(1)   Tactful choice of words and speech inflection.

    _____(2)   Swearing at them.

    _____(3)   Exerting political pressure.

    _____(4)   Use of police force.

7. (T — F)   True communication necessitates a sympathetic interest in individual differences.

8. (M. C.)   The characteristic of the scientific attitude which makes better communication possible is:

    _____(1)   The limited range of interest.

    _____(2)   The absorption in pure science.

    _____(3)   The mind open to new ideas.

    _____(4)   The technical level of vocabulary.

9. (T — F)   Ideas do not always accompany the words that express them.

10. (T — F)   The spirit essential to communication is the conviction that you have a good idea to which you must convert others.

Number VI-10

Services of the Exchange

(Reprinted from the pamphlet *The Nations Market Place*,
by permission of the New York Stock Exchange)

——————— WAIT FOR SIGNAL TO BEGIN READING ———————

Early development

Having come into existence when the First Congress of the United States created the need for a market place for securities, the New York Stock Exchange closely parallels, in its history, the entire course of our nation's life. It was in the third year of George Washington's first administration — in 1792 — that a few business men who traded in the securities of the day decided to appoint a place and a regular time for their meetings.

New York City was then scarcely more than a town by today's standards. It had forty thousand people and occupied five square miles.

Congress, which first met in 1789, had authorized an issue of eighty millions of dollars in "stock" to refund the cost of the Revolutionary War. Banks and insurance companies were springing up in a number of places, and public improvements were being started.

To pay for the Revolutionary War and finance these other activities, stocks and bonds had to be sold to the public. But the people naturally were unwilling to invest in securities unless they could be easily resold. The need for a market place for securities was as clearly apparent to these early settlers as it is to us today.

When these pioneer brokers decided, more than a century and a half ago, to meet every day under the wide branches of an old button-wood tree — it was located only a few blocks away from the site of the present New York Stock Exchange — they fulfilled one of the most vital financial needs of a young Republic. These men were the original members of the New York Stock Exchange. Twenty-four in number, they dealt only in Government "stock" and a few issues of bank and insurance company shares. For their trading "floor" they had simply a small plot of ground protected by the branches of a tree.

World-wide in scope

Today the New York Stock Exchange is a greatly broadened, highly mechanized, and efficiently organized unit, world-wide in the scope of its services. But, in essentials, the market place experienced no fundamental change by going under a roof. It is still an auction room where the securities of our largest and best-known business enterprises, representing the savings of the people, are continually appraised by a world consensus; and where these securities may be readily converted into cash, and cash exchanged for securities.

The many millions of people who own stocks and bonds listed on its market have a direct, personal interest in the New York Stock Exchange. Estimates of the number of stockholders in the nation range as high as 15,000,000. People from all walks of life, with small incomes and large, own stocks. In many leading business corporations the average stockholder owns no more than 40 or 50 shares.

There is also a vast, although indirect, public participation in Stock Exchange securities among the owners of insurance policies, and people who receive income from private trusts or from corporate pension funds. A substantial part of these financial resources is invested in stocks.

The Stock Exchange does not, as is supposed by some, buy or sell securities, nor does it in any manner establish their prices. The Exchange is a market place, a vital public convenience for the purchase and sale by investors of the listed securities of America's Industries.

The New York Stock Exchange is an association of brokers who have qualified for membership. Their day-to-day business consists of handling investors' orders to buy or sell a few shares or hundreds of shares of stock. In contrast with the small number of 24 pioneers who first conducted such business in

1792, the Exchange today is comprised of 1,375 members, 2,400 allied members and some 625 member firms, conducting business in 396 cities across the country.

Many long dividend records

Instead of a mere handful of securities, the present Exchange has a trading list that includes the securities of more than 1,200 different companies, embracing virtually every department of industry and business. Some 302 of these companies have paid a dividend on their common stocks every year for as long as 20 years to more than a century; some 377 more have paid a dividend every year for 10 to 20 years, 700 ⇄ and another 137 for five to nearly 10 years.

Sixty-three issues of Federal and State government bonds are also listed on the Exchange, together with 185 security issues of foreign governments. The number of corporate bonds listed is 656. Corporate stock issues number 1,478. The market value of all stocks and bonds listed on the Exchange is approximately 203 billions of dollars.

A company, in order to list its securities on the New York Stock Exchange, must be a substantial, going concern; must be legally organized and the securities validly authorized and issued; there must be 800 ← sufficient distribution of the securities to assure an adequate market in them, and the company must comply with the Exchange's requirements respecting periodic reports to owners of its securities and to the public.

The New York Stock Exchange is the nation's principal market for securities; just and equitable principles of trade prevail. Opinions as to security values from all parts of the world are reflected. Buyer and seller meet on perfect equality. The man in San Francisco or Portland, Maine, gets the same service as the man just around the corner from the Exchange.

Auction market

Trading follows the rules of the auction market. 900 ← The highest first bid has priority, as has the lowest first offer. The market on the Exchange is a double auction. Bidders seek to buy stock from sellers at the lowest possible price. Sellers want to get the highest price for the shares they are offering.

When a buyer's bid and a seller's offer arrive at a mutually acceptable price, a transaction is completed.

Each transaction ends the auction and new market is then started. All bids and offers are made orally, in an audible voice. Secret transactions are not permitted, and the prompt publicity given to prices by 1000 → means of the stock and bond ticker tapes makes deception in respect to prices of listed securities impossible. The only function the Exchange has with respect to prices is to publish them.

This is the kind of market that public demand has evolved, through more than one hundred and fifty years, upon the floor of the New York Stock Exchange. Aided by the mechanism of security markets, corporations are able to obtain funds with which to build plants and equip them with machinery. Thus this country converts the surplus funds of its 1100 → people into the real savings of our nation.

Through the Stock Exchange public ownership of industry is spreading throughout the nation to many investors all over the country. The biggest single reason given by some 15,000 people when interviewed and asked the question "Why did you decide to buy the stock you own?" was that they hoped and expected the price would go up. Dividend income was the second most popular reason.

Those are good reasons, of course; the long-range trend of security prices, for instance, has been upward for decades. And there are hundreds of com- 1200 → panies which have paid dividends annually for ten years to more than a century.

But it is also true that share prices of even the strongest companies move down as well as up, that corporations may earn good profits one year and in another may not. So prudent investors should consider the risks of share ownership as well as the potential rewards.

The story of the New York Stock Exchange is one with the development of our country. The essence of progress is the flow of capital into productive enterprise. Our nation has learned to build immense factories and transportation systems and to under- 1300 → take efficient methods of mass manufacture far beyond the resources of individual man. The result is the highest standard of living ever known to the world — a standard incomparably better than that of any other time or any other place. The New York Stock Exchange takes pride in its vital contributions 1350 → to this progress.

————STOP — ASK FOR YOUR TIME————

Record time immediately on next page
and answer the questions on content.

Time _____ Sec.	RATE (from table on page 305):	R. _____
No. Errors: _____	COMPREHENSION: (100 − 10% for each Error):	C. _____
VI- 10	EFFICIENCY: (R × C):	E. _____

ANSWER THESE QUESTIONS IMMEDIATELY (VI-10)

1. (M. C.) The New York Stock Exchange developed because of the needs of:

   ____(1)   British landlords during colonial times.

   ____(2)   The American Colonies during the Revolution.

   ____(3)   American businessmen during the early years of the republic.

   ____(4)   Northern capitalists during the period of the Civil War.

2. (T — F)   The first meeting of the Exchange was in the office of a New York Banker.

3. (T — F)   The activities of the Exchange reflect only the price trends in the United States of America.

4. (M. C.)   The purpose of the New York Stock Exchange is:

   ____(1)   To serve as a merchant in buying and selling securities for a profit.

   ____(2)   To provide a market place for people to buy and sell securities.

   ____(3)   To set fair price standards on all securities sold.

   ____(4)   To print and distribute new stocks and bonds.

5. (T — F)   Over 300 companies in the Exchange have paid annual dividends regularly for over twenty years.

6. (C)   The Stock Exchange trading follows the pattern of an _____ type market.

7. (T — F)   The Exchange is instrumental in spreading public ownership of industry over the whole country.

8. (C)   The only function of the Exchange in respect to prices is to _____ those prices.

9. (T — F)   An investor can always expect good dividends if he invests in a well-established company.

10. (T — F)   The most common reason for buying stock is the expectation of an increase in the value of that stock.

Communication and Propaganda

(Reprinted from Chapter IX, *Guidebook for Prospective Teachers*, Ohio State University Press, 1948, by permission of the authors, Lyle L. Miller and Alice Z. Seeman)

──────────── WAIT·FOR SIGNAL TO BEGIN READING ────────────

Communicating with others

Can you imagine yourself living under conditions such that it would be impossible to communicate with other people? You could not get in touch with anyone by using the telephone, telegraph, or letter; you could not turn on a radio and hear other people; you could not attend a motion picture or look at a television screen; you could not get in touch with anyone by writing, talking, painting, reading, or playing any musical instrument. Without some means of communication you would be living in complete isolation. You would be unable to transmit your ideas to other people and unable to receive any **100** ideas from anyone else.

Methods of evaluating communications

In this modern world we are constantly subjected to a barrage of information and misinformation, persuasion, deception, and variations of opinion. In our democracy we prize freedom of speech and freedom of the press. This means that we place on the individual a tremendous responsibility for evaluating the ideas which are relayed to him through the radio, press, movies, newspapers, magazines, and personal contacts. Americans are readers of many kinds of material.

As a citizen you have a responsibility for deciding what to believe and what not to believe; what to **200** read and what not to read; what sources are representing special interests and what sources are striving to be fair. This is a process of evaluation which you will have to continue for life. Teachers have a more important task of helping young people to develop some standards for evaluating the material which they receive from the various media of communication.

One of the purposes of education is to develop individuals who will maintain suspended judgments until all available evidence is collected, act intelligently in terms of available information, and evaluate **300** their activity in terms of other evidence that becomes available. Schools should help to give students a range of knowledge that will enlarge the outlook of their minds. But schools must recognize that there are groups which do not wish to encourage the development of that kind of a thinking citizen. Many groups use methods of mass communication to get individuals to make conclusions on partial, cross-sectional, or distorted information. They are desirous of leading people into attitudes which will make them jump to conclusions without paying much attention to available evidence. These attempts to lead people to emotional thinking are usually called **400** *propaganda*. This threat to clear thinking is used on a large scale in the world today. It may not always be "anti-something," but it may be used to lead you to the support of some cause by painting a rosy picture of all the nice aspects of it. A thinking person should beware of communication channels that appeal to his emotions and that encourage him to act quickly without giving careful consideration to the matter at hand. Propaganda can often be detected by some general techniques which are commonly used to mislead your thinking.

500 *Name calling* — Bad names are given to those the propagandist would have us condemn; good names to those he would have us favor. Examples are: "progressive teacher," "Communist," "bureaucrat," "Conservative," "Jew," "Fraternity Man," "Socialist," "regular fellow," etc.

Glittering generalities — We are told that "the American system is threatened" and are lured with such attractive phrases as "social justice," "the more abundant life," "economic freedom," "the welfare of the common man," etc. These vague terms may have different meanings to everyone, and we frequently put our own meanings into the mouth of the speaker rather than try to decide what he really means by seeing how his actions define his terms. 600 ←

Flag waving — The propagandist associates his cause with the American flag, the Christian religion, or with some person of great prestige. He attempts to make you feel that loyalty to your God and your country dictates that you agree with him.

Slogans — The propagandist finds some catchy phrase which may stick in one's mind. Then he tries to get it generally accepted without an analysis of its meaning. Examples are "democratic way of life," "it's Luckies 2 to 1," "The skin you love to touch," "For men of distinction," "good to the last drop," etc. Applying the question, *why, what,* or *how* to 700 ← some of these slogans may help you see how superficial many of them are.

Repetition and fabrication — The propagandist loves to take an incident and magnify its importance. He is similar to the old gossip who likes to make the story just a little better before she passes it on. By repeating it over and over he attempts to make you accept its validity. You may protect yourself from this to some extent by trying to get at the source of some of your information which you question.

Band-wagon technique — You are led to believe you 800 ← should do something because "everybody's doing it," "it's smart to be seen at the Cliff Cafe," etc. Campaign managers and advertisers know the human tendency to follow the crowd and will invariably predict victory for their candidate or widespread use of their product. Here again you need to question, "Who is everybody?" "Why is it smart?"

Suppression and distortion of facts — Many of the socioeconomic cartoons lead to considerable distortion of the facts. Many of our labor journal cartoonists would have everyone believe that employers and capitalists are all bloated bigots with tall silk hats. Each politcial party has cartoonists 900 ← who try to make the other party look ridiculous. Pictures showing only a limited view of a situation are often used to distort reality. The things that are omitted in a news report may be just the things that you need to know to reach a wise decision. By withholding the whole truth from you, you may be led to reach a decision which the propagandist favors.

Ambush and showmanship — Wealthy interests and pressure groups sometimes use the ambush method of winning public opinion. They may use pressures

1000 → to get their employees or their debtors to promote their ideas. They may organize "front" organizations which take on an attractive name and carry on the publicity. They may give large sums to philanthropic institutions and then make the institution fight their battles. Oratory many times appeals to the emotions and does not present any facts. In case of doubt, you might try to discover who is financing the group or speaker in question.

These and many other methods may be used to lure the gullible thinker into false and sometimes dangerous conclusions. The tenseness of our international situation and the war of ideologies now 1100 → going on make it important for you to consider carefully the ideas to which you are exposed.

One of the most important factors influencing the communication of ideas is the reader's understanding. Dr. Edgar Dale, has suggested several questions which might be asked in an effort to evaluate your own ability as a reader. Although these questions apply to reading of newspapers primarily, you can frame some parallel questions to apply to magazines, radio programs, movies, speakers, etc.

1. Am I familiar with a number of newspapers, not only the good ones but the poor ones as well?
1200 → 2. Do I plan my reading in terms of (a) time spent, (b) material read, and (c) the order and speed in which the material is read?
3. Have I examined all parts of the material to find out what's in it?
4. Can I find desired information quickly by using the index, summary, etc?
5. Am I familiar with the way a typical news story is constructed?
6. Do I get the most out of the big news stories by following them day by day as they develop?
7. Am I able to read, understand, and criticize the editorials in daily newspapers?
1300 → 8. Do I have an efficient speed and comprehension in reading?
9. Am I familiar with some important factors which influence the nature and accuracy of news: (a) the reader, (b) ownership of the paper, (c) political affiliations, (d) the reporter, (e) the editor, (f) the make-up editor, (g) space restrictions, and 1350 → (h) advertising?

————STOP — ASK FOR YOUR TIME————

Record time immediately on next page and answer the questions on content.

Time _____ Sec.   RATE (from table on page 305):   R. _____

No. Errors _____   COMPREHENSION: (100 − 10% for each Error):   C. _____

VI-11   EFFICIENCY (R × C):   E. _____

ANSWER THESE QUESTIONS IMMEDIATELY (VI-11)

1. (C)   In a democracy the evaluation of ideas presented to the public is the responsibility of the_____
_____.

2. (T — F)   Teachers should evaluate all materials presented to students to protect them from misunderstanding the ideas.

3. (T — F)   Some people do not believe that students should be taught to analyze and evaluate the material they read.

4. (C)   Attempts to lead people to emotional thinking are called _____.

5. (M. C.)   The technique which appeals to ones own definition of terms such as "economic freedom" and "American way of life" is called the technique of:

    _____(1)   Repetition.

    _____(2)   Suppression of facts.

    _____(3)   Flag waving.

    _____(4)   Glittering generalities.

6. (T — F)   The author suggests that you apply the questions "why," "what," and "how" to any slogan approach.

7. (T — F)   The "Band Wagon" technique is described as that which uses a popular "name band" to gain attention.

8. (T — F)   Socioeconomic cartoons usually present an accurate view of a situation.

9. (T — F)   The "Ambush" technique implies the use of some "front" organization to expound the ideas.

10. (M. C.)   According to the author one of the most important factors influencing the written communication of ideas is:

    _____(1)   The reader's understanding.

    _____(2)   The political affiliation of the writer.

    _____(3)   The size and style of type used by the publisher.

    _____(4)   The newspaper which carries the story.

Maps as Teaching Aids

BY CLARENCE SAMFORD AND EUGENE COTTLE

(An excerpt from the book, *Social Studies in the Secondary School*.
Reprinted by permission of the authors and the publishers, McGraw-Hill Book Company, Inc.)

──────── WAIT FOR SIGNAL TO BEGIN READING ────────

Maps as teaching aids

Teachers of the social studies have probably made more use of maps over a longer period of time than they have of any other visual aid. Perhaps the map may have seemed to be a more integral part of the social studies than some other visual aids. An examination of textbooks in social studies will reveal that among the visual aids included, maps are usually second to pictures in number. One text revealed over fifty maps; another carried more than thirty. Despite this, maps are not always used properly, nor their full value realized, by pupils in the social studies. 100 Maps vary in purpose and consequently require various skills of those who would make adequate use of the information shown. The establishment of these skills in pupils is a responsibility of the social studies teacher. The supervised study period with the preparatory planning and succeeding activity stages offers the opportunity for the teacher to conduct drill work with the class or to provide individualized instruction, to develop map skills.

A map is a representation of the world or a portion of the world, and the best presentation of the idea of a map of any part of the world is by means of a 200 globe. As the pupil examines a globe, he observes more accurately the relationship in size and distance of the various features of the earth. A map usually distorts the shape of some of the geographic elements, and this condition must be called to the pupil's attention together with the explanation. The meaning of latitude and longitude must be understood, and how these devices are used must become ready knowledge of the pupils. Parallels of latitude indicate degrees of distance north or south of the equator and are always parallel to the equator. Distances 300 east or west are marked by meridians of longitude,

which run from pole to pole with the prime meridian passing through Greenwich, England. The scale of miles is a further device to give the map more meaning, by indicating the distance on the map in proportion to the actual distance. Certainly the pupil must become aware of the cartographer's use of color and symbols to indicate surface features and significant details of the specific map in question. With the revision of world geographic relationships through air transportation, pupils need to develop 400 mental images of the map of the United States in relation to other nations from the point of view of air travel.

Map information

For most adequate use of maps in the social studies, it is desirable that two or more maps be used simultaneously to illustrate relationships. For example, a map showing industrial areas used with one showing natural resources helps pupils to realize economic problems and processes resulting from the locations of the two phenomena under consideration. A relief map may be used to explain population distribution as well as such economic factors as the location of transportation lines.

Pupil participation in map work

500 In addition to the use of the map as a tool in learning, it may sometimes seem desirable for pupils to construct maps. When the pupil engages in this activity, his purpose should be the justifiable one of an experience which carries meaning for him. By doing this particular bit of creative work, he will acquire an emphasis on some knowledge, or some information will become more significant. Pupils

will become map-conscious to the degree that they are guided into study activities involving maps. When a pupil shows interest in constructing a map, he must be guided into meaningful and valuable activities relating to the map-construction process. Neatness, accuracy, and an evidence of knowledge applied to a specific problem must be found in the completed work. It is more desirable that a sense of relationship between geographic factors and map be shown by the map than that the map be merely an artistic product which has cost much time and labor, but which does not contribute to a pupil's knowledge. There may be times when it seems desirable for the entire social studies class to work on map construction. For example, a class in United States history may have discussed the Gadsden Purchase and, realizing that it was the last contiguous territory added to the United States, may have become interested in glancing over a map of the entire United States boundary. The question can so easily be raised, "How did the boundary of our country happen to follow the lines it does?" With such a problem calling for an investigation of the treaty settlements and purchases, the class may be launched on a map project to decide what sections of the national boundary were established by certain specific historic agreements. When such occasions arise, the teacher and pupils should discuss the problem of map making from the point of view of the purpose of the map and the various techniques necessary for the pupils to produce an adequate map. Such items as a map legend, lettering, the title, its size in relation to other lettering, the scale of miles, color, and the signature are important.

Map equipment for the social studies classroom

The present output of map equipment for schools provides unusual opportunity to the teacher to equip the social studies classroom with valuable teaching aids at not too great a cost. It is the responsibility of the teacher to see to it that this essential equipment is a part of the laboratory facilities of the social studies classroom. The teacher must plan the room's map equipment in terms of needs and money available. To buy inexpensive maps is not necessarily a saving. Neither should the teacher make a heavy investment if funds are not adequate to cover all needs in proportion.

In selecting maps for the social studies room the teacher must consider various factors of room environment. In choosing the mounting for large maps the teacher must keep in mind the pupils' ease of viewing the maps. Some maps are mounted on a heavy pedestal base stand, while some are supported by a metal tripod. The tripod seems to require more floor space and in a room of limited size is easily in the way of moving about the room. The wall-arm mounting, which swings from a hinged base fastened to the wall, allows two maps to be viewed readily by the swinging of the arm. This type serves best when space permits it to occupy a wall center removed from a corner. In small rooms roller maps have the advantage of being rolled up when not in use.

Accuracy of information and the amount and kind of information are significant items to consider in map selection. Some authors give more information on their maps than do others, although the teacher should examine the maps to see that information is easily read and that the map is not crowded in content.

The globe seems to be an essential for the social studies classroom. Here again room space may influence the teacher's choice of a globe. Sizes range from a small desk model to the large floorstand type. A 16-inch globe seems to be a practical size, and a holder which allows the globe to be placed in any position is desirable.

The blackboard outline map is a helpful teaching device, as it permits pupils and teacher to demonstrate map details by drawing in such items as may relate to the unit under discussion.

The social studies teacher will probably accumulate a variety of maps from many sources. It is desirable for a teacher to build a file of maps, arranging them by subject, mounting small sizes on lightweight cardboard and rolling large sizes for cupboard storage. In addition to these various ways in which the social studies teacher will plan the equipment of the room, the selection of textbooks will afford a further opportunity to bring map resources into the room. Present-day writers of our social studies textbooks recognize the value of the map as a visual aid to understanding textbook material, and many textbooks supply the pupil with excellent maps.

————STOP — ASK FOR YOUR TIME————

Record time immediately on next page
and answer the questions on content.

Time _____ Sec.	RATE (from table on page 305):	R. _____
No. Errors _____	COMPREHENSION (100 − 10% for each error):	C. _____
VI—12	EFFICIENCY (R × C):	E. _____

ANSWER THESE QUESTIONS IMMEDIATELY (VI-12)

1. (T — F) The large number of maps found in social studies textbooks are very easy for the pupils to use without help.

2. (C) A map is a representation of the _____ or a portion of it.

3. (C) A cartographer uses _____ and symbols to indicate surface features and significant details.

4. (M. C.) Population distribution and economic factors may be explained by use of a:

　　　____(1) Globe.

　　　____(2) Relief map.

　　　____(3) Blackboard outline map.

　　　____(4) Pupil-constructed map.

5. (T — F) Only neatness and accuracy are important on a pupil-constructed map.

6. (T — F) A teacher must consider room space in selecting types of maps.

7. (T — F) A map giving the most information will be the teacher's best buy.

8. (T — F) A map usually distorts the shape of some of the geographic elements of the earth.

9. (T — F) The relationship in size and distance of the various features of the earth may be more accurately observed on a globe.

10. (M. C.) The greatest need of the social studies classroom seems to be a:

　　　____(1) Roller map of the United States.

　　　____(2) A permanently mounted blackboard outline map.

　　　____(3) Globe suspended from the ceiling for easy use.

　　　____(4) A file of a variety of types and kinds of maps.

Number VI-13

Stamping Out Horror Comics

(Reprinted from the January, 1955, issue of *Machinists Monthly Journal*,
by permission of the publishers)

─────────────── WAIT FOR SIGNAL TO BEGIN READING ───────────────

Have you looked at a comic book your children have been reading recently? Do you assume that they are being entertained by the playful antics of animated animals and the innocent pranks of fictitious comedians? Do you help them to select the comic books they read or are you maintaining a hands-off policy? Many organizations have been urging parents to take a more serious interest in the comic book reading habits of their children. The following article is one that has been published by the International Association of Machinists to stimulate thinking by its members.

Down with horror comics

Will the current crusade to rid the nation of millions of "horror comic books" succeed? Or will it be a "flash in the pan?" For that matter, are crime and juvenile delinquency actually encouraged by wild-eyed stories about sex, crime and horror?

Those questions are being asked across the nation as groups of citizens, in increasing numbers, move to wipe the country's bookstands clean of trashy publications. Churches, Unions, Parent-Teachers Associations, American Legion posts and other groups are active in the drive.

The campaign got under way during the summer months and is still going. As this article is being written it's still too soon to predict full success or failure. But the latest drive, unlike earlier efforts to eliminate gory comics, seems to be growing in intensity.

One of the earliest community drives took place in Hartford, Conn. There, in a neighborhood rife with juvenile delinquency, a small girl was killed. A newspaper columnist found the area swarming with horror comics. He wrote a series of stories describing the magazines. Hundreds of Hartford citizens and organizations joined in a clean-up fight. Now most of the horror comics have disappeared in Hartford and throughout the state.

In Chicago, two teen-age girls saw a three-year old youngster toddle up to a newsstand and purchase one of the most "lewd" comics available. It turned out the little girl was making the purchase for her father, who was ashamed to buy the magazine himself. The two teen-agers began circulating petitions asking Congress for a ban. They now have obtained more than 30 thousand signatures and are aiming at another 30 thousand.

In Oklahoma City and Houston, local churches and clubs conducted a hard-hitting campaign. Both cities passed ordinances banning crime and horror comics. In Los Angeles, Santa Barbara, Long Beach and other California cities an incessant campaign against the gruesome comics is being carried on by the newspapers and combined groups of parents.

Attitudes of publishers

The campaign ran so strong in New York that one of the biggest horror-comic publishers suddenly announced he was stopping publication of the books in response "to appeals by American parents." The publisher is William M. Gaines.

Last spring, testifying before the Senate Sub-committee on Juvenile Delinquency, Gaines insisted that one of his comic-book covers showing an ax-wielding man holding the severed head of a woman was "in good taste." When Senator Estes Kefauver of Tennessee queried Gaines further, the publisher said the scene would only be in "bad taste" if the head "were held a little higher so the neck would show blood dripping out." But in the months that followed the Senate investigation, Gaines said his sales dropped off a third. He promised customers he'd substitute "new lines" for his horror and suspense books. He announced the "capitulation" in one of his magazines. "We give up; we've had it," Gaines wrote.

The Comics Magazine Association

Two days before Gaines gave in, an alarmed comic

industry announed it had set up the Comics Magazine Association of America to self-police the industry. 600 ← Most of the nation's 27 comic book publishers joined the organization. The Association hired Charles F. Murphy, a New York City magistrate with nine years on the bench, as a "czar" of the industry. Murphy was given a code of ethics with which to work.

Cardinal points in the code were: crime shall not be presented so as to arouse sympathy for the criminal; good shall triumph over evil; scenes of excessive violence and brutality shall be prohibited; and law enforcement officials, judges and the Government must be respected at all times. Murphy said that he would enforce the code vigorously and that pub- 700 ← lishers who violate it would be publicly expelled from the Association. "I am the last word on what is going into comic books," Murphy declared.

Police action

But the great body of citizens behind the campaign aren't resting on their two big laurels — the Gaines decision and the publishers' self-policing. In city after city, church and other community groups, aided by deeply-concerned parents, vow there'll be no rest until the worst of the comics are off the market — and off for good. With regard to the Association's decision to police itself, those engaged in the crusade say they're adopting a "wait and 800 ← see" attitude. "In the meantime, we'll not relax our efforts," declared a Washington, D. C., youth conservation leader.

In Columbus, Ohio, where the city has taken action to establish a board of censorship, Judge Clayton W. Rose of the Domestic Relations Court, reminded citizens that the comic-book industry had attempted self-regulation several years ago but that after the public clamor died down, the publishers went back to turning out vile publications. Other civic leaders, familiar with the problem, contend that the Association can't do an adequate job. No code, they say, can touch the "fly-by-night" operator who 900 ← publishes a couple of volumes of depravity, then folds up — only to reappear a few weeks later, perhaps in another city, with a new line of horror material.

From comic books to crime?

As the campaign moves ahead the question posed at the beginning of this article is being asked in many quarters. Can a comic book turn a youngster to crime?

Gaines, a publishing tycoon at 32, is probably the outstanding spokesman for those who say "no". He contends that horror stories provide a harmless outlet for hates that are normal to children — hates on 1000 ←

paper. "I don't think anyone was ever harmed by anything they read," the publisher said. "Neuroses are caused by real, emotional experiences. Anyone who has studied psychiatry knows that."

Many publishers side with Gaines, and so do some psychiatrists. The blame, they say, lies deeper — in the home and in the neighborhood.

But a mass of testimony on the question indicates that a majority of psychiatrists, law enforcement authorities and juvenile officials disagree. While not absolving the parents or the community in the least, they emphatically believe that horror and crime 1100 → comics are a "contributing factor" to juvenile delinquency!

Dr. Reginald Steen of New York, leading child psychiatrist, states bluntly: "The sadistic type of comic book is harmful to all children — and to certain unstable adults."

Senate investigating committee

The strongest indictment of comic books comes from Senator Robert C. Hendrickson of New Jersey. Hendrickson, who headed the Senate investigation that pored over hundreds of comics, said his committee found, "That for ten cents a copy our children devour tales — illustrated in gory detail — of murder, rape, burglary, extortion and kidnapping. Half-rotted corpses rise from their graves to pillage. 1200 → Vampires go forth to drink the blood of children."

"Why are such books published? Because there is money in it," Senator Hendrickson flatly stated, adding, "Not even the Communist conspiracy could devise a more deadly way to demoralize, disrupt and confuse our future citizens."

The future for comics

No one knows exactly how many horror comics are published each year. Conservative estimates place the figure at 15 million. It's certain that the all-out campaign against them has cut the figure considerably and will reduce it still further. The voice of protest grows louder each passing day. Perhaps Publisher Gaines, in announcing his plans 1300 → to cut off his horror productions, foresaw success for the present campaign when he said, "It seems to be what American parents want."

The key to a successful campaign is found in that statement. For certainly if enough American parents are properly concerned about the threat of horror 1350 → comics, they will succeed in stamping them out.

————STOP — ASK FOR YOUR TIME————

Record time immediately on next page and answer the questions on content.

Time _____ Sec.	RATE (from table on page 305):	R. _____
No. Errors _____	COMPREHENSION (100 − 10% for each Error):	C. _____
VI-13	EFFICIENCY (R × C):	E. _____

ANSWER THESE QUESTIONS IMMEDIATELY (VI-13)

1. (M. C.) One of the earliest community drives took place in:

    ____(1) Oklahoma City, Oklahoma.

    ____(2) Houston, Texas.

    ____(3) Hartford, Connecticut.

    ____(4) Los Angeles, California.

2. (T — F) The Comics Magazine Association of America was organized by aroused parents to exercise controls on the publication of certain comics.

3. (T — F) Judge Charles Murphy is supposedly the last word on what goes into comic books.

4. (T — F) Citizens are content that the work of Murphy and the Comics Magazine Association will solve its problem.

5. (T — F) Publisher William Gaines promised customers he'd substitute a new line for his horror and suspense books.

6. (T — F) Civic leaders believe the Association can do an adquate job of controlling all comic magazine publications.

7. (C) Local authorities and Commission officials will find the _____ operator the most difficult to control.

8. (T — F) Gaines contends that people cannot be harmed by what they read.

9. (C) A majority of psychiatrists, law enforcement authorities, and juvenile officials believe that horror and crime comics are a contributing factor to _____.

10. (M. C.) The key to a successful campaign in eliminating horror comics lies in the long range attitude of:

    ____(1) Publishers.

    ____(2) Customers.

    ____(3) The Senate Investigating Committee.

    ____(4) American parents.

No Margin for Error

(Reprinted from the November, 1962, issue of the University of Southern California
Alumni Review, by permission of the editor)

───────────────── **WAIT FOR SIGNAL TO BEGIN READING** ─────────────────

Clipboards in hand, the men walked silently through the fields, stopping now and then to examine in painstaking detail some new piece of aircraft wreckage they found strewn in front of them — as if thrown there by a giant hand moving in anger.

From metal cases some of the men carried, they took magnifying glasses, goose-neck lights and micrometers to aid them in their examinations of the twisted, scorched and broken parts.

Before they moved on, each piece of what had once been a powerful aircraft was inventoried and its position plotted on the clipboard sheets.

Which federal agency had sent these men here? 100 What new aircraft tragedy were they investigating?

The men with the clipboards represented no governmental agency. They were students in a unique school — the University's Aviation and Missile Safety Division, only one of its kind in the world.

The crash they were investigating was not a new one. It happened years ago and in a different place. But the pieces — all 2,314 of them — now lay in the same relative positions as those in which they were found when the airplane broke up on impact with the ground.

Today the parts, reassembled in the original crash 200 pattern along a 1,000-foot "crash course," provide a field investigation problem for the men who attend this unusual school. Everything is there — skid and impact ground marks, oil stains included.

Considering the hundreds who have followed this "Crash course" in a succession of classes, the accident is doubtlessly the best-investigated crash in U. S. aviation history.

But each new student, with the investigative skills learned in his class and laboratory sessions, must find anew the answer to: What caused this plane to crash and why?

Although only a detail of the instruction, the 300 question ranks in importance with a semifinal exam.

A select group

In all, more than 3,500 men have attended the Aviation and Missile Safety Classes in the last nine years.

Members of this very select group — the only formally trained aircraft accident investigators in the world — are found today in key positions related to aircraft and missile safety and accident investigation.

They are flight safety officers in the air forces of half the nations of the world. Two of them are astronauts: Lt. Cmdr. Walter M. Schirra Jr., who recently made a six-orbit space flight, and Lt. Comdr. 400 James A. Lovell Jr., one of America's nine new astronauts. Spaceman Schirra studied here in 1957, and Lovell, in 1961.

Many of the graduates can be found behind the executive desks of aeronautics manufacturing companies and related firms. Many have positions with the U. S. aviation agencies, and many are airline captains. And some have been brought into the insurance business and the underwriters of aviation's risks.

Youngest of this new breed are those trained in the safe handling of ballistic missiles. Classes in this area began a little more than a year ago, and now hundreds of missile safety officers are performing their duties 500 at various missile installations throughout the United States.

The men who have come from across the country or from around the world, as scores have done, to attend these classes at the University have emerged with an amazing, often Sherlock Holmes-type capacity for solving the fatal riddles of aircraft crashes. It is not unusual that a hardened "expert" has been impressed by the accuracy with which a broken aircraft part becomes a tell-tale clue to disaster — once the lessons have been applied.

Just how penetratingly accurate can an Aviation and Missile Safety Division student be on the scene of an aviation tragedy?

David Holladay, head of the aircraft accident pre- 600 vention and investigation section of the division, lists a few of the things which these students can accurately determine by careful investigation of a crashed aircraft.

Even the fractured remains of a tiny vacuum tube will tell the trained investigator whether or not there was any electrical energy in the tube at the time the plane hit the ground.

Was there a fire aboard the aircraft while it was airborne? Or did the fire break out after ground impact? Instructor Holladay says in many cases this is a relatively easy question.

He picks up a part from the crash course on which 700 his men have been working and points to a fracture in the metal: "The differences in metal fractures will tell you whether the break came on impact."

If fatigue in the metal was the cause of the break, the investigator who has learned his lessons will be able to tell you whether the break was the result of up-and-down stress, or twisting — and sometimes the sequence of the stress in the lifetime of the aircraft.

Whether the landing gear was up or down, the exact setting of the wing flaps in degrees and whether or 800 not the craft had a fuel supply at the time disaster struck — all these are basic training lessons for the students.

Important as these investigative skills are rated, the underlying purpose of this training is even more significant. Expressed in the words of Division Director George Potter, is this over-riding goal:

"Accident investigation is for the sake of accident prevention. This program, our texts, our curriculum, the human centrifuge, the 'crash course,' our 'museum' of aeronautical mistakes — they all contribute to the skills we know already have saved thousands of lives and millions of dollars worth of property." 900

The courses offered by the Aviation and Missile Safety Division not only include accident investigation but courses in aeronautical engineering, aviation physiology, aviation psychology, and communication principles and techniques.

One of the unique aspects of the program is the use made of the human centrifuge, only such apparatus on a university campus in the United States. It is used for indoctrination and research, giving the students an opportunity to experience and witness various effects of exposure to G-forces under conditions where they are not charged with responsibility

1000 for control of an aircraft. The centrifuge duplicates the forces encountered when banking steeply or pulling out of a dive.

Birth of the idea

How and why did this school come about?

According to Dean Carl Hancey of University College, it was the huge loss of personnel and equipment which the U. S. Air Force suffered in the peacetime years following the end of World War II that brought the one-and-only school into being. In 1951 the Air Force Inspector General's Directorate of Flight Safety Research urged establishment of a flying safety officer course — a course where pilots would be 1100 taught the characteristics and capabilities of an aircraft; where they would learn to investigate aircraft accidents scientifically and emerge with recommendations and procedures which could be used to prevent similar accidents.

The problem landed in USC's lap less than a year later when the University was given a research contract to study skills and information needed by such personnel.

Under the direction of Dean Hancey the program curriculum and methodology of the then-Aviation Safety Division was thoroughly researched, refined, drafted and made operational.

Dean Hancey says: "The Air Force came to us with a serious problem. It's the business of a private 1200 university such as USC to solve such problems. And creation of this program was a natural, direct result of that need."

Rapid growth

After the Air Force came the Navy and then the Army for the training of Flight Safety Officers. Today the University maintains 8 to 12-week courses for all these, plus courses for officers of Allied Nations through the Military Assistance Program. Just begun, in addition to these, is a special set of classes for the Federal Aviation Agency.

Growth of the Division has been phenomenal and the University now has 14 full-time and 17 part-time 1300 personnel engaged in the instruction of these classes and in their administration.

With a decade of experience the Aviation and Missile Safety Division today sets it sights far beyond the basics of aviation accident investigation and prevention. The Division hopes ultimately for clearer channels by which all aircraft accident investigators may funnel their knowledge to the aeronautics 1350 industry.

————STOP — ASK FOR YOUR TIME————

Record time immediately and answer the questions on content.

Time _____ Sec.	RATE (from table on page 305):	R. _____
No. Errors _____	COMPREHENSION (100 — 10% for each Error):	C. _____
VI-14	EFFICIENCY (R × C):	E. _____

ANSWER THESE QUESTIONS IMMEDIATELY (VI-14)

1. (T — F) The Aviation and Missile Safety Division is an important federal agency.

2. (T — F) A "crash course" is a field investigation problem for students at the Aviation and Missile Safety Division.

3. (C) Two astronauts who attended this unique school are Lovell and _____.

4. (M. C.) The most recent addition has been the training of men for:

   ____(1) the safe handling of ballistic missiles.

   ____(2) executive positions in aeronautics manufacturing firms.

   ____(3) positions with the U. S. aviation agencies.

   ____(4) positions as airline captains.

5. (T — F) An investigator can determine whether a part failed from fatigue or on impact by studying the differences in metal fractures.

6. (T — F) The investigative skills taught to the students are an important factor contributing to the underlying purpose of their training.

7. (C) Division Director George Potter stated, "Accident investigation is for the sake of accident _____ _____."

8. (M. C.) Which of the following is *not* a course offered by the Aviation and Missile Safety Division?

   ____(1) Aviation psychology.

   ____(2) Aviation physiology.

   ____(3) Use of the human centrifuge.

   ____(4) Communications and techniques.

9. (T — F) The school came into being because of losses of personnel and equipment suffered by the Air Force during World War II.

10. (T — F) The growth of the Aviation and Missile Safety Division has been retarded by lack of instructors.

Number VI-15

The Story of Western Union

(Reprinted from a pamphlet of the same name, by permission of Western Union)

────────── WAIT FOR SIGNAL TO BEGIN READING ──────────

From smoke signals to talking wires

The streamlined telegraph era of today is a far cry indeed from the primitive fire, smoke and flag signals of early times. A thousand years before this era of highspeed selective switching systems, radio beam telegraphy and multi-channel, printing telegraphy, man wished for rapid communications. In medieval times, knights flashed their burnished shields to communicate with each other. Argonauts used colored sails on their ships to convey a meaning. The Greeks, Romans and Aztecs used relay runners. In the days of Julius Caesar, sentinels were stationed in towers at regular intervals to shout messages from ⇌100 one to the other, covering as much as 150 miles in a few hours.

The jungles of Africa and islands of the South Pacific still echo with the throbbing of native tom-toms, or drums, to communicate with distant villages. Our American Indians signaled by day with puffs of smoke, and at night by waving torches and shooting flaming arrows into the sky. The huge fortune of the Rothschilds was made in part through information they obtained by use of carrier pigeons. Semaphore towers were used by George Washington during the Revolutionary War, and more than a century ago systems of Semaphore Towers, with ⇌200 arms that were moved to various positions to convey messages, were built for hundreds of miles in France, England and the United States. Early forms of rapid communication, however, were all slow. Men constantly rebelled against the limitations of time and space.

The first man to direct thought to the use of electricity for communications was Roger Bacon, in 1267, and he was put in jail for twenty years for dealing in black magic. The burgomaster of Magdeburg, Germany, Otto Von Guericke, made the first electricity-producing machine in 1650. It was a sulphur

⇀300 ball that he charged by rubbing his hands on it, just as we can charge our bodies by rubbing our feet on a thick rug. Wood, of England, found in 1726 that electricity could be conveyed by a metal conductor, and a few years later Gray and Wheeler sent electricity through 800 feet of wire. Thus the basic principle of telegraphy was known more than 200 years ago.

After that time, literally hundreds of men carried the knowledge of electricity forward, each adding something that helped in the invention of the telegraph. Oersted showed that current exerts a force ⇀400 which will deflect a magnet; LaPlace advanced the idea that a magnetic needle might be deflected to receive messages at a great distance; and Ampere put magnetic needles at the ends of 26 wires, so that deflections would signal the letters of the alphabet. In 1820 Baron Schilling, a gay captain of Hussars in the Russian Army, produced a telegraph which he operated by the use of five magnetic needles.

Harrison Grey Dyar operated a telegraph line on Long Island, N. Y., in 1826. Joseph Henry, a school teacher at Albany (NY) Academy, operated an electromagnetic telegraph in his room in 1830 and ⇀500 '31. He also built a line which he operated between two buildings at Princeton University in 1836. Gauss and Weber devised a simple magnetic telegraph in 1833 at the University of Goetingen, and Steinheil improved on their system in 1836. In the following year, Sir Charles Wheatstone and Sir William Cooke obtained a patent in England for their telegraph, the first in England.

Samuel Finley Breese Morse

The first really practical telegraph system was invented by Samuel F. B. Morse, a distinguished American painter who founded the National Academy of Design.

Returning from a trip to Europe on board the

Packet Ship "Sully" in 1832, Morse received his 600 ⇌ great inspiration. He realized that, if he could transmit intelligence and record it at a distance, he could revolutionize communications. He thought of signs which could be transmitted over a wire, and realized that the dot, dash and space were three signals which could be easily communicated. Morse was appointed professor of the Literature of the Arts of Design at New York University in 1835. This gave him a small salary, and provided the rooms in Washington Square where he built his first telegraph instrument, a crude affair constructed on a picture frame, with an ordinary 700 ⇌ lead pencil suspended by a pendulum to make the dots and dashes.

Morse demonstrated his first apparatus before a group of friends in his rooms at New York University on September 2, 1837. One of those present was Alfred Vail, son of Judge Stephen Vail, of the Speedwell Iron Works at Morristown, N. J. Young Vail became Morse's partner, providing money and building new and better instruments. These instruments were shown before an audience in the Geological Cabinet of the New York University, January 24, 1838. General Thomas S. Cummings was present, and when Morse asked for a message to be sent, a 800 ⇌ friend of Cummings wrote a facetious military command: "Attention, the Universe! By Kingdoms, Right Wheel!"

Morse exhibited the telegraph before President Van Buren and his Cabinet at Washington, D. C. Members of Congress called it a crazy scheme. Morse tried for years to get Congress to appropriate money for an experimental line, and finally his bill was passed on March 3, 1843. News of the Bill's passage was brought to him by Annie Ellsworth, daughter of the Commissioner of patents, and he gave Annie the honor of preparing the first telegram. The first telegraph line, built between Washington, D. C. 900 ⇌ and Baltimore, was opened before a distinguished group in the Supreme Court Chambers, on May 24 1844. The first telegram, handed to Morse by Annie Ellsworth, was "WHAT HATH GOD WROUGHT!"

The experimental line was exhibited for a year, but government officials decided the telegraph was an interesting toy that never would earn enough money to support itself. Morse then persuaded a skeptical public to buy stock and finance the telegraph as a private enterprise. The telegraph industry has been a private enterprise ever since, far outgrowing the subsidized, government-operated telegraph systems of foreign countries. More than a third of the world's 1000 ⇌ telegraph mileage is in the United States.

Morse and his associates extended the Washington-Baltimore telegraph line to New York City in 1846. Others obtained licenses from Morse and built lines between New York and Buffalo, New York and Boston, and other eastern cities. Western Union now has over 2,500,000 miles of carrier system circuits, many of which carry as many as 288 messages simultaneously.

Western Union — How it started

Over fifty telegraph companies were in operation in 1851 when a group of Rochester (NY) men led by Hiram Sibley, Ezra Cornell, Samuel L. and Henry 1100 → R. Selden organized to found the New York and Mississippi Valley Printing Telegraph Company. Lines to operate the House Printing Telegraph System, which printed the received message in plain Roman letters instead of dots and dashes, had been built prior to 1850 between New York and Boston, and between New York and Philadelphia. The group of Rochester men acquired rights to extend the House System throughout the United States.

Thirteen other companies were operating short lines in the five states north of the Ohio River. It was not easy to send a telegram a great distance; 1200 → it had to be transferred from one line to another and the charges of each line had to be paid. Service was slow and unreliable. Two of these lines were sold for debt, and the others were in such an improverished condition that the New York and Mississippi Valley Company bought them out. The Company was named Western Union Telegraph Company, indicating the union of the western lines in one system, on April 4, 1856. This name was insisted upon by Ezra Cornell, pioneer line builder, who used a part of the telegraph fortune he made to found Cornell → University. Western Union continued its policy of 1300 merging with other companies and building new lines, rapidly extending telegraph service over the nation.

This continued growth and expansion was accompanied by study and research into the improvement of machines and services. Consequently Western Union was able to provide better service to its cus- 1350 → tomers with each passing year.

—————STOP — ASK FOR YOUR TIME—————
Record time immediately on next page
and answer the questions on content.

Time _____ Sec.	RATE (from table on page 305):	R. _____
No. Errors _____	COMPREHENSION (100 − 10% for each Error):	C. _____
VI- 15	EFFICIENCY (R × C):	E. _____

ANSWER THESE QUESTIONS IMMEDIATELY (VI-15)

1. (M. C.) Which of the following methods of communication was not used in the early days?

    ____(1) Flashing of sunlight from shields.

    ____(2) Coded colored sails.

    ____(3) Sending messages by wire.

    ____(4) Shouting messages through signals.

2. (C) The one thing which all early forms of communication had in common was that they were all
_____.

3. (T — F) Early ideas of using electricity for communication brought accusations of black magic.

4. (T — F) The basic principles of telegraphy were unknown before the 20th Century.

5. (T — F) Samuel Morse invented the first really practical telegraph system.

6. (T — F) The major contribution which Alfred Vail made to Morse's invention by his partnership was his financial assistance.

7. (T — F) Members of Congress were enthusiastic after Morse's demonstration in Washington, D. C.

8. (C) The money for the building of the first experimental telegraph line was provided by _____
_____.

9. (T — F) In 1851 there was only one major telegraphic company operating in the United States.

10. (M. C.) The company which was the forerunner of Western Union was the:

    ____(1) New York and Mississippi Valley Company.

    ____(2) House Printing Telegraph Company.

    ____(3) Ohio River Telegraph Company

    ____(4) Sibley — Cornell — Selden Telegraph Company.

Whence Came This "Ism"?

BY PETER TIMERSON

(Reprinted from the September, 1954, issue of *Machinists Monthly Journal*, with the permission of the editor)

──────── WAIT FOR SIGNAL TO BEGIN READING ────────

Trade unionism

On the advent of another Labor Day, it might be appropriate to pause for a moment to reflect on the institution of that segment of our society and economy which we know as trade unionism. What motivated its conception? From whence did it come? While the locale of its origin may not be definite, it can reasonably be assumed that man's finer instinct for correcting injustice, coupled with the elemental instinct of combining for self-preservation, motivated its origin.

Development of early trade unions

History tells us that the equivalent of trade unions existed in Europe long before Columbus $\overset{100}{\leftarrow}$ discovered America. These early equivalents of trade unions were not, of course, the trade unions that we know today, but they did come into existence for the same purpose, which then was that of self-protection among what were peasants or serfs, long prior to the industrial revolution of the nineteenth century. These organizations were subjected to the same suppression that was later imposed upon trade unions.

In the early days, it was the land owners, and governments which were under the influence of the land owner, which sought suppression, and in later years, the suppression was imposed by industrialists, $\overset{200}{\leftarrow}$ and governments who were under the influence of industrialists.

Labor scarcity and wages

The Great Plague in England, in the middle 1300's, brought about a scarcity of labor, and workmen forced wages up because of this labor scarcity. This resulted in legislation, influenced by the wealthy, to force workers to accept wages the same as existed prior to the plague. There is evidence that the peasants of those days subscribed money to pay fines, and to defend those who were prosecuted because of this unjust legislation.

Later on in the century, authorities of the city of $\overset{300}{\rightarrow}$ London prohibited gatherings of workmen and we had the famous "Peasants Revolution," or "Wat Tyler's Rebellion," against the wealthy for attempting to force down wages. Those who violated these statutes were branded as vagabonds and condemned to slavery for a period of two years. If they attempted to escape, they were branded as slaves for life. If they continued to persist in their objection to the statutes, they were usually hanged.

Local justices or magistrates had the power to fix wages until the early 1800's, but, as is evidenced in our own day, attempts made to legislate wages or $\overset{400}{\rightarrow}$ working conditions, were doomed to failure, as the workers affected formed organizations in defiance of the authorities.

Because of this suppression by the wealthy land owners and legislators under their influence, the history of the worker for centuries is a sad story. It was not until 1871 that trade unions were recognized as legal societies in Great Britian, and the same pattern was followed in other European countries.

The organization of craftsmen

Following the medieval equivalent of trade unions, and with the expansion of trade, came guilds or societies comprised of craftsmen such as tailors, shoemakers, etc. The members of these guilds event- $\overset{500}{\rightarrow}$ ually became owners of small plants and shops, and admission to a craft society was limited to cope with the amount of business.

Journeymen craftsmen in these societies usually looked forward to one day becoming shop owners themselves, and it is now the consensus that this guild tradition of restriction of craftsmen retarded the evolution of trade unionism. However, with the industrial revolution of the nineteenth century, the guilds, naturally, went into discard, journeymen craftsmen no longer hoping to become businessmen on a small scale, as establishments which employed a few craftsmen grew into large plants employing many hundreds.

The early American colonists, because of their ⁶⁰⁰ origin, adopted the same attitude towards the workers as that of the English working class towards their "inferiors." The craftsmen did organize the equivalent of the European guilds, but when they did organize, they had to stipulate they would not engage in activities regarding hours of labor or wages. As a result their organizations were, for the most part, more of a fraternal nature, providing benefits for their members in times of sickness, etc. However, there were some craft unions organized on the eastern seaboard of the United States in the latter part of the eighteenth century, whose activities were devoted to matters of ⁷⁰⁰ hours and wages.

The problem of labor surplus

The economic situation after the Civil War produced a surplus of labor, thus leading to wage reductions and other hardships to which the workers reacted by organizing. Prior to and after the Civil War, several efforts were made to create national labor organizations, but none survived until the 1880's, when the American Federation of Labor came into existence.

Trade unionism today

Trade unionism today is an accepted factor in the social and economic structure of most of the free nations of the world. For many years we have had ⁸⁰⁰ international labor organizations culminating in the present I.C.F.T.U., but the evolution of trade unionism has not had an easy road to travel, and it can be well said that it has developed through a number of stages.

There was first, attempted subjugation; second, in the latter half of the nineteenth century, a stage of what might be called toleration; and in the twentieth century, the stage of acceptance and respect. There are other stages yet to come! Will the next stage be more prominent participation and responsibility in the governing of peoples?

Trade unionism originated from the activities of ⁹⁰⁰ minority groups who had the intestinal fortitude to demand an equitable share of the wealth which they produced. Every assult made by trade unionism on what is commonly termed, "the vested interests," resulted in considerable loss of blood as well as many hardships. For the preservation of unionism blood has flowed in coal, steel, and other industrial centers here in our own country.

Minorities lead

On a New England meadow in April, 1776, a small group of soldier farmers gave birth to the greatest nation on earth. Our own IAM was originated ¹⁰⁰⁰ by a small group of men seeking redress for injustices in an engine pit in a roundhouse in Atlanta, Georgia over 66 years ago.

A good analogy of what has emanated from the activities of minorities in the institution of trade unionism comes from an Anglo-American lecturer, John Ballentine Gough, (1817-1886):

"What is a minority? The chosen heroes of this earth have been in a minority. There is not a social, political, or religious principle that you enjoy today that was not bought for you by the blood and tears and patient suffering of the minority. It is the minority that has stood in the van of every ¹¹⁰⁰ moral conflict, and achieved all that is noble in the history of the world."

Trade unionism, in itself, is a paradox of idealism and hardhearted practicability. While idealism is the motivating force, the objectives are obtained by forceful, practical leaders supported by militant followers.

Unionism must be vigilant

Trade unionists should be ever vigilant and not allow themselves to be absorbed by, or integrated into, any other "ism". Trade unionism should always retain its identity and continue its activities to better the lot of suppressed peoples everywhere. It has ¹²⁰⁰ proved to be an effective factor in the fight against Communism in its program of enslavement.

The benefits obtained by trade unions are legion and cannot be enumerated here, but it is a far cry from fighting for a crust of bread and sufficient rags to cover nakedness, to the standard of living now enjoyed by trade unionists in the United States and Canada. Workmen's and unemployment compensation, as well as paid vacations, are but a few of the benefits obtained.

So, however you are enjoying Labor Day, do not think of it as just another holiday, but as a day dedi-¹³⁰⁰ cated to the founders of trade unionism. Neither should you think that Utopia has been reached; there is yet much to be done. Adequate housing and medical care are but two of the objectives yet unattained.

To paraphrase that great American, Oliver Wendell Holmes, Jr., "The race may be over but the work is ¹³⁵⁰ never done."

————STOP — ASK FOR YOUR TIME————

Record time immediately on next page
and answer the questions on content.

Time _____ Sec.   RATE (from table on page 305):   R. _____

No. Errors _____   COMPREHENSION (100 — 10% for each Error):   C. _____

VI- 16   EFFICIENCY (R × C):   E. _____

ANSWER THESE QUESTIONS IMMEDIATELY (VI-16)

1. (T — F) Organizations of serfs, similar to trade unions, were unknown until 1500 A.D.

2. (T — F) The Great Plague in England brought about a control of wages by legislation.

3. (M. C.) Trade unions were first recognized as legal societies in:

    ____(1) France.

    ____(2) United States.

    ____(3) Great Britian.

    ____(4) Germany.

4. (T — F) The guild tradition of restriction of craftsmen retarded the evolution of trade unionism.

5. (C) With the _____ of the nineteenth century the guilds went into discard as many journeymen craftsmen lost their aspirations to become owners.

6. (T — F) Several national labor organizations which were formed immediately after the Civil War are still in existence today.

7. (M. C.) The first permanent national labor organization in this country was the:

    ____(1) CIO.

    ____(2) AFL.

    ____(3) I.C.F.T.U.

    ____(4) IAM.

8. (T — F) Trade unionism originated from the activities of minority groups.

9. (C) _____ is the motivating force behind trade unionism.

10. (T — F) Workmen's and unemployment compensation are the only two benefits obtained by the trade unions.

Length: 1350 words

Number VI-17

Readability Score: 36

Using Current Materials

By Clarence Samford and Eugene Cottle

(Reprinted from the book, *Social Studies in the Secondary School,*
by permission of the authors and the publishers, McGraw-Hill Book Company, Inc.)

───────────── WAIT FOR SIGNAL TO BEGIN READING ─────────────

Free and inexpensive publications

One of the characteristics of our industrial age which may at times seem to be a wasteful consumption of materials is the abundance of published material emphasizing a product or a process, but it often will include helpful information upon a general topic which relates to a unit of work in the social studies. Since these materials are usually intended primarily to advertise, the teacher will face the problem of careful selection in order not to appear to be encouraging the use of some product. Most commercial advertisers realize the educational value of these publications, which may be recognized as 100 contributing a helpful service to the public. For example, the history of some business development can be of much value in a general description. The particular product whose manufacturer is publishing the pamphlet may be representative of several which are typical of the business development which is the significant element in some study unit. A teacher is soon able to build up a considerable file of these publications.

Some advantages in using free and inexpensive materials

As school curricula have exhibited a growing trend toward general education, social studies teachers have recognized the great supply of helpful material 200 available in free and inexpensive form as one of the chief sources of information to be used by their classes in studying the problems so closely related to everyday living as emphasized in this program. Thus it seems that this material does lend itself to such use.

The slow reader may also find a benefit in some of these materials, although they may not be written with him in mind. The pamphlets seldom carry lengthy discussions, and they usually include simple explanations of the technical phases of their contents. 300 Such writing enables the slow reader to achieve an understanding of what he reads, and thus the material becomes a source of satisfaction to him. The pamphlets frequently include illustrations and graphic representations which add to their attractiveness.

The use of these materials may encourage in the pupils the habit of using more than one source to arrive at conclusions. The pupil enjoys the variety of these publications, and as he makes use of several different kinds in the process of gathering information about a topic, he experiences pleasure in the exploration and a challenge in organizing his findings.

These materials may also serve as supplementary 400 sources in units of study which are based upon a textbook. In this use they may aid the teacher in providing material for some particular pupil interest.

Materials from periodicals and newspapers

Magazine and newspaper articles are of great value in building up the file of information on some topic. When pupils are encouraged to read periodicals and newspapers with an eye toward the building up of resource files on various topics, their reading becomes a more worth-while experience as they examine the contents of an article with a given topic in mind. 500 The periodical may frequently be one that carried in each issue a certain department, which affords opportunity for the pupil to gather a sequence of articles and data upon a topic or series of topics. By becoming well-acquainted with some given periodicals or newspapers, the pupil forms reading habits involving taste and appreciation which are of permanent value to him. As indicated earlier in this chapter, certain periodicals seem to be of particular interest to the social studies. It is frequently possible to build discussion periods around a particular magazine. The need for pupil understanding of current topics calls for such use of periodicals. Consistent use of periodicals whose value in social studies is $\underset{\leftarrow}{600}$ recognized encourages pupils not only to read these particular publications but to evaluate other materials which they will read.

Using the newspaper

The daily newspaper is an important element in our culture and affords great opportunity for the social studies teacher to guide pupils in their reading habits concerning current happenings. The radio news broadcast reaches many people, but it is of necessity brief in time and does not allow freedom of selection and range in contacting the news as does the newspaper. Teachers are in error when they assume that because the newspaper is so common an $\underset{\leftarrow}{700}$ element in our civilization, pupils are acquainted with all the make-up of a paper. One of the most interesting, as well as valuable, units in the social studies can be one based on getting acquainted with newspapers.

A beginning on such a study can be made by having the class examine copies of large-city daily newspapers. Local newspaper agencies are usually cooperative in giving day-old papers to the school for such study purposes. It is a valuable experience for pupils to become acquainted with the names of papers. As these papers are examined, pupils will discover $\underset{\leftarrow}{800}$ many differences in form and in the style of publication. Recognition of these differences will raise questions which can lead to a valuable investigation of the newspaper.

The department of a newspaper must be recognized and evaluated in terms of the type of news contained within that portion of the paper. Pupils need to understand the purpose of headlines and how to evaluate them. Becoming acquainted with the style of writing in a particular newspaper is a worthwhile experience. Pupils realize by their own experience how news may affect the reader, as they compare news write-ups in different papers. Probably one of $\underset{\leftarrow}{900}$ the most significant values for the pupil to develop from the study of the newspaper is an appreciation of editorial writing. Just as the class may set up criteria to evaluate a news article, so may they also decide on the characteristics of a good editorial. Learning to know the style of writing and the philosophy of a columnist increases pupil ability in using the news-

paper. When such a study project is undertaken, the teacher will find it developing in various ways after the first stages of becoming acquainted with news- $\underset{1000}{\longrightarrow}$ paper organization. This study sets the stage for valuable pupil experiences and growth as various tangent topics arise from pupil interest and reaction. It should be included in the year plans of all social studies teachers.

Building resource units

The trend toward general education courses has caused the social studies teacher more and more to depend upon a variety of materials and new activities in which the textbook with its prearranged material is no longer adequate. The total plan and listed materials together with many explanations of topics for a given unit of work may be described as a re- $\underset{1100}{\longrightarrow}$ source unit. It is the full explanation for the teacher of all the probable lines of development which might occur in a large problem area or general overall topic. When a class studies a unit involving some particular area, the teacher has at hand the guiding subject matter materials and possible plan in his resource unit. Each year additions to the resource unit from new practices, activities, and materials will enrich it as a resource. As some phases seem to be no longer practical or efficient, these may be withdrawn from the resource-unit file. With the resource $\underset{1200}{\longrightarrow}$ unit as a guide the teacher can share the planning of the pupils' unit with them, pointing toward desirable objectives suggested by the resource unit and giving suggestions to aid the pupils in the careful and judicious planning of their unit; for the resource unit gives cautions and characterizes as inefficient or less helpful certain procedures and activities recorded from past experience with this general topic.

Some commercially prepared resource units may be available for the social studies teacher, but such aids must be used in a way most beneficial to the specific class situation. With experience the social studies teacher will find that his own planning and $\underset{1300}{\longrightarrow}$ collection of materials is of greatest value to him, although he will always watch for new approaches and materials. It will probably be through the building of several resource units that the social studies teacher will lose the dread of trying new curricular procedures where no previously planned outline of $\underset{1350}{\longrightarrow}$ work exists.

———STOP — ASK FOR YOUR TIME———

Record time immediately on next page
and answer the questions on content.

Time _____ Sec.	RATE (from table on page 305):	R. _____
No. Errors _____	COMPREHENSION (100 − 10% for each Error):	C. _____
VI- 17	EFFICIENCY (R × C):	E. _____

ANSWER THESE QUESTIONS IMMEDIATELY (VI-17)

1. (T — F) The abundance of published materials in advertising is a wasteful consumption of materials.

2. (C) These materials are usually intended primarily to _____.

3. (T — F) The habit of using more than one source to arrive at conclusions may be encouraged in pupils by use of these materials.

4. (M. C.) The material becomes a source of satisfaction to the slow reader because the pamphlets:

    ____(1) Present interesting information.

    ____(2) Include lengthy explanations of technical phases.

    ____(3) Include no explanatory pictures.

    ____(4) Present sample explanations of technical phases.

5. (T — F) Newspaper articles are of less value than magazine articles in building up a file of information on some topic.

6. (T — F) Teachers may assume that pupils are well acquainted with newspapers and the ways to use them.

7. (M. C.) One of the most important values for the pupil to develop from the study of the newspaper is the recognition of:

    ____(1) The publisher of the newspaper.

    ____(2) The differences in form and style of different papers.

    ____(3) The arrangement of the editorial page.

    ____(4) The style and size of headlines used.

8. (T — F) The textbook with its prearranged material is no longer adequate in teaching social studies.

9. (C) The _____ is the total plan and listed materials together with many explanations of topics for a given unit of work.

10. (T — F) Purchase of commercially prepared materials is not necessary for successful learning of social studies.

Number VI-18

Electronics—Your Chance to Shape the Future

(Reprinted from the pamphlet "Electronics," by permission of the
Executive Vice-President of Electronics Industries Association)

───────── WAIT FOR SIGNAL TO BEGIN READING ─────────

Career horizons unlimited!

In science and engineering nowadays there is an often used word. That word is "exotic." Exotic implies something strange and wonderful. Career opportunities in electronics promise to be exotic. In fact, new opportunities continually arise — not only for the creative scientist and engineer, but for every eager searcher whatever his special interests may be. The situation is almost parallel to that time-worn dream of romantic inventors — perpetual motion. It works this way. Laboratory experiments require new kinds of electronic instruments that develop into new fields of gadgetry which branch out into new discoveries about the laws of nature that lead to 100 ← new kinds of industry which again branch out into new household conveniences, more effective methods of communication, better ways to control illnesses, safer and faster travel, more efficient techniques in education, more luxuries to enjoy cheaper products through automatic mass-production, speedier ways to solve complex problems, highly accurate air defense and alarm systems to assure your security, as well as an over-all increase of precision throughout almost every endeavor stimulated by modern society. A few examples are automatic pilots for aircraft and sea-going craft, electronic controls in factories, hearing aids, tape recorders, and manned spaceflight.

The rapid and continuous application of electronics 200 ← provides jobs for everyone: scientists and engineers evolve new principles, engineers design devices based on those principles, technicians and craftsmen use their skills to construct the devices, salesmen see that the devices are distributed, field technicians install and maintain the devices, and teachers train students in all of these techniques.

As an electronics specialist, you can be involved in the excitement of building and operating analog or digital computers, giant radar installations, micro-wave relay systems that span the continent, missile tracking and detection systems as well as automatic 300 → countdown systems for checking out and launching the big "birds," radio telescopes at the great observatories, television transmitters and cameras (both black and white and full color) and perhaps one day stereophonic installations at FM radio stations, and remote-control handling systems in the nuclear or industrial manufacturing fields. These are only random choices of challenging activities that are available for you today. Tomorrow's will be even more extensive.

Astrionics

Someday men are going to land on the moon and planets to colonize those alien bodies. They will be able to accomplish this mainly because of a new 400 → branch in electronics. Astrionics is the field of application of the electronics technology involved with spaceflight, just as avionics is the field of application of electronics to flight within the Earth's atmosphere. In each case electronics provides navigational and control equipment that performs tasks with precision and speed beyond the capability of human beings. Electronic devices also assure communications that give the pilot and crew vital information, including the isolation and warning of a malfunction to the craft. Astrionics further includes an entirely new area that is just now getting under way: satellite communications system. There will be electronic repeater-stations in 500 → space that can relay voice, television, facsimile and teletype signals from any one point in the world to distant points. They will be unaffected by weather conditions on Earth or magnetic storms on the Sun, because they will use microwave radio. Another young and rapidly growing technology, this uses electromagnetic waves of such short wavelength that they can pass through the spaces between raindrops or electrified particles in the gases of the upper atmosphere. Already experimental models of these re-peater-stations have been successfully orbited in space.

Intellectronics

As this coined word implies, it describes another new field of electronics — the processing and storing $\overset{600}{\leftarrow}$ of information. Ultimately, all information presently stored in books may be much more efficiently stored by electronic means. This would have a powerful effect on the processes of education — since at the push of a button, so to speak, any kind of special information on whatever subject could be retrieved and displayed in a matter of seconds. Certainly this would be a great help to you in researching a theme paper. It would also help your teacher devise ways to build up your background of knowledge faster. The scientist, engineer, and technician too, would be saved a vast amount of valuable time that they now $\overset{700}{\leftarrow}$ use up in searching through technical literature for solutions to problems. Intellectronics is a wide-open field to those of you with a mathematical bent. It depends upon the development of new approaches to information theory, computer-logic, and on non-linear differential equations. Yet those of you who like to tinker experimentally, build gadgets, or are curious about natural phenomena also have a place in intellectronics.

Low temperature electronics — Cryogenics

This is the realm of extremely low-temperature phenomena (sometimes referred to as cryogenics). It is becoming increasingly important in electronics, since electrical conductivity increases as temperature $\overset{800}{\leftarrow}$ drops lower and lower. At the temperature of liquid helium some metals become superconductors. The general reason is that almost all the atoms which form the material cease their thermal vibrations in crystalline lattice structures and offer virtually no resistance to the passage of electrons from one to another. Cryogenic electronics could be your dish, if you have an exploring kind of mind that likes to delve into the physical properties of nature and adapt them to useful work on new levels. Take your choice; you can be either an electronics physicist or electronics engineer and still find a place in cryogenics. $\overset{900}{\leftarrow}$

MHD and plasma electronics

"MHD" stands for magnetohydrodynamics. It deals with the motion of an electrically conducting fluid in the presence of a magnetic field. A plasma is a gaseous mixture of charged particles — negative electrons and positively charged molecules of gas. After acceleration by a magnetic field these particles possess enormous energies, evidenced by kinetic temperatures of thousands to millions of degrees. The thermonuclear reaction possible with this phe-

nomenon could lead to the direct conversion of matter into electricity. Designers are already at work on MHD engines for space ships. Such engines could $\overset{1000}{\longrightarrow}$ accelerate a space craft to half the speed of light. Other types of space engines being actively worked upon by electronics engineers include electrostatic as well as ion-driven ones. The problems involved with MHD are formidable. Ultra high temperatures can be maintained for but brief fractions of a second. The problem of confining the high temperature plasma by a magnetic field is waiting to be solved.

Electronics at home

After all this talk about extremely low and extremely high temperatures, it may appear rather prosaic to discuss electronics in the home. Yet it's $\overset{1100}{\longrightarrow}$ not prosaic at all, for electronics is exciting in all of its many forms. Increasingly, electronics engineers have been creating more and more automatic devices for the home. With the tremendous advances made in miniaturization through solid-state electronics much equipment can be packed into a small space. Normally, hi-fi amplifiers require areas covering one-half to one full square foot of space. Micro-miniaturization has made it possible to produce an amplifier in a space no larger than a dime. An entire computing system can be built into a cubic foot or less.

Career summary

Because electronics forms a vitally important sustaining part of so many other areas of endeavor, it $\overset{1200}{\longrightarrow}$ is practically impossible here to make a job-by-job listing of all available positions. Most electronics work is usually accomplished by teams. A given project may offer work to persons ranging in education from high school graduate to Doctor of Science or Philosophy. In terms of varied skills, electronics runs the gamut from factory assembly-line to research engineers. In terms of opportunities, there are vast areas of specialization within industry and the military. In terms of salaries, those in the electronics industry are well above those of technical industry in general.

Electronics is moving forward at such a pace that $\overset{1300}{\longrightarrow}$ alert, well-trained and interested people must be found to help both the military and industry keep up with technological progress. Training may be either academic or technical or both. Such training most assuredly requires a solid and well-planned high school education as a basis with additional reading $\overset{1350}{\longrightarrow}$ and tinkering on your own.

———STOP — ASK FOR YOUR TIME———

Record time immediately and answer the questions on content.

Time _____ Sec.	RATE (from table on page 305):	R. _____
No. Errors _____	COMPREHENSION (100 − 10% for each Error):	C. _____
VI-18	EFFICIENCY (R × C):	E. _____

ANSWER THESE QUESTIONS IMMEDIATELY (VI-18)

1. (M. C.) The way in which new opportunities continually arise in the field of electronics may be compared to the inventor's dream of:

    _____(1) laboratory experiments.

    _____(2) automatic mass production.

    _____(3) perpetual motion.

    _____(4) manned space flight.

2. (T − F) An electronics specialist can be involved in the excitement of building and operating analog and digital computers.

3. (C) _____ is the field of application of the electronics technology involved with space flight.

4. (T − F) Intellectronics involves the new area of satellite communications.

5. (T − F) Intellectronics is a wide-open field to those with a mathematical bent.

6. (T − F) Cryogenics is a field dealing with extremely high-temperature phenomena.

7. (M. C.) The thermonulcear reaction possible with the "MHD" phenomenon could lead to:

    _____(1) the direct conversion of matter into electricity.

    _____(2) the formation of a gaseous mixture of charged particles.

    _____(3) the development of a magnetic field.

    _____(4) the production of negative electrons.

8. (T − F) Electronics engineers are creating fewer and fewer devices for the home.

9. (T − F) Miniaturization is the process which has made it possible to produce many household devices which fit in very small places.

10. (C) In terms of educational training, most jobs in electronics require at least a _____ education.

Number VI-19

Using Community Resources

BY CLARENCE SAMFORD AND EUGENE COTTLE

(An excerpt from the book, *Social Studies in the Secondary School.*
Reprinted by permission of the authors and the publishers, McGraw-Hill Book Company, Inc.)

──────── WAIT FOR SIGNAL TO BEGIN READING ────────

Using the community as a resource

For the social studies the local community affords a kind of source material which surpasses almost all other materials in value for the pupil. In considering the community as a resource for the social studies, teachers are not only seeking to recognize the school as a functional part of the community but they are finding within it those materials necessary for social understandings. Seen in their actual relationship within the community, all the elements of community life become more vital and meaningful for the pupil than when these same elements are discussed from a textbook without actual experience. More ⭢100 and more social studies courses are utilizing the life of the local community in providing ways in which to achieve objectives which pupils recognize as significant.

There are many activities in which pupils may engage which can establish new social understandings and attitudes resulting from pupil participation in such community projects as may be open to youth. Nearly all communities carry on such welfare programs as the annual Community Chest Drive. Pupils in social studies classes may become more aware of their responsibilities of citizenship in their community through a unit of work centering around this annual ⭢200 community project. Pupils may share in such a project in various ways, such as distributing literature and announcements, taking turns by groups at Community Chest headquarters as messengers, and managing some office administrative tasks assigned by the citizens' committee in charge.

In some communities the recreational facilities for youth are inadequate but need not continue so. A social studies class, aware of its local problem, can publicize the situation by a house-to-house canvass, by a committee's visit to the city council to present the problem and to urge the community administration to consider some means to provide

⭢300 for the recreational needs of the community, by writing a series of newspaper articles explaining the situation, or by selecting committees to appear before church groups and service organizations to arouse public interest in the problem.

During a national campaign to inform the public on the dangers of cancer, a social studies class, in cooperation with the school health classes, planned and carried out a community project in which each pupil interviewed people on the streets and in their homes asking such questions as the following;

1. Do you know about how many deaths occur annually from cancer?
⭢400 2. Do you know what some possible symptoms of cancer are?
3. Do you know what should be done by each person to help prevent cancer deaths?

Such projects as those mentioned above, in addition to acquainting pupils with their community more intimately, provide experience in meeting and talking with business and professional members of the community and with housewives. From such personal contacts pupils gain new attitudes and understandings; they become aware of points of view other than those of their own family or social group. When community and school work together, pupils see no ⭢500 separation of the school from the life of the community and their participation in community enterprises is a natural activity.

The Citizenship Education Project conducted by Teachers College, Columbia University, is giving outstanding leadership in the trend toward school-community participation in local projects. This program attempts to vitalize the fundamental of citizenship by providing opportunities for pupils to experience many of the community processes about which pupils have up to this time usually had only a reading knowledge.

Planning the use of community resources

Before the community can be used by the social studies class, the teacher must have made some careful study of the community and must be aware of its 600 ← chief characteristics, its history, its chief institutions, its basic economic structure, its organization, and many other details. A part of the training of a social studies teacher should involve such practice experiences as will give him a background for this important phase of his teaching career. Too often the teacher in training has been removed from the specific examples of social living by a curriculum which has stressed theory and has given too little attention to the life of the community as a means of preparation for teaching. The teacher must see the community in all 700 ← its processes in order to guide pupils intelligently. In learning to know the community, the teacher will be one with the pupils, especially when he is new in the town. Much of his spare time should be given over to a concentrated effort to become acquainted with local institutions and to achieve a knowledge of the community in general.

Some suggestions for community study

The social studies teacher may wonder how to begin using within the classroom the resources of the local scene. It is obvious that the teacher must guide the pupils in becoming aware of community problems 800 ← or activities worthy of consideration. Perhaps one approach for the teacher may be the planning for himself of what experiences might seem desirable for the pupils. When the teacher is a newcomer to the community he may need to give much time and thought to becoming acquainted with the area. Some of the possible points of consideration for the teacher may be:

1. What are the characteristics of the local population?
2. What environmental factors dominate the economic scene?
3. Is the community mindful of the recreational needs of its citizens?
4. How is the community related to other nearby 900 ← centers of population?
5. What is the employment situation in the community?
6. What transportation and communication facilities exist in the community?
7. From observation do any conditions appear which might be improved for the general welfare of the community?

From this list of suggestions the teacher will be led to think of others perhaps more pertinent to his own situation.

The daily discussion of news events is a fruitful source of projects for community activities by pupils. When it is observed that local news items are followed by a newspaper editorial comment, the project nearly 1000 → always has an established significance. For example, a city is considering the addition of a fluorination process to its water purification, and the local newspaper will carry news items concerning the proposal. The resulting discussion in the community will lead to editorial comment in the newspaper concerning the desirability of such a process. From the discussion in the social studies class of this community problem a class has the opportunity to investigate the process, to interview citizens for opinions concerning the proposal, and to aid in any campaign of education of the public for what may be a worth-while community development.

1100 →
The field trip

Pupil observance of community activities is carried on in the form of field trips. The entire class may go on a trip, a committee from the class may go, or an individual pupil may investigate a given community activity and report his findings to the class. The field trip is a valuable device in teaching, but its worth depends upon the teacher's careful planning and organization.

The individual citizen resources

Within every community there are individuals whose lifework or experience can be of great interest and value to pupils in the social studies. Members 1200 → of the professions may visit a class to tell of some of their professional responsibilities, aims, and activities as guidance in vocational planning. Representatives of community organizations or institutions, such as a police officer, a sanitation engineer, a member of the fire department, or an official from a welfare agency, can bring valuable information into the classroom. A visit from an elderly person who is able to describe earlier times in the community is frequently a very instructive experience for pupils, as the past is brought to them by someone who remembers it. As with the 1300 → field trip, a visit from an individual requires preparation by the class. The visit should be planned in relation to the unit of study, and pupil questions need to be planned in anticipation of the visit. A discussion of points of information gained and pupil reaction to the visit must follow, to hold the valuable 1350 → experience for the class.

————STOP — ASK FOR YOUR TIME————

Record time immediately on next page
and answer the questions on content.

Time _____ Sec.	RATE (from table on page 305):	R. _____
No. Errors _____	COMPREHENSION (100 − 10% for each Error):	C. _____
VI-19	EFFICIENCY (R × C):	E. _____

ANSWER THESE QUESTIONS IMMEDIATELY (VI-19)

1. (T — F) In considering the community as a resource for the social studies, teachers are only seeking to recognize the school as a functional part of the community.

2. (C) Textbooks plus _____ cause the elements of community life to become more meaningful for the pupil.

3. (M. C.) Which of the following activities was not mentioned as a worthwhile learning experience for students?

    ____(1) Publicize needs in a house-to-house canvass.

    ____(2) Serving as messengers at Community Chest headquarters.

    ____(3) Soliciting funds in a house-to-house canvass.

    ____(4) Visiting the city council meeting.

4. (T — F) Too often the teacher in training is faced with a curriculum which puts too little stress on theory.

5. (T — F) The teacher must see the community in all its processes in order to guide pupils intelligently.

6. (T — F) From the contacts of personal interviews, pupils gain new attitudes.

7. (T — F) There is little to be gained from pupil participation in a community problem.

8. (C) The _____ must guide pupils in becoming aware of activities worthy of consideration.

9. (M. C.) The field trip is a valuable device in teaching but its worth depends on the preparation by the:

    ____(1) School principal.

    ____(2) Pupils.

    ____(3) Community leaders.

    ____(4) Teacher.

10. (T — F) Individuals in the community can be of great value to pupils in the social studies.

Number VI-20

Words Under the Sea

(Reprinted from the pamphlet *The Story of Western Union*, by permission of Western Union)

─────────────── WAIT FOR SIGNAL TO BEGIN READING ───────────────

The submarine cables

With the Civil War scarcely over, Western Union in 1865 began building an audacious, globe-girdling overland line westward to Europe. Led by the Clipper ship Nightingale, a flotilla of twenty-two vessels was sent forth from San Francisco to commence construction of the telegraph line which was to run northward from San Francisco to Portland, through British Columbia and the unexplored wilderness of Russian-America (now Alaska), across Bering Strait by cable, and through Siberia to the mouth of the Amur River, where it was to join a 7,000-mile line under construction from St. Petersburg.

Exploration and construction of the line was ⟵100 progressing rapidly over thousands of miles when Cyrus W. Field laid the first permanent and successful Atlantic Cable on July 27, 1866. The need for an overland line to Europe then was ended. The expedition was called off, but the negotiations for the right-of-way for the line by Western Union's President Sibley on a trip to St. Petersburg, led to the purchase of Alaska by the United States.

A cable expedition led by Cyrus W. Field had laid the first transatlantic cable in 1858, but that cable was ruined in a few weeks by the use of too much ⟵200 electrical current. Enough current to operate a cable can be generated in a thimble, but the engineers of 1858 did not know that. Field tried again and again, and in 1866 the first permanently successful Atlantic cable was laid. Others followed.

In 1882 Western Union entered the cable business by leasing from the American Telegraph & Cable Company two transatlantic cables which that company had laid between Penzance, England, and Canso, Nova Scotia, with land wire connections between Canso and New York. The lease, for fifty years, would have expired in 1932, but Western Union purchased the cable company in 1930, and thus ⟵300 acquired the cables.

In 1912 Western Union leased a complete transatlantic system of five cables, and subsequently laid three loaded or permalloy cables, one to England and two to the Azores, making ten in all, which with cables to Cuba and one to Barbados, connecting there to South America through the Western Telegraph Company, constitute the main arteries of the Western Union cable system. For the care of the cables the company has two cable ships, the "Lord Kelvin" and the "Cyrus Field."

A new type cable

400⟶ From the time the first successful transatlantic cable was laid in 1866 until 1924, no material change in the design of ocean cables was made. In 1924 Western Union inaugurated a new era in cable development by laying a cable between New York and Horta, Azores, in which the single copper conductor was wound with wafer-thin ribbon of metal known as "permalloy". At slightly increased cost this greatly increased the capacity of the cable for transmitting words. To utilize the large capacity the cable is operated in a number of separate channels, each used as an individual unit.

500⟶ Then cables similar in design, but embodying still further improvements, were laid between Newfoundland and Horta, Azores. Each of the three Western Union permalloy cables can transmit a total number of words equal to the combined capacities of the company's seven cables of older design. The cable between Newfoundland and Horta was designed by the engineers for simultaneous operation in both directions, and it has been operated at a speed of 1400 letters per minute each way, establishing the highest record thus far for any transoceanic cable.

Speed of the New York-Bay Roberts-Penzance permalloy cable has been increased by Western Union engineers from 1600 to 2400 letters per minute, ⟶ providing eight channels of 300 letters each. The 600 cable has been working satisfactorily at this speed in direct operation between New York and London. One channel has been extended from New York to

239

Montreal and Toronto thus providing direct working between those cities and London, and one channel has been extended from London to Amsterdam for direct working between Amsterdam and New York.

Current operations

Western Union maintains and operates offices in sixteen cities in Great Britain and Ireland, and maintains eleven branch offices located in convenient sections of London. The Company operates in Paris and Havre, France, also in Antwerp and Brussels, Belgium. It maintains its own office 700 in Amsterdam, Holland, and in Italy it is associated with the Italcable Company which maintains offices in the principal cities in Italy. The company's submarine cable system totals 30,500 nautical miles.

Western Union operates a combination of landline and submarine cables to Havana where the company maintains its own offices. The circuits extend beyond Havana to provide direct service between New York with Santiago, Cuba, Kingston, Jamaica, and San Juan, Puerto Rico. From these four key cities a highly dependable service is maintained with all places in the West Indies. The Company operates 800 a combination landline-submarine service from New York to Bridgetown, Barbados where a through connection is had with the Western Telegraph Company serving all countries on the South American continent.

Western Union also handles telegrams to and from Canadian and Mexican points through an exchange agreement with telegraph companies in those countries. In Canada, the Canadian National Telegraphs and the Canadian Pacific Railway Company originate and terminate messages for Western Union, while the Mexican National Telegraphs performs the same function in that country.

The Western Union Telegraph Company impartially represents all international cable and radio systems connecting with the United States. Customers may 900 specifically route their business via the international carrier of their choice by simply writing on their message the word "via" followed by the name of the Company to which the message is to be transferred at the point of exit from the United States. These routings will be honored by Western Union. All other international messages will continue to be sent over the various normal routes on international carriers operating between the several points of exit in the United States and the different overseas destinations.

How to write international messages

International cable and radio messages are constructed similarly to domestic telegrams, except that 1000 registered (abbreviated) code addresses may be used to save tolls, and code words (secret language) are permitted in the Full-Rate classification. Each word in the address, text and signature is counted and charged for.

In addressing international cable or radio messages, the name of the country of destination is seldom necessary. Unregistered addresses should not be unduly shortened, since senders are responsible for incorrect or insufficient addresses and corrections or amplifications can be made only by sending a paid service message at the Full-Rate.

International services

The ordinary or Full-Rate classification of international 1100 service is subject to a minimum charge for five words. It is the standard fast service for messages in plain language, in secret (code of cipher) language, or in a combination of plain and secret language.

The Letter Telegram classification of international service, which is for messages in plain language only, is charged for at one-half of the per word rates applicable to Full-Rate messages, with a minimum charge for twenty-two words. This is an overnight service with delivery generally being made the day after the filing date. Letter Telegram messages are designated 1200 by the indicator "LT" which is placed before the address and counted and charged as one word.

Cable Money Orders — This service provides the quickest, surest way to send funds to many foreign countries. The money is deposited at the nearest Western Union office, and a fast Cable Money Order is sent abroad. Payment is made through one of the company's many foreign offices.

Shore-Ship Messages — Communication with ships at sea in all parts of the world is provided by Western Union in association with connecting radio-telegraph companies. However, only the full-rate message classification is available.

IMCO Service — International Metered Communications Service is a form of shared private line service in which certain facilities and apparatus of Western Union are used by subscribers and correspondents on a two-point basis for the teleprinter transmission of record communication between New York City and London. Transmission is direct between each subscriber's station and the correspondent's station, providing either one-way or two-way communica- 1350 tion.

————STOP — ASK FOR YOUR TIME————

Record time immediately on next page and answer the questions on content.

Time _____ Sec.   RATE (from table on page 305):   R. _____

No. Errors _____   COMPREHENSION (100 − 10% for each Error):   C. _____

VI-20   EFFICIENCY (R × C):   E. _____

ANSWER THESE QUESTIONS IMMEDIATELY (VI — 20)

1. (T — F) The first globe-girdling overland line from America to Europe started from the United States westward.

2. (M. C.) According to this author, negotiations for the right of way for this overland line eventually led to:

____(1) The purchase of the Trans-Siberian Telegraph Co. by Western Union.

____(2) The U. S. Government's purchase of Alaska.

____(3) The Russo-Japanese War.

____(4) The establishment of a World Union Telegraph service.

3. (T — F) The first permanently successful Atlantic cable was laid in 1866.

4. (C) The American Telegraph and Cable Company which owned some of the transatlantic cables was later purchased by _____.

5. (T — F) Permalloy cables are 7 times as efficient as the cables of the earlier design.

6. (T — F) Western Union has no offices in Europe.

7. (C) The companion company to Western Union serving South America is called the Western _____ _____ Company.

8. (T — F) Western Union is the major telegraph company in Canada.

9. (T — F) Secret language is not permitted in international telegrams.

10. (M. C.) The "half-rate" service which allows for a twenty-two word message which is delivered the following day is called:

____(1) IMCO service.

____(2) Ordinary classification.

____(3) Letter-Telegram classification.

____(4) Ship-shore message.

SERIES VII
Study Reading Drills

These exercises provide practice in a self-recitation type of reading. They are designed to help you understand some of the principles of self-recitation and spaced review. In a limited sense they provide a practical illustration of the fact that it is easier to remember soon after reading than it is to allow a lapse of other reading or other activities to intervene. In actual practice, however, you will provide your own questions for the self-recitation periods.

Here the stress is still on increasing the reading speed and the reading level, but there is also a stress on a study technique which will help improve long range retention of material read. Here you expose yourself to ideas not only by reading about them but by pausing frequently to think about them and to apply them to practical questions on the material. You should find that this technique helps to break the monotony of reading and to enable you to read with less tension and less fatigue because you bring into use more than one type of study approach.

These exercises are matched — number for number — with those in series VI for readability, length, and type of questions asked. Comparisons of your reading rate and reading efficiency scores on these drills with the comparable exercises in Series VI will give you some measure of your progress in mastering this technique of self recitation as you read.

General directions on these exercises are the same as for those in Series V except that you do not call for your time until you have finished the tenth question in the exercise. You then compute your *rate, comprehension, and efficiency* as before and record on the graph for study reading on page 291. Keys are on pages 312 and 318.

Family Insurance

By Clarence Woodbury

(Reprinted from the November 1951 issue of the *American Magazine*,
by permission of the editor)

─────────── WAIT FOR SIGNAL TO BEGIN READING ───────────

You can do everything with insurance, from protecting your children against poverty to avoiding a lawsuit over an accident. Some people have too much insurance, but most of us don't have enough. These simple do's and don't's will help you decide exactly what you need.

Are you fully insured?

A friend of mine, whom I'll call George Anderson, thought he was fully insured. He had life, health, fire, and auto insurance. He and his family were protected against windstorms, falling aircraft, riots, burglary, and theft. Even had a meteor dropped on his home, Mr. Anderson could have taken it in his ⟵100 stride.

But one afternoon he transplanted a shrub in his yard and neglected to pack down the earth when he refilled the hole he had made. That evening an elderly neighbor woman toddled over to call on Mrs. Anderson. She stepped in the soft dirt, fell, and fractured her hip in three places. When she got out of the hospital she sued Mr. Anderson, and was awarded $18,000 in damages.

That was not an unreasonable judgment, considering the extent of the old lady's injuries, but it ruined the Andersons. Paying off the $18,000 cost them their home, their savings, and a slice of Mr. Anderson's ⟵200 salary for several years. This could all have been avoided if he had had an inexpensive public-liability policy which would have protected him against lawsuits. But he didn't have one. He and his family were not adequately insured after all!

1. (T — F) Mr. Woodbury believes the courts were very unjust in awarding the old lady such large damages.
2. (C) The type of insurance which Mr. Anderson had failed to provide for his family was a_____ policy.

The right kind of insurance

Similar cases occur every day. We are the most heavily insured nation the world has ever seen. In ⟶300 1950, the American people spent $15,135,000,000 (more than $100 per person) for various types of insurance. Mostly, this money was wisely invested. But millions of us don't have the *right kind* of insurance. It often represents the most important family purchase of a lifetime, yet many of us give less thought to the selection of policies than we do to buying a new suit.

The sensible man doesn't buy a suit which is too small for him, or too large, or one without pants. ⟵400 That is exactly what a lot of people do when they select insurance coverage. Through carelessness or lack of foresight they pick policies which don't fit their needs or even cover their nakedness.

I discovered this when I set out recently to find out what kind of insurance program the average family should have. I talked with many of the nation's leading authorities in the fields of life insurance, casualty insurance, inland marine insurance, and the other main branches of the risk business. I consulted with so many purveyors of insurance, in fact, that in the end I found myself buying some more of their commodity.

⟶500 Without exception, these experts deplored the unwise manner in which many people pick their insurance. They cited many horrible examples of policy-holders who had been imprudent or plain dumb in selecting coverage. In no other realm are so many if-he'd-only-been-smarter stories floating around as in the insurance field.

I was told about a California oil man, for example, who carried $100,000 worth of temporary, low-cost term life insurance for many years. He always figured he would get around to buying some permanent policies later on. When he reached 45 his term policy ⟶600 expired, and by then he was in such poor health he couldn't renew it or get insurance of any kind. He died a couple of years later without leaving his family a dollar.

In Michigan, a railroad employee recently bought a new ranch house. He insured it against fire, but failed to take out extended coverage, giving protection against windstorms and other disasters. He thought he'd save a few dollars a year on that. Soon after he moved into his new home an auto collided with a chemical truck on the street outside. The resultant explosion blew the ranch house to smithereens. The railroad man couldn't collect a dime.

3. (T — F) Mr. Woodbury is convinced that 700 many people do not give enough thought to the planning of their insurance programs.

4. (M. C.) The experts gave the author many examples of people who:
   ____(1) Waited too late to buy insurance.
   ____(2) Planned their insurance carefully.
   ____(3) Were unwise in selecting insurance coverage.
   ____(4) Paid too much for their insurance.

Planning is important

In countless cases like these, just a little forethought would have paid off in a big way. You don't have to be a Philadelphia lawyer to map out an adequate insurance program for yourself and your family. 800 By following just a few simple rules, anyone can provide coverage that will protect him and his loved ones from most of the financial hazards of life.

5. (T — F) The author thinks it is very difficult to plan an adequate insurance program.

Advice — From whom?

The very first thing to do in considering your insurance problem, the experts say, is to call in some professional advisers. Ordinarily, you'll need two — a life-insurance agent and a property-insurance agent. In some small towns one man handles both life and property insurance, but that's rare. In most cases two agents are needed. 900

The chances are you won't have any trouble finding a life-insurance man. He'll probably find you, if he hasn't already done so. But property-insurance agents aren't quite so beagle-nosed in hunting down prospects, and you may have to seek one out. If you live in a small town or a residential neighborhood of a big city, you'll no doubt locate one right on a main streek back of a sign which says, "Real Estate and Insurance." You may discover that he also practices a bit of law and dabbles in politics in his spare time.

In any event, you're sure to find him an amiable 1000 1350 character. Selling is his main business, and if he has been purveying insurance in the community for any

length of time you can be pretty sure he is trustworthy. If you have any doubts about the company or companies he works for, however, you can check up on them by dropping a line to your state insurance commission.

6. (T — F) The first step in planning insurance is to secure sound professional advice.

7. (C) You need two kinds of advisers — the life-insurance man and the_____ _____insurance man.

1100 8. (M. C.) You may check on the reputation of any insurance salesman by writing to:
   ____(1) The mayor of your town.
   ____(2) The state insurance commission.
   ____(3) The home office of his company.
   ____(4) The federal bureau of standards.

What will you bet on?

Having located a property agent you like and trust, the next thing is to tell him what you want to bet with him about. All insurance is a form of gambling and, for a stipulated premium, the firm or firms which your agent represents will assume the risk for practically any damage which might befall your worldly 1200 goods.

If you're afraid it may rain next Fourth of July, for example, and ruin the gate receipts at an outdoor sporting event you're planning on that date, you can get an insurance company to bet with you that it won't rain. If you're fearful you may bean someone with a golf ball, or that your newborn baby may have to have a costly tooth-straightening job at the age of 14, you can insure yourself against such an emergency.

In all probability, however, if you are an average householder of moderate means there are just 5 1300 kinds of property insurance you need. They are:
   1. Fire insurance and extended coverage.
   2. Automobile insurance.
   3. Burglary-and-theft insurance.
   4. Inland-marine insurance.
   5. Public-liability insurance.

9. (T — F) All insurance is a form of gambling.
10. (T — F) In the long run, you will need only two basic types of insurance.

————STOP — ASK FOR YOUR TIME————

Time _____ Sec.	RATE (from table on page 305):	R. _____
No. Errors _____	COMPREHENSION (100 — 10% for each Error):	C. _____
VII — 1	EFFICIENCY (R × C):	E. _____

Number VII-2

On Minding One's Own Business

By William Graham Sumner

(Reprinted from the publication *In Brief*,
by permission of the Foundation of Economic Education, Inc.)

(This material is selected from Chapter VII of William G. Sumner's book,
What Social Classes Owe to Each Other, published in 1883.)

─────── WAIT FOR SIGNAL TO BEGIN READING ───────

The passion for dealing with social questions is one of the marks of our time. Every man gets some experience of, and makes some observations on social affairs. Except matters of health, probably none have such general interest as matters of society. Except matters of health, none are so much afflicted by dogmatism and crude speculation as those which appertain to society. The amateurs in social science always ask: What shall we do? What shall we do with Neighbor A? What shall we do for Neighbor B? What shall we make Neighbor A do for Neighbor B? It is a <u>100</u> fine thing to be planning and discussing broad and general theories of wide application. The amateurs always plan to use the individual for some constructive social purpose, or to use the society for some constructive individual purpose. For A to sit down and think, "What shall I do?" is commonplace; but to think what B ought to do is interesting, romantic, moral, self-flattering, and public-spirited all at once. It satisfies a great number of human weaknesses at once. To go on and plan what a whole class of people ought to do is to feel one's self a power on earth, <u>200</u> and to clothe one's self in dignity. Hence we have an unlimited supply of reformers, philanthropists, humanitarians, and would-be managers-in-general of society.

1. (T — F) The author expresses the basic feeling that people find it more interesting to plan what someone else should do than to plan what they should do themselves.

The first duty

Every man and woman in society has one big duty. That is, to take care of his or her own self. This is a social duty. The matter stands so that the duty of making the best of one's self individually <u>300</u> is not a separate thing from the duty of filling one's place in society, but the two are one and the latter is accomplished when the former is done. The common notion, however, seems to be that one has a duty to society, as a special and separate thing, and that this duty consists in considering and deciding what other people ought to do. Now, the man who can do anything for or about anybody else than himself is fit to be head of a family; and when he becomes head of a family he has duties to his wife and children, in addition to the former big duty. <u>400</u> Then, again, any man who can take care of himself and his family is in a very exceptional position if he does not find in his immediate surroundings people who need his care and have some sort of a personal claim on him. If, now, he is able to fulfill all this, and to take care of anybody outside his family and his dependents, he must have a surplus of energy, wisdom and moral virtue beyond what he needs for his own business. No man has this; <u>500</u> for a family is a charge which is capable of infinite development, and no man could suffice to the full measure of duty for which a family may draw upon him. Neither can a man give to society so advantageous an employment of his services, whatever they are, in any other way as by spending them on his family. Upon this, however, I will not insist. I recur to the observation that a man who proposes to take care of other people must have himself and his family taken care of, after some sort of fashion, and <u>600</u> must have an as yet unexhausted store of energy.

2. (C) According to Mr. Sumner, man's first duty is to take care of _____ _____.

3. (T — F) The author believes that man has an obligation to go beyond his duty to his family and to take care of others outside the family.

A twofold danger

The danger of minding other people's business is twofold. First, there is the danger that a man may leave his own business unattended to; and, second, there is the danger of an impertinent interference with another's affairs. The "friends of humanity" almost always run into both dangers. I am one of humanity, and I do not want any volunteer friends. 700 ⟵
I regard friendship as mutual, and I want to have my say about it. I suppose that other components of humanity feel in the same way about it. If so, they must regard any one who assumes the *role* of a friend of humanity as impertinent. The reference of the friend of humanity back to his own business is obviously the next step.

4 & 5. (M. C.) The author says that the two dangers of minding other people's business are:

    ____(1) Basic ignorance.
    ____(2) Political power.
    ____(3) Rash dictatorship.
    ____(4) Slandering gossip.
    ____(5) Voluntary servitude.
    ____(6) Slighting one's own busi- 800 ⟵ ness.
    ____(7) Losing all one's friends.
    ____(8) Impertinent interferences.

Social quacks

The amateur social doctors are like the amateur physicians — they always begin with the question of *remedies*, and they go at this without any diagnosis or any knowledge of the anatomy or physiology of society. They never have any doubt of the efficacy of their remedies. They never take account of any ulterior effects which may be apprehended from the remedy itself. Against all such social quackery the obvious injunction to the quacks is, to mind their own business.

6. (T — F) The author believes that social doctors 900 ⇄ are more concerned with remedies than with causes or effects.

The most needed reform

The greatest reforms which could now be accomplished would consist in undoing the work of statesmen in the past, and the greatest difficulty in the way of reform is to find out how to undo their work without injury to what is natural and sound. All this mischief has been done by men who sat down to consider the problem, What kind of a society do we want to make? When they had settled this question 1000 → *a priori* to their satisfaction, they set to work to make their ideal society, and today we suffer the consequences.

Society, therefore, does not need any care or supervision. If we can acquire a science of society, based on observation of phenomena and study of forces, we may hope to gain some ground slowly toward the elimination of old errors and the re-establishment of a sound and natural social order. Whatever we gain that way will be by growth, never by any reconstruction of society on the plan of some enthusiastic social architect. Society needs first of all to be 1100 → freed from these meddlers — that is, to be let alone. Here we are, then, once more back at the old doctrine — *Laissez Faire*. Let us translate it into blunt English, and it will read, "Mind your own business."

7. (T — F) The author believes that society needs some care and supervision in order to assure individual freedom.

8. (T — F) The basic need of society, as seen by Mr. Sumner, is to be left alone.

The root of dictatorship

We never supposed that *laissez faire* would give us perfect happiness. We have left perfect happiness 1200 → entirely out of our account. If the social doctors will mind their own business, we shall have no troubles but what belong to Nature. Those we will endure or combat as we can. What we desire is, that the friends of humanity should cease to add to them. Our disposition toward the ills which our fellow-man inflicts on us through malice or meddling is quite different from our disposition toward the ills which are inherent in the conditions of all human life.

To mind one's own business is a purely negative and unproductive injunction, but, taking social 1300 → matters as they are just now, it is a sociological principle of the first importance. There might be developed a grand philosophy on the basis of minding one's own business.

9. (T — F) Mr. Sumner believes that a "laissez faire" system would bring us complete happiness.

10. (C) The basic idea of this article is that 1350 → people should _____.

————STOP — ASK FOR YOUR TIME————

Time ____ Sec.   RATE (from table on page 305):   R. ____

No. Errors ____   COMPREHENSION (100 — 10% for each Error):   C. ____

VII — 2   EFFICIENCY (R × C):   E. ____

The Enchantment With Enhancement

By Ernest Swift

(Reprinted from the December, 1962, issue of *Wyoming Wildlife*, by permission of the editor)

— WAIT FOR SIGNAL TO BEGIN READING —

An enticing connotation

Recently, two articles on super-highways appeared in *Conservation News*. They brought a mild protest to the effect that the editorials were of a negative nature, and that relations could be improved with the road builders if they were praised for having given some thought to beautification, the prevention of erosion and the preservation of wildlife habitat.

In this regard the word enhancement has come into common use with reference to highways, high dams and reservoir construction. Enhancement has an enticing connotation. It apparently lulls the less perceptive into the notion that more is being gained than lost. 100

Realists know that such construction will continue. They are not being altogether enchanted by the word enhancement, but are insisting on a minimum of destruction.

1. (T — F) The word *enhancement* apparently lulls some people into the notion that more is being gained than lost.

A compromise

There are ever-increasing demands for the re-routing of highways where they would cut ugly gashes through a country beautiful. And, endless numbers of high dams are destroying the once mighty Pacific salmon runs. These problems have brought many a conservation group into a death struggle with these behemoths of progress.

The earth movers, the concrete builders and the 200 economists of both private enterprise and public bureaus have cared little in the past about the consequences of their programs. Techniques have reached a point of proficiency to alter drastically the face of the earth. Few if any of them want any truck with such philosophies.

To minimize the irritations caused by such dreamers the road and high dam builders talk persuasively of enhancement. Talk does not increase construction costs. Nevertheless, there is insistent public demand for reducing needless damage.

Webster defines *enhance:* To raise, augment, increase, to increase worth or value; to beautify.

Where highways level slum districts the word en- 300

hancement might be correct. But where a farm unit is split and becomes an uneconomical operation because of the highway, the owner sees no enhancement. It is also difficult to rationalize enhancement when waterfowl or fishing areas are drained or filled for road construction. Then, some miles further on, gravel pits are flooded and called enhancement.

A flooded gravel pit may minimize total destruction of some wildlife species in the region, but calling it enhancement is a misuse of the word. Nor can the 400 relocation of a highway to save a park, a wilderness, a vista or a trout stream in any sense be termed enhancement. It is simply a compromise between two opposing ideologies.

2. (M. C.) Which of these phrases is *not* used by Webster to define the word *enhance?*
   ____(1) To raise.
   ____(2) To mitigate loss.
   ____(3) To increase worth.
   ____(4) To beautify.

3. (C) The term *enhancement* has been used as a _____ between two opposing ideologies.

A matter of interpretation

Inquiries and comments coming to the National Wildlife Federation have brought a great divergence of opinion. One state, with a natural resources committee of which the highway department is a member, 500 has set up study committees. Their recommendations have resulted in the change of road specifications, rights of way maintenance, the creation of impoundments and shrubbery planting. This state also has a mandatory law that requires notification of the conservation commission on new road construction, or altering or discontinuance. This is certainly all to the good, and shows maturity and progress. Still, by close definition it is more of a matter of mitigating losses than one of enhancement.

Storage reservoirs in some of the water-starved plains states create boating and fishing areas. There 600 was a time when such flowages were one-purpose projects for holding water. Their worth for recreation has radically changed the thinking and increased the out-of-doors potential for their localities. Such projects have enhanced the communities recreationally and economically.

On the other hand, valuable timber, winter game yards and fish spawning grounds are often destroyed by flooding, especially in the mountain country. Here is a case of attempting to mitigate losses, of some salvage, where talking of enhancement is simply a play on words.

As the wetlands in the Dakotas are drained with taxpayers' monies, farm ponds have been built with money from the same source. The biggest delusion $\underset{\rightleftarrows}{700}$ of all is that they are enhancement to waterfowl. There are not enough of them to compensate for the drainage of natural ponds, and ducks do not like ponds with spoil banks that obstruct their view. That is the nature of the critter.

On the lower Mississippi where flood control is carried on by the army engineers, the loss of waterfowl habitat has been greater than any compensations. Again, enhancement becomes a myth.

What may happen to the Pacific salmon is brought to light in a speech by Mr. J. C. Swidler, chairman of the Federal Power Commission. Here is a section $\underset{\leftarrow}{800}$ of his address before the American Power Association on May 15, 1962. "By far the most troublesome problem is to reconcile the construction of dams with the preservation of a favorable environment for game fish. However, we cannot allow the fish problem to paralyze the Commission in acting on hydroelectric licence applications."

Further on in the address is this statement: "If on the record in a particular case the fish problems are insurmountable and more would be lost than gained by approving the license, we shall of course deny the license application."

It is rather difficult to make these two statements $\underset{\leftarrow}{900}$ dovetail. Whether the latter one is crumbs for the peasants is a matter of individual interpretation.

4. (T — F) A state law requiring notification of the Conservation Commission on new road construction is a good example of true enhancement.

5. (T — F) The flood control on the lower Mississippi has resulted in more waterfowl habitat.

6. (T — F) J. C. Swidler made contradicting statements in reference to the fish problem and hydroelectric licenses.

A trick word

Since revolutionary times this nation has developed certain fixations regarding land-use. Time-honored priorities based on past economic standards have $\underset{\leftarrow}{1000}$ become quite deep-rooted. Testing their validity under the present conditions of these fast-moving times has been a wrench to the traditional thinking of many people.

For decades agriculture had an incontestable priority over all land uses. As a result, millions of acres of sub-marginal land were farmed. Often valuable timber or grass cover was destroyed in the process.

Only land wholly unsuited for farming east of the Mississippi was left in forests until cut. Then followed sporadic farming efforts and tax delinquency. Producing techniques finally increased crop surpluses, and returned many an abandoned farm to regrowing $\underset{\rightarrow}{1100}$ timber. These methods also made possible a soil bank program, which on the prairies was beneficial to wildlife.

But looking back to original native game populations that once used the prairies, this respite in growing crops was hardly enhancement. Some would question going back that far, and so enhancement becomes a trick word.

7. (T — F) In the past, only land wholly unfit for raising timber was left to farming.

8. (M. C.) Which of the following was *not* a result of producing techniques in land use?

    ____(1) Destruction of farms.
    ____(2) Increased farm surpluses.
    ____(3) Regrowth of timber.
    ____(4) Soil bank program.

$\underset{\rightarrow}{1200}$ ## Realism versus fancy phrases

Is pollution control an enhancement? Or is it simply an abatement of industrial and municipal filth? A stump prairie replanted to trees comes under the accepted term of enhancement. But if the timber tract has been selectively cut with a residual stand left and protected from fire, the enhancement could be considered more valid.

Fancy phrases are no substitute for realistic thinking. In-roads of a destructive nature will continue on many resources. They will raise questions of gain or loss according to what values are considered paramount.

Let us not use the word enhancement unless it $\underset{\rightarrow}{1300}$ definitely fits the occasion. It is far more realistic to educate the public to demand a reduction of losses.

9. (C) Fancy phrases are no substitute for _____thinking.

10. (T — F) $\underset{\rightarrow}{1350}$ The public should be educated to demand a reduction of losses.

————STOP — ASK FOR YOUR TIME————

Time ____ Sec.	RATE (from table on page 305):	R. ____
No. Errors ____	COMPREHENSION (100 — 10% for each Error):	C. ____
VII-3	EFFICIENCY (R × C):	E. ____

Number VII-4

From Seed to Syrup

(Reprinted from the pamphlet *The Story of Sugar Cane*,
by permission of the American Sugar Refining Company)

───────────── WAIT FOR SIGNAL TO BEGIN READING ─────────────

Commercial production of sugar cane is begun by planting cuttings about a foot long, each containing two or three seed buds. A plant soon grows with several shoots forming a clump of cane. One such planting on virgin soil in Cuba is sufficient to produce crops annually for ten to fifteen years. New plants, termed "ratoons," spring up from the stubble after each harvesting. The first crop, known as plant cane, is ordinarily harvested about 18 months after planting. After the first crop, sugar cane is normally harvested every 12 months, although in some areas, notably Hawaii, at longer intervals. 100

The sugar cane stalks are quite similar in appearance to growing corn, but often attain heights of from fifteen to eighteen feet. They are thick and unbranched with broad, flat leaves, about three feet in length.

When the cane is ready for harvest, the stalks are cut near the surface of the ground. In most areas these operations are performed by hand; in others mechanical harvesters are used. An expert workman, using a heavy machete, can cut and load about six tons of cane a day. After cutting, the leaves are stripped from the stalks which are then loaded into 200 ox carts. While the ox cart is still common in Cuba and much of Asia, the harvested cane is carried to the mills in every type of conveyance ranging from the most primitive to the most modern. The trend in harvesting and transportation of the sugar cane is steadily toward mechanized handling, for greater efficiency and economy.

1. (T — F) Sugar cane has to be replanted each year.
2. (T — F) Most sugar cane is harvested by hand.

From field to mill

Within easy hauling distance of each cane field there is usually a railroad siding and loading station. 300 These loading stations are equipped with cranes which lift the load and deposit it into waiting railroad cars.

Locomotives haul the loaded cars to the raw sugar mill or "central" and are switched onto tilting tables. The cars have hinged sides so that, when these tables are tilted to a sufficient angle, the sugar cane slides from the car to conveyors which carry the cane stalks to the crushing rolls. These consist of pairs of corrugated cylinders placed one above the other, which shred the cane by twisting as it passes through. This operation separates the fibers and prepares 400 them for the grinding mills but does not press out the juice.

The shredded cane now passes through a series of heavy horizontal steel rollers, revolving with tremendous pressure against each other, bursting the sugar cane cells and pressing out the juice. Toward the end of this operation sprays of water facilitate the extraction of any remaining juice. The fibrous residue, known as "bagasse," generally provides the fuel for generating the power to operate the mill and the steam for evaporation and crystallization of the juice. Bagasse also forms the basic material for the 500 manufacture of fiber insulation board used in building construction. The sugar cane juice, which constitutes about 80% of the entire weight of the cane, is now ready for further processing to produce raw sugar.

3. (M. C.) Most sugar cane is carried from local growing areas to central sugar mills by means of:
   ____(1) Airplanes.
   ____(2) Steamboats.
   ____(3) Truck-trailers.
   ____(4) Railroads.
4. (C) The first major step in the sugar mill is to run the cane through corrugated rollers which _____
   the cane without crushing out the juice.

Raw sugar

The juice is first heated, after which lime is added to neutralize acidity and precipitate certain impurities which are then removed by settling and filtration. 600

Concentration of the juice into syrup starts in huge evaporators. The syrup is then boiled in vacuum pans which are large dome-shaped tanks, where crystallization takes place. It is essential to avoid caramelization or burning of the syrup that would result from boiling at elevated temperatures. Since liquids boil at lower temperature under a partial vacuum than in open air, a vacuum pump in connection with a condenser is employed to create a partial vacuum within the pan. The resulting mixture of sugar crystals and molasses then goes to centrifugal machines.

700 ←

A centrifugal machine consists of a round basket-like container with screen sides, suspended on a vertical shaft within a circular metal shell. The shaft spins the basket at a speed of 1000 to 1200 revolutions per minute. The centrifugal force thus developed throws the molasses off through the screen sides, and the sugar crystals are retained inside the basket. The resulting product is rather sticky, ranging from grayish to reddish brown in color, and is known as centrifugal raw sugar. Raw sugar is not suitable for food or as a component of foods unless further processed.

5. (T — F) Impurities are removed from the juice by settling and filtering. 800 ←

6. (T — F) Centrifugal raw sugar is in a form quite suitable for food.

The refining process begins

The raw sugar is packed in large burlap bags and is ready for shipment to the nearest seaport, where it is shipped to cane sugar refineries in the United States. In recent years new methods have been developed for loading the raw sugar in bulk directly into ships, which are then unloaded by huge conveyors at the refinery wharves.

Sampling and weighing take place upon arrival, the samples being subjected to laboratory analysis to establish in conjunction with the weights, a basis for settlement of customs duty, if any, and the purchase value. 900 ←

From the wharves the bags of raw sugar are carried to stations, where the bags are opened and the raw sugar emptied into a hopper that feeds a mechanical crusher, breaking up any large lumps that may have formed.

From the crusher a bucket-type chain elevator carries the raw sugar to the top of the refinery where it is emptied into mixers, known as "minglers." The addition of syrup at this point forms a thick paste called "magma." From the mingler the magma flows by gravity into centrifugal machines where it is washed to remove the thin film of dark molasses that still surrounds each crystal of the raw sugar. 1000 ←

The removal of this film might be termed the first step in the refining process. From the centrifugals the washed sugar crystals are conveyed to melting tanks where they are dissolved in warm water.

7. (C) Most of the sugar refining is done in (what country) _____.

8. (T — F) The first step in the actual refining process is the removal of the thin film of molasses from each crystal of raw sugar. 1100 →

Filtering processes

To this sugar solution is added diatomaceous earth, an exceedingly porous, finely divided material which assists in the removal of impurities. It is then passed through pressure filters which contain circular screen discs covered with cloth. The cloth holds back all suspended impurities together with the added diatomaceous earth.

The liquid, which has a high sugar content after leaving these pressure filters, is clear but amber in color. To assure a high quality refined sugar, the removal of this color is essential, and this is accomplished by flowing the liquid through char filters. The char filters are huge, cylindrical tanks about 20 feet high, containing granular bone char. The liquid runs brilliant and colorless from the char filters, and then passes to what is called the liquor gallery to be graded. Such small quantities of the sugar liquor as retain traces of color are returned to the filters, while the fully decolorized liquor passes to the "pan-house." When the char is used for some time it becomes inefficient. Its decolorizing properties are then restored by washing and burning processes permitting the use of the char over and over again. 1200 ←

1300 →

9. (M. C.) The amber color of the sugar is removed by:
____(1) Adding diatomaceous earth.
____(2) Filtering through granular bone char.
____(3) Running through pressure filters.
____(4) Allowing it to settle out in the "pan-house."

10. (T — F) This decoloring agent can be used only once and then must be discarded. 1350 →

————STOP — ASK FOR YOUR TIME————

Time _____ Sec.	RATE (from table on page 305):	R. _____
No. Errors _____	COMPREHENSION (100 − 10% for each Error):	C. _____
VII — 4	EFFICIENCY (R × C):	E. _____

Number VII-5

The Leader Was A Critic

By Seymour Lieberman

(A digest of an original article which appeared in the February, 1955, issue of *Adult Leadership*, reprinted by permission of the author)

—————————————— WAIT FOR SIGNAL TO BEGIN READING ——————————————

History records many instances where men have been thrust headlong into new and critical roles. Abdications and assassinations have created kings and presidents overnight. These new leaders are apt to start off confused and bewildered, not knowing how to carry out their functions. But after a while they often "grow" into their new job. Why do they?

Are leaders made or born? The answer to the time-worn question would seem to be: both.

The potential leader has certain latent characteristics before he steps into the leadership role — certain skills, abilities, know-how. But it takes being in the leadership role to bring out and fully develop these 100 abilities.

In other words, a person learns to lead by leading. Previously he might have looked nothing like a leader, nothing like a person who could be responsible for guiding the group along the path toward achievement of its goals. The man may not have chosen the role, but if he has basic potentialities and abilities, the role may make the man.

The success of any organization depends largely on how well its leaders carry out their jobs. And how well leaders do their jobs is determined largely by whether or not they hold attitudes which motivate 200 them to perform their duties well. Only by accepting the goals of the group and having the interests of the group at heart can a club president fulfill his obligations to the other members.

1. (T — F) The author states that leaders are made, not born.
2. (C) A person learns to lead by _____ _____.
3. (T — F) Many potential leaders might not look like a person who could be responsible for guiding a group.
4. (M. C.) The success of any type of organization depends largely on:
   ____(1) How workers are selected.
   ____(2) Cooperation between labor 300 and management.
   ____(3) How well leaders carry out their jobs.
   ____(4) Strict discipline.

The all-important attitudes

Having attitudes appropriate to a role doesn't mean that a person should be extremely pro or anti in his leanings. How can we ensure that the leaders of an organization will possess attitudes appropriate to their roles? There are two possible solutions. One solution is to select those people who already have the desired set of attitudes and orientations. The second solution is to let the role itself do the trick. 400 Place a person in a leadership role and see if the role itself produces the desired pattern of attitudes and orientations.

How should we choose our leaders? Should we select them "already made?" Or should we depend on the role to make them? Some clues and insights are obtained from a recent study.

5. (T — F) Having attitudes appropriate to a role means a person should be extremely pro or anti in his leanings.

The Rockwell story

The study was carried out in a medium-sized factory engaged in the production of home appliance equipment. Let's call it the Rockwell Home Appliance Corporation. Rockwell is situated in a small 500 Midwestern town with a population of around 12,000. Most of the workers are on semi-skilled jobs and have some high school education.

In 1951, we administered paper-and-pencil attitude questionnaires to the entire rank-and-file, non-supervisory factory population at Rockwell — roughly 2,500 in all. There was a wide variety of questions dealing with the workers' jobs.

In the next 12 months, during the normal course of things, a number of personnel changes took place in various leadership positions at Rockwell. On managements' side, some new departments were created and some old ones expanded. On the union's 600 side, annual steward elections were held. As a result, a number of rank-and-file workers moved into leadership positions. By going back and re-interviewing these workers after they had changed roles, as well as some workers who had not changed roles, we had an excellent opportunity to study two kinds of questions:

(1) What are the characteristics of workers who are chosen for leadership roles at Rockwell? What are their attitudes and orientations? Are pro-management workers the ones who tend to be selected as foremen? Are pro-

union workers the ones selected as stewards?

(2) What happens to workers once they are placed in leadership roles? Do the roles change <u>700</u> their attitudes and orientations? Does being placed in the foreman role result in a worker's becoming more pro-management? Does being made a steward make a worker more pro-union?

By comparing the attitudes of workers both before and after they changed roles, we had the basic data to answer our questions.

6. (T — F) The Rockwell study was carried out in a typical large factory in New York.

What did we find?

Are pro-management workers made foremen? Are pro-union workers made stewards? The answer to both questions seems to be: no! If anything, there was some indication that the workers who were <u>800</u> later chosen for leadership roles tended to be anti-management and anti-union. They were critical of both management and union policies. Management and the union were apparently — although not consciously — choosing their leaders from the more dissident, dissatisfied elements of the rank-and-file worker population.

Although the leaders-to-be were somewhat critical of the company and the union, they also had a number of positive traits. They tended to be better educated than the rest of the workers at Rockwell. They were more verbally facile — they did a better and more complete job of filling out the questionnaires. They were ambitious and interested in getting ahead — they wanted to become foremen or stewards, although <u>900</u> not because they were pro-management or pro-union. These traits seem to add up to a picture of the leaders-to-be as being alert, able, and competent — traits which might be partly responsible for their tendency to be dissident and critical.

Apart from whether the leaders-to-be were able and competent, an equally crucial question is: did their dissidence or dissatisfaction prevent them from taking on the values of managment or the union once they were made representatives of management or the union? Apparently not. Both groups came to see things in a new light. The role itself — along with various forces associated with it — had ap- <u>1000</u> parently done the trick!

7. (C) The Rockwell Study showed that the _____ management workers are most often made foremen.

8. (T — F) The study showed that management apparently chose leaders from the more dissatisfied employees.

Applying the Rockwell findings

The question then becomes: how can we channel the recalcitrant's involvement and energies into paths that are useful for the effective functioning of the organization? One solution that is suggested here is to give him important duties to carry out. From this new vantage point, he will be more likely <u>1100</u> to accept the goals and values of the organization.

A number of studies has shown that giving group members greater participation will go a long way toward bringing about greater involvement in the goals of an organization. Morse found that the morale of clerks in an insurance firm went up when they were given more authority and responsibility in deciding how their jobs were to be carried out and in controlling various other aspects of their job situations.

A lament is often heard about the lack of leadership material to choose from in selecting leaders. <u>1200</u> One reason that leadership material seems to be scarce is that we find it difficult to visualize people who occupy one role as occupying another role.

How many of us can readily "see" a non-supervisory worker as the boss, or the boss as a member of the rank-and-file? A danger may be present in giving responsibility to people who are not qualified to handle it, but equally dangerous may be our reluctance to yield the reins of control to people who are qualified to handle it.

9. (M. C.) The article mentioned several positive traits of the critical leaders-to-be. <u>1300</u> Which of the following is not one of them?
   ____(1) They came from higher-skilled jobs.
   ____(2) Tend to be better educated.
   ____(3) Desire to become foremen because they were pro-management.
   ____(4) Ambition.

10. (T — F) Other studies show that giving group members greater participation causes interest in the goals of the organization. <u>1350</u>

————STOP — ASK FOR YOUR TIME————

Time _____ Sec.	RATE (from table on page 305):	R. _____
No. Errors _____	COMPREHENSION (100 − 10% for each Error):	C. _____
VII — 5	EFFICIENCY (R × C):	E. _____

Number VII-6

Gateways to the World

By Lou Phillips

(Reprinted from *An Air View of Portugal Today*, by permission of the publisher,
Pan American World Airlines)

—————— WAIT FOR SIGNAL TO BEGIN READING ——————

Three ports

The capital city, Lisbon, has a population of over 800,000 and is also the chief seaport of the land. It is a city radiant with color. Seen at a distance from the Tagus it shines white in the sun but as one approaches its buildings the different pastel shades of various houses becomes evident. Some facades are pink, yellow, light blue, almond green or white under roofs covered with red tiles. Some are completely encrusted with delicately glazed tiles which sparkle like jewels. The city has many parks, palaces, churches and gardens and its sub-tropical vegetation maintains a 100 luxurious green hue all through the year.

Oporto is the second city of Portugal and stands on the steep, rocky, right bank of the Douro River in the northern part of the country about 165 miles from Lisbon. Owing to a bar at the mouth of the river, an Atlantic harbor has been constructed four miles farther north. The famous Port Wine comes from the city of Oporto (and the equally famous Madeira from the Madeira Islands). Within the confines of the city are seven principal churches, including a Cathedral built by Henry the Navigator; a polytechnic academy; an observatory; scientific 200 collections; and other academic institutions. There are universities at both Lisbon and Oporto but the oldest and most famous college is found in Coimbra which is called the nation's Seat of Learning. The annual enrollment at these colleges is over 15,000.

The other principal port of the country is Setubal located about seventeen miles southeast of Lisbon. It is one of the important tuna and sardine canning centers of the country. Portuguese sardines are famous the world over. At all times rows and rows of fishing boats can be seen in its harbor against a background of lovely churches and battleworn fortresses. At the 300 outskirts of the city, orchards and vineyards producing oranges and muscatel grapes are found.

1. (M. C.)   The oldest, most famous college is found in the nation's Seat of Learning which is:
    ____(1) Coimbra.
    ____(2) Lisbon.
    ____(3) Oporto.
    ____(4) Setubal.

2. (T — F)   Lisbon is one of the important tuna and sardine canning centers of the country.

The fruit of the land

Agriculture is the most important occupation of the people. In the warmer sections, oranges, lemons and olives are grown in abundance. The most important fruit is the grape from which the nations' 400 famous port wine is made. About one-third of the land is devoted to the raising of cereals. Great numbers of cattle, sheep, goats and hogs are raised. Fish, next to wine, is the most important product of export and is confined mostly to tuna and sardine canning.

About one-fourth of the land is forested, the most important trees being the cork and the oak. There are also chestnut groves. Crude cork is one of the nation's most important products of export, and the production of resin and turpentine is also an important industry. Portugal possesses considerable mineral 500 wealth, but for want of electric power and cheap transportation valuable mines remain unworked. At present there are only a little over 2,000 miles of railway and 9,000 miles of highways so the country must rely heavily on the Tagus and Douro Rivers for transportation to the ocean. There are, however, known deposits of coal, copper, lead, sulpher and tin.

Textile production is the principal manufacturing industry but one of the most characteristic of the land is the manufacture of azulejos or porcelain tiles. This was inherited from the Moors, and tiles are used extensively for interior and exterior decoration of public and private buildings. At Sacavem, 600 near Lisbon, a large factory makes tiles and chinaware. In Peniche, an old fishing village on the north coast of Lisbon there is a local pillow lace industry and the Island of Madeira is also famous for embroideries.

3. (C)   _____ is the most important occupation of the people.

4. (C)   _____ is the most important product of export.

5. (M. C.) Portugal's mineral wealth remains unexploited for want of:
_____(1) Cheap labor.
_____(2) Capital.
_____(3) Sufficient raw materials.
_____(4) Electric power.

6. (T — F) The making of porcelain tiles is the principal manufacturing industry of $\overset{700}{\leftarrow}$ the land.

Portugal and the United States

The chief imports of Portugal are fuel-oil and coal, steel, raw materials and some heavy industry products. Its chief customers as well as suppliers are Great Britain and the United States. Portugal is among the sixteen Western European Nations who have accepted the Marshall Plan but the Portuguese Government declined financial aid in the first year of the program's operation. The monetary unit is the escudo which is worth four cents in American money.

During World War II the country remained neutral. This neutrality was held under an agreement with Spain to keep the Germans behind the Pyrenees. $\overset{800}{\leftarrow}$ On the other hand, Portugal's help to the Allies proved important through the allowance of strategic bases on the Portuguese Islands in the Atlantic which were used by the Americans and the British to defect the U-boat threat in that area.

At the end of World War II Portugal was frankly prosperous. In spite of wide-spread individual poverty and hardship, partly traditional and partly due to the higher cost of living, there were substantial gold reserves and dollar credits. But at war's end Portugal, as every other nation, bought feverishly from the United States. Purchases ran the gamut from motor $\overset{900}{\leftarrow}$ vehicles to novelty toys and toilet requisites. As a result before long we were selling to Portugal much more than we were buying in return. To further aggravate the situation Britain and Germany which used to supply Portugal's coal needs could no longer do so and coal had to be purchased from the United States. This increased the flow of dollars out of the country. Moreover the mounting austerity of life in Britain precluded such luxuries as port wine and tinned sardines which are among Portugal's richest exports. Sales to the United States also decreased in $\overset{1000}{\leftarrow}$ the face of competition from exporters in North Africa and Spain who offered cork or sardines at lower prices. The Government became alarmed at the outflow of United States currency and started to clamp down on dollar imports, banning luxury articles altogether. In addition a ceiling of $3,600 was imposed on the retail prices of automobiles which resulted in the disappearance of most American cars from the Portuguese market. In contrast, trade with Great Britain was increased, due in part to ancient commercial ties and also to the fact that as a result $\overset{1100}{\rightarrow}$ of wartime purchases England was in debt to Portugal for about 80 million pounds. Repayment was naturally made in English pound sterling. By the latter part of last year automobiles, commercial vehicles and coal were arriving mainly from Great Britain.

When the Portuguese had available dollars they preferred American goods and they will undoubtedly buy our merchandise again as soon as they can afford to do so. Portugal cannot pay its bills, hower, unless it can sell products to the United States or provide Americans with services which will earn dollars. The pleasantest means of getting these dollars abroad $\overset{1200}{\rightarrow}$ is for American visitors to take them over. Each one left behind will ultimately be spent in the United States. Moreover the dollars spent in Portugal will open up a new world, for the whole way of life and standard of living there is very different from that enjoyed in the United States. The visting American will find a land of sunshine, beautiful scenery, peasant costumes and customs, decorative village fairs and local wines. Travelers will delight in shops crammed with luxury goods and will enjoy bullfights, shooting, golf, swimming and yachting.

7. (T — F) Portugal's chief customers and suppliers are Great Britain and France.

$\overset{1300}{\rightarrow}$ 8. (T — F) During World War II the country remained neutral.

9. (T — F) At the end of World War II Portugal was quite prosperous and bought feverishly from the United States.

10. (T — F) At the present time the Portuguese $\overset{1350}{\rightarrow}$ cannot afford to buy American goods.

———STOP — ASK FOR YOUR TIME———

Time _____ Sec.   RATE (from table on page 305):   R. _____

No. Errors _____   COMPREHENSION (100 — 10% for each Error):   C. _____

VII — 6   EFFICIENCY (R × C):   E. _____

Number VII-7

How to Criticize the Schools

By William G. Carr

(Reprinted from the November, 1954, issue of the *NEA Journal*, by permission of the editor)

——— WAIT FOR SIGNAL TO BEGIN READING ———

William G. Carr, Executive Secretary of the National Education Association, is only one of many who have been disturbed by the published articles criticizing the public schools. Believing this matter of public criticism to be one of the most important problems of the year, he chose this as his topic for the speech at the Education Magazine Editor Conference in New York City. The following excerpt from that speech was published in the NEA Journal for November, 1954.

How to criticize the schools

The big national magazines are now printing well over 200 articles a year about education. These magazines have a great opportunity to serve the ←100 existing public interest in our schools — and to arouse an even greater and more informed interest. Here are some tips for them.

Criticize to improve, not to destroy

There are certain people in this country who think our public schools should be destroyed. In an effort to bring this about, they are spending substantial sums of money to buy or infiltrate the means of communication and to spread their propaganda. One of their favorite devices is to identify public education with socialism or communism.

Fortunately, these people are not numerous, and they defeat their own purpose by the intemperance ←200 and inaccuracy of their statements.

1. (T — F)   There are people who desire to control the means of communication in order to spread propaganda.

Consider the results of criticism

The critics who want to help improve education, rather than weaken or destroy it, have a special responsibility to consider the results of what they say or write or publish. After all, the schools are an essential ingredient of the American way of life. It is not necessary to approach them with reverence, but it is wise to use the usual safeguards for reaching sound →300 conclusions. This means care in generalizing from too narrow a range of inspection and rigorous checking on the validity of data.

The serious teacher shortage justifies the profession in asking the molders of public opinion to exercise unusual care. To encourage competent young people to prepare for teaching and to make it their career, everything possible is being done by the profession.

A widely read magazine article which casts unjustified doubts upon the integrity or good judgment of teachers is bound to have an adverse effect upon the number of qualified new teachers we are able to bring →400 into the schools.

2. (T — F)   Everyone in this country realizes that our school system must be continued and improved — not weakened or destroyed.

3. (T — F)   Schools are essential to the American way of life and should be approached with reverence.

4. (C)   The serious _____ justifies the profession in asking publishers not to publish articles which cast unjustified doubts upon the integrity or good judgement of teachers.

5. (C)   One of the most serious results of the criticism of our schools is that it _____ those young people who might make teaching their career.

→500 Use the help of the profession

I am not saying that magazines should never publish articles which mention such professional foibles and follies as our calling may possess. Teachers are just as concerned as other citizens in the matter of better schooling and will not resent honest criticism of their work. In fact, self-criticism has become a hallmark of the teaching profession.

The NEA has no desire to cover up the many defects in our schools. We want whatever weak spots that do exist in education to be called to public attention in order that these shortcomings may be →600 examined and corrected.

6. (T — F)   Teachers are as concerned as other citizens in the matter of better schooling and do not wish to cover up defects in our schools.

Balance the accounts

The kind of schools which America wants and needs will cost money — probably a great deal of money. It is a poor system of educational appraisal which talks about school costs, but says no word about the economic results of general education. A good school system pays for itself, and much more besides. The costs of the schools must be balanced against their economic productivity, against their great contribution (in the face of adverse conditions) $\overset{700}{\rightleftharpoons}$ to health, safety, prosperity, and happiness. For example:

(1) In spite of the seductions of a materialistic age, in spite of the hardships of the depression, the cruelties of war, and the frustrations of the present epoch, the schools have continued to develop moral, spiritual, and esthetic standards which exalt human life.

(2) In spite of the heavy economic demands of a war and defense spending, the productive skills of the American people have been so increased that a rising standard of living has been maintained.

(3) Altho they have provided universal education for practically every American child, the $\overset{800}{\leftarrow}$ schools have also sent into the professions a body of competent leaders.

(4) In spite of hostile ideologies, the schools have continued to give American youth the knowledge, habits, and loyalties of citizens who can govern themselves.

A fair chance to tell the whole story of the schools, good and bad, is all that the teaching profession asks. But that much it does ask. The opportunity to hear the full truth is something that the American people have a right to expect from the editors and publishers of magazines and from educators.

7. (M. C.) The author states that there are $\overset{900}{\rightleftharpoons}$ several contributions of the school which should be considered carefully before criticizing the costs. Of the following, which was not mentioned as such a contribution?

____(1) An increased standard of living.

____(2) A number of competent leaders in many fields.

____(3) A pattern of moral, spiritual, and esthetic standards.

____(4) A greater understanding of our military and political history.

Judge your schools by modern standards

If your schools today duplicate the ones of 20 or 30 years ago, they are probably poor schools. "It was good enough for me and therefore is good enough for the younger generation" is a doctrine $\overset{1000}{\leftarrow}$ profoundly hostile to the American spirit. We adults have not handled affairs so skillfully that we may assume the education we received was ideal.

Children now entering school will spend most of their lives in the last half of the twentieth century. While every other phase of life is transformed, the schools cannot remain unchanged.

Comparison of the "good old days" with the supposed shortcomings of the present is a sure way to get public attention. In evaluating such comparisons, we need what Charles Beard liked to call the $\overset{1100}{\rightarrow}$ Socratic elenchus. This was a device used by Socrates in his teaching. It consisted essentially of responding to every overconfident assertion by asking the irritating question, "Is that so?" This teaching device was, in fact, so annoying that the Athenians decided to eliminate the elenchus by eliminating Socrates.

But we have to ask, or ought to ask, "Is that so?" Is the evidence reliable? Were there no errors in arithmetic 20 years ago? Did every child write and spell impeccably?

As Disraeli said, "It is easier to be critical than correct." I might add that it is not only easier but $\overset{1200}{\rightarrow}$ also more fun. But when we are dealing with the education of our youth, we touch on a topic where it is important to be both critical and correct.

8. (T — F) If your schools today are similar to those of 20 or 30 years ago, they are probably good schools.

9. (T —) Socrates was annoying to critics in his day because he asked them to examine the overconfident assertions they frequently made.

10. (M. C.) Which of the following is not one of Dr. Carr's suggestions?

____(1) The critics who want to help improve education must consider the results of what they say.

____(2) Magazines should not publish articles which mention shortcomings and professional follies.

____(3) Do not criticize school costs without mentioning their contribution to health, safety, prosperity, and happiness.

____(4) It is best not to judge today's schools by the standards used 20 or 30 years ago.

$\overset{1300}{\rightarrow}$

$\overset{1350}{\rightarrow}$

————STOP — ASK FOR YOUR TIME————

Time ____ Sec.	RATE (from table on page 305):	R. ____
No. Errors ____	COMPREHENSION (100 − 10% for each Error):	C. ____
VII — 7	EFFICIENCY (R × C):	E. ____

Insurance for Life

By Clarence Woodbury

(Reprinted from *Family Insurance* from the November 1951 issue of the *American Magazine*, by permission of the editor)

———————————— WAIT FOR SIGNAL TO BEGIN READING ————————————

Four types of life insurance

Most family life insurance falls into 4 main categories — term insurance, ordinary life, limited-payment life, and endowment. Your agent will get out his little black book and give you details about each variety, but here are some general facts you should know.

Term insurance

Term insurance provides temporary coverage only. It runs for a limited number of years, usually 5 or 10, and then expires unless renewed, always at a higher premium rate necessitated by the increased age of the policyholder. For a young person it is much the cheapest kind of insurance, and can provide valuable $\overset{100}{\leftarrow}$ protection for temporary periods.

But term insurance has serious disadvantages. Its cost becomes prohibitive as one grows older and it usually has no cash or loan value. If your health fails, you may not be able to renew your coverage without a medical examination. The insurance pays off only if the policyholder dies. Insurance experts say no family should depend upon term insurance alone for any length of time.

1. (C) Although low in cost, term insurance $\overset{200}{\leftarrow}$ has the disadvantage of providing only _____ coverage.

Ordinary life

Ordinary life, which is often called straight life or whole life, is the most popular form of life insurance. As its name implies, its purpose is to provide lifetime protection, and it does this at a premium rate which can never increase. Premiums are determined by your age at the time you take out the policy (the younger you are, the lower they are), and are payable as long as you live.

The face value of an ordinary life policy is payable only at death but such policies have, in addition, attractive investment features. As time passes, they acquire an increasing cash value and can be converted into dollars and cents if you need money for an $\overset{300}{\leftarrow}$ emergency or no longer have dependents to protect.

Moreover, you have the privilege of borrowing money on an ordinary life policy or can put it up as collateral for a loan. For all these reasons most

experts think the average family should build its insurance program around at last one ordinary life policy.

2. (C) Premiums on ordinary life insurance are determined by your _____ when you take out the policy.

Limited payment life

Limited-payment life insurance is exactly like ordi- $\overset{400}{\rightarrow}$ nary life, except that premiums are paid for a limited number of years instead of for life. Usually, after a period of either 20 or 30 years, the policy becomes paid up, and the policyholder remains insured from then on without having to spend another cent on premiums.

Many young people prefer these limited-payment policies because they don't like to look forward to paying premiums as long as they live, but they have one drawback: the premiums are a good deal higher than those of ordinary life, and the young breadwinner, whose income and babies are both apt to be small, can't get as much protection for his money as $\overset{500}{\rightarrow}$ he could if he bought ordinary life.

A better type than 20- or 30-year payment life for most young people, the top authorities say, is life paid up at age 65. This gives relatively low-cost protection for one's family, yet doesn't require continuing premiums after the normal retirement age.

3. (T — F) On limited-payment life insurance one pays a fixed premium for as long as he lives.

Endowment

Endowment policies carry a far greater investment element than either ordinary life or limited-payment life policies. This kind of insurance is very expensive for the amount of protection afforded, but if you buy $\overset{600}{\rightarrow}$ it you are assured of collecting the full face value of your policy at the end of a specified number of years. Or your beneficiaries collect if you die before the policy matures.

When I was 21, I took out a modest 20-year endowment policy. Not long ago, when I reached 41, I collected the full value of the policy and applied it against a mortgage on my home. That worked out very well, but, looking back, I feel I was rather foolish. Had I turned up my toes at any time during the

20 years, my dependents would not have received $\xleftarrow{700}$ nearly as much cash as they would have if I had put the same amount of premiums into another type of policy.

When the endowment matured I was in good health, fortunately, and able to replace it with ordinary life coverage, but had that not been the case my family would now be unprotected except for a group policy which I have.

4. (T — F) Endowment policies are much more expensive than the other three types for the same amount of coverage.

Which types for you?

In considering the 4 principal types of policies I have described, remember you don't have to select $\xleftarrow{800}$ just one kind. Your needs may call for several types of policies.

If you are a breadwinner of 30, for example, have two children, are just making ends meet, but expect to have a larger income in a few years, you may find it wise to buy a comparatively small ordinary life policy and even smaller endowment coverage for your kids' college costs, but a big slice of term insurance to protect your family until you can afford more permanent insurance. In this case, it is important to be sure your term insurance can be converted into permanent insurance. $\xleftarrow{900}$

5. (T — F) Mr. Woodbury says you need to select the one type of insurance which will give you the most protection for your money.

Family income policies

Before doing this, though, you should ask your agent about *family-income* and *family-maintenance* policies. These are combinations of ordinary life and term insurance which have been specially designed to help young families over their lean years.

On the other hand, if you are now earning a lot of money but expect a reduced income later, you may wish to invest in a *life-annuity contract*. There are many $\xleftarrow{1000}$ different kinds of annuities, but they all have one thing in common: they provide the insured person with a regular income from a specified date until death.

6. (M. C.) A combination of ordinary life and term insurance commonly used by young families is called a:
   ____(1) Family-income policy.
   ____(2) Child support policy.
   ____(3) Life annuity contract.
   ____(4) Ordinary term life insurance policy.

Four suggestions

There are 4 final tips, however, which the risk experts have for every insurance purchaser.

1. Read the fine print on any policy you buy and be sure you understand it.

$\xrightarrow{1100}$ 2. Pay your premiums annually or semiannually instead of on a monthly or quarterly basis. You'll save a good deal of money that way over the years.

3. Keep your policies in a safe place, preferably in your home, and let the person who will settle your affairs in the event of your death know where they are. A safe-deposit box is safe, but it generally has the disadvantage that after the death of the insured it may not be opened except by court order.

$\xrightarrow{1200}$ 4. Review both your property and life insurance programs at regular intervals. Changing family needs frequently require changes in insurance. Students of the subject told me every family should re-examine its program at least once every 3 years.

While all insurance is a form of gambling, it is gambling which permits you to play safe. "The essence of the business," Winston Churchill once said, "is bringing the magic of averages to the rescue of the millions."

This magic, if intelligently applied, can provide an inestimable amount of security for you and your family.

7. (T — F) Premiums are the same each year whether paid quarterly or annually.

$\xrightarrow{1300}$ 8. (T — F) Reading the fine print in a policy may protect you from buying worthless insurance policies.

9. (M. C.) You will save money by arranging to pay your insurance premiums:
   ____(1) Monthly.
   ____(2) Weekly.
   ____(3) Annually.
   ____(4) Whenever you can.

10. (T — F) Mr. Woodbury recommends that families re-examine their insurance policies at least once every three $\xrightarrow{1350}$ years.

————STOP — ASK FOR YOUR TIME————

Time ____ Sec.	RATE (from table on page 305):	R. ____
No. Errors ____	COMPREHENSION (100 — 10% for each Error):	C. ____
VII — 8	EFFICIENCY (R × C):	E. ____

Try California

By Horace Sutton

(Reprinted from the September, 1953, issue of *The Elks Magazine*, by permission of the editor)

─────────────── WAIT FOR SIGNAL TO BEGIN READING ───────────────

If everything goes according to pattern this year, Labor Day will be the usual signal for the vacationers to beat it for home, the kids to beat it for school, and the resort owners to fold up the scenery and drain the lakes until the new season rolls around in the spring. The only trouble with the system is that it seems to leave a rather numerous collection of people utterly and simply vacationless with no place to get a sunburn except from a barber shop lamp. This is where California comes in.

The lower half of the West Coast real estate enjoys $\overset{100}{\rightleftarrows}$ what the local boosters like to think of as a "second summer," a bonus of good weather all through September and October, and running into November. Mountains, valley, desert and seashore offer subtropical atmosphere at the same time, and since no single area has any particular climatic advantage over any other the rates are rather sensible. It is past the "high rate" season at the beaches and the mountains, and the astronomic scale has not gone into effect yet on the desert oases.

1. (T — F) The big disadvantage of traveling in Southern California in late summer is $\overset{200}{\rightleftarrows}$ the high cost.
2. (T — F) Southern California offers mountains, deserts, valleys, and the seashore to the visitor.

Cool and dry

At the same time the weather is moderate too. All during September a man standing with a thermometer in the center of Los Angeles would strike an average of 77.3 degrees. In October the slip does down to 73.8, in November to 70.8. But what makes September especially interesting is that the rainfall average is down to two tenths of one inch, and October is only six-tenths of an inch. Despite the wisecracks of the radio comedians broadcasting from $\overset{300}{\rightleftarrows}$ the West Coast, the Weather Bureau says there is only one day in September with 1/100 of an inch of rain or more, only two such days in October and three in November.

On the other hand, there is plenty of water along Southern California's 200 miles of sea, and although the rates sink when school starts, the weather goes on being amiable for another 60 days or so. All manner of fall events are scheduled along the seaside in the second summer months. Oceanside in San Diego County holds a swimming race on September $\overset{400}{\rightarrow}$ 7, an excuse for visitors to take the short drive out from Los Angeles. Spectators will crowd the pier, otherwise used for fishing, among other attractions, while the race begins at the beach, continues through the breakers, around the milelong pier and back to the beach. While this race is for hardies, there are others for junior boys and girls and for senior gaffers of 45 or more.

Oceanside is an entrance to Palomar Mountain, site of the world's largest observatory which is open during the day to visitors. San Diego has been building for tourists, too, especially at Mission Bay, a $20- $\overset{500}{\rightarrow}$ million aquatic park development that has attracted a 302-unit resort motel. Forty-eight units were completed this summer, opening under the name of the Bahia Hotel. Coming soon is a salt water swimming pool, restaurant, cocktail lounge, cabana and boating facilities. If you wander about with a trailer hooked on your back bumper, a new 900-unit deluxe trailer park is going up on De Anza Point in another corner of Mission Bay.

Down at San Pedro, world's largest fishing port, the town does honor to its most important industry, fish. The San Pedro Fisherman's Fiesta comes off $\overset{600}{\rightarrow}$ September 19 to 21 and for three days the place is decked out in bunting and loaded with celebrants. Everything comes to a climax in a water parade of 100 fishing boats, each decorated with flags and flowers, and representing something nautical — character, song, or situation.

Way down near the Mexican border at the south end of San Diego Bay, where the names and the atmosphere are tinted with tortilla, the city of Chula Vista holds its Moon Festival, the Fiesta de la Luna, September 24 to 27. Here old Spain and the new West mix amiably and citizens in both costumes hold $\overset{700}{\rightarrow}$ a flower show, a horse show, a chuckwagon breakfast for all visitors and a gigantic Fiesta Parade. If the moon is cooperative it will rise over San Diego Bay and the evening's entertainment will feature its arrival.

3. (T — F) The biggest attraction in the San Diego area during the second summer is the fishing.

4. (C) The world's largest _____ is near Oceanside.

5. (T — F) The biggest attraction of the season in the San Pedro area is the Fisherman's Fiesta.

6. (C) Chula Vista near the Mexican border is the scene of the _____ Festival in September.

800 ←

The desert in October

Since it is vastly too hot for a mortal to venture into the desert area during the first summer, the ranchlands of Southern Cal don't get under way until the second summer is fully at hand. Palm Springs, that famous retreat of the glamorous West, starts things off with Western Week, October 23 to 25 and offers a swimming pool with virtually every large hotel or apartment house. You can cycle the surroundings, golf on the 9-hole course, picnic in a canyon, take your pick of well over 100 hotels and apartments, half of them called the Casa Something or other and the other half the El Something or other.

900 ←

In the matter of getting West, in case you are not already there, The Overland Route from Chicago follows the path blazed by the nation's early fur trappers in the 1800's, and worn smooth by the covered wagons of the Mormons. Now you run west over the combined rails of the Chicago and Northwestern, the Union Pacific, and the Southern Pacific from Chicago to Salt Lake City to Reno to San Francisco. The Golden State Route takes you via Southern Pacific south from Chicago to El Paso, then up through Tucson, Phoenix and Los Angeles. The Sunset Route is for Southerners coming via New Orleans, Houston, San Antonio and so west. All trains offer chair cars or Pullmans. For late vacationers in the Northwest, the California second summer can be reached on the Shasta Route running south from Portland to San Francisco over 718 miles of

1000 ←

woods, lakes and mountains which you can enjoy in full daylight.

7. (T — F) Almost every hotel in Palm Springs features a swimming pool.

8. (T — F) The Overland Route is recommended for all Southerners.

Package tours

1100 → Another way to do it if you would rather keep your own car in the garage is to fly west with United and take one of their tours. You can either travel by bus or pick up a rented car at the airport and the price of your transportation and your lodging is figured in one bundle. For instance, there is a seven-day Hollywood vacation as low as $26.83 plus tax and air fare. It includes hotel accomodations at the Hollywood Plaza at the corner of Hollywood and Vine for six nights, plus a sightseeing tour of town, 1200 → and tickets to radio and TV shows emanating from the west coast.

A more comprehensive visit takes in Southern California for one week and a week-end, starting from Los Angeles and visiting Hollywood, Beverly Hills and the Beaches, Santa Barbara, San Diego and crossing into Mexico at Tijuana. You'll have a look at the Sunset Cliffs, La Jolla, and San Juan Capistrano, and an evening at Ciro's back in Hollywood. U-drive tours are available to Riverside (1 day), Santa Barbara (1 day), San Diego (2 days), Los Angeles to San Francisco (3 days or 5 days). As a matter of 1300 → fact there are all manner of extensions, California being a big and persuasive state.

9 & 10. (M. C.) Which two of the following places were not mentioned as possible "package tours"?
_____(1) Pasadena.
_____(2) Riverside.
_____(3) Hollywood.
_____(4) San Juan Capistrano.
_____(5) Santa Barbara.
_____(6) San Diego.
_____(7) Tijuana.
1350 → _____(8) San Bernadino.

————STOP — ASK FOR YOUR TIME————

Time _____ Sec.

No. Errors _____

VII — 9

RATE (from table on page 305):   R. _____

COMPREHENSION (100 — 10% for each Error):   C. _____

EFFICIENCY (R × C):   E. _____

Number VII-10

California's Colossus

BY LEE SCHWANZ

(Reprinted from the February-March, 1963, issue of *National Wildlife*, by permission of the editor)

— WAIT FOR SIGNAL TO BEGIN READING —

Water for all in a thirsty land

California is in desperate need for more water for its booming population. More than a thousand people move into the state every day — mostly in the southern two-thirds of the state, where all the available water is now being used up. New supplies must be found — soon — or this growth must stop.

The population growth is astonishing. The number of residents has doubled since World War II, and is now approaching 17 million. By the turn of the century there may be 50 million — and half of them will live in the nine counties in the Los Angeles ⟻100 area.

"Our main problem in California comes down to the fact that nature has not provided the right amount of water in the right places at the right times," observes Director William E. Warne of the Department of Water Resources. "Around 70 percent of our water is in the northern third of the state, but 77 percent of the water *need* is in the southern two thirds."

With this pressing need for more water, it would be easy to forget the requirements of fish and wildlife and to ignore the great value of water for recreational ⟻200 uses. But that's not true in California. Their vast new water project, designed to meet the needs of its population over the next 30 years, considers all needs.

The great new water system can only be described as colossal. It is the greatest water system in the world — perhaps the greatest in all man's history. The only effort that approaches it in scope is the irrigation system of ancient Babylon.

"Southern California is in a critical water situation," declares Director Warne. It is almost completely using up its allotment of water from the Colorado River and the Ownes Valley, and is drawing water from local ⟻300 wells faster than it can be restored. By 1970, the area must have water from far north of the Tehachapi Mountains or its growth will stop.

This, then is the problem that the California Water project must meet: It must collect water in the mountains to the north, control its flow into storage and channeling structures, and get the water to the distant users — all without disturbing the water supply in the northern part of the state and with provisions for wildlife and recreation uses along the ⟻400 way. It will be the largest, most expensive state project ever undertaken, with a $2 billion price tag.

1. (T — F) California's main problem is that the water supply is not properly located to fulfill its needs.

2. (T — F) This project is smaller than many other projects already completed.

The project begins in the tributaries of the Feather River, 750 miles north of thirsty Los Angeles. First of the upper dams is Frenchman Dam on Little Last Chance Creek. Antelope Valley Reservoir, Dixie Refuge, Abbey Bridge and Grizzly Valley Reservoir complete that part of the system.

Downstream, on the Feather River itself, will be 500→ huge Oroville Dam, highest in the country at 735 feet. Capacity of its reservoir will be 3,485,000 acre feet — a year's household needs for California's entire population!

From Oroville, water will be released downstream toward the Delta country of the Sacramento River. This flow will be tapped by the North Bay Aqueduct to serve cities north of San Francisco.

At the southern end of the Delta, giant pumps will lift the water from its meandering channels into the California Aqueduct. A concrete-lined channel 450 miles long and up to 150 feet wide and 30 feet 600→ deep, it will truly be a man-made major river.

Halfway down the valley, the big channel will deliver water to the San Luis Reservoir to irrigate the fertile San Fernando Valley. Next withdrawal is at Avenal Gap, where the Coastal Aqueduct will carry away water for San Luis Obispo and Santa Barbara counties.

Then comes the greatest engineering feat of all — the lift over the Tehachapi Mountains to the thirsty Los Angeles basin. Five pumping stations, with a total lift of 3,580 feet, will raise more water to a greater height than ever before in history.

700→ Once over the hump, the water will flow through the West Branch into Costiac Reservoir above Los Angeles, and through the East Branch to Cedar Springs and Perris Reservoirs, which serve other southern cities.

The master plan calls for a total of 21 dams, hundreds of miles of aqueducts, dozens of new recreation areas, and facilities for extensive fish and wildlife programs. The plan is now in the third year of construction, with eight to go. Completed, it should be adequate for California's needs for 30 years.

3. (C)   The project begins in the tributaries of the _____ River.

4. (M. C.)   The greatest engineering feat will be the:

    _____(1)   drainage of wetlands.   800 ←
    _____(2)   lift over the Tehachapi Mountains.
    _____(3)   construction of Oroville Dam.
    _____(4)   construction of the Pacific Flyway.

5. (T — F)   The system will be adequate for 60 years.

Water for wildlife

While engineers have been planning watercourses, biologists are studying the effects of water flow changes on wildlife. The Water Resources Department has contracted with the California Fish and Game Department to study the problems of changes in salinity, current, habitat and other factors involving wildlife.

Perhaps the greatest challenge to the planners is the Delta. A vast, diverse area with 700 miles of waterways, it supports a heavy population of fish, 900 ← birds and animals. The lower reaches are salt or brackish water; its upper sections are fresh. One important project is a survey of the effects of salinity changes on the spawning habits of resident fish.

Other problems include the huge pump intakes, which could pull young fish into the aqueduct, and which could disturb the plankton on which the young fish feed. These and other problems must be solved before the Delta region plan can be approved.

Drainage of wetlands presents another wildlife habitat problem. The Central Valley area, with the Tule Lake-Klamath complex to the north, are vital 1000 ← to waterfowl moving along the Pacific Flyway, and the Suisan Marsh is one of California's best duck hunting areas. Even with millions of acre feet of water being withdrawn, good hunting can be preserved through good management, reports Robert L.

Jones, project leader for the Delta Fish and Wildlife Protection Study.

6. (C)   While engineers are studying watercourses, _____ are studying the effects of waterflow changes on wildlife.

7. (T — F)   The Delta supports a heavy wildlife population.

Water for recreation

All the way from the Feather River to the end of 1100 → the aqueduct, the project will provide more recreation for everyone. Recreation areas are being planned wherever possible on the reservoirs by the state Department of Parks and Recreation. The big Oroville Reservoir, which now sees almost no recreational use, is ultimately expected to provide 10 million visitor-days of recreational use each year.

The Delta area now provides about three million man-days of recreation a year, two thirds of which is fishing. When the project is complete, it is expected to support 15 million man-days of all kinds of recreation — a whopping increase made possible by the 1200 → improvement of water quality and access.

Along the big California Aqueduct, 19 potential reservoir sites will provide multiple-use recreation areas for fishing, camping, boating, and the related water and shore sports. The same water will encourage wildlife, too.

The giant project is right on schedule. When completed, it will not only supply water, but also outdoor recreation, for California's booming population. For if Mother Nature neglected to put their water in the right places, the Californians are hard at work correcting her oversights.

8. (M. C.)   Greatest increases in recreational uses will be seen in:

    _____(1)   Abbey Bridge and Grizzly Valley.
    _____(2)   Antelope Valley and Frenchman Dam.
    1300 →
    _____(3)   Abbey Bridge and Oroville Dam.
    _____(4)   Oroville Dam and the Delta.

9. (T — F)   The Delta area is expected to provide facilities for fishing only.

10. (T — F)   Multiple-use recreation areas will be 1350 → located along the California Aqueduct.

————STOP — ASK FOR YOUR TIME————

Time _____ Sec.   RATE (from table on page 305):   R. _____

No. Errors _____   COMPREHENSION (100 — 10% for each Error):   C. _____

VII-10   EFFICIENCY (R × C):   E. _____

Number VII-11

High Soars the Eagle

By Dick Kirkpatrick

(Reprinted from the January, 1963, issue of *National Wildlife*, by permission of the editor)

─── WAIT FOR SIGNAL TO BEGIN READING ───

Our national bird

When the Continental Congress chose the "American Eagle" as our national bird on June 20, 1782, their choice seemed a logical one. The native bald eagle is a strikingly handsome, regal-looking bird, and the eagle has been a symbol of freedom, valor and strength dating back beyond the earliest historical records.

Surprisingly, his nomination met some stout resistance among the founding fathers — and an occasional detractor still takes a pot shot at his selection.

Despite all resistance, and against the arguments that the bald eagle is a thief (he is), a timid coward (sometimes), a carrion eater (partly right), and a **100** bully (right again), he became our national symbol.

The most dedicated eagle detractor, however, can not deny that he is a fine-looking bird. The dark-brown body and darker brown wings contrast sharply with the pure-white head and tail feathers, which glisten in the sunlight in flight and stand out strongly against the dark browns and greens of his native forest backgrounds. A large adult female bald eagle can weigh over 14 pounds with a flat-stretched wing-span of over 90 inches and a body length of over a yard. The adult eagle has few, if any, enemies other **200** than man, and can prey on almost any animal in sight at one stage of its life or another. Though their primary and favorite food is fish, eagles commonly kill and eat other birds and small mammals — chiefly rabbits and other small rodents — with occasional spectacular attacks on much larger animals.

1. (M. C.) The eagle's detractors have described him as:

    _____(1) a thief and a bully.

    _____(2) a symbol of the feudal system.

    _____(3) a homely, timid-looking bird.

    _____(4) an appropriate choice as national bird.

2. (T — F) An adult female bald eagle may have a wing span of over 7 feet. **300**

3. (C) The primary and favorite food of the eagle is _____.

Symbol of might or overrated bully?

These are the source of many eagle legends, and the reason for much of the bird's reputation as a varmint. There are records of eagle attacks on almost every species of animal — even humans — and one impressive account of three bald eagles cooperating in bringing down, killing, and feeding on a three-quarters-grown pronghorn antelope.

There is record of a near-successful attack on a two-year-old Hereford heifer, and many records — mostly exaggerated — of attacks on human children **400** (including one ridiculous tale of an eight-year-old boy being lifted 75 feet and carried 200 feet). There are, however, authenticated records of attacks on children — logical in view of records involving larger animals where the eagle attempts to kill but not to carry off its victim.

The term "carrion-eater" is probably another unearned libel on the eagle's reputation, depending on your definition of the word "carrion." Like any predator, the eagle takes its food in the easiest way possible, certainly welcoming the windfall of a dead fish washed up on shore. Since most estimates of the **500** eagle's diet are made from analysis of stomach contents, it's hard to estimate the original freshness of the partly-digested findings. Such washed-up spawners are the main food of the northern bald eagle during the salmon spawning season.

What ever the circumstances, the strike of the bald eagle can be a fearsome thing. He will follow and attack a diving duck under water, strike and kill a big Canadian goose in midair, and pick a mountain goat kid off a lofty crag. Even in his most unpopular hunting activity — robbing the smaller osprey of his hard-caught fish dinner — he is impressive.

Another shortcoming of the bald eagle, often **600** pointed out by scientists brave and agile enough to reach an occasional aerie, is the bird's apparent reluctance to defend his own nest. Though occasional individuals will attack an intruder, there are few records of their actually striking him. By far the more usual conduct is for the eagle to retire to a safe distance, perhaps crying out, but offering no resistance. Against other predators and the annoyances of smaller birds, however, the eagle will defend itself, and will sometimes put up a fierce struggle when cornered or trapped. At the same time, many eagles have been observed under attack by smaller 700 birds and seen to retire in order with a dignified indifference. In general, however, in his conduct under pressure, the bald eagle is regarded by many authorities as a plain coward.

One really impressive feature on the eagle's side, however, is his nest-building capacity. Building in tall trees near water when possible, and returning to the same nest year after year, a pair will add another foot to the nest's height each season until it attains enormous proportions. Construction is mainly of sticks, branches and other available structural members in a sort of rampart, filled on the inside with smaller materials, then lined in the center with softer 800 stuffs. The sheer bulk of the nest accounts for one of the eagle's few natural hazards — weather. High winds and structural failure can bring down the massive nest before the eggs are hatched or while the eaglets are still unable to fly.

4. (T — F) Records show that an eagle will not attack a human child.

5. (M. C.) Because the eagle sometimes feeds on dead fish washed ashore he has been termed a:

_____(1) scavenger.

_____(2) spawner.

_____(3) coward.

_____(4) carrion-eater.

6. (T — F) Despite other shortcomings, a bald 900 eagle usually will defend his own nest against attack.

7. (T — F) One feature in the eagle's favor is his nest-building capacity.

Preservation of population

At the time of that debate by the Continental Congress, the bald eagle ranged over the entire North American continent, though most commonly around bodies of water that assured a good supply of fish. Since that time, however, man's depredations, both from hunting and from civilization's many changes in habitat, have greatly reduced their numbers. One new hazard is that of indirect poisoning through pesticides. However, the bird is not thought to be in danger of 1000

extinction anywhere. In June of 1940, the "American Eagle" came under government protection under the Bald Eagle Act, though the then-Territory of Alaska was not included. The 34 years of bounty hunting in that territory is believed to have resulted in the killing of at least 100,000 eagles. After years of debate and the passage of much conflicting legislation, the Alaskan Territorial Legislature repealed its eagle bounty law on March 2, 1953. The birds may still be killed when "committing damage to fishes, other wildlife, domestic birds and animals." With the end 1100 of bounty hunting, which had become an important source of income to many Alaskans, it is expected that the eagle population may return to "normal" within a few years.

Since the bald eagle is not a prolific breeder, it is hoped that protection throughout the continent will enable the population to achieve and maintain a balance. It may even increase, though not to a point of becoming an important predator again. A pair of eagles normally only produces two eggs — sometimes as many as three. They often manage to raise only one eaglet to maturity. The eggs have been described as 1200 "ridiculously small for so large a bird"; consequently the eaglet takes quite a long time to develop into a self-sufficient individual. Often they mate and nest while still in their juvenile plumage. Even so, their slow rate of reproduction caused Alaskan ornithologists to fear that even inefficient bounty hunting could render them practically extinct.

Whatever his shortcomings, the loss of our bald eagle population would be a tragedy. Despite his detractors, he will remain our national bird, and the general public, ignoring his shortcomings and those detractions, will probably continue to regard him as an excellent choice.

8. (C) 1300 The Bald Eagle Act of 1940 provided protection for "American Eagles" everywhere in the United States except _____.

9. (T — F) Because the bald eagle is a prolific breeder, there is little chance of population depletion.

10. (T — F) A pair of eagles normally produces two eggs, often raising only one eaglet to maturity. 1350

————STOP — ASK FOR YOUR TIME————

Time _____ Sec.   RATE (from table on page 305):   R. _____

No. Errors _____   COMPREHENSION (100 − 10% for each Error):   C. _____

VII-11   EFFICIENCY (R × C):   E. _____

Number VII-12

The Problem of Personality

BY JESSIE RUNNER

(A digest of an original article which appeared in the December, 1954, issue of *Adult Leadership*, reprinted by permission of the author)

―――― WAIT FOR SIGNAL TO BEGIN READING ――――

Personality — what is it? It is not a sharply definable scientific term. It is an everyday word used to describe the characteristic responses which we make to various elements of our daily lives, under ordinary conditions. The conditions, and our responses, are much the same from day to day. Our own particular feelings and attitudes and our characteristic ways of expressing our feeling, make up our personality pattern.

Personality is a phenomenon of life as it is lived. It is a continual process of living, feeling, acting, wishing, thinking, as we use our energy in the pursuit of ends of our own, however dimly we perceive ← 100 them. Even the idlest and most purposeless personalities show some direction in their life course, if only toward the satisfaction of successfully avoiding effort.

It is not the characteristics of an individual that create his personality. It is his attitudes toward them. As I see it, personality is not what we are, in terms of our characteristics, but what we decide to do about them, or with them. It is our way of life, under the conditions of our own lot, in a real world of frustration and opportunities.

Interpersonal relations may be studied in terms of 200 ← a social field of force. The concepts of electrical charge of brainwaves, or the neurological correlates of personality phenomena and processes, may, in days to come, furnish a truly scientific explanation of personality differences of feeling, thought, and action. But for the present, the study of personality must stay on the commonsense level of trying to account for the great differences in the feeling, activities, and goals of various persons, in terms of what needs to be done.

1. (C)   Personality is used to describe the characteristic _____ we make to elements in our daily lives.

2. (T — F) The characteristics of an individual 300 ← create his personality.

3. (T — F) The concepts of electrical charge and brainwaves furnish a scientific explanation of personality differences.

The questions which press for immediate answer are practical questions. What is it that the person actually wants from his life activity? How does he go about getting his life satisfactions? What is he good for, from the social point of view? How can we predict what he will feel and do in unknown situations? How can we give him insight and understanding which might make him more adequate in 400 → handling his life problems?

The need to understand the processes of personality is becoming acute in an increasingly organized world, where persons must operate together and fulfill highly specialized functions. The cost, in human dissatisfaction and discontent, of misplacing personalities in the social mechanism, of putting them in situations where they do not fit, it saddening to contemplate. Even more saddening are the evidences of unnecessary strife and misunderstanding between persons.

The first problem that the student of personality must solve is how he shall analyze the phenomena in a meaningful way for the purposes at hand. What 500 → shall he look for? What variables shall he choose in trying to understand, and control, and predict, the feelings and behavior of given personalities in given situations? The decisions he makes will be determined by what he thinks personality is.

I feel that if any given personality is to be understood, meaningfully and predictively, it is necessary to know, quite definitely, the inner nature of the person's attitudes and purposes, plus the characteristic ways he expresses himself outwardly. The student should be able to put himself, mentally, in the position of the person he is studying, and see and feel 600 → life as that person perceives it — not as he, himself, would perceive it under similar circumstances. Obtaining sufficient significant data for such a purpose is a problem of scientific observation and testing procedures, but putting the findings together again, in order to reconstruct the living personality, is a matter of insight and synthetic logic.

4. (T — F) The need to understand the processes of personality is becoming more urgent.

5. (M. C.) Which of the following will determine the decisions of the student of personality.
   ____(1) What he thinks personality is.
   ____(2) The subject's attitude.
   ____(3) Outward behavior of subject.
   ____(4) Subconscious emotions of ⤺700 subject.

6. (T — F) A student must be able to think how he would act under a set of circumstances similar to that of the person he is studying.

Fortunately for the researcher, he is able to obtain more and better data than is available to ordinary observation, by means of suitable planned tests. He can discover some very fundamental kinds of attitudes that lie back of large segments of behavior. Take, for example, the individual's attitude toward personal freedom and the satisfactions involved in making his own decisions as to what he shall think and what he shall do. To some people the opportun- ⤺800 ity to be free to do their own thinking and to live their own lives in their own way is almost a first necessity if they are to find satisfaction in life. They feel personally threatened by restraints.

The wish or need for personal freedom is, however, by no means universal. The average person prefers the controlled and structured life of conformity to the group pattern. The big, inclusive attitudes of personality, such as the pleasure of freedom or of control, are certainly of great importance in understanding given persons in relation to their life cir- ⤺900 cumstance; but from the point of view of the individuality within this large area, it is the personal focus of interest and effort that is of major importance in understanding the personality. It is usually possible to discover some dominating attitude, some overall wish, or purpose, or need, which acts as a control over the development of the other attitudes and integrates the whole personality.

7. (T — F) The author states that the average person prefers a controlled life of conformity to the group pattern.

8. (M. C.) Which of the following is of major importance in understanding the personality:
   1000→
   ____(1) The pleasure of freedom or control.
   ____(2) The personal focus of interest and effort.
   ____(3) Characteristic outward expression.
   ____(4) Interpersonal relations.

In order to test out our knowledge of a given personality, there are certain searching questions which we should try to answer. For instance, what kind of problems would a certain person be likely to get involved in? Thus, people whose attitude toward money is that its only usefulness is to be spent, quickly, for the things one wants, will be lucky not to have financial problems. People whose 1100→ affections are intense and free-floating, will find themselves involved in romantic difficulties. Those who find pleasure in increasing their own feeling of status by disparaging the status of others, will have interpersonal troubles. We make our own problems, in large measure, by reason of our own attitudes, and they are not likely to be easily solved so long as the causative attitudes persist.

Having decided what kind of problems a certain person might make for himself, we must then ask ourselves how he will try to answer them. Will he try to blame someone else for them? Ascribe them to 1200→ his bad luck and do nothing much? Withdraw into some kind of a fantasy world? Or will he take a good look at them, find out what caused them, and what the best available solution would be.

If we can answer questions of that sort, then it becomes possible to see life as this other person sees it, to realize the emotional response he will make to given situations, and what he will be likely to do about them. If we can do this, it may be possible to make predictions not only concerning his own attitudes in given situations, but what his associates will think 1300→ of him, and what, in general, their response will be to him.

9. (C) The author seems to believe that in large measure we create our own problems by reason of our own
_____.

10. (T —F) People usually have some dominating attitude which controls the develop-
   1350→ ment of other attitudes.

————STOP — ASK FOR YOUR TIME————

Time _____ Sec.	RATE (from table on page 305):	R. _____
No. Errors _____	COMPREHENSION (100 − 10% for each Error):	C. _____
VII — 12	EFFICIENCY (R × C):	E. _____

An Air View of Portugal Today

By Lou Phillips

(Reprinted by permission of the publisher, Pan American World Airlines)

──────── **WAIT FOR SIGNAL TO BEGIN READING** ────────

If Henry The Navigator, princely patron of mariners and King of Portugal during the fifteenth century, were to return to Lisbon today, he would probably be a bit saddened but very proud of the tiny 40,000 sq. miles of land which are closer to the United States than any other part of the European Continent. It is true that Portugal does not play so dominant a part in world affairs as in Henry's day when its ships showed the way to India, The Isles of Spices and the Rivers of Brazil. Since then man has conquered the air as he did the sea, Clippers of the sky have 100← succeeded their surface-bound counterparts and a whole new field of aerial navigation has been developed. But Portugal's strategic situation on the globe and the far-flung empire it still controls would stir Henry's imagination and prompt him, as it has over eight million Portuguese of today, to plan to play an important role in the Air Age.

Portugal is located in the western part of the Iberian Peninsula and its frontiers in Europe are almost seven centuries old. On the west and south lies the Atlantic Ocean giving the country a coast 200← line of nearly 465 miles. On the north and east is Spain. Although there is no great natural barrier between Spain and Portugal the character of the landscape changes completely when one crosses over the frontier. The Portuguese nation has experienced over eight hundred years of independent existence, defending its soil in many bitter battles, and its people have developed strong traditions distinctly apart from the Spanish. They have both a language and a culture all their own.

1. (T — F) Portugal is closer to the U. S. than any other part of the European continent.
2. (T — F) There is a great natural barrier be-300← tween Spain and Portugal.
3. (T — F) The Spanish and Portuguese are very much alike in culture and language.

The age of Portuguese glory

Portugal gained its independence as a kingdom in 1147 and its territorial acquisitions on continental Europe were completed in the early days of the thirteenth century with the occupation of the southern part of the country. The great role of Portugal in the world's history came in the reign of King Joao I (John) when the Portuguese settled in North Africa and started their grand enterprise of 400→ navigation and discoveries. Under the inspiration of Prince Henry, son of Joao I, the nation's sailors explored nearly two thirds of the inhabited globe. Vasco da Gama reached India, Cabral discovered Brazil, and all the Indian Ocean and the China Sea were familiar to the Portuguese before the first quarter of the sixteenth century. Magellan, a Portuguese, leading Spanish ships in the area accorded to Spain by a treaty, sailed the Pacific in the first voyage around the world.

Henry loved the sea and under his guidance Portugal entered in a fierce race with Spain for the 500→ legendary wealth of distant countries. Its ships were the fastest and most seaworthy and its seamen were reputedly the best in all Europe. But the Prince also believed that mariners should be trained for such dangerous voyages so he founded a school of navigation and brought the finest astronomers and mathematicians there to instruct the seamen. Their explorations brought both fame and riches to Portugal for a lively trade sprang up between that nation and the newly discovered lands.

But the people of Portugal also suffered in this gigantic drive. Its manpower, ravaged by the epi-600→ demics of the times, was drawn upon too heavily by all these undertakings. Gradually much of the enormous Portuguese Empire was lost to other powers, mostly to Holland and England. In 1792 King Joao became involved in a war with Napoleon which resulted in occupancy of the nation until the French were driven out by the British in 1808. During this time the royal family abandoned Lisbon and transferred the seat of government of the country to Brazil. For twelve years Rio de Janeiro was the capital for the United Kingdom of Portugal and Brazil. When the King returned to Portugal he left his eldest 700→ son in Brazil who became Emperor in 1822 as Pedro I.

Under Portuguese rule Brazil advanced rapidly but because of a desire for a democratic government, a republic called the United States of Brazil was established in 1889. The daughter of the Emperor of Brazil became Queen of Portugal and her descendants ruled the country until 1910 when the Monarchy was replaced by a Republican Regime.

The early years of the new republic were troubled by political and social unrest. In 1926, a military government took control of the country. Soon after, Marshal Carmona was elected President and in 1932 Ollveira Salazar became Premier. The Marshal has ⁸⁰⁰← been reelected three times, his third term ending in March 1949. According to the Constitution of 1933 the country is a Corporate Republic. The president is elected for a seven year term and the National Assembly for four year terms. The president appoints a premier who selects a cabinet but is responsible directly to the president and not to the National Assembly.

4. (M. C.) Portuguese independence as a kingdom dates back to about
——(1) 1850
——(2) 1150
——(3) 1500
——(4) 750

5. (T —F) Under Prince Henry's rule Portuguese sailors explored nearly ninety percent ⁹⁰⁰← of the uninhabited globe.

6. (T —F) The success of the Portuguese exploration was due in part to the school of navigation established by King Henry.

7. (C) During the French occupancy the seat of the government was transferred to ——————————————.

8. (C) When this article was written, Portugal was organized politically as a
——————————————————.

Portugal overseas

Portugal still holds great parts of its territorial discoveries and conquests. It has possessions in Africa — Guinea, Angola, Mozambique, the Cape Verde Islands and the Islands of Principe and S. Tome; in Asia — Portuguese India and the Island of Macao; and in Oceania — the eastern portion of ¹³⁵⁰→ the Island of Timor. Each territory is governed by an ¹⁰⁰⁰

appointive Governor assisted by a local Advisory Assembly. The exports from these colonies are mostly agricultural but in many areas there are gold, diamond and other mineral mines. This colonial empire of over 803,000 square miles and with more than 10,800,000 inhabitants is out-ranked by only those of England and France.

Portugal's empire is one of her greatest potential assets in the Air Age. Because of it the nation has, dispersed throughout the world in convenient ¹¹⁰⁰→ locations, cities and islands which could serve admirably as bases for international air transport. Only Great Britain of all other nations is better supplied with such strategic, potential bases. Although France possesses excellent aerial centers many are far removed from each other and from the regions of great commercial activity. The United States, in contrast, has relatively few potential bases and must negotiate with other nations for the use of foreign facilities. In 1930, a Franco-Portuguese aviation company obtained a thirty-year concession for the exploitation of commercial aviation within Portugal and a monopoly of air routes between that country and its colonies.

¹²⁰⁰→ The chief airport on the Portuguese mainland is Portela de Sacavem, the landplane base at Lisbon. Pan American Clippers land there 5 times a week 19 hours after leaving New York. New 60-passenger Boeing Stratocruisers are expected to complete the three thousand mile trip in less than 10 hours. Before land-planes were used over the Atlantic, Pan American World Airways flying-boats used to land on the River Tagus at Cabo Ruivo, a seaplane anchorage near Lisbon. Even before landing in continental Portugal, Clippers have already touched the territory of the Portuguese Republic on its way in ¹³⁰⁰→ Horta, in the Azores, where refueling takes place.

9. (T — F) Portugal's colonial empire is out-ranked only by those of England and France.

10. (M. C.) The new Stratocruisers are expected to complete the trip from New York to Lisbon in about
——(1) 10 hours
——(2) 16 hours
——(3) 19 hours
——(4) 60 hours

—————STOP — ASK FOR YOUR TIME—————

Time ———— Sec.	RATE (from table on page 305):	R. ————
No. Errors ————	COMPREHENSION (100 — 10% for each Error):	C. ————
VII — 13	EFFICIENCY (R × C):	E. ————

Number VII-14

What Is a College?

BY EDGAR C. CUMMINGS

(Reprinted from the introductory issue of *School and Society*,
by permission from the editor and author)

───────────── WAIT FOR SIGNAL TO BEGIN READING ─────────────

Confusion exists concerning the real purposes, aims, and goals of a college. What are these? What should a college be?

Some believe that the chief function of even a liberal arts college is a vocational one. I feel that the vocational function of a college, while important, is nonetheless secondary. Others profess that the chief purpose of a college is to produce paragons of moral, mental, and spiritual stamina — Bernard MacFaddens with halos. If they mean that the college should inculcate students with the highest moral, ethical, and religious standards by precept and example, I am willing to accept the thesis. 100 ←

I believe in attention to both social amenities and regulations, but I prefer to see our colleges get down to more basic moral and ethical considerations instead of standing in loco parentis for four years when the student is attempting, in his youthful and awkward ways, to grow up. It has been said that it is not our duty to prolong adolescences. We are singularly adept at it.

1 & 2. (C) The author believes that a college should inculcate students with the highest moral, _____, and _____ standards by precept and example.

Some complain that a college is not extolling the 200 ← merits of a given religious denomination. I am not decrying the benefits to be derived from a healthy church relationship for a college, for religion and education have a stake in one another. I am criticizing the tendency of many religious denominations, both Catholic and Protestant, to regard a college as a place where education takes second place to religion, and where the strings may be pulled by those who are confused about the chief tasks of an educational institution. I favor the general requirement that each student have a course in religion, but only on condition that this course leads to a questioning of 300 ← and strengthening of the student's faith. It is of little concern to me whether or not a student can recite the "begats" or the Bible chapters from Genesis to Revelations; an atheist can do that, too.

3. (T — F) If a religious class leads to the questioning of and strengthening of the student's faith, the author believes it should be included in the college curricula.

There are those who maintain that the chief purpose of a college is to develop "responsible citizens." This is good if responsible citizenship is a 400 → by-product of all the factors which go to make up a college education and life itself. The difficulty arises from a confusion about the meaning of responsible citizenship. I know of one college which aims mainly to produce, in a kind of academic assembly line, outstanding exponents of our system of free enterprise. While really free enterprise has much to commend it, I hesitate to commend to posterity students who live according to the gospel of John D. Rockefeller or Engine Charlie Wilson. Likewise, I hesitate to praise the kind of education which extols 500 → one kind of economic system to the exclusion of the good portions of other kinds of economic systems. It seems to me therefore, that a college should represent a combination of all the above aims, and should be something else besides — first and foremost an educational experience, the center of which is the intellectual exchange between teachers and students.

Even after the departure of one of the great university leaders of our history — David Starr Jordan, the aura of Jordan still hung over the campus and electrified it. Despite poor buildings, little equipment, and small student body and faculty, 600 → education was the magic watchword of that time and there was hardly a student who had not fought his way there or who was not motivated by a now forgotten fervor to gain knowledge and culture for the sake of knowledge and culture. Not yet arrived was the time when going to college was "the thing to do," or when the almost automatic receipt of a diploma somehow opened the door to all enterprises. In those days, apparently, a college education still emphasized the gaining of knowledge the hard way, the thesis that mental discipline is a necessity and not something that modern psychologists and experts on education have discarded as obsolete. **700 ←**

4. (T — F) According to this author, David Starr Jordan was one of the great university leaders of our history.

5. (T — F) Years ago a university was a luxury for playboys and a diploma didn't mean too much.

Along with the times, curricula have changed and multiplied as new vistas of knowledge have been opened up. Along with genuine new intellectual avenues, however, we have indulged ourselves in some so-called intellectual activities and subjects which must have the ancients or the early leaders of our higher education in stitches. It remains to be seen whether a college is foresighted or merely **800 ←** foolish when it offers a course in "Travel in Outer Space." I should advise students not to rush to make their reservations for a trip to Mars or the moon; they still have time left.

Along with the change in times has, I fear, come a change in the attitudes of many students toward a college education. I have read entirely too many statements such as this one on admissions application papers: "I want a college education because I feel that this will help to support me and my family." I suspect that a job as a bricklayer would help this **900 ←** student to support himself and his family much better than a college education.

6. (T — F) The author believes that a college education is primarily for vocational purposes.

In an address, April, 1953, to the Ohio Association of College Presidents and Deans, Charles Allen Smart said, "When I see silly floats in student parades, and fraternity and sorority house decorations, I wonder whether our art departments aren't slipping. When I note the energy that goes into campaigning for 'prom-kings' and 'prom-queens,' while the students remain relatively indifferent to actual politics or, much worse, have learned that there is less **1000 ←** **1350 →** and less room and safety for unorthodox opinions in this country, I begin to wonder what goes on in the

classes in the various social sciences. When I see how vulgarly and publicly the students choose to make love, I wonder whether I myself, as a teacher of literature, expounding texts from Chaucer, Shakespeare and Browning, for example, in which love is felt and made most beautifully, have not failed to make these passages come alive in my students' minds in such a way as implicitly to expose and so **1100 →** lessen their own vulgarity. I happen to share Cardinal Newman's conviction, as I understand it, that if education does not strongly help to make ladies and gentlemen, there is something wrong with the education. He seems to say that liberal education can and should do nothing else, and if we accept his broad and deep definition of a gentleman, I am inclined to agree with him."

7. (T — F) After observing students participating in parades, campaigns, etc., Mr. Smart believes the college student is obtaining valuable educational experiences.

8. (T — F) Cardinal Newman believes that if **1200 →** education does not strongly help to make ladies and gentlemen, there is something wrong with an education.

A college should be an educational institution. This should not have to be said, but so many colleges and universities (and students) have become sidetracked concerning the matter that it needs to be restated, trite as it may sound. A college is a place where the teacher and the student are the two most important people; where young people should improve their thinking and deepen it, broaden it, refine it, and make it rational and objective. It is a place **1300 →** where they should, first and foremost, find the tools and the knowledge on which this thinking will be predicated.

9 & 10. (M. C.) According to this article the most important people in a university are the: (check two)

_____ (1) President.
_____ (2) Trustees.
_____ (3) Custodians.
_____ (4) Students.
_____ (5) Alumni.
_____ (6) Teachers.
_____ (7) Student body officers.
_____ (8) Parents.

————STOP — ASK FOR YOUR TIME————

Time _____ Sec.

No. Errors _____

VII — 14

RATE (from table on page 305):

COMPREHENSION (100 — 10% for each Error):

EFFICIENCY (R × C):

R. _____

C. _____

E. _____

Number VII-15

Mass Investment

BY G. KEITH FUNSTON

(Reprinted from the February, 1954, issue of *The Exchange*, published by
the New York Stock Exchange, by permission of the author, G. Keith Funston)

──────── WAIT FOR SIGNAL TO BEGIN READING ────────

Industry and business are working with the New York Stock Exchange and with other segments of the securities business to create a nation of share owners and a stronger America. Our ultimate goal is a direct ownership interest in the tools of production for every family in this country — or, to put it another way, we would like to see to it that every American who is able to, owns a share of American business.

It is our deep conviction that capitalism in the United States cannot even survive without direct public participation and support. We cherish our political democracy — now, to safeguard that political ⟵100 freedom, we must seek true economic democracy.

The most prosperous year in our history has just ended. At the start of 1954 the immediate future is clouded by such factors as declining new and unfilled orders in the hands of manufacturers, a rise in business inventories, a slight increase in unemployment, retail sales a little smaller than they might have been. It is quite possible that the current year may see a number of readjustments. That is the short-term outlook — and with it go all the qualms which accompany any attempt to gauge exactly the im- ⟵200 mediate future.

1. (T — F) Industry and business are working with the exchange to increase the number of share owners.
2. (T — F) The Exchange would like to see everyone everywhere own shares of American industry.
3. (T — F) According to this author, economic democracy is necessary to safeguard political freedom.

Long view

But if we step back a bit and try for a longer perspective, we get a different view and the ruts that look so ominous when they are under our noses seem to level off. In my opinion the future of America's industrial development is still in the toddling stage. ⟵300 A growing population is demanding a bewildering variety of goods and services which didn't exist even a couple of decades ago. Lest this may sound like overly optimistic theorizing, I should like to mention a comment made a few days ago by Crawford H. Greenewalt, President of Du Pont.

"It is also interesting to note," he said, "that when anyone in the past has attempted to predict the long-term future, his forecast has turned out to be hopelessly shortsighted and pessimistic."

We are just starting to learn the potentialities of 400⟶ such industries as electronics, petro-chemicals, antibiotics — while stretching ahead, still to be explored, is the incalculable range of atomic energy. The pressure for more and better products must grow indefinitely; and the pressure must come from a fully employed and increasing labor force which has income to satisfy its wants and needs.

Industry itself knows that its own vitality hinges upon figuring out new and better ways to satisfy the American public — and is spending more than one billion dollars a year on research with that ultimate aim in mind. This often spectacular technological progress, of course, is translated every year into 500⟶ the construction of new plants and equipment.

Funds needed

Industry cannot afford to rely on a limited number of people for capital to finance future expansion. The money that is needed must come from millions of people who are not now investors — the investors of the future who will share in the ownership of American industry.

Now, how does all this affect the New York Stock Exchange? How can the Stock Exchange make the maximum effective contribution to the national welfare? The answer, it seems to me, lies in the honest and efficient discharge of the Exchange's responsibilities to the public and to industry.

600⟶ Mass production and mass distribution are two modern phenomena on which American prosperity is founded. But to exploit those two concepts for the maximum benefit of the maximum number of people, a third concept must be added — mass investment. It's no secret that a great many people, including myself, were disturbed by the disclosure in the Brookings Institution census of share owners that only 6,500,000 people had an ownership stake in our corporate wealth at the close of 1951. That figure must be multiplied again and again — if we want capitalism to work at maximum efficiency.

4. (T — F) America's industrial development is in its infancy.
700⟶

5. (C) The author believes he is justified in being _____.

6. (M. C.) Capital to finance future expansion must come from
____(1) Increased profits.
____(2) Future investors.
____(3) Borrowed money.
____(4) Retained earnings.

7. (M. C.) At the close of 1951 how many people shared as owners of our corporate wealth?
____(1) 5,000,000
____(2) 3,500,000
____(3) 3,000,000
____(4) 6,500,000

Primary job

I regard it as a primary job of the Stock Exchange to make true economic democracy part of our way of life and not merely a catchy phrase.

In recent years the Exchange has conducted an ←800 intensive educational campaign to tell people about the importance of the investment process to our economy. We intend to intensify and broaden that effort. In January of this year, as part of our campaign to encourage share ownership, one of the most significant developments in financial history was made available to the public by the Exchange's member firms: The opportunity to purchase the securities of our great corporations on a pay-as-you-go basis. The Monthly Investment Plan, as it is popularly known, clears the road — for the first time — to mass investment.

New departure
900→

The Monthly Investment Plan represents a radical step for the Stock Exchange community — just as radical in its way as General Electric's use of Bing Crosby and Ken Carpenter to discuss the importance of investment before a nationwide radio audience — just as radical as Pennsylvania Railroad, Chrysler, Socony-Vacuum, Monsanto Chemical and Allied Chemical utilizing the street floor windows of Exchange member firms to graphically tell to the public their own story and the contribution of investment to their growth.

Simply as a matter of self-preservation, industry must go to the public for a larger share of the funds needed for new plants and equipment. But the ←1000 investor must be protected, too, whether he is already a share owner or is becoming one for the first time.

The Stock Exchange, of course, has its own regulations for the protection of the investor — such safeguards as insistence on sound corporate accounting practices by its listed companies, frequent and full reports to their share owners, and that supervision which has given member firms a record of integrity and fair dealing.

8. (T — F) The primary job of the Exchange is to protect investors.

1100→ 9. (C) The Monthly Investment Plan clears the road to _____.

Taxation

The Exchange has a responsibility in other areas in which the interests of the investor are at stake — the responsibility to fight against confiscatory, unfair and crippling Federal Tax legislation. Freedom of capital has been the cornerstone of our business system since this nation was founded. Yet the Capital Gains Tax and double taxation of dividends have seemed to be almost deliberately contrived to impede the freedom of capital and to discourage investment. These are unjust laws. It is our obligation to oppose them — and I am pleased to report that the new 1200→ administration appears to be as aware as we are of their inherent defects.

In his State of the Union Message, President Eisenhower said: "We should now revise the more glaring tax inequities, particularly on small tax payers; reduce restraint on the growth of small business, and make other changes that will encourage initiative, enterprise and production."

A free market

We have still another responsibility: To maintain a marketplace where the securities of the nation's leading corporations can be bought and sold quickly. The need for such a marketplace led to the foundation of the New York Stock Exchange 162 years 1300→ ago. The need today is greater than it was then and the need tomorrow will be greater still. We provided such a marketplace in George Washington's day — we shall provide it for the America of tomorrow, the prosperous nation built by mass investment.

10. (T — F) Tax legislation can't harm the interests of investors.
1350→

————STOP — ASK FOR YOUR TIME————

Time _____ Sec.   RATE (from table on page 305):   R. _____

No. Errors _____   COMPREHENSION (100 — 10% for each error):   C. _____

VII — 15   EFFICIENCY (R × C):   E. _____

Number VII-16

The Story of Sugar Cane

(Reprinted from a pamphlet of the same name,
by permission of the American Sugar Refining Company)

───────── WAIT FOR SIGNAL TO BEGIN READING ─────────

This is the story of cane sugar — the sparkling white sugar you stirred in your coffee and sprinkled on your cereal at breakfast; as well as the sugar that plays such an important part in creating the satisfying flavor of your favorite dessert at dinner. Sugar is an essential ingredient in every meal and it would be almost impossible to satisfy the food requirements of our modern civilization without it.

Refined cane sugar is a pure, wholesome, naturally occurring carbohydrate technically known as *sucrose*. There is a whole series of related carbohydrates known to chemists as sugars, but in everyday language the 100 word "sugar" refers solely to sucrose.

About two-thirds of the world's sugar supply is derived from the sweet juice of sugar cane. It is a tropical plant, thriving only in a warm, moist climate. The principal growing areas are Cuba, Puerto Rico, India, Java, the Philippine Islands, the Hawaiian Islands, South America, Egypt, South Africa, Formosa and Australia. In the United States, sugar cane is grown principally in the State of Louisiana and, to a lesser extent, in the State of Florida.

There are definite indications that sugar cane was known and its juice highly valued hundreds of years 200 before the birth of Christ. The earliest written mention of sugar cane appears in records of the expedition of Alexander the Great down the Indus River in 325 B. C. Writing of their explorations, Nearchus, one of the emperor's admirals, said they found "honey-bearing reeds."

Linked together in the Bible as articles of great value are Incense from Sheba and Sweet Cane from a far country. Another reference is by Dioscorides, a Greek physician who lived during the time of the Roman Emperor Nero. "There is a sort of hard honey," he wrote, "which is called saccharum (sugar) found upon canes in India. It is grainy like 300 salt and brittle between the teeth, but of sweet taste withal."

By 600 A.D. sugar had become known throughout the Orient. Taitsung, Emperor of China (627-650 A.D.), sent envoys to India to learn the art of extracting a syrup from sugar cane. The syrup in turn was boiled until it became a thick, dark mixture of sugar and syrup. It is believed this was somewhat similar in color to the darkest brown sugar we have today.

1. (C)   The technical name of sugar is
            _____.

400 2. (M. C.) About what portion of the world's sugar supply comes from sugar cane?
            ____(1) One-third.
            ____(2) One-half.
            ____(3) Two-thirds.
            ____(4) Ninety per cent.

3. (T — F) Discovery of sugar as a food was made only recently.

A basis of commerce

In the 8th century, a crude kind of refining process was devised by the Egyptians. Sugar cane was introduced on the Island of Sicily by Arab traders from the Nile Valley. Growing successfully in Sicily, sugar cane spread to Spain and to other Mediterranean border countries. Records showing the income of the Sultan of Turkey in the 11th century include 50,000 pounds of sugar as part of his revenue.

500 From the Moslems, the Crusaders learned the art of preserving meat with spices. From the Moslems, too, they acquired a taste for sugar. Returning home, the armies of the Crusades spread word of these new food wonders. This created a demand resulting in brisk trade between Europe and the countries of the Far East. This trade prospered until 1453, when the Turks captured Constantinople and began to levy high tribute on passing caravans. Prior to this conquest, the Italian Republics of Venice and Genoa were the principal European seaports on the 600 Mediterranean. They had become rich and powerful because through their ports passed most of the trade between the Far East and the Northern European countries. Restriction of that commerce by the invading Turks was the principal reason why Columbus sought a new route to India and discovered America.

In the 15th century an inventor, living in Venice, received 100,000 crowns for devising a method of molding sugar. The molded sugar became known as "pains de Venise" or Venetian loaves. The process of molding sugar into cones was the last step in refining practiced for over 400 years and to a limited extent is employed to the present day. Granulated $\overset{700}{\leftarrow}$ sugar as we know it today is a relatively modern innovation.

4. (T — F) Distribution of sugar in Europe was hampered by the conquests of the Turks.

5. (T — F) A Venetian inventor in the 15th century developed the process for making granulated sugar.

6. (M. C.) For almost four hundred years the most common form of commercial sugar was:

____(1) Molded sugar cones.
____(2) Granulated sugar.
____(3) Cube sugar.
____(4) Irregular lump sugar.

Sugar in the new world

Columbus carried cuttings of sugar cane to the new world on his second voyage. His letters told how $\overset{800}{\leftarrow}$ he planted the cuttings in fertile soil and described the luxuriant growth of the sugar cane. Columbus quickly observed that articles of food were always gratefully received by the Indians. According to Washington Irving's biography, to win the friendship of the wary natives whom Columbus prevailed upon to visit aboard his ship, he "gave them beads, hawks' bells and sugar and sent them highly gratified on shore."

Although sugar had been known to Europeans since the return of the Crusaders in the Middle Ages, ancient modes of transportation, crude refining methods and lack of an efficient distribution $\overset{900}{\leftarrow}$ system prior to the 19th century combined to make sugar an expensive luxury for only the wealthy to enjoy. In fact, from an old print which features a price list of food products, we learn that sugar sold at $2.75 a pound in London in 1742.

Modern methods of refining, packing and distribution have resulted in a greatly improved product, offered in a variety of forms at prices within the reach of all. The people of the United States are among the largest consumers of sugar and our principal sources of supply are Cuba, Puerto Rico, Hawaii and the Philippine Islands, with the largest percentage $\overset{1000}{\leftarrow}$ coming from Cuba. It is interesting to note that the most progressive countries of the world have the highest per capita consumption of sugar, while that

of the more backward nations is the lowest.

7. (C) Sugar was brought to America by _____.

8. (T — F) Sugar has always been inexpensive.

9. (T — F) The people of the United States are among the largest consumers of sugar.

The American Sugar Refining Company

Organized in 1891, the Company manufactures and distributes three well known brands of sugar — Domino, Franklin and Sunny Cane. The Company owns and operates five large refineries, located at $\overset{1100}{\rightarrow}$ Boston, Brooklyn, Philadelphia, Baltimore and New Orleans. These modern, efficient refineries are capable of turning out about 17 million pounds of pure cane sugar each working day.

The individual refinery laboratories and a Central Quality Control Laboratory constantly keep close watch on the raw materials, manufacturing operations and the packaging procedures of these products. The Company's Research and Development Laboratory is located in Philadelphia. In addition to conducting its important basic and applied researches on new sugar products and products derived from sugar, it is engaged in the development of improved refining processes and new uses for sugar products. $\overset{1200}{\rightarrow}$ These activities have the objective of providing the consumer with sugar products of the highest possible quality.

The Company also conducts extensive raw sugar operations in Cuba through its Cuban subsidiary, Central Cunagua. Its Cunagua and Jaronu mills serve a cane producing area of about 700 square miles, with a working population of 20,000 persons. The property contains some 200 miles of company operated, modern railroad facilities — and during the grinding season, these two mills crush more than forty million pounds of sugar cane every twenty-four hours — representing the harvest of approximately $\overset{1300}{\rightarrow}$ 1,000 acres.

Notwithstanding the magnitude of these operations, the raw sugar produced by Cunagua and Jaronu represents only a small part of the total raw sugar requirements of the Company's five domestic refineries.

10. (T — F) The American Sugar Refining Company operates extensive research programs as well as refining operations.

$\overset{1350}{\rightarrow}$

————STOP — ASK FOR YOUR TIME————

Time ____ Sec.	RATE (from table on page 305):	R. ____
No. Errors ____	COMPREHENSION (100 — 10% for each Error):	C. ____
VII — 16	EFFICIENCY (R × C):	E. ____

Sweet Crystals

(Reprinted from the pamphlet, *The Story of Sugar Cane*,
by permission of the American Sugar Refining Company)

———— WAIT FOR SIGNAL TO BEGIN READING ————

How sugar crystals form

After filtration, the clear sugar solution is conveyed to large, dome-shaped vacuum pans where steam, passing through copper tubes or coils, furnishes the necessary heat for evaporation of the water and subsequent formation of crystals. Vacuum pans are necessary, as explained before, to enable the sugar solution to boil at a low temperature, without burning. Boiling the sugar to form crystals of the proper grain size is one of the important steps in the refining of sugar. Through experience and with the assistance of instrument controls, the operator is able to produce the maximum quantity of crystals of 100 ⇆ the required size.

When the desired grain size has been obtained through the boiling process and the greatest number of crystals have formed, the contents of the vacuum pan are emptied into a mixer resembling a huge trough, located on the floor below. Revolving paddles maintain a uniform mixture of the warm sugar crystals and syrup, known as the "magma," to prevent the mixture from hardening. Now the sugar crystals must be separated from the syrup which still surrounds them. This is done in more centrifugal machines, similar to those used at the start of the process.

1. (T — F) Experience and accurate controls are 200 ⇆ necessary for a workman to produce sugar crystals of a uniform size.
2. (C) Evaporation of sugar solutions without caramelization (or burning) can be accomplished only in a _____ type container.

Pure white granulated sugar

After the syrup is thrown off, the sugar crystals deposited on the screen sides of the centrifugal machine are sprayed with clear water while the machine is still spinning, to remove the last traces of adhering syrup from each grain. When the machine is stopped, the crystalline sugar remains in the basket, sparkling white and pure. The sugar is 300 ⇆ discharged from the bottom of the centrifugal onto conveyors to be carried to huge revolving drying drums were a strong current of heated air absorbs the remaining moisture from the sugar. The dried granulated sugar now passes across inclined vibrating screens which grade the crystals according to size.

After screening, the refined sugar moves to large bins or directly to the weighing and packing machines. Under the guidance of skilled operators, these modern packaging machines automatically fill, weigh and pack the many varieties of pure cane sugar in the sanitary, convenient and accurately weighed packages 400 → so familiar to American housewives and manufacturers.

3. (C) After drying, the granulated sugar crystals are graded according to _____.
4. (T — F) Most of the weighing and packaging of the processed sugar is done by hand.

Other varieties of sugar

Brown or so-called "Soft" sugars are prepared by crystallizing and centrifuging the sugar remaining in the syrup spun off by the centrifugal machines during the processing of white granulated sugar. Brown sugars contain a nominal amount of mineral salts and possess a delectable cane or cane-molasses flavor.

Confectioners XXXX or "Icing" sugar is made by 500 → grinding pure granulated sugar to a very fine powder.

Cube and tablet sugars are formed by pressing pure moist granulated sugar in individual molds on a rotating cylinder. The individual cubes or tablets are ejected onto metal plates which are transferred to ovens for drying and hardening to retain their form.

There is also another interesting process by which tablets are manufactured. This is the so-called Adant Process, used in the United States exclusively by the American Sugar Refining Company. In this process the highest purity sugar syrup of exceptional clarity and brilliance is obtained by char-filtering the sugar 600 → solution *twice*. The syrup is evaporated in vacuum pans and is then discharged into iron molds with dividers closely spaced where, after cooling, crystallization is completed. The crystallized mass still in the molds is sprayed with crystal-clear syrup to remove all traces of color. This syrup is then spun off in centrifugal machines. The slabs of sugar are removed from the molds, slowly dried in ovens, then sawed and clipped into tablets of superlative whiteness and brilliancy — Crystal Domino Tablets.

5. (M. C.) Brown sugar is prepared from the by-product of the:
    _____(1) Cane crushing operation.
    _____(2) Vibrating screen operation.
    _____(3) Evaporation process.
    _____(4) Final centrifugal separation $\underset{\leftarrow}{700}$ process.

6. (T — F) One of the features in the manufacture of "Crystal Domino Tablets" is a double char-filtration.

Sugar syrups

Sugar refiners manufacture sugar syrups also known as "liquid" sugars — which are becoming increasingly important among various types of food manufacturers. The development of these products has been accelerated by significant savings in handling costs since they can be readily transported from the refinery in stainless steel tank trucks and in railroad tank cars to the manufacturer's plant, easily stored there and subsequently pumped to any part of the plant for instant use in processing. These sugar syrups are usually made from refinery sugar solutions $\underset{\leftarrow}{800}$ that have not undergone the final crystallization process but which have been decolorized and otherwise purified. They are essentially saturated solutions of sugar and/or invert sugar and are available at densities ranging from 66% to 80% solids content, depending upon the relative proportions of sugar and invert sugar present.

7. (T — F) A disadvantage of sugar syrups is the difficulty of transportation.

8. (M. C.) Sugar syrups contain about how much solid sugar?
    _____(1) 10 — 30 per cent.
    _____(2) 30 — 60 per cent.
    _____(3) 60 — 80 per cent. $\underset{\leftarrow}{900}$
    _____(4) 80 — 100 per cent.

Sugar — An important nutrient

Sugar today plays an important part in our daily lives. It has long been in such general use that few have ever considered how changed our mode of living would be without it. The common use of sugar in scores of prepared foods and beverages and as a staple in home cooking, canning and table use not only affords fuel for our body's energy needs but contributes highly to the palatability of our foods.

Everyone knows that carbohydrates are necessary in our diets for their energy value, but it is also important to know that carbohydrates serve other $\underset{}{1000}$ important functions. For example, they assist in the utilization of fat and spare protein for body-building and tissue repair. Fortunately, the human body is well equipped to use carbohydrates. Since carbohydrates are the main source of our body's fuel supplies, sugar, being a pure wholesome carbohydrate, has a very definite place in the normal diet. Moreover, sugar is an economical source of the energy and body fuel needed for balanced, healthful diets.

Because the true value of sugar in the normal diet is becoming better understood, we now know that $\underset{\rightarrow}{1100}$ we can use it frequently and liberally without endangering good nutrition — contrary to the expressed opinions of many food faddists. We all recognize the value of the basic food groups as a guide to better nutrition and, fortunately, we have a much greater choice of foods today which afford well balanced, wholesome, nutritious diets. Therefore, a liberal allowance of sugar need not displace nor interfere in any manner with adequate daily requirements of vitamins, minerals, fats and proteins.

Refined cane sugars, both white and brown, are wholesome, easily utilized sweeteners, rich in energy. They contain no waste, are freely soluble, require $\underset{\rightarrow}{1200}$ no further processing and keep indefinitely.

Sugars for home use

There are Domino pure cane sugars for every baking, cooking and serving need. These varieties of sugar are refinery packed in small, convenient cartons and bags for all household purposes. Some of the most popular types are:

Extra-fine granulated — for general table use and in cooking, baking, candy making, preserving and canning.

Confectioners XXXX — A powdered sugar of extremely smooth texture, used for making frostings, fondants and uncooked cake icings.

Old fashioned brown — gives a rich cane-molasses flavor to baked beans, baked apples, and fruit cake.

$\underset{\rightarrow}{1300}$ *Light brown* — adds a delicate cane flavor to waffles, puddings, sauces and candies.

9. (T — F) As a basic food type, sugar is classified as a carbohydrate.

10. (T — F) One of the greatest losses to the sugar companies is the loss through deterioration of the processed sugar before it reaches the market.

$\underset{\rightarrow}{1350}$

————STOP — ASK FOR YOUR TIME————

Time _____ Sec.   RATE (from table on page 305):   R. _____

No. Errors _____   COMPREHENSION (100 — 10% for each Error):   C. _____

VII — 17   EFFICIENCY (R × C):   E. _____

How to Produce an Idea

By Helen Rowan

— WAIT FOR SIGNAL TO BEGIN READING —

Degrees of creativity

The six-year-old child who succeeds in repairing his broken tricycle bell has a creative experience, New York University psychologist Morris I. Stein is fond of pointing out, but no one would claim that the repaired bell constitutes a "creative product" in the generally accepted meaning of the term.

It is possible, in other words, to differentiate roughly between individual creativity and social creativity. If you have an idea, it may be creative in comparison to all the other ideas you have ever had, which certainly represents individual creativity, or it may be creative in comparison to all the ideas 100 *everyone* has ever had; this represents social creativity of the highest order.

In short, the basic difference may be one of *degree* rather than kind. The highly creative person may be so because of the kind of problem he sets for himself and the quality of his response to it, but his creative process is not necessarily very different from what everyone goes through, or at least can go through.

It is necessary to bear this in mind because of the aura of mystery which has surrounded the creative process — a mystery which has been augmented rather 200 than dissipated by the numerous accounts left by the geniuses of history. Almost to a man — ancient or modern, writers, artists, musicians, scientists — they have gladly committed to paper accounts of how they did what they did and how they felt while they were doing it. The trouble with this kind of evidence, fascinating as it is, is that it is impressionistic, imprecise and incomplete. Furthermore, one aspect has tended to overshadow all others in the public mind; this has to do with the role of "inspiration" in the creative process.

It is true that most highly creative individuals, 300 even those as different in temperament and field as Samuel Coleridge and Bertrand Russell, do report flashes of insight, of sudden "knowing," but when these bursts of inspiration are seen in the context of the entire process of which they are a part, they take on different significance.

1. (T — F) The child who successfully repairs a broken tricycle bell has produced a "creative product" in the generally accepted meaning of the term.

2. (C) The basic difference between social and individual creativity may be one of _____ rather than of kind.

The four stages

400 To most people who have studied the problem, it seems apparent that the creative process occurs in four (or five, as some would have it) stages, while others say that what knowledge we have of the various stages is of little help because it is sheerly descriptive.

But for whatever it is worth, many participants and observers have described the stages of the creative experience in the following terms:

Preparation.
Incubation.
Illumination.
Verification.

Some break the preparatory stage into two parts, saying that in a sense one's entire life — the gaining of experience, education, the mastery of a medium, 500 whether it be pigments or words or mathematical symbols — is preparation for the act of creating. Then next (or first) comes the stage of intensive preparation: The individual works, consciously and hard, on whatever problem he is trying to solve. This preparation involves enormous effort and eventually, in many cases, great frustration, with accompanying tension and anxiety.

3. (M. C.) The four stages of the creative process as described by many participants and observers are:

___(1) preparation, incubation, illumination, variation.

___(2) preparation, incubation, illumination, verification.

___(3) preparation, experimentation, incubation, verification.

___(4) preparation, incubation, experimentation, variation.

600 4. (T — F) Some people say that the preparatory stage may be divided into two parts, claiming that one's lifetime experiences, which are preparation for the act of creating, prelude the stage of intensive preparation.

The creator withdraws

Then the creator often withdraws from the problem, perhaps for a very short time, perhaps for a long period. There is no certain knowledge of what occurs during this period, but some psychologists believe that the subconscious is at work. Some believe that the period of incubation frees the individual of previous fixations, and that he is then able to see the problem with new eyes when he returns to it, while 700 others would add to this hypothesis the idea that during the withdrawal period the creator is receiving helpful cues from his environment and experience.

Whatever it is that happens, next comes the moment everyone yearns for: the burst of insight, an experience of the "Aha" or "Eureka!" type that we all have had in some degree. But when considered in the light of all that has gone before, it loses some of its mystery. Remember that the individual has already established an outside criterion against which he may check his idea or insight; he has been desperately looking for something; he sees it, recognizes it, and cries, 800 "Eureka!" (To give a homely example that has nothing to do with creativity, set yourself the task of finding a red-headed man who is speaking German and wearing green socks, and when you see him, you, too, will have an "Aha" experience.)

Following the illumination comes the period of verification or completion, in which time the individual applies all his skills and craft and intelligence to make solid the original insight and finish the creation.

A distinctive characteristic of highly creative individuals seems to be their ability to maintain an exceedingly delicate balance between the most intense 900 effort, on the one hand, and suspension of conscious effort on the other. Even though few would go as far as Edison did in saying that genius is only one percent inspiration, the other 99 percent being perspiration, all genuinely creative people do show that "transcendent capacity for taking trouble" that Carlyle said made genius. But other kinds of traits seem to be just as essential to their creativity. Many observers have mentioned the attitude of playfulness highly creative individuals reveal — the ability to get both enjoyment and amusement from juggling ideas or paints or words or whatever. They also 1000 show a certain kind of restraint: They are not driven to pursue their purposes implacably and directly at all times, nor to force a solution arbitrarily, but they seem to trust themselves to recognize *the* right solution when it emerges, and have enough confidence to wait for it.

5. (T — F) The period of withdrawal from the problem that a creator often experiences is referred to as the incubation stage.

6. (C) The stage of the creative process in which the creator experiences a burst of insight and recognizes his goal is called the stage of _____.

1100 →
7. (M. C.) The stage of verification is the period of time in which the creative individual:

____(1) withdraws from the problem to gain a more objective view.

____(2) establishes some outside criterion by which to obtain insight.

____(3) recognizes the ultimate creation he has desperately been seeking.

____(4) applies his skills, craft, and intelligence to stabilize the original insight.

8. (T — F) A distinctive characteristic of highly creative individuals seems to be their inability to maintain a balance between the most intense effort and the suspension of conscious effort.

1200 →
9. (T — F) Creative individuals are driven to pursue their purposes implacably and directly at all times, showing little or no restraint.

No how-to-do-it books

The "how-to-do-it handbook of creativity" has never been written and probably never could — or should be. Nevertheless, it seems possible that all of us might increase somewhat the degree of creativity we show in our daily lives by making deliberate attempts to develop the kinds of attitudes, habits, and modes of operation that mark highly creative individuals. There is pretty general agreement that conscious effort alone cannot produce a creative achievement, but conscious effort may put us in a position where creative achievement is more likely.

1300 →
10. (T — F) The author feels that all might increase the degree of creativity shown in their daily lives by attempting to develop the kinds of attitudes, habits, and modes of operation that are characteristic of highly creative individuals.

1350 →
———STOP — ASK FOR YOUR TIME———

Time _____ Sec.   RATE (from table on page 305):   R. _____

No. Errors _____   COMPREHENSION (100 − 10% for each Error):   C. _____

VII-18   EFFICIENCY (R × C):   E. _____

Lightning in a Nutshell

(Reprinted from the pamphlet "Electronics," by permission of the
Executive Vice-President of Electronics Industries Association)

─────── WAIT FOR SIGNAL TO BEGIN READING ───────

The magic of electronics

Electrons are everywhere! They form the pictures on your television screen; they carry the music through your hi-fi set; every time you get your feet wet in a thunderstorm, they're splashing all around you; they're behind the cause of the rich brown suntan that you get on the beach each summer; they even flow abundantly in and out of stars googollians of miles away from you in space. It took a long time for men to understand these things, but when they did, a new branch of engineering was born — electronics.

The future of electronics abounds with magic — like 100 the lamp the genie gave to Aladdin; if you handle it the right way, there is no wish too fantastic to be granted.

So what is this magical electronics? Electronics is a branch of science and engineering which explains and exploits the magic of electrons for the use of mankind, but what are electrons? As Joseph J. Thomson discovered, they are lightweight charges of negative electricity that neutralize the heavier positive electrical charges in every atom.

James Chadwick, an English physicist, discovered that this atomic core or nucleus also contains even heavier particles called neutrons because they are 200 neutral and have no electrical charge. For his world shattering discovery of the neutron, Chadwick received the Nobel Prize in 1935. The possible existence of the neutron had been postulated by Lord Ernest Rutherford in 1920, but Chadwick's brilliant experimental work was responsible for its discovery. The electron's charge was first measured by Robert Millikan, and it was proposed as a kind of shell to the atom by Niels Bohr. Albert Einstein inferred (and it was later proved) that electrons, as well as protons and neutrons, become heavier the faster they are made to travel, but of the three basic subatomic particles, 300 the electron could be impelled to the highest speeds by far. Since the electron is only one-2000th as heavy as the proton and the neutron, it can be accelerated very nearly to the speed of light by energy sources that engineers have been able to build.

1. (T — F) Electronics is an area of science and engineering which explains and exploits the magic of electrons to benefit mankind.

2. (T — F) Joseph J. Thomson discovered that electrons are lightweight charges of positive electricity that neutralize the heavier negative charges in the atom.

400 3. (M. C.) The electron can be accelerated to greater speeds than either the neutron or proton because:

_____(1) it has a neutral charge and is highly flexible.

_____(2) more information is available in relation to the electron.

_____(3) the electron is much lighter than the proton or the neutron.

_____(4) the electron becomes lighter as its speed is accelerated.

The application of electrons

How do you accelerate an invisible, infinitesimal speck of matter? Because it has an electrical charge, it can be accelerated by a magnetic field or another electrical charge. Electromagnets in combination with 500 charged plates are used in television picture tubes to guide beams of electrons to the screen. As the electrons strike the screen in a particular pattern, the screen glows intermittently to produce a picture.

Accelerated electrons produce the light in fluorescent lamps and neon signs, and the opposite approach works too, for the energy in a beam of light falling on certain materials can cause electrons to flow in the materials, this latter effect being the one that makes solar cells generate electricity.

There are many kinds of electromagnetic radiation, some visible (light) and some invisible (radio, infra- 600 red, ultraviolet, and x-ray) to the human eye. Each kind can be used to generate or transfer some type of energy — electromagnetic, electrical, thermal or mechanical — by focusing or directing it into a gas, a liquid or a solid. By exploitation of such phenomena engineers have made certain crystals into transistors that detect and amplify radio impulses, opening a whole new field — solid-state electronics. The same phenomena have made microminiaturization possible, when different solid materials are "fused" together, each responding differently. By joining together the right combination, you can build a radio receiver (or transmitter, or computer unit, etc.) the size of a matchstick or smaller, like lightning contained in 700 a nutshell!

The total range of electromagnetic waves covers the higher energy gamma, X- and ultra-violet radiations all the colors of the rainbow from deep violet to deep red in visible light, through the lower energy infrared, microwave and longer radio radiations. All of these have applications in electronics, and most of the possibilities are still undreamed.

The brain and nervous system are themselves electronic-like, a fact that forms the basis of a new field of interest to research engineers called cybernetics, which concentrates on a study of the relationship between this human "electronic" network and man-made machines. A new school of psychologists has 800 been inspired by electronics to investigate the possibilities of what they call "SBS," which stands for "Synthetic Behavior Systems" and has as its goal the development of electronic machines based on human behavior patterns — machines that think for themselves and learn from their own mistakes. Engineers working in this same area call their objective "Artificial Intelligence." Machines using these concepts could be sent off to the moon or planets to determine whether or how a human being could survive there.

4. (C) An example of electromagnetic radiation visible to the human eye is

_____.

5. (T — F) The phenomena which allow engineers 900 to develop transistors have opened a new field — solid state electronics.

6. (T — F) The field of cybernetics involves investigation of the microminiaturization phenomenon.

7. (M. C.) The goal of the researcher participating in the "SBS" investigation is:

_____(1) to discover a higher energy gamma radiation.

_____(2) to develop a method of fusing together different solid materials.

_____(3) to increase knowledge of solid-state electronics.

_____(4) to develop electronic machines based on human behavior patterns.

The realm of electronics

What is the domain of electronics? It extends

through all the sciences, from biology to astronomy; 1000 it has created entirely new and exciting engineering fields; it is vital to the exploration of outer space; it is vital to national defense; it is vital to education, to industry, to medicine, to communications; and most significantly, it can be the basis of your own future.

How far can you go in an electronics career? Only the laws of nature can stop you — and new laws are always being discovered. Someday you may discover one yourself, or you may apply new laws to the invention of new devices. Or perhaps you'll uncover a 1100 new slant on the old laws and establish a breakthrough like television, or radar, or the electron and ion microscopes. Whatever career you choose in the wide realm of electronics, whether as scientist, engineer, teacher, technician, or even salesman — you'll have endless opportunities to contribute to mankind's progress and your own satisfaction.

Since World War II, electronics has expanded with the lightning speed of the particles after which it is named. According to Secretary of Commerce Luther Hodges, "During the past ten years, the manufacture of electronics products expanded twice as fast as the (total) national output . . . research and development 1200 in electronics accounted for expenditures of an estimated $2 billion . . . . New scientific knowledge led to the establishment of entirely new enterprises which did not exist before the war, or existed only as laboratory curiosities . . . ."

One breakthrough leads to another; each fans outward like a searchlight beam to illuminate new ideas, new applications, new products. In electronics you will be working at new frontiers, with the most powerful and stimulating forces of nature — electricity, magnetism, and the mysterious "glue" that holds together the parts of an atomic nucleus.

Is there a future in electronics? The Universe itself is your only limit!

1300 8. (C) The domain of electronics extends throughout all the _____, from biology to astronomy.

9. (T — F) In the past ten years the manufacture of electronic products expanded half as rapidly as the total national output.

10. (T — F) Electronics is a desirable area of occupation because it is as unlimited as 1350 the universe.

—————STOP — ASK FOR YOUR TIME—————

Time _____ Sec.   RATE (from table on page 305):   R. _____

No. Errors _____   COMPREHENSION (100 — 10% for each Error):   C. _____

VII-19   EFFICIENCY (R × C):   E. _____

Number VII-20

Wilderness

BY STEWART L. UDALL

(Reprinted from the Spring-Summer, 1962, issue of *The Living Wilderness*,
by permission of the author and the editor)

——————————— WAIT FOR SIGNAL TO BEGIN READING ———————————

Out of the wilderness — Mother of Resources — has come the raw material with which Americans have fashioned a great civilization. Our forbears molded the wilds: Trees became boards, prairies became pastures, iron became steel, and with such developments came the highest material standard of living yet known. Our ancestors were molded by the virgin continent in return — rugged, self-reliant, independent.

At first the effect of America on her new masters was less apparent than theirs on the land, but slowly Americans have come to realize that the wilderness has been an influence upon the national character, as well as a reservoir of abundance, and is responsible <u>100</u> for both the high spiritual and the material quality of American life.

The inspirational values of the American wilderness have moved an impressive roster of men to become advocates of wilderness preservation: Henry David Thoreau, Daniel Boone, John James Audubon, Jim Bridger, Theodore Roosevelt, and many others.

But not until the current decade did public concern about wilderness reach a crescendo.

We can no longer trust to the accidents of history to preserve for our enjoyment those few acres that have so far escaped exploitation. Inaccessibility will not be protection in the face of an increasingly <u>200</u> efficient technology.

Today the public has abundant leisure time, and more crowded living conditions than ever before in American history. People look increasingly to wilderness areas for recreation, for the renewal of routine-wearied bodies and jaded minds that have been deprived of once-familiar refreshing primeval influences.

Our society needs a benchmark, a check of natural conditions against which to measure the soundness of its values.

Wilderness preservation is the first element in a sound national conservation policy.

Preservation of wilderness is a tribute to "America the Beautiful," a demonstration of faith in her future and an ability to learn from her past. It demonstrates <u>300</u> to the world that the United States is an inspired democracy, not exploiting every material resource in every cranny of the land, but wisely living on a sustained interest, not capital.

1. (T — F)   Public concern about wilderness pres-ervation has reached a crescendo in recent years.

2. (T — F)   The first element in a sound national conservation policy is wilderness pres-ervation.

Opportunity

The American wilderness heritage exists in some state and private areas but for the most part is in our federal jurisdiction. Wilderness areas occur in <u>400</u> the National Park System, in wildlife refuges and ranges, and in parts of the national forests that are classified as wilderness, wild, primitive, or canoe areas. The uses of wilderness in all these classifica-tions are compatible with, and essential to, the management objectives of the areas involved. . . .

Because of the rapid expansion of our society, our entire national land estate is facing competing, some-times harmonious, sometimes conflicting, demands for usage of areas. The Constitution assigns to the Congress responsibility for public lands. Thus land administrators of the federal government have recom-mended to Congress legislation which emphasizes the proper responsibility of Congress to decide what <u>500</u> areas may be preserved as wilderness for the American public. . . .

National status for wilderness lands in a National Wilderness Preservation System now can be achieved without having to acquire lands, without transferring areas from one jurisdiction to another, without establishing a new agency of government, or dis-rupting commercial or recreational enterprises. The option may not last long, if unused. It can be readily realized now, and at almost no cost in dollars and cents, or significant sacrifice.

3. (T — F)   Most of the wilderness areas are re-stricted to state and local jurisdiction.

<u>600</u> 4. (M. C.)   The Constitution assigns the respon-sibility for public lands to:

_____(1)   Congress.
_____(2)   the President.
_____(3)   state officials.
_____(4)   local authorities.

Requirements

The concept of wilderness that has been cherished by Americans is the idea of lands where man and his works do not dominate the landscape, where the earth and its whole community of life are untrammeled by man, where man himself is a visitor who does not remain.

Wilderness, therefore, is that condition of nature which affords man the ultimate opportunity for solitude and the kind of recreation that is primitive and unconfined. Any area of wilderness must be large enough to make practicable its preservation and ⟵700 use in an unimpaired condition.

The United States Forest Service administers 29 "wild areas," and 14 "wilderness areas," in which primitive conditions are maintained. Designation of these areas has been based upon careful review of the multiple purposes of national forest lands. The Forest Service also administers 39 "primitive areas" which are under study to determine which portions are suitable for permanent designation, and which portions are not predominantly of wilderness value.

The National Park Service administers 48 units that contain wilderness suitable for preservation in a national program. Within the next ten years, the Park Service will need to take inventory of these units ⟵800 and advise the Nation as to which parts of each unit should be developed for intensive visitor access, and which parts of the back country should be retained in wilderness condition.

Expansion of our society has made these appraisals of the national wilderness estate mandatory. At the same time a national wilderness program must continue to be sufficiently flexible to permit continued livestock grazing and the use of aircraft and motorboats where these are already well-established, as well as management provisions for dealing with fire, blight, and other emergencies. Commercial enterprises, roads, motorized equipment, and installations ⟵900 that would impair a wilderness environment should be precluded.

Requirements for national wilderness protection include definition of wilderness conditions and boundaries, and at the same time recognition of emergency or resource scarcity conditions which might make non-conforming uses of wilderness areas essential to the overriding national interest.

5. (C)   Wilderness is that condition of nature which affords man the opportunity for _____ and recreation that is primitive and unconfined.

6. (T — F) The designation of lands as "wild," "wilderness," or "primitive" areas has been based on review of the multiple purposes of the lands.

7. (M. C.) Which of the following is *not* included ⟵1000 as a requirement for national wilderness protection?

___(1) Definition of boundaries.
___(2) Recognition of emergency conditions.
___(3) Recognition of resource scarcity.
___(4) Realization of a national profit.

Prospect

The public has demanded assurance that the wilderness remnant will be protected for the recreation and re-creation of the American people.

A national program for wilderness preservation involves a great and enduring benefit at remarkably small cost. It calls for no new administrative agency, no transfer of jurisdiction over any public lands, no new lands, no new funds. It eliminates no established 1100→ commercial or recreational uses.

A national wilderness program provides for specific study and appraisal of lands now managed as wilderness to determine their eligibility for a Wilderness System. It requires special specific action by Congress to extend Wilderness System protection to any new areas.

The National Wilderness Preservation System which is part of a national program provides protection as wilderness for some 2% of the United States, about an eighth of an acre per citizen by the year 2000. Future generations through this program will be assured the opportunity to experience the primeval 1200→ which has contributed so much vigor to American character. Youth will be assured the opportunity to gain from the primeval the initiative, self-reliance, confidence, stamina which their forbears needed to accomplish their tasks — attributes which are needed equally today to perpetuate their achievements.

America has yet to prove that she is willing to balance material abundance with spiritual benefits. Our people deserve both. Through preservation of wilderness, there is within our grasp a lasting testament to the maturity of our society and a lasting legacy for the well-being of our people.

8. (T — F) 1300→ A disadvantage of a national program for wilderness preservation is that the great and enduring benefits are realized only at remarkably high cost.

9. (C)   The National Wilderness Preservation system provides protection as wilderness equalling _____ acre per citizen by the year 2000.

10. (T — F) America has proved repeatedly that 1000→ 1350→ she is willing to balance material abundance with spiritual benefits.

————STOP — ASK FOR YOUR TIME————

Time _____ Sec.   RATE (from table on page 305):   R. _____
No. Errors _____   COMPREHENSION (100 − 10% for each Error):   C. _____
VII-20   EFFICIENCY (R × C):   E. _____

Vocabulary List

List of all key words missed *and* all words underlined by mistake. Study these until you have added them to your vocabulary.

1.

2.

3.

4.

5.

6.

7.

8.

9.

10.

11.

12.

13.

14.

15.

16.

17.

18.

19.

20.

21.

22.

23.

24.

25.

26.

27.

28.

29.

30.

31.

32.

33.

34.

35.

36.

37.

38.

39.

40.

41.

42.

43.

44.

45.

46.

List of all key words missed *and* all words underlined by mistake. Study these until you have added them to your vocabulary.

1.	24.
2.	25.
3.	26.
4.	27.
5.	28.
6.	29.
7.	30.
8.	31.
9.	32.
10.	33.
11.	34.
12.	35.
13.	36.
14.	37.
15.	38.
16.	39.
17.	40.
18.	41.
19.	42.
20.	43.
21.	44.
22.	45.
23.	46.

List of all key words missed *and* all words underlined by mistake. Study these until you have added them to your vocabulary.

1.	24.
2.	25.
3.	26.
4.	27.
5.	28.
6.	29.
7.	30.
8.	31.
9.	32.
10.	33.
11.	34.
12.	35.
13.	36.
14.	37.
15.	38.
16.	39.
17.	40.
18.	41.
19.	42.
20.	43.
21.	44.
22.	45.
23.	46.

List of all key words missed *and* all words underlined by mistake. Study these until you have added them to your vocabulary.

1.	24.
2.	25.
3.	26.
4.	27.
5.	28.
6.	29.
7.	30.
8.	31.
9.	32.
10.	33.
11.	34.
12.	35.
13.	36.
14.	37.
15.	38.
16.	39.
17.	40.
18.	41.
19.	42.
20.	43.
21.	44.
22.	45.
23.	46.

READING PROGRESS CHART

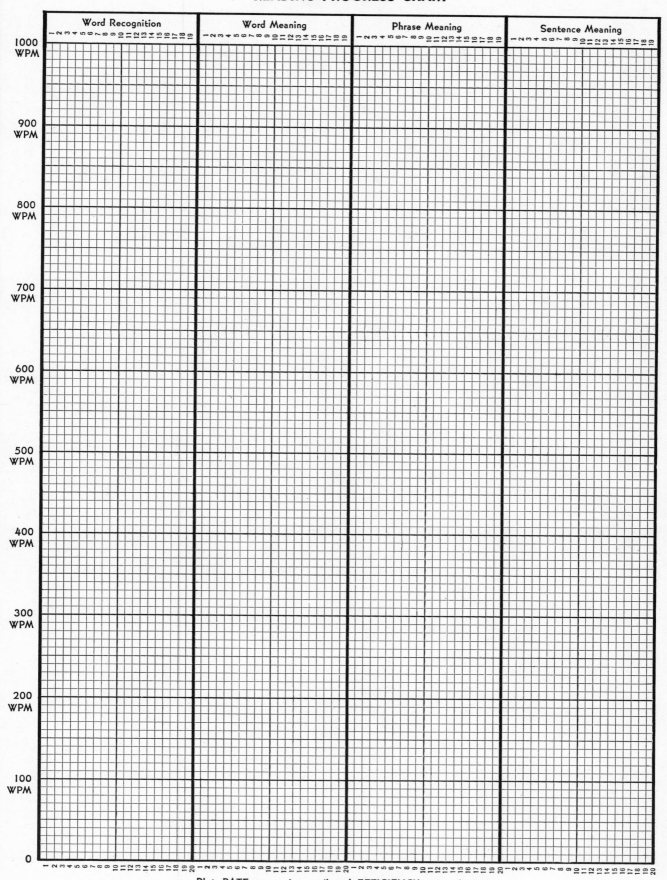

Plot RATE scores in pencil and EFFICIENCY scores in pen

READING PROGRESS CHART

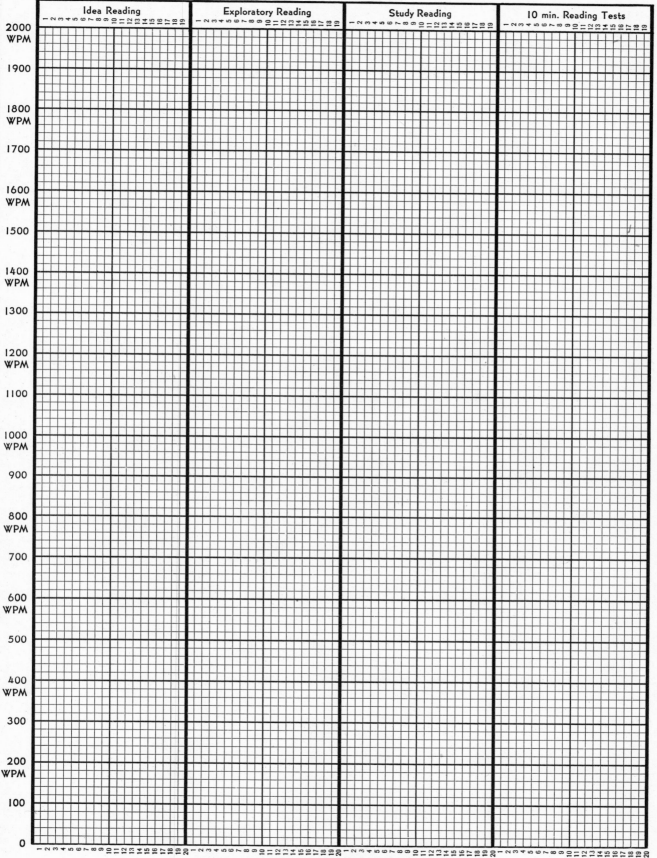

Idea Reading   **Exploratory Reading**   **Study Reading**   **10 min. Reading Tests**

Plot RATE scores in pencil and EFFICIENCY scores in pen

EXTENSION OF READING PROGRESS CHART

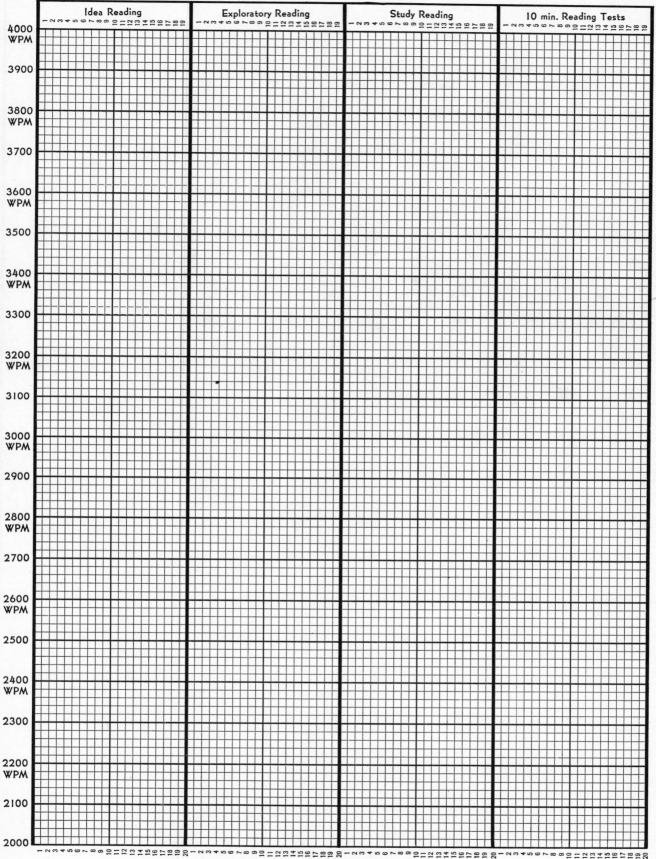

Plot RATE scores in pencil and EFFICIENCY scores in pen

EXTENSION OF READING PROGRESS CHART

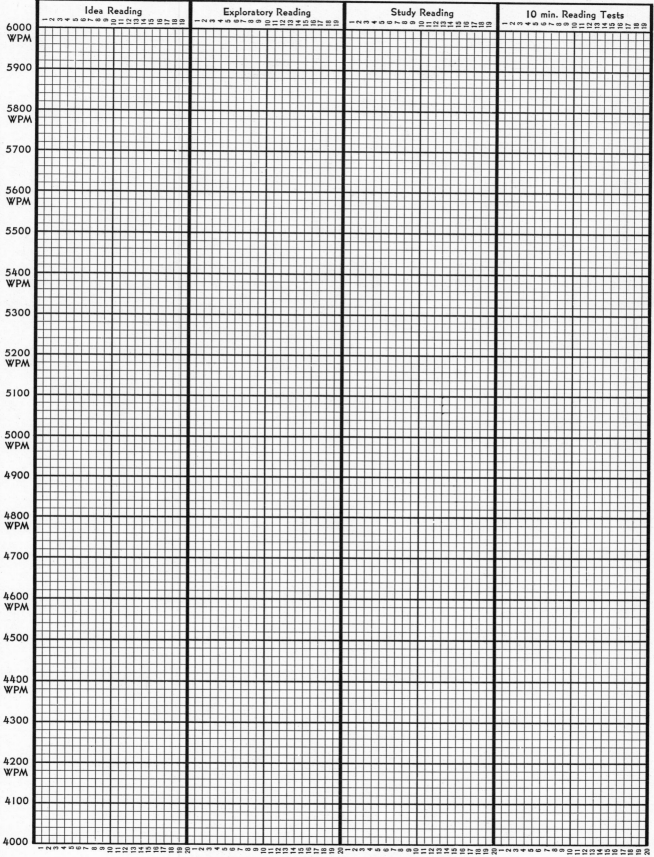

Plot RATE scores in pencil and EFFICIENCY scores in pen

KEY FOR COMPUTING RATE ON SERIES I AND II

Use for the word recognition drills and the word meaning drills.

Look up your time in Column I and read your rate in Column II.

I	II	I	II	I	II	I	II	I	II
1	9000	31	291	61	148	101	89	182–185	49
2	4500	32	281	62	145	102	88	186–189	48
3	3000	33	273	63	143	103–104	87	190–193	47
4	2250	34	265	64	141	105	86	194–197	46
5	1800	35	257	65	138	106	85	198–202	45
6	1500	36	250	66	136	107	84	203–206	44
7	1286	37	243	67	134	108–109	83	207–211	43
8	1125	38	237	68	132	110	82	212–216	42
9	1000	39	231	69	130	111	81	217–222	41
10	900	40	225	70	129	112–113	80	223–227	40
11	818	41	220	71	127	114	79	228–232	39
12	750	42	214	72	125	115–116	78	234–240	38
13	692	43	209	73	123	117	77	241–246	37
14	643	44	205	74	122	118–119	76	247–253	36
15	600	45	200	75	120	120	75	254–260	35
16	563	46	196	76	118	121–122	74	261–268	34
17	529	47	191	77	117	123–124	73	269–276	33
18	500	48	188	78	115	125	72	277–285	32
19	474	49	184	79	114	126–127	71	286–295	31
20	450	50	180	80	113	128–129	70	296–305	30
21	429	51	176	81	111	130–131	69	306–315	29
22	409	52	173	82	110	132–133	68	316–327	28
23	391	53	170	83	108	134–135	67	328–339	27
24	375	54	167	84	107	136–137	66	340–352	26
25	360	55	164	85	106	138–139	65	353–366	25
26	346	56	161	86	105	140–141	64	367–382	24
27	333	57	158	87	103	142–144	63	383–400	23
28	321	58	155	88	102	145–146	62	401–418	22
29	310	59	153	89	101	147–148	61	419–439	21
30	300	60	150	90	100	149–151	60	440–461	20
				91	99	152–153	59	462–486	19
				92	98	154–156	58	487–514	18
				93	97	157–159	57	515–545	17
				94	96	160–162	56	546–580	16
				95	95	163–165	55	581–620	15
				96	94	166–168	54	621–666	14
				97	93	169–171	53	667–720	13
				98	92	172–174	52	721–782	12
				99	91	175–178	51	783–857	11
				100	90	179–181	50	858–947	10

RATE TABLE FOR SERIES III — PHRASE MEANING

Look up your time (to the nearest 5 seconds) in Column I and read your rate in the Column under the appropriate exercise number. If your time is more or less than the limits of the table, or if you desire to compute your time more accurately to the exact second, divide the time (No. of seconds) into the "Division Constant" for that exercise.

Time	Exercise #1–4	Exercise #5–8	Exercise #9–12	Exercise #13–16	Exercise #17–20
# words	300	350	400	500	600
Division Constant	18,000	21,000	24,000	30,000	36,000
# seconds					
5	3600	4200	4800	6000	7200
10	1800	2100	2400	3000	3600
15	1200	1400	1600	2000	2400
20	900	1050	1200	1500	1800
25	720	840	960	1200	1440
30	600	700	800	1000	1200
35	514	600	686	875	1029
40	456	525	600	750	900
45	400	467	533	667	800
50	360	420	480	600	720
55	327	382	436	545	655
60	300	350	400	500	600
65	277	323	369	462	554
70	257	300	343	429	514
75	240	280	320	400	480
80	225	263	300	375	450
85	212	247	282	353	424
90	200	233	267	333	400
95	189	221	253	316	379
100	180	210	240	300	360
105	171	200	229	286	343
110	164	191	218	273	327
115	157	183	209	261	313
120	150	175	200	256	300
125	144	168	192	240	288
130	138	162	185	231	277
135	133	156	178	222	267
140	129	150	171	214	257
145	124	145	166	207	248
150	120	140	160	200	240
155	116	135	155	194	232
160	113	131	150	188	225
165	109	127	145	182	218
170	106	124	141	176	212
175	103	120	137	171	206
180	100	117	133	167	200
185	97	114	130	162	195
190	95	111	126	158	189
195	92	108	123	154	185
200	90	105	120	150	180

RATE TABLE FOR SERIES IV — SENTENCE MEANING

Look up your time (to the nearest 5 seconds) in Column I and read your rate in the Column under the appropriate exercise number. If your time is more or less than the limits of the table, or if you desire to compute your time more accurately to the exact second, divide the time (No. of seconds) into the "Division Constant" for that exercise.

Time	Exercise #1 — 6	Exercise #7 — 14	Exercise #15 — 20
# words	120	160	200
Division Constant	7200	9600	12,000
# seconds			
5	1440	1920	2400
10	720	960	1200
15	480	640	800
20	360	480	600
25	288	384	480
30	240	320	400
35	206	274	343
40	180	240	300
45	160	213	267
50	144	192	240
55	131	175	218
60	120	160	200
65	111	148	185
70	103	137	171
75	96	128	160
80	90	120	150
85	85	113	141
90	80	107	133
95	76	101	126
100	72	96	120
105	69	91	114
110	65	87	109
115	63	83	104
120	60	80	100
125	58	77	96
130	55	74	92
135	53	71	89
140	51	69	86
145	50	66	83
150	48	64	80
155	46	62	77
160	45	60	75
165	44	58	73
170	42	56	70
175	41	55	69

RATE TABLES FOR SERIES V — IDEA READING DRILLS

Look up your time (to the nearest second interval shown) in the column at the left, then find reading rate in the column under the appropriate exercise. For times beyond the limits of the table or between the intervals on the table, compute rate by dividing the time (number seconds) into the "Division Constant" for the appropriate column.

Exercise #	10, 19	1, 3, 5, 14, 17, 18	6, 9, 11	2, 4, 7, 8, 12, 13, 15, 16, 20	Exercise #	10, 19	1, 3, 5, 14, 17, 18	6, 9, 11	2, 4, 7, 8, 12, 13, 15, 16, 20
Word Count	500	600	750	800	Word Count	500	600	750	800
Division Constant	30,000	36,000	45,000	48,000	Division Constant	30,000	36,000	45,000	48,000
# seconds					# seconds				
5	6000	7200	9000	9600	105	286	343	429	457
6	5000	6000	7500	8000	110	273	327	409	436
7	4286	5143	6429	6857	115	261	313	391	417
8	3750	4500	5630	6000	120	250	300	374	400
9	3333	4000	5000	5333	125	240	288	360	384
10	3000	3600	4500	4800	130	231	277	346	369
11	2727	3273	4091	4364	135	222	267	333	356
12	2500	3000	3750	4000	140	214	257	321	343
13	2308	2769	3462	3692	145	207	248	310	331
14	2143	2571	3214	3429	150	200	240	300	320
15	2000	2400	3000	3200	155	194	232	290	310
16	1875	2250	2813	3000	160	188	225	281	300
17	1765	2118	2647	2824	165	182	218	273	291
18	1667	2000	2500	2667	170	176	212	265	282
19	1579	1895	2368	2526	175	171	206	257	274
20	1500	1800	2250	2400	180	167	200	250	267
21	1429	1714	2143	2285	185	162	195	243	259
22	1364	1636	2045	2182	190	158	189	237	253
23	1304	1565	1957	2087	195	154	185	231	246
24	1250	1500	1875	2000	200	150	180	225	240
25	1200	1440	1800	1920	205	146	176	220	234
26	1154	1385	1731	1846	210	143	171	214	229
27	1111	1333	1667	1778	215	140	167	209	223
28	1071	1285	1607	1714	220	136	164	205	218
29	1034	1241	1551	1655	225	133	160	200	213
30	1000	1200	1500	1600	230	130	157	196	209
35	857	1028	1284	1371	235	128	153	191	204
40	750	900	1125	1200	240	125	150	188	200
45	666	800	1000	1066	245	122	147	184	196
50	600	720	900	960	250	120	144	180	192
55	545	654	818	872	255	118	141	176	188
60	500	600	750	800	260	115	138	173	185
65	462	554	692	738	265	113	136	170	181
70	429	514	643	686	270	111	133	167	178
75	409	480	600	640	275	109	131	164	175
80	375	450	563	600	280	107	129	161	171
85	353	424	529	565	285	105	126	158	168
90	333	400	500	533	290	103	124	155	166
95	316	379	474	505	295	102	122	153	163
100	300	360	450	480	300	100	120	150	160

RATE TABLE FOR EXPLORATORY READING AND STUDY TYPE READING DRILLS
SERIES VI AND VII

Since all the exercises in Series VI and VII have been standardized to a length of 1350 words, rates for any of these exercises can be found by looking up the time in Column I of this table and reading the rate from Column II. Times are given at 5 second intervals. For an approximate time you may take the time figure nearest your actual time.

For any time figures beyond the limits of this table or between the intervals, the rate may be computed by dividing the time (in seconds) into 81,000.

I	II	I	II	I	II	I	II
5	16,200	105	771	305	266	505	160
6	13,500	110	736	310	261	510	159
7	11,571	115	704	315	257	515	157
8	10,125	120	675	320	253	520	156
9	9,000	125	648	325	249	525	154
10	8,100	130	623	330	245	530	153
11	7,333	135	600	335	242	535	151
12	6,750	140	579	340	238	540	150
13	6,231	145	559	345	235	545	149
14	5,786	150	540	350	231	550	147
15	5,400	155	523	355	228	555	146
16	5,063	160	506	360	225	560	145
17	4,765	165	491	365	222	565	143
18	4,500	170	476	370	219	570	142
19	4,263	175	463	375	216	575	141
20	4,050	180	450	380	213	580	140
21	3,857	185	438	385	210	585	138
22	3,667	190	426	390	208	590	137
23	3,522	195	415	395	205	595	136
24	3,375	200	405	400	203	600	135
25	3,240	205	395	405	200	605	134
26	3,116	210	386	410	198	610	133
27	3,000	215	377	415	195	615	132
28	2,893	220	368	420	193	620	131
29	2,793	225	360	425	191	625	130
30	2,700	230	352	430	188	630	129
35	2,314	235	345	435	186	635	128
40	2,025	240	338	440	184	640	127
45	1,800	245	331	445	182	645	126
50	1,620	250	324	450	180	650	125
55	1,473	255	318	455	178	655	124
60	1,350	260	312	460	176	660	123
65	1,246	265	306	465	174	665	122
70	1,157	270	300	470	172	670	121
75	1,080	275	295	475	171	675	120
80	1,012	280	289	480	169	680	119
85	953	285	284	485	167	685	118
90	900	290	279	490	165	690	117
95	853	295	275	495	164	695	117
100	810	300	270	500	162	700	116

SERIES II (ODD NUMBERS)

NO. 1	NO. 3	NO. 5	NO. 7	NO. 9
1. forehead	light	parched	trifle	crocodile
2. tease	support	inferior	obscure	stigma
3. bed	smell	hood	mark	devote
4. tranquillity	cupola	twist	port	salary
5. ice	fowl	economical	manservant	affection
6. sound	furnish	overlook	bent	lift
7. brisk	honor	prevent	rodents	discourse
8. dent	bare	goddess	dynamo	need
9. fine	cut	victim	remember	rule
10. tatter	wealthy	soothe	leg	danger
11. stick	ravage	song	vowed	vast
12. direction	slope	blemish	mist	sign
13. tired	stay	scribe	relieve	hum
14. mournful	degrade	stick	youthful	pretend
15. father	signal	scorch	yield	law
16. dash	postpone	bear	ball	hook
17. trip	avid	get	thigh	voice
18. score	anger	dress	costume	adorn
19. hotel	cage	chart	stately	power
20. powder	crazy	threat	enigmatic	form
21. heathen	ancient	pageant	drudge	verbal
22. craft	liable	headlong	penitence	bow
23. rare	scour	clean	criminal	pastoral
24. trap	dough	brace	seduction	chipmunk
25. dictator	daze	pure	eruption	shake

NO. 11	NO. 13	NO. 15	NO. 17	NO. 19
1. heard	shoeless	stir	terrify	indignantly
2. bovine	estimate	flower	benevolent	concerned
3. woman	cheat	truism	conclusion	convert
4. style	condone	distribute	forever	lasting
5. gaze	seriousness	pecuniary	mournful	cyclone
6. fever	drunk	weighty	killer	yet
7. limestone	intellectual	observe	recede	also
8. excursion	bundle	hill	hurtful	bias
9. clear	estimate	spoil	railroad	chickens
10. isolate	wise	oppose	subservient	litter
11. hidden	uncertainty	sully	replace	stainless
12. rude	escort	silent	rare	convey
13. nut	front	cascade	illiterate	feast
14. box	lift	rub	cutter	spine
15. limpidness	entrust	tuber	university	waterfall
16. mature	refuse	vicious	scholar	formal
17. starve	haze	serious	prolific	trap
18. shout	dully	liberty	sense	renounce
19. pitcher	infirm	throw	powerful	hellish
20. change	city	solitary	rural	stonework
21. endure	melancholy	incubator	region	disregard
22. ruin	taste	pretense	trellis	origin
23. pretense	soft	bone	trust	satisfy
24. distrust	tuft	ruler	fabric	stop
25. helpful	strength	diplomacy	distant	rational

SERIES III (ODD NUMBERS)

NO. 1	NO. 3
1. a precious stone	physical vigor
2. to say something	even surface
3. an opening for	scarcity of food
4. divide evenly	exhibiting envy
5. quite happy	close at all times
6. about medium	to reveal openly
7. one fully grown	in great need
8. a violent wrong	a cheerful person
9. to go ahead of	true to life
10. articulate sound	a modest person
11. view critically	with promptness
12. a rascal	quickness of action
13. rather meager	lighter than water
14. to lean down	made imperfectly
15. to amuse	open to view
16. a big tree	act of dominating
17. for smelling	show preference
18. has mild temper	brought about by
19. morning hymn	to frighten suddenly
20. a search for game	to set free

NO. 5	NO. 7
1. some incentive	a common junction
2. to move ahead	to bid farewell
3. man of decision	eternal existence
4. not using care	act of liberation
5. a sudden calamity	keeping a secret
6. act of forgetting	comes to an end
7. the threshold	an exhibit of humor
8. completely worthless	correct position
9. gain full meaning	that which is beyond
10. no set price	being very busy
11. show satisfaction	to fascinate
12. confirm the deed	likely a quarrel
13. to take turns	considerable amount
14. something odd	with promptness
15. in all probability	regular procedure
16. on the offensive	a severe look
17. make a thrust	join in a group
18. a trivial matter	absence of sound
19. have no boundary	honesty of mind
20. serve as a guide	not completed

SERIES III (ODD NUMBERS — *cont'd*)

NO. 9

1. to mix confusedly
2. to be outstanding
3. a decisive moment
4. more than is needed
5. thought to be absurd
6. especially suitable
7. covering all phases
8. to comprehend
9. usual way of doing something
10. where one lives
11. the last in the series
12. boundary line
13. a sound like a moan
14. a scenic painting
15. not public in nature
16. to set back
17. a solitary existence
18. provide financial aid
19. a tidy person
20. an act of good will

NO. 11

a feeling of thirst
not certain to occur
to be obedient
that which is to come
showing hilarity
an acquired holiday
one who is a criminal
pass quickly from sight
to be in right accord
of his own free will
choosing from several
to come together
simplicity of style
roughly sketched
state of being strong
a short hurried view
only one of a kind
changed in appearance
to stand still
to be thankful

NO. 13

1. associated with the press
2. usual course of events
3. capacity of receiving impressions
4. one who displays strength
5. one who is not selfish
6. overwhelming amazement
7. an amiable person
8. an ample amount of anything
9. set apart from others
10. adhering to a set plan
11. all over everywhere
12. to anticipate the outcome
13. becoming more complex
14. that which is dispersed
15. thought to be significant
16. related to the truth
17. authorized by proclamation
18. to withhold a privilege
19. an act which is illegal
20. to be potentially obtainable

NO. 15

considered to be brilliant
a surface injury to flesh
that which is awarded
something awkward or unhandy
in a contrary or reverse way
a perplexing and frustrating experience
buildings for lodging soldiers
not capable of producing vegetation
a battle between two individuals
be reduced to a state of beggary
rise and fall of the voice
cancel out the effects of
the capital city of a state
a state of being careful
the cause of an event
taking a census of the population
that which is indisputable
a summons to fight
to assemble or accumulate together
to contend in rivalry

SERIES III (ODD NUMBERS — *cont'd*)

NO. 17

1. the monarch of a kingdom
2. that which is relatively low
3. to enlarge either in fact or appearance
4. a representation of the surface of the earth
5. a martyr for the sake of principle
6. using the faculty of remembering
7. reproduced on a miniature level
8. the sixtieth part of an hour
9. which is within reasonable limits
10. a system of teaching morals
11. a moderately feeble-minded person
12. a complex situation or mystery
13. to have very narrow limits
14. quality or state of being neutral
15. a state of being nominated
16. does not deviate from the average
17. that which stands in the way
18. counted as obsolete in style
19. to vindicate or justify an act
20. under the oppression of a tyrant

NO. 19

1. the earth upon which we live
2. to develop and cultivate the mental processes
3. the practice of referring overmuch to oneself
4. to be envious of the other person
5. to be equal in quantity or degree
6. an error in the way a person thinks
7. that which becomes extinct
8. to be supported by evidence based on facts
9. to have a prescribed or set form
10. terror excited by sudden danger
11. to be full or complete in quantity
12. the accumulation or increasing of profits
13. a gesture used to enforce an opinion
14. to give a gift to someone
15. the act or action of gliding
16. the goal to obtain in winning the race
17. a meeting face to face with a client
18. to supply water to the land by canals
19. that which is regarded as an island
20. January, named after the Latin deity, Janus

SERIES IV (ODD NUMBERS)

	NO. 1	NO. 3	NO. 5	NO. 7	NO. 9	NO. 11	NO. 13	NO. 15	NO. 17	NO. 19
1.	S	D	S	D	D	S	D	S	S	S
2.	D	D	D	S	S	D	S	D	D	D
3.	S	D	S	S	S	S	D	D	D	D
4.	D	S	D	D	S	D	D	D	D	S
5.	D	S	D	D	D	S	D	D	S	D
6.	S	D	D	S	D	D	S	D	D	S
7.	D	S	S	D	D	D	D	S	S	S
8.	D	D	D	D	D	D	D	D	S	S
9.	D	D	D	D	D	S	S	D	D	D
10.	S	D	S	S	D	S	S	S	S	D

SERIES V (ODD NUMBERS)

	NO. 1	NO. 3	NO. 5	NO. 7	NO. 9	NO. 11	NO. 13	NO. 15	NO. 17	NO. 19
1.	2	2	1	4	3	3	1	4	4	2
2.	T	F	F	T	T	F	F	T	F	F

SERIES VI (ODD NUMBERS)

	NO. 1	NO. 3	NO. 5	NO. 7	NO. 9	NO. 11	NO. 13	NO. 15	NO. 17	NO. 19
1.	F	Germans	F	light	community	Individual	3	3	F	F
2.	Paul Bunyan	F	delinquent	F	T	F	F	slow	advertise	experience
3.	2	T	2	gas	F	T	T	T	T	3
4.	F	T	1	T	mind	propaganda	F	F	4	F
5.	T	1	T	T	F	4	T	T	F	T
6.	T	T	T	2	1	T	F	T	F	T
7.	F	F	T	3	T	F	"fly-by night"	F	2	F
8.	T	F	F	F	3	F	T	U.S. Congress	T	teacher
9.	3	Lancaster	F	F	T	T	juvenile delinquency	F	resource unit	4
10.	open-pit	4	J. Edgar Hoover	T	F	1	4	1	T	T

SERIES VII (ODD NUMBERS)

	NO. 1	NO. 3	NO. 5	NO. 7	NO. 9	NO. 11	NO. 13	NO. 15	NO. 17	NO. 19
1.	F	T	F	T	F	1	T	T	T	T
2.	public liability	2	leading	F	T	T	F	F	vacuum	F
3.	T	enhancement	T	F	F	fish	F	T	size	3
4.	3	F	3	teacher shortage	observatory	F	2	T	F	light
5.	F	F	F	discourages	T	4	F	optimistic	4	T
6.	T	T	F	T	Moon	F	T	2	T	F
7.	property	F	anti	4	T	T	Brazil	4	F	4
8.	2	1	T	F	F	Alaska	Republic	F	3	sciences
9.	T	realistic	3	T	1	F	T	mass investment	T	F
10.	F	T	T	2	8	T	1	F	F	T

SERIES II (EVEN NUMBERS)

NO. 2	NO. 4	NO. 6	NO. 8	NO. 10
1. cot	glimpse	cook	keen	humiliated
2. polite	charlatan	house	ministers	headland
3. mount	settlement	fish	eat	boast
4. falsehood	steps	gutter	empty	dominion
5. resin	hamper	blaze	pork	deny
6. predicament	cry	grass	jangle	incompetent
7. memory	sharp	level	lose	enrage
8. dromedary	sop	affront	medicine	inflexible
9. measure	hat	braid	concerning	possessions
10. conceal	afflict	intended	cutlery	muffler
11. contaminate	killer	weep	levy	stalks
12. green	melt	saving	disgusting	bag
13. dabbler	salary	plant	gas	biological
14. price	friendship	prayer	brush	see
15. shell	child	chest	vanquish	cheat
16. doctrine	short	inlet	pigeon	divinity
17. dart	drop	revise	holder	hasten
18. fortunate	struggled	scowl	pawn	dealer
19. contract	practice	assert	smaller	concept
20. tidy	ignited	chance	trap	hash
21. gait	cornucopia	western	harbor	resound
22. dwell	choose	advance	fury	restoration
23. pat	answer	part	furtive	form
24. befall	exhausted	relieve	coagulate	wooer
25. pocketbook	taut	ripped	squander	useless

NO. 12	NO. 14	NO. 16	NO. 18	NO. 20
1. embarrass	plentiful	wrong	obscure	covetous
2. testimony	stake	bearer	assemble	rustic
3. morn	teach	heal	consider	naive
4. outbreak	industrious	guide	homemaking	robin
5. temerity	plume	crepe	penalty	cloth
6. ask	listen	angry	nose	inscrutable
7. weighty	succulent	spite	vegetable	elevation
8. foreign	wet	path	immunity	grateful
9. adventure	tormentor	wisdom	tolerable	manufacture
10. elder	depend	secure	fanciful	gratify
11. element	site	adhered	person	acknowledge
12. compassion	compassion	below	esteem	base
13. receive	oscillate	foolish	competency	road
14. injured	change	perplex	watch	disaster
15. staff	wife	perimeter	law	science
16. delve	official	relate	closet	producer
17. cringe	bureau	get	beguile	trade
18. tools	anticipate	chasm	final	thankfulness
19. house	useless	jewel	statement	consultation
20. ray	probable	accident	teacher	fair
21. aspect	torment	confined	degraded	hunter
22. director	bag	denial	buyer	mend
23. manifested	quit	tray	unite	depression
24. expanded	drench	shrewd	grand	exist
25. conquer	flung	unaffected	confusion	omnipresent

SERIES III (EVEN NUMBERS)

NO. 2

1. to recognize again
2. precious metal
3. a high polish
4. to empty out
5. a belief held
6. prose fiction
7. of little breadth
8. to belong to
9. infinite in size
10. entertains another
11. surface of earth
12. to poke something
13. made independent of
14. to make peace
15. leave it out
16. possessing dignity
17. an enormous animal
18. administer justice
19. not correct
20. one who expects

NO. 4

correct position
gentle animal
a gradual decline
diminish in size
abundant harvest
be flustered
upright position
to be stable
rather sleepy
ruinous condition
neglect of duty
expressive of pain
marked boundary
to annihilate
this very instant
ramble along
most valuable part
being clumsy
to collapse
to complicate

NO. 6

1. hurrying for aid
2. nearly as easy
3. more than needed
4. very small quantity
5. one or the other
6. a great error
7. plain to see
8. not interested in
9. scandalous conduct
10. just the opposite
11. at the beginning
12. a surviving part
13. obviously clear
14. about dawn
15. he who is a criminal
16. craving something
17. offer your service
18. avoiding something
19. being historical
20. dislike to work

NO. 8

rising in power
should be allowed
according to facts
to dispose of
to reach the peak
brought about by
prepared to go on
exclusive of others
not very busy
death by violence
decent in character
free from reproach
keep from falling
a great outcry
very necessary
completely exhausted
place for vacations
one who is punctual
one who is courageous
shattered to pieces

SERIES III (EVEN NUMBERS — *cont'd*)

NO. 10

1. punishment for an offense
2. an act of entering
3. in complete contrast
4. to pronounce guilty
5. to complicate matters
6. free from blame
7. to throw with violence
8. from this time forward
9. a military foe
10. to come to an end
11. the art of carving
12. a large river barge
13. to have an aversion to
14. to be part of an audience
15. anything very old
16. rough in countenance
17. pleasant salutation
18. one mad dog
19. to rush some place
20. to be in a safe place

NO. 12

consecrated as sacred
betray a trust
not according to facts
bottom of the scale
training for an event
that which is immense
an act of teaching
prove to be right
an orderly arrangement
one of the seasons
a table in a room
in a close-by vicinity
to answer yes
to be against
one noble in spirit
lack of attention
that which is interior
retain ownership of
to present for acceptance
to pause undecidedly

NO. 14

1. possessed with a severe handicap
2. soon to be indispensable
3. as often as necessary
4. an annual event or happening
5. the appendix of a book
6. to engage with close attention
7. close to correctness
8. to submit to arbitration
9. a military organization
10. something made without skill
11. to assault another person
12. the acceptance of an assumption
13. quality of being atrocious
14. to make trials or experiments
15. sale of goods to highest bidder
16. that which is authentic
17. to establish by authority
18. that written by his own hand
19. feeling of aversion toward something
20. a belief of some sort

NO. 16

to have and to keep
that which is tormenting
that which is done instantly
a confusing predicament
be on your guard
the part that is taken away
having gone astray
to arrange into chapters
idle chat in a conversation
the leader of the organization
to clarify the issue or report
to group or segregate in classes
instrument such as a clock
any system of rules or principles
that which is beyond
that which lies next to
to receive with intention or returning
that which is the bottom
to apply a brake to
characterized by brevity

SERIES III (EVEN NUMBERS — *cont'd*)

NO. 18

1. to make plain by means of interpretation
2. closely acquainted or familiar with
3. that which is in fashion
4. that which is without strength or solidity
5. a kind of a watertight structure
6. the foot of an animal or a person
7. to be eternal or infinite in duration
8. that which happens or occurs
9. a person who gives evidence as to what happened
10. extremely good of its kind
11. that which exceeds what is usual
12. personal conduct motivated by expediency
13. something considered as abnormal
14. living under false pretenses
15. sequence with no interval or break
16. in the nature of an enchantment
17. consecrated to a noble purpose
18. a habitual course of action
19. that which has a deceptive appearance
20. that which happens early

NO. 20

1. an allowance to one retired from service
2. that which is perplexed
3. pertinent to the present condition
4. formative in nature as clay or plastic
5. quality or state of being popular
6. the duties of a porter
7. within the powers of performance
8. a precaution taken in advance
9. a query relative to a problem to be solved
10. safeguarded by divine care and guidance
11. to puzzle out a mystery
12. a vessel holding one quart
13. to ramble or wander with no set goal
14. a place where anything is kept in store
15. a long loose outer garment
16. a part presented for inspection
17. to separate in different directions
18. coming first in logical order
19. to be slow or tardy in action
20. the guard going the rounds

SERIES IV (EVEN NUMBERS)

	NO. 2	NO. 4	NO. 6	NO. 8	NO. 10	NO. 12	NO. 14	NO. 16	NO. 18	NO. 20
1.	D	D	D	S	S	D	D	S	S	S
2.	D	S	S	D	S	D	D	D	D	D
3.	S	S	D	D	S	S	S	S	S	D
4.	S	S	S	D	S	S	S	D	D	D
5.	D	D	D	D	D	S	S	D	D	D
6.	D	D	D	S	D	S	D	D	D	D
7.	D	S	D	D	D	D	S	S	S	D
8.	D	D	D	D	S	S	D	D	D	S
9.	S	D	D	S	D	D	D	S	S	D
10.	D	D	S	D	D	D	D	D	D	S

SERIES V (EVEN NUMBERS)

	NO. 2	NO. 4	NO. 6	NO. 8	NO. 10	NO. 12	NO. 14	NO. 16	NO. 18	NO. 20
1.	3	4	4	2	4	3	3	4	2	1
2.	T	T	F	F	F	T	T	T	F	T

SERIES VI (EVEN NUMBERS)

	NO. 2	NO. 4	NO. 6	NO. 8	NO. 10	NO. 12	NO. 14	NO. 16	NO. 18	NO. 20
1.	F	F	F	autumn	3	F	F	F	3	T
2.	3	T	T	1	F	world	T	T	T	2
3.	2	medicine man	amphi-theater	F	F	color	Schirra	3	Astrionics	T
4.	Joseph Hayden	2	1	F	2	2	1	T	F	Western Union
5.	F	T	F	T	T	F	T	Industrial Revolution	T	T
6.	T	F	F	3	auction	T	T	F	F	F
7.	T	F	T	T	T	F	prevention	2	1	Telegraph
8.	adoption	T	T	F	publish	T	3	T	F	F
9.	T	patient	Glacier	colleges	F	T	F	idealism	T	F
10.	F	2	3	T	T	4	F	F	high school	3

SERIES VII (EVEN NUMBERS)

	NO. 2	NO. 4	NO. 6	NO. 8	NO. 10	NO. 12	NO. 14	NO. 16	NO. 18	NO. 20
1.	T	F	1	limited (or short term)	T	responses	ethical	sucrose	F	T
2.	himself	T	F	age	F	F	religious	3	degree	T
3.	F	4	agriculture	F	Feather	F	T	F	2	F
4.	6	shred	wine	T	2	T	T	T	T	4
5.	8	T	4	F	F	1	F	F	T	T
6.	T	F	F	1	biologists	F	F	I	illumination	T
7.	F	United States	F	F	T	T	F	Columbus	4	4
8.	T	T	T	T	4	2	T	F	F	solitude
9.	F	2	T	3	F	attitudes	4	T	F	⅛
10.	mind their own business	F	T	T	T	T	6	T	T	F

CROSS REFERENCE

	RATE TABLES	KEY	PROGRESS CHART
SERIES I	297	None Needed	289
SERIES II	297	307 & 313	289
SERIES III	299	308 & 314	289
SERIES IV	301	311 & 317	289
SERIES V	303	311 & 317	291
SERIES VI	305	312 & 318	291
SERIES VII	305	312 & 318	291